The Rise
and Fall of
Modern
Japanese
Literature

The Rise
and Fall of
Modern
Japanese
Literature

JOHN WHITTIER TREAT

The University of Chicago Press
Chicago and London

The University of Chicago Press, Chicago 60637
The University of Chicago Press, Ltd., London
Published 2018
Printed in the United States of America

27 26 25 24 23 22 21 20 19 18   1 2 3 4 5

ISBN-13: 978-0-226-81170-3 (cloth)
ISBN-13: 978-0-226-54513-4 (paper)
ISBN-13: 978-0-226-54527-1 (e-book)
DOI: https://doi.org/10.7208/chicago/9780226545271.001.0001

The University of Chicago Press gratefully acknowledges the generous support of the
Suntory Foundation toward the publication of this book.

Published with the assistance of the Frederick W. Hilles Publication Fund of
Yale University.

Library of Congress Cataloging-in-Publication Data

Names: Treat, John Whittier, author.
Title: The rise and fall of modern Japanese literature / John Whittier Treat.
Description: Chicago ; London : The University of Chicago Press, 2018. | Includes
    bibliographical references and index.
Identifiers: LCCN 2017041010 | ISBN 9780226811703 (cloth : alk. paper) | ISBN
    9780226545134 (pbk. : alk. paper) | ISBN 9780226545271 (e-book)
Subjects: LCSH: Japanese literature—19th century—History and criticism. | Japanese
    literature—20th century—History and criticism.
Classification: LCC PL726.55 .T68 2018 | DDC 895.609—dc23
LC record available at https://lccn.loc.gov/2017041010

Contents

Introduction

Modern, Japanese, Literary, History

In Italo Svevo's novel *The Confessions of Zeno,* Zeno Cosini is seated in a café when he overhears one man tell another how fifty-four bones in the human foot must work in perfect coordination for a human to walk. When Cosini rises to leave, he finds himself limping, now so aware of the theoretical complexity of bipedal locomotion that he can no longer do what was once natural. The predicament of Svevo's hero resembles that of anyone today who would write literary history, or *any* history predicated on causality so abridged as to be easily articulable. Indeed, apropos another academic discipline that has stalled before the difficulty of synchronizing the complex, Clifford Geertz named "the hallmark of modern consciousness . . . its enormous multiplicity."[1] Anthropologist or historian, we are now so cognizant of the manifold subtleties of cultural artifacts, their genealogies, and our interpretations of them that we hardly know where literally or figuratively to begin tracing their trajectory. Cosini only hopes to walk across the room. The literary historian must circumambulate his subject's entire edifice.

Literary history's charge to us was once ambitious but straightforward. It was to tell a story that combined other stories—our fiction, poetry, and plays—with their moment in time, and thus model history. It was by necessity a hybrid genre, encompassing criticism, biography, and intellectual or social historiography but organized under and by a narrative of progress. We are now more skeptical about the utility of history and narrative. Indeed, the illusionary coherence with which we now indict any narrative, but perhaps especially the historical, is a sign of how far the assumptions of literary modernism, already apparent in the nineteenth century, have undermined the foundations of many arenas of knowledge. So axiomatic is our skepticism that a book even as casually structured and argued as the present one, purporting to narrate something as elusive as literary history, must either coyly renounce the aims it pursues (by insisting, for instance, that history has nothing to do with the past but still signifies *something*) or install an apology as a coda. I do the latter. I am interested in how something called modern Japanese literature coalesced, and I believe answers can be found in the archive. But at the same time (here comes the apology) I understand that no resulting literary history claims durable authority. For while each subsequent attempt will doubtlessly add to the immense inventory of how and why writers write what they have, the accounting is never total as long as one deduction only begs another to amend it.

The search in Western literary history for a chain of determined causes and effects in modernity is, in Japan, often a search for West–East influences and effects and just as quixotic. The generation of Japan's literary historians who sought something definitive to say about Japan's century and a half of print culture, including Hirano Ken, Nakamura Mitsuo, Isoda Kōichi, and Etō Jun, is gone. We are left with *kasō bungakushi*: hypothetical literary history whose subject is no longer always literature but its systems (*seido*), ranging from the now unfashionable busywork of sorting writers into schools (Naturalist, Proletarian, Neo-Perceptionalist, New Third Generation, etc.) to the hypercommercialized business of awarding prizes to new and not so new writers.[2] That is not to say that all pretensions to literary history have to be bracketed as contingent because history itself is. Things do not have to be fully true to still be true. Just because René Wellek conceded that our attempts at evolutionary history have failed, this does not mean that any sort of history is futile or misleading.[3] But to be true, the arguments of a literary historian have to reconcile with an enunciable theory of the historical, a word I prefer to history because an attribute is easier to live with than an entity, and much less messy philosophically. I am aware that our current reduction of history is the consequence of our modern abandonment of a certain kind of metaphysics.[4] Whether we are right about that, though, hardly matters: what should be obvious in our present time of undoing is the "need to resist the understandable suspicion that codified literary history is a bankrupt enterprise. The truth is that we cannot escape from it and, even if we could, should not."[5]

The historical is commonly construed nowadays as radically subjective in determination. In Michel Foucault's words, it is "the most cluttered area of our memory." But that subjectivism nonetheless constitutes a real, insofar as history "is equally the depths from which all beings emerge into their precarious, glittering existence."[6] The question of the historical and the real is deferred to speculating what that depth could be: psychology, sets of discourses, even as ineffable a thing as the human spirit. Literary history without the question of just how "beings emerge" would be as tedious as literature itself without that same inquiry. What we modern beings are is a matter of social practices that, while conditional and variable, are the product of a logic as well as accident. My working assumption in this book is that the history of modern Japanese literature may be impossible to tell without taking note of the odd quirks of individual novelists, but that it also obeys what we understand as the form (read history) of culture in a modern nation-state that has preserved certain institutions and habits of its non-Western past. Literature and so too literary history are themselves integral parts of Japanese modernity and therefore also partake of a worldwide developmental model if with identifiably Japanese elaborations of that model.

This is an uneasy cohabitation, and its fragility plagues those who attempt the history of modern Japanese literature. To the extent that we have learned culture — "that complex whole," in E. B. Tylor's definition, "which includes knowledge, belief, art, morals, law, custom, and any other capabilities and habits acquired by man as a member of society"[7] — is not a vulgar production of social or economic relations, we are also tempted to retreat into a naïve ethnography of Japanese literature that never queries how our categories of study are themselves the legacy of the same history we pursue. These two temptations are why the history of modern literature in Japan, like in many places, is a history of prose fiction. This book will have relatively little to say about poetry or drama. It is with modernity and not just Japanese modernity that public and private life are integrated in ways that call for a literary genre that encompasses both historiography and biography. Novels do not succeed if their characters are no more than symbols of some collectivity or if their characters live in some purely private inaccessible space. A deceptively simple genre in some ways, the novel endorses a complex historical process but within a surprisingly stable and co-herent structure because of, as has been observed of the novel in English, "its unrivaled power both to formulate, and to explain, a set of problems that are central to early modern experience."[8]

That said, the structures of many Japanese novels in this regard do not cor-respond with what readers raised on their Western equivalents might expect. Japanese history since the early seventh century CE has been so shaped by its interrogative responses to the significance of the foreign models imported or imposed (Chinese, Korean, Euro-American) that its novels will inevitably trace a singular history.[9] More important is a far briefer history than literate Japan's millennium-plus: that of the opportunities or accommodations that literature has pursued or been consigned to within Japan's prison-house of modernity. My history of modern literature in Japan is not the result of an arbitrary period-ization. I believe in modernity as a distinct and describable episode, and one I suggest in the last chapter that has come to an end and a beginning. Despite the modern period's brevity, two of the three truly major events in all of Japanese history—the 1868 Meiji Revolution (usually referred to as the Meiji Resto-ration) and the Second World War in the mid-twentieth century—occurred within it. Western modernity, now over three hundred years old, registered that moment when the word modern came to mean "now," but defining the modern is harder than dating it, and so it is in Japan. It has been identified with the rise of a self-conscious subjectivity *and* with our status as objects of technological modernization; with rationality and faith in progress, the rise of capitalism and the ascendancy of the bourgeoisie *and* with the critique of those ideas as an inevitable ensemble; with an attitude toward historical chronology that posits origins *and* with life as a sense of the fleeting and ephemeral that lacks histor-ical reference; with structures *and* with their impossibility; with a structure of feeling toward contemporary reality *and* with social orders where feelings mean nothing; with the contradiction of being both individuals *and* interrelated. The modern has been linked with the sureness of scientific truth *and* the honesty of both madness and the imagination; with a split between some meanings that are firmly anchored to their referents *and* those that are not; with Enlightenment values *and* the efficiency of Auschwitz; and with both the empowerment and containment of human potential.

These definitions, gleaned from thinkers as diverse as Baudelaire, Marx, Darwin, Dewey, Nietzsche, and Foucault, were once intended to be only de-scriptive of modernity in the West. Moving beyond Europe and its colonies, the nature of the modern has to become more complex if only because so much of it is grafted upon places and cultures whose own histories interact with it both well and badly. To be sure, many cogent observers have identified Japanese modernity, whether native or borrowed, in terms cognate with those used in and for the West. Fukuzawa Yukichi argued across his oeuvre that civilization (*bunmei*) commences with doubts generated within the self, but he was only the first to note critical subjectivity as indispensable to it. More materially, all that Japan aspired to since 1868—W. G. Beasley's wish list was "constitutions, conscript armies, factories, Western-style novels and art"[10]—has long been analyzed as congenitally related desires embodying universal, not merely Western, values. If since the 1950s, the notion of a non-Western modernity largely congruent with the West's experience has been replaced by that of modernization, it is only because world events such as the Chinese Revolution, decolonization and the Cold War required, in Jürgen Habermas's words, a term that "dissolves 'modernity' from its modern European origins and stylizes it into a spatio-temporally neutral model" amenable to ideological machinations.[11]

It is nonetheless impossible to speak of modernization without the model of modernity, destined to be imprecisely derived worldwide since modernity is a process of local subjectification as well as rationalization. In Japan, we can find many examples of modernity (*kindaisei*) defined as a functional model, which is to say a society with certain sets of features that largely coincide with those found in Euro-American societies. One of Japan's leading literary historians, Miyoshi Yukio, defines modernity for Japan in just such terms as the period (*jidai*) of capitalist and democratic civil societies that prize notions of human liberty and freedom and the dignity of the individual.[12] But this model is best illustrated by the descriptions of Japanese modernity/modernization produced by the 1960 Hakone Conference, at which Japanese and foreign scholars (largely American) came together to describe the rise of modern economic production, social rationalization, and enfranchisement in Japan and implicitly elsewhere in the non-Western world via a model largely devoid of historical determinism. At the time, dialectical materialism was an ideal dangerously Marxist in its implications given the worldwide stakes of the Cold War and the local challenge to American hegemony. In hindsight, historian Victor Koschmann concludes with little effort that the Americans were in Hakone on a political mission fueled by values and ideology even as they seemed eager to promote a "value-free" definition of modernization.[13] For a conference strikingly devoid of insights from cultural or literary studies, one contribution was telling: Katō

Shūichi's characterization of the lists of features to be found in modern societies (urbanization, a high degree of use of inanimate energy, mass communications, etc.) as akin to the symptoms of a disease. Katō, an important figure in postwar literary circles as well as a trained physician, recommended that his fellow conferees consider these symptoms' "relationship in a syndrome so as to obtain a complete picture."[14] John Whitney Hall, the dean of the American scholars gathered at Hakone, responded that "the syndrome of symptoms described in our revised list . . . serves then to isolate a process of change and a condition of society," an isolation that in Hall's view exempted the Hakone Conference's work from political ideology.[15]

Do we know better now? There are many ways we can reconstruct the ideological work performed at Hakone, such as the twentieth-century imperative to move from an earlier Orientalist discourse on the uniqueness of the West to one which insisted just as vigorously on the necessity that Japan draw from the well of whatever made Western modernity modern. But in retrospect another reconstruction might be Foucault's clever critique of the idea of a symptom in the first place. In Europe in the eighteenth century, the same century that gave rise to the suprahistorical vision that enabled the practice of literary history, medicine codified the "uniquely privileged" observation of symptoms to know the invisible disease itself, leaving "the essence of the signified—the heart of the disease" "entirely exhausted in the intelligible syntax of the signifier." The literary work in literary history is no more history than the "cough, fever, pain in the side, and difficulty in breathing" are pleurisy: but they are all we can see, or read. Just as "the blueing of the nails is an unfailing announcement of death," the new lyric or story presents change but is not change, which is invisible.[16]

Despite the tendency of modernization theory to downplay it, modernity—including its literary configurations—has a geopolitical history equally unseen aside from its presumed indications. It is, if nothing else, a term for the "modes of social life or organization which emerged in Europe from the seventeenth century onward and which subsequently became more or less worldwide in their influence."[17] It is a history that in Japan occurred for the most part subsequent to Europe's but before the rest of East Asia's. It is also a history that unfolded at a geographical periphery, two facts related to each other. Just as modernity in Europe was reaching maturity (or decadence, in the view of some), Japan was grappling with structures and attitudes willed from what, while perhaps not too accurately termed a feudal past, certainly contested key features of basic modernization. These are features that, following sociologist Anthony

Giddons and others, I find in Japanese novels and stories to be the primacy of sexual or friendship relations over those of kinship, the proliferation of abstract systems across time and space, and the widespread fear no longer of nature or a god's wrath but instead the fragile (un-)certainties of modernity itself.

It is a basic question whether any setting outside Europe and its immediate offspring can sponsor modernity independent of the West's historical precedent. If the impetus for modernity comes from without, as it did in a Japan genuinely threatened by the West, then the dependency of the periphery on the center denies it the vital requisite of agency, the self-fashioning so important to how we understand modernity. Under the threat of foreign encroachment, native systems were not at stake so much as the defense of the realm. Japanese were well aware of the Opium Wars and the subsequent infringements on Japan's own sovereignty represented by Commodore Matthew Perry's arrival in 1853. In the realm of modern Japanese literature, this question of authenticity has typically been asked within the ongoing debate over Japanese literature's originality versus its mimicry of foreign exemplars. One answer is pessimistic: while Japan can have the world's fastest trains or safest streets, the intellectual project of modernization, though not without its successes (affluence, democracy, scientific breakthroughs, Nobel Prizes in Literature, etc.), is seen as inherently contradictory and disappointing because it could not have been spontaneous. But some answers have been less fatalistic. During the Second World War, a cohort of Japanese intellectuals linked their empire's forced eviction of the Western colonial powers with an overall critique of a modernity perceived, too, as a colonial ploy. Unfortunately, Japan's own colonialism was built, brick by brick, upon that same indicted modernity. More successful in the view of some has been the accommodation of a peripheral modernity with what is, in effect, a newer idea of just what modernity may mean—or rather, a definition that emphasizes less the functional model that the Hakone Conference endorsed and more a specific, historical product that is recognizable not so much by its resemblance to older, pre- or proto-modern features but to the uncanny talent of dominant social agents and institutions to manage change, defuse crises, and accommodate changing international conditions.

How Japan accomplished this is no mystery. It has happened elsewhere, too. This modernity counts among its indicators the emergence of the subject and the Foucauldian sciences of order that both produce and limit that subject. But it is also attested in the consolidation of the individual to the authority of the modern nation-state and the irony of a people increasingly permitted physical and intellectual liberties at the same time the repressive powers of society are internalized and consolidated. It has been cited as evidence of Japan's so-called incomplete modernity that a fully individuated citizenry never emerged, or that its state never fully converted its power into the logic of that citizenry's everyday life. But that is not so much incomplete as it is what Japanese modernity— yes, fully formed—*is*. Japan's modern success is also said to have achieved great material benefits and social entitlements despite (and occasionally because of) being non-Western. However, that view, in addition to being patronizingly Orientalist, fails to see that in Japan, as elsewhere, the specific things and rights in which those achievements are found also express how power is exercised within its modernity. One aim of this book is to reexamine certain key conjunctions in the history of Japan's modern literature where we can excavate just how literary texts came to embody emerging, dominant or resistant strategies of power in society. My attempt here is to map modern Japan's "governing metaphors" in two senses: how the terms of literary language were policed by the state ("state" being convenient shorthand for coordinated institutions of central authority), and how those terms themselves exercised their own power, governing in turn various critiques of the state or its logic. As Hayden White remarked, echoing Nietzsche, every discipline has to be defined in large measure by what it forbids its practitioners to do, as well as what it may enable.[18]

Two early efforts at writing literary history in modern Japan illustrate how the project was imbricated with modern Japanese society and governance from the start. Literary historiography is an enterprise launched in and by modernity, commencing in the West's eighteenth century. With the formation of modern nation-states in Europe, literary history was outfitted with the enabling new technology of modernity. If we differentiate literary history from literary criticism by declaring the former concerned with literature as creation and the latter with it as an institution, then literary history joins a host of other contemporary projects dedicated to the construction and not just description of cultural legacies as part of modernity's architecture with the reorganization of postmonarchial Europe into nations requiring, among other things, literary pedigrees. By the nineteenth century the genre had become truly popular. Hippolyte Taine's 1863 *History of English Literature* was a best seller in its day. With the injection of the ideas of Hegel and the Schlegels, it became self-consciously intellectual, a ground for the rehearsal of ideas on race, dialectics, and the pedagogy of modern citizens. Later, Marx, Darwin, Spengler, Weber, Adorno, and, in our own time, Foucault and Geertz lent further grand designs to a literary practice that was, until the late twentieth century, generally a triumphant narrative: a description of transitions from one state of affairs to another propelled by a chain of causes and their effects. In this developmental model, the early history of the novel has to start with something that is *not* the novel (diaries, newspapers, the epic) and then proceed, with the confidence of inevitability, to the feat of modern prose fiction. Nietzsche's *The Birth of Tragedy* is a good example: it is literary history with a plot, a protagonist in the form of an immaterial Zeitgeist. Like all literary histories in the West that owe something to the genre's impetus under Romantic thought, Nietzsche's was riveted by origins. Like other literary histories governed by a belief in historically inevitable nationhood—certainly the case in Japan—it needed to culminate in the satisfactory account of a great national classic in the past and the potential of a nation's great modern novel in the present. Literary history often had its *telos* in the heralded moment of a country's national unification, or definitive separation from a colonial power's own cultural hegemony. "We study literature in a discipline," writes Timothy Brennan, "with roots in a philological tradition first formulated with ideas of nations in mind, in the very period when modern nation-states were first being formed."[19] The ideological work of literary history was to confirm that each of its canonized texts embodies the national culture's singular, splendid history. In Japan, that work meant a focus on *junbungaku* (pure literature), a term coined in the late nineteenth century to counter the alien tradition of *kanbungaku* (writing in Chinese) and *gesaku* (frivolous literature) at home that fairly dominated the first half of that century.

At the same time, literary history was dogged by the accusation that it failed to explain aesthetic achievement adequately. If a literary history did not account for genius, then it proved Benedetto Croce's contention that the genre was impossible to begin with since every work of art was unique and therefore could not be categorized or generalized. There was indeed an aporetical problem with literary history at the level of the modernity it attempted to theorize. As a kind of representational narrative, its own claims to realism were always as problematic as those made by the novels it sought to explain. Other assaults on literary (and not just literary) historiography identified other knotty contradictions. Do texts produce the classifications they are placed within, or the other way around? Is there a closed hermeneutic circle between texts and the concepts that organize them (or are organized *by* them)? What is the relationship between a historical process and the values that are alternatively credited for being its result, or cause? The greatest charge of literary history's implausibility came when the genre was effectively left for dead in the West after attacks from Russian formalism and its scholastic heir, New Criticism. By the late—and increasingly Sophist—twentieth century, the only new literary histories being written were avowedly postmodern and paralyzingly ironic. (I have the 1987 *Columbia Literary History of the United States* and the 1989 *New History of French Literature* in mind.) In his influential 1970 essay "Literary History and Literary Modernity," Paul de Man argued that literature, history, and modernity were all hopelessly incompatible words. Modernity would forsake the notion of history; literature, with its "obsession with a *tabula rasa*, with new beginnings" would be equally antithetical.[20] This and other skeptical ideas that insinuated themselves into the common sense of literary scholars was the death warrant of traditional literary history. Where it survives, it is largely an antihistory, not much more than a record of ruptures and discontinuities, all of which are as suspect as the unities and continuities they have replaced.

Still, habits persist. Lawrence Buell surveys three examples of American literary histories and concludes that all share the same unexamined convention: the concept of the literary work as a sociogram, defined as "the encapsulated formation of a work's significance as historical artifact and national product."[21] The same is observed of recent literary historiography in Japan. Kamei Hideo points out that while a turn away from analysis of a work's content has served to disengage the significance of a work from its moment, the concomitant turn toward structure in the work has rejoined the two.[22] Such coincidences are not guaranteed. While the rise and fall of literary history in the West influenced Japan, its own literary history traces a markedly different path. Literary historiography in Japan started in the late 1870s with government tracts such as the Ministry of Education's *Nihon kyōiku shiryaku* (A Brief History of Japanese Learning, 1877) and Taguchi Ukichi's Western-influenced *Nihon kaika shōshi* (A Short History of Japanese Civilization, 1877–82), but it was never rendered wholly cynical, as happened in the West. It is a continuing process for reasons that have to do with the distinct track not only of Japanese literature but of Japanese modernity and its present-day residual effects. Those reasons comprise my prolegomenon for writing literary history today.

The emerging modern Japanese state's first attempt to tell the story of its country's literature, *Nihon kyōiku shiryaku*, was prepared with Philadelphia's 1876 Centennial International Exhibition in mind; the audience was the world. It takes a Sinocentric, Confucianist approach. It begins with little reference to literature but eventually declares that Japanese *bungaku*, in the sense of scholarship, is essentially *kanbungaku* writings in Chinese. Medicine, for example, is regarded as *bungaku*, since it teaches the proper conduct of one's life. Japanese literature is advertised as a particularly talented branch of Chinese culture (*kangaku*), but a branch nonetheless. But even this earliest example of literary historiography in modern Japan cannot be understood properly without knowing it was initially proposed—by an English employee of the ministry, David Morley—for the benefit of visitors to Philadelphia who might think Japan has no claim to a literature.[23] Or more precisely, without the benefits that Westernization was conferring, ten years into state-sponsored modernization, on a tradition that once may have valued the lyric over prose but now celebrated the practical (*jitsugaku*) over the poetic.

The earliest example of Japanese literary history after the Meiji Revolution is seldom read without attention to a West that challenged it. For the Ministry of Education, the West was an adversary to be impressed in part to defuse its threat; for Taguchi Ukichi (one of the most important figures in Meiji Japan for economics as well as historiography), the West was a place that, like China before it, could provide Japan with intellectual vigor even as it menaced it with military and commercial prowess. Taguchi's *Nihon kaika shōshi* is much more than a history of Japan and its culture. Published in six substantial volumes from 1877 (when Taguchi was only twenty-three) to 1882, it surveyed Japanese civilization from its origins to the start of the Meiji era. Like those histories that followed, his *Shōshi* relied not only on the writings of Tokugawa-period (1603–1868) historians such as Rai Sanyō and Arai Hakuseki, but on Western predecessors Henry Thomas Buckle (*History of Civilization in England*), Herbert Spenser, Thomas Macaulay, and John Stuart Mill. For Taguchi, literature, per se, was always a dialectical play between two forms of writing: *jō* (sentiment, what we might now call the subjective) and *chi* (knowledge, or the objective). But for literature to progress in Taguchi's estimation, it had to privilege *chi* over *jō*, prose over poetry, and the lives of the common people over those of the elites. Both views were not wholly contrary to that expressed in the *Shiryaku* or indeed the predominant opinion of the Japanese intelligentsia ten years into Meiji, a period when national concerns remained fixed on Japan's existential competition with the Western powers.

Taguchi, writing under the combined influence of Western modernity and Confucianism adapted over the Tokugawa period to accommodate an emerging native humanism, defined literature (*bungaku*) as "the manifestation of the human soul" (*hito no kokoro no kenzō nari*).[24] In this context, traditional definitions of *bun* (literature) were significantly reworked. Long opposed to *bu* (weapons), *bun* was the pre-Meiji term for what would become *bungaku*, and it was essentially a Sinitic, nominally Confucian concept. *Bun*—better understood as learning or scholarship—was proximate to the concept of the Way (Chinese *tao*). As Hayashi Razan succinctly puts it, "Where there is the Way, there is *Bun*; where there is no Way, there is no *Bun*."[25] In short, *bun* was instrumental. It referred to the intellectual and ethical means for keeping men in good order. More specifically, it referred to the study of the practical means of government.[26] The source of this knowledge, and therefore the principal idiom of *bun*, was the Chinese classics and their commentaries.

The rise of *kokugaku* (national learning) in the mid- to late Tokugawa began to challenge this worldview, and in the Meiji period the definition of *bun* (soon *bungaku*) underwent a revealing and decisive shift. It was not until half a dozen years into the Meiji period that the term *bungaku* appeared in print, and it was not until the late 1880s that the word came to be used predominantly in the sense that it is today, that is, as imaginative writing.[27] It is an irony of history that Western terms for literature were rendered into Sinitic Japanese with the morpheme *gaku*, or, "learning."[28] Prior to the Meiji period and in keeping with the Chinese organization of knowledge, literature was everything *but* fanciful prose. By the end of the Meiji period, classics such as the *Man'yōshū*, *Genji monogatari*, and *Kōshoku ichidai otoko*, once *uta* (poem), *monogatari* (narrative), and *ukiyozōshi* (popular fiction), respectively, were all subsumed under the omnibus of literature (*bungaku*).[29] In 1890, when *bungaku* was defined as "all proper knowledge and all proper emotions" that make us human, the term had obviously traveled far from neo-Confucian definitions of *bun* in the Tokugawa period.[30] But its transformation was not done. In his 1908 novel *Gubinjinsō* (Poppies), Natsume Sōseki (1867–1916) qualified what Japanese today call *bungaku* as pure (*jun*) literature, since the term still retained Tokugawa nuances of all knowledge, not simply that garnered or conveyed via what was awarded, or relegated, to the faculty of imagination. But more significantly, by Sōseki's time, just what was *bungaku* was a more unruly matter than definitions in the few early literary histories. To draw the fuller picture, this book attends to matters of the day not immediately literary at all.

This turn in the episteme of the literary from *bun* to *bungaku* was facilitated by the evolving taxonomy of academic knowledge within the confines of Japan's preeminent institution of higher learning, Tokyo Imperial University. In 1887, the university established the curricular and research divisions of English literature (*Igirisu bungaku ka*) and German literature (*Doitsu bungaku ka*). In 1889, a French literature unit (*Furansu bungaku ka*) joined them. This is important to note since Japanese intellectuals who, beginning in the 1880s, were using the word *bungaku* in terms congruent with those in England (literature), Germany (*Literatur*) and France (*littérature*) were institutionally linked with Tokyo Imperial University. Like so many words of the day, such as *kenpō* (constitution), *keizai* (economics), *geijutsu* (art), and so forth—Sinitic vocabulary expediently coined for an age of modernization and therefore signs of a hybrid modernity—*bungaku* was another index of what has been called the bastard child (*otoshigo*) of mid-Meiji's drive toward Westernization.[31]

Tsubouchi Shōyō (1859–1935), author of the 1886 theoretical manifesto *Shōsetsu shinzui* (Essence of fiction) was one such Tokyo Imperial University graduate. That his work was so entitled instead of "Essence of Literature [*bungaku*]" had something to do with how his alma mater deployed these terms. In the mid-Meiji period, *bungaku* referred to the *classics* of Chinese and Japanese literature but not yet to modern fiction, a genre for which *shōsetsu* was reserved but not yet subsumed under the *-gaku* of *bungaku*, an addition that literary historian Isoda Kōichi declared an irony of history a century later.[32] Shōyō and others of his generation were ambivalent about the worth of fiction and literature, as the varied career of his protégé and collaborator Futabatei Shimei (1864–1909) illustrates. Vacillating between a government career and his ambitions as a novelist, Shimei's résumé recalls the diverse and not always consistent meaning of the word *bungaku*. From the start, *bungaku* was deemed necessary for Japanese modernity but also critical of it, as Shimei's own *Ukigumo* (Floating Clouds, 1887–89), often hailed as Japan's first modern novel, attested, with its story of a bureaucrat both educated and rendered superfluous by the Meiji state. This ambiguity was evident by the late 1870s and in works of literary history such as the *Shiryaku* and the *Shōshi*, both of which attempted to resolve it through the regulatory work of literary history (*bungakushi*). At stake was not only Japan's reputation as a civilized nation but the definition of its proof, a national modern literature. Was it to be, in the spirit of the first decade of the Meiji period, a branch of practical learning? Or alternatively, was it to be like the great imaginative works of Western literature, objects of envy in Japan? Our twentieth-century sense of the word *bungaku* is the legacy of Japanese literary history's efforts early in the Meiji period but culminating in the last decade of the nineteenth century. British philologist and Tokyo Imperial University professor Basil Hall Chamberlain might have been able to claim in the early 1880s with some justification that the Japanese, in their frantic "pursuit of the advantages of the material side of European civilization" were exhibiting a "disdain for everything poetic, or even literary."[33] But that was to change soon enough, as the Japanese extended their work in building a new nation-state to literature. If true that nations are most appropriately distinguished by the way they are imagined, then Japanese intellectuals and officialdom made full use of their country's past and present hoard of literary texts to guide just how and where that imagination would be cultivated. There was ample precedent. The Meiji period was when many of Japan's national traditions were variously invented, systematized, and ideologized as state apparatuses. There was, for example, philologist and lexicographer Ueda Kazutoshi's German-influenced theory of Japanese as a national language (*kokugo*), a parallel with a national citizenry (*kokumin*) and a nation-state (*kokka*).

Still, we do not conjure out of thin air. Historian Mary Elizabeth Berry has shown, citing a great deal of premodern fiction, that there was a firm grasp of "'our country,' regularly identified with 'our people,'" by the turn of the eighteenth century.[34] Ethnologist Orikuchi Shinobu used the new word *kokubungaku* (national literature) in talking about the earliest Japanese written records and their mention of "marvelous visitors" (*marebito*) a millennium earlier.[35] The question of a nation-state (*kokka*) may be another matter, but the Japanese were always going to be a nation on account of "the fatality of language and the necessity of citizenship in the modern world."[36] Just how they did so is what made them less than fully commensurate with the rest of the world. Perhaps what we do instead of constructing our traditions is remember and promote them selectively, and here is one role that modern literary history in Japan has played. The nomination of a national literature was the direct product of a national literary history (*kokubungakushi*), not the other way around. To illustrate how this happened, and with what consequences, it is useful to look at the 1890 *Nihon bungakushi* (History of Japanese Literature) written by Mikami Sanji and Takatsu Kuwasaburō, classmates of Ueda Kazutoshi at Tokyo Imperial University. This work, like Taguchi's decades earlier, cannot be discussed without reference to Western literary history in addition to the burgeoning Japanese cultural nationalism. Taine and H. M. Posnett influenced Mikami, and his *Nihon bungakushi* shared with them Spencerian ideas of social organization and, more importantly, the belief in a national literature as the expression of Taine's troika of race, milieu, and moment. In his own somewhat tautological phrasing, Mikami defined a national literature as "something through which the country's people [kokumin] express the nation's unique thought [shisō], emotion [kanjō], and imagination [sōzō] in the written form of its national language [kokugo]."[37] There were local reasons for why and how these ideas found fertile ground. Mikami and his colleagues were heir to eighteenth-century kokugaku, in which Japanese literature, in the process of differentiating it from Chinese literature, was endowed with ineffably Japanese characteristics derived from or parallel to equally ineffable ethnic, cultural qualities.

The preface to Nihon bungakushi makes clear its debt to the Meiji discourse of practical learning when it declares its objective to be the demonstration, based on scientific research, of the use of literature (bungaku no kōyō) and the value of literary history (bungakushi no kachi). The authors insist theirs is the first true literary history in Japan, however hastily it was written. They had to familiarize themselves with the discipline of literary history in the West as well as confer with other writers and intellectuals in Japan to produce an amalgam to explain and evaluate the development of literature in Japan and its writers' styles. The end result of the "unprecedented . . . comprehensive organization" of their history is to prove, they hope, that Japan's literature is in no way inferior to any other nation's—and that it is destined to rise "like the morning sun" even farther.[38]

Literary history, the authors argue, is subsumed under historiography in general and therefore comes in two varieties: world history and national history. If what makes a Japanese literary history literary is its narrative of "the origins, development and transformation of literature," what makes it national is its restriction to those phenomena told historically within the context of a single nation.[39] Indeed, a national literary history is also the history of a nation; a national literature rises and falls with the history inseparable from each nation's "innate signs of vigor." Literary history, then, is a part of the history of civilization (bunmeishi), even if literary history, to be truly historical, must note what is low and vulgar as well what is as high and refined. Literary historians must take notice of political, social, religious, and other contexts of writing in addition to the writing itself. It is vital, Mikami and Takatsu insist, that Japan, too, have its narrative history of a rich literature, a history that will deepen the love of the Japanese citizenry (kokumin) for their country.

Unlike the earlier Shiryaku, Nihon bungakushi does not regard writing in Chinese (kangaku) as properly Japanese literature. Moreover, it departs from the Sinitic view of the literary as essentially the poetic when its authors declare they focus on prose writing above all other genres. "Fiction," they rule, "is simply one variety of elegant literature [*bibungaku*]. It would be impossible to speak of the proper progress of literature had it not developed in tandem with rational disciplines [*ribungaku*] such as history, philosophy and political science."[40] Moreover, *Nihon bungakushi*—whose second volume was planned as a textbook—has an explicitly pedagogical purpose. Japanese literature needs to be taught in the schools lest literature be thought of as a frivolous plaything (*ganrōbutsu*): like the endorsement of fiction, a necessary conceit for both Japanese literature's modernity and its vital role in the collateral construction of the nation-state. In the first chapter of *Nihon bungakushi* Mikami and Takatsu categorically define the object of their history as literature (*bungaku*). All that is literary, they stipulate, must satisfy four conditions. It must have an identifiable style derived from the talent (*myō*) of each writer. It must demonstrate human thought, sentiment, and imagination. It has to edify and entertain. Lastly, it is required to speak to great numbers of people, not few. At the same time the literary is to be differentiated from other types of writing. Of course literature has relationships with such things as jurisprudence and ethics, but just as in recent times Japan has seen the increasing differentiation of labor occupations, for example, so have scholarly discourses witnessed their own necessary fragmentation. Aesthetics and political economy are naturally literary to the extent they are expressed in language, but Mikami and Takatsu note that universities specialized these sorts of writing institutionally. The authors insist what makes literature distinct is the requirement it possess *omoshirosa*, "interest," "charm" or "pleasure." When we read law, we are interested merely in the meaning the words can supply us. But when we read literature, the words must somehow be an end in themselves. That is by no means a decadent goal, they quickly add, for it is only via pleasure that literature can hope to successfully improve *kokumin no seishin*, the "spirit of the national citizenry."[41]

This is true, they concede, of literature in all nations. But that is not to say that all national literatures are alike. Hegel had already accounted for cultural differences in terms of just how aware each evolving nation was of its spirit (*Geist*). Were each nation's sentiments, climate, geography, language, and customs alike, then so would be their literatures, and we would be saved the need for national literary histories. Each country has its national distinctiveness (*kokumin kokuyu no tokusei*), and Mikami and Takatsu give examples of how the Japanese diverged from the Chinese in the past and the West at present. They say it is the burden of literary history to explore and elucidate these differences fully. In this sense, then, literary history must be at the same time the history of civilizations. Mikami and Takatsu declare, in other words, that their literary history expresses the national distinctiveness of their country and that its utilitarian function is to further national achievement through its pedagogy. For them, Japanese literary history is conceived as a national allegory. The dialectical nature of the evolution of literature, passing through encounters with various foreign cultures and drawing strength from each, is much the same story told of the Japanese nation as a whole at this time. Indeed, *kokubungaku* (national literature), a neologism that had won out by the third decade of the Meiji period over such competitors as *wabungaku* (Japanese literature), was developed as a codified disciplinary regime of texts in lockstep with other material and discursive systems of the Meiji nation-state, all of them to some degree a conflation of culture (*bunka*), race (*jinshu*) and populace (*minzoku*). Modernization, it may be said generally, transforms agrarian societies and their structures with the notion of culture, a new form of identity largely cognate with nationality, and requires the kind of literacy, education, and construct of cultural homogeneity that literary history is precisely charged with supplying.

Critics and theorists in the West, such as Fredric Jameson, though they have on occasion exempted "great eastern empires" (one supposes Japan), have regarded non-Western literature, particularly those genres developed from "western machineries of representation, such as the novel," as invariably national allegories due to the absence of what Jameson, for one, regards as the crucial absence of a subjective split between the public sphere and the individual.[42] While such a view fails to satisfactorily account for the various morphologies of the modern Japanese novel, I agree with Jameson that the history of the modern novel outside the West, even in great Eastern empires, cannot be written without taking the presence and authority of the West into account, and in ways that point to a pressure on non-Western intellectuals to tell their stories coordinate with the exigencies of the histories their nations, emergent or otherwise, face. Any literary history today must explore contexts, conventional or otherwise, but contexts overlap if not neatly coincide with discourses of national identity and distinctiveness. This is hardly literary history's unique claim. If the question in Western Europe is the correlation between the rise of the novel and the rise of the middle class, then for a history of the novel in modern Japan we must additionally inquire: what is the correlation between the rise of *shōsetsu* (fiction) and the rise of the modern national subject (*Nihonjin*)? The assumptions and processes at work in nineteenth-century Japan were hardly unique, or even rare. Historian of American literature Larzer Ziff notes that in the early decades of the Republic, the literary was coextensive with political culture, "even as literature was coextensive with knowledge."[43] The two were rapidly divided in a rupture repeated a hundred years later in Japan's Meiji period. Just why this should be so in two modern(-izing) nations so different in their histories is one of the problems I explore in this book, and I state as a preface that the modern, whether it migrates between regions of the globe or evolves independently *and* similarly, has been observed to take roughly parallel interests in the morphology of its discourses, among them that of the literary. Language and writing have tended to be organized in comparable ways in modern nation-states. Any literary history other than the simply taxonomical has to ask why.

It is neither radical nor original to argue that the history of modern literature is inextricably linked with the history of the modern in general, though for a variety of reasons some historians have sought to inoculate these histories from each other. Literary history always requires something other than literature itself. As René Wellek observed, literature's history is the only one that can be that of something else. However discontinuous we may believe history to be, at some point we are forced to organize it, or as Jameson made a maxim after complaining about the necessity of doing so, "We cannot not periodize."[44] What a history of texts always entails are fewer diachronic narratives and more synchronic descriptions: con-texts. The historicity of a novel is not the same as its historical context, nor will it do to declare that literature has an historical context, which is close to meaningless since that includes everything temporally contingent or variable, infinite to the point of being indescribable. Just what narrower range of context the literary historian chooses is motivated by any one or combination of the factors David Perkins has enumerated: "tradition, ideological interests, the aesthetic requirements of writing a literary history, the assertions of authors and their contemporaries about their affinities and antipathies, the similarities that the literary historian observes among authors and/or texts, and the needs of professional careers and the politics of power in institutions."[45]

Without context there is no interpretation, though interpretation need not decide what a work is about. Rather, the goal always remains "to appreciate what plural constitutes it," as Roland Barthes put it.[46] Our reflex has been to establish a work of literature as evidence of something *else*, be it the author's life or his milieu. This instrumentality of literature is now often blamed for misunderstanding how literature, always a social practice, is less a second-order representation than an active agent in how the contradictions of lived reality are lived *and* how the social relations that produce such contradictions are guaranteed reproduction. Just *which* contexts to choose is the rub. Historicisms multiply whenever we minimize the distinction between texts and con-texts. The old story is told of Japanese ceramics experts being summoned to the Victoria and Albert to appraise the value of the museum's tea bowls, but being unable to do so since the curators had unwittingly discarded the original boxes upon which key information of provenance, and so forth was noted.[47] None of this is really new. Quintilian said, "Not only what we say and how we say it is of importance, but also the circumstances under which we say it."[48] But just what constitutes a circumstance has changed. Thanks to the vogue of New Historicism and its cultural poetics of a generation ago, few contexts strike us any longer as too far-fetched; anecdotes generate their own synecdochal auras of totality. If we now believe that literary texts and nonliterary texts circulate inseparably in complex networks, it is in part because some historiographical practices are energized by a free-fall faith in the power of contingency to explain everything. To say that texts are historically embedded and must be studied in the full range of their specificity sounds intuitively right but does not get us far. A better map is required. There may be "no escape from contingency,"[49] but we are trapped within it with other, less casual things.

Foucault noted that modern ethnology established a dichotomy between structure (the thinkable) and event (unthinkable, irrational). The event is an absolute contingency, which for better or worse led to its rejection (and that of history too) by the mainstream of modern anthropology. Foucault's reaction was: let's distinguish among events and be sure to "differentiate the networks and levels to which they belong."[50] He had his own problems with an insufficient theory of the historical, but there is more here than in the toolbox of many literary historians. The danger, noted by Hayden White, is that we uncritically ascribe to (real) events a "coherence, integrity, fullness, and closure of an image of life that is and can only be imaginary."[51] Still, these insights have on occasion been taken literally, if ironically. There may indeed be a world of factual chaos out there for which belief in contingency is an attractive antidote, but there are others. Carrying historically contingent contextualism too far is a risk in literary history. Contextual explanations can never be conclusive, if only because the path that runs from event to text, from anecdote to novel, is too faint to mark. Too often the context (for example, exorcism) of a text (*Lear*) locks the work of art in an effective structure of necessity which has to guarantee its effects even before it has been enacted. When Stephen Greenblatt ruled that the "task of understanding then depends not on the extraction of an abstract set of principles, and still less on the application of a theoretical model, but rather on an encounter with the singular, the specific, and the individual," he in no way freed himself from the need of principles or a theoretical model to know what is meant by "the singular, the specific, and the individual."[52] Everything ends up sewn neatly with no loose threads at its plainest, or circular at its cleverest.

One alternative is to *really* abandon our affection for causes and effects and simply describe correspondences between texts and events. Some of the events I discuss are anointed in Japanese history as *jiken* (major incidents). Others are hardly of note. Other histories by other people, using a similar method, could be written with reference to different events marking either crises replete with the ambiguities, rhetoric and ideological dodges that works of literature have laid bare, or crises that works of literature themselves have created. In any case, correspondences between these events and history are less relations than they are articulations, the construction of one set of relations out of another. This is still a theory of contexts, but not as background. They are what Gilles Deleuze and Félix Guattari reserved the metaphor of "rhizomes" for, assemblages of interactions. A context has to be defined as a structured field within which texts have varying near and far linkages with other social and material practices, none of which is predictable beforehand.

The project of reconstructing this kind of historical context has nothing to do with literary history's hope for grasping a whole society in its presumed reality. That is a romantic (and Romantic) ambition that literary historians of Japan (whether Japanese or not) have clung to long and tightly. One problem plaguing Japanese literary historiography has been the belief that Japan's modern literature is radically *estranged* from context, and therefore, its history from contextualism. "The distinguishing characteristic of the modern Japanese novel," wrote Nakamura Mitsuo, "is the fact that it developed in a manner quite removed from the context of the surrounding environment. This applies not only to the novel or to literature alone, but is characteristic of everything which has ever gone by the name of 'culture' from the Meiji period until our own day."[53] But it is impossible for anything we would want to deem cultural to develop free of context. Self-appointed guardian of literary studies Harold Bloom may want to dismiss cultural criticism as "astonishing garbage,"[54] but the articulations between literary text and the rest of modern Japanese culture are where we discover how that culture allows its people both to overcome the contradictions they face in their lives and to make sure the means of social production are guaranteed reproduction.

The Rise and Fall of Modern Japanese Literature voices my objection to Nakamura's view by suggesting that the contexts in which modern Japanese literature developed were not wholly arbitrary. The relationship between text and context is tautological, but not entirely. The history of modern Japanese literature is coordinate with how the exercise of power—on behalf of the state and against it—was woven in ways both Japanese and generically modern. To prove that, I discuss Japanese authors and works: some canonical but some not. In addition I write about contexts bearing on Japanese literature but not themselves literature: newspaper journalism, theater, the influence of Western fiction, and that of the fine arts. Ralph Cohen spoke for a generation of literary historians when he called "inadequate a conception of literature . . . that takes no account of paintings that include writing or illustrate writing, that disregards the music in sung prayers and oratorios, that sees no relation between Descartes' *Meditations* and the meditative poem or Shaftebury's and Mandeville's dialogues and the development of the novel, between the narratives of criminals and the parodies of affairs of state."[55] But there is also talk of things not yet found in Japanese literary histories: stock exchanges, spinning mills, the writing of constitutions, television, theories of multiple personalities, and handheld digital pets. I think about Korea, boogie-woogie music, and a serial murderer, all parts of Roland Barthes's plural. I do not aim to be either conclusive or exhaustive. Neither do I intend to let the literary dissolve within a grab bag of culture, as did the 2009 *A New Literary History of America*. Still, with David Perkins, I believe that the "contextual explanation of literary texts rests ultimately on faith, on an intuition."[56] I mean to sketch a surface best graphed by reference to how Japanese literature has been shaped in ways congruent with how the nation evolved from an oligarchic state to a constitutional monarchy; from an industrial-militarist power to a modern, democratic and rich capitalist nation; and now, in the early twenty-first century, into something upon whose precipice we stand and are barely peering into and can only name at the risk of soon looking foolish.

I place my book amid other recent histories of modern Japanese literature and acknowledge my debt to them while explaining why I have added another. One could easily account for the many literary histories that continue to be written in Japan, or by foreign scholars of it, by noting how relatively late the genre came to Japan. Japan might be allowed at least a good century and half of literary historiography before it, too, finds the practice depleted or déclassé. I suggest that Japanese literary histories, such as those by Donald Keene, Katō Shūichi, and Konishi Jin'ichi, continue to be written because the history of Japanese modernity, whether it is over or not, continues to press certain issues more insistently than is done in the West. Keene, Katō, and Konishi are informative and useful; each proceeds from a different repertoire of reading, but they share a commitment to the canon as a measure of literary merit and to the construction of a chronological line that embeds that canon sequentially. (Japanese literary history's ever-present adjunct, the *nenpyō* [chronological table], retains its influence today.[57]) Each of their histories accepts Jameson's demand for periods, and within each period a pyramid of literary value. Each has appeared in both English and Japanese. Undergraduates regularly consult them, and they are what *The Rise and Fall of Modern Japanese Literature* will be compared to. I, along with my predecessors, accept canons as inevitable as long as we continue to print, teach, and critique some works and not others. I also accept the commonsense deployment of a forward chronology, since writers can be cognizant only of what comes before them, not after. But then we part company. In 1991, the government-funded National Institute of Japanese Literature dedicated its annual international conference to the theme of Japanese literary history. The highlight of those three days was the unprecedented appearance before the audience of all three scholars who had recently made literary history in Japan so popular: Keene, Katō, and Konishi. I was in the audience. Each was asked why he decided to write a literary history. Keene replied he wanted to give his readers something with *eiensei* (permanence). His literary history was one, he believed, that would not require amendment. It would be the *truth* of modern Japanese literature rather a cultured appreciation of it.

This is the naïve dream of some historians: to fix and make a sure record of the past. David Perkins has pointed out the obvious, that "partisanship and simplification are very common in literary histories."[58] Keene's history of Japan's modern literature, *Dawn to the West*, uses language that leaves no doubt of the author's confidence. Masamune Hakuchō (1879–1962) is "unendearing"; Satomi Ton (1888–1983) is a "lightweight . . . immoralist." The "truths" of Kamura Isota (1897–1933) are dismissed as "insufficient," while Mishima Yukio's (1925–70) *Kamen no kokuhaku* (*Confessions of a Mask*, 1949) was somehow never "fully understood." While these views were in dispute at the time that Keene voiced them and even more so today, he was not inclined to revisit them.

"Once I completed a chapter and moved on to the next one," Keene wrote, "the temptation has been to think with relief that I 'disposed' of it."[59]

Keene's ambition for the longevity of his literary history was unsurprisingly met with incredulity at the conference, from his fellow panelists especially. But I wish to defend *Dawn to the West*—not on the grounds of its advertised permanence but for opposite reasons. While Keene's history may be the least erudite of the three, it is also the most promising because it opened the door to the demonstrable multiplicity of reception and interpretation. Even Keene, in his rhetoric, admits to a certain problem with ascertaining the value of the books and stories he discusses. He uses more than one yardstick in measuring literariness, and with that multiplicity falls apart any hope of the evaluation of literature being unitary now or ever. Throughout *Dawn to the West* he refers to "the Japanese reader" and "the Western reader." Leaving aside the question of just what these archetypes are or how they have been arrived at, Keene treats his readerly categories as if he were neither, or rather both, having unobstructed access to the minds of the Japanese and those of us not. There is the Japanese reader, the Western reader, and then there is Donald Keene, the voice of the presiding literary historian/judge who would forgo talk of his own particular perspective in order to render permanent verdicts.

Of Shimazaki Tōson (1872–1943), Keene writes that his "*Spring* [*Haru*, 1908] has little appeal for Western readers, but Japanese readers . . . can be stirred by the youthful hopes of the Meiji past."[60] Just *how* Keene knows this is irrelevant. The point is that by positing the existence of *two* novels entitled *Haru* by Tōson—one for us and one for them—Keene places the determinant of a text's worth not in the words themselves, or the author's intent, but in the reception of the text by its variegated readers. Keene is torn in two directions: Keene as belletristic arbiter and Keene as amateur anthropologist eager to point out how often unique and incomparable experiences of Japanese and Western reading can be. The obvious critique aside, this latter insight of Keene's should be encouraged. His intuition saves his literary history from the datedness and naïveté of earlier times. His solipsistic dichotomy of the Japanese reader and the Western reader, though heir to Orientalist canards, leads to the possibility of literary history that is no longer an encyclopedic catalog of great works, but instead a self-conscious and even humble investigation into the sociology of reading within a given linguistic and cultural milieu at a given time. In effect this would be a study of reception, by which I mean a study of literacy, its technologies, and its telos.[61] "Consciousness and subjectivity are unrepresentable," writes Fredric Jameson, "only situations of modernity can be narrated."[62] The history of literary modernity has to be interdisciplinary and drawn on knowledge far beyond the ken of the narrowly literary. Given the vast charge of such a study, it has to be strategically interrogative rather than confidently narrative. What previous literary histories have done may be incomplete or prejudiced, but that invites us to do something else. My own effort, *The Rise and Fall of Modern Japanese Literature*, argues that the course of Japan's modern literature is no passive reflection of its national, cultural modernity, but instead one of the technologies that actively produced it. At the same time, remembering that a novel, in the words of Edward Said, "is neither a frigate nor a bank draft,"[63] I mean to explore the particular and often autonomous work of art. It is there, in the work of metaphor, that the vitality as well as the strictures of the modern is possible. But governing metaphors reminds us that the state and its array of apparatuses are no strangers to rhetoric and how it rules our everyday lives and the imagination of something, which is not everyday. "Literary history cannot simply be a genealogy of what has been written," writes one Japanese critic; "it has to include the gulf between the written and what is not."[64]

One scholar has stated, "Twentieth-century Japanese fiction has been plagued by a dearth of imagination."[65] That is not true. No modern society can *be* without a cultural life that is not its expression but its fantastical complement; it is there to compensate for the real and virtual insufficiencies of an otherwise totalized modern life. The metaphors for modernity that literature supplies us are the rhetoric through which perception is conditioned, generated, and go on to govern. The chapters that follow argue that the imagination plays an intrinsic role in the history of modern Japan. They look not just at what modern Japanese literature *says*, but at what it *does* and for whom. The gaps in my survey are many. Writing in the early twenty-first century, Kawanishi Masaaki spoke for the field when he said the history of modern Japanese literature is a hundred and twenty years old, dated from Shimei's *Ukigumo* and divided neatly in two by defeat in the Second World War.[66] I devote little attention to either. Japan is home to two Nobel Prize winners in literature, but neither laureate gets his own chapter. Some clamor for an "entirely new 'Japanese literary history'" that accounts for the imaginative power of anime and manga in media and society.[67] One critic has attempted it with movies and rock music, another with baseball.[68] A valiant attempt was made to tell its ancient history as the embodiment of *moe*, an affect only recently discovered in present-day euphoric attachments to stuffed toys or action figures.[69] This is none of those. I will soon be lectured on all my omissions, but that is why literary history, despite its much-heralded death, persists. Half a century ago the journal *New Literary History* asked its own existential question: "Is Literary History Obsolete?" But then, just what is this excited, resuscitated talk today of "world literature," if not the yearning to write literary history all over again?

The "modern," wrote Henri Lefebvre, "is a prestigious word, a talisman, an open sesame, and it comes with a lifelong guarantee."[70] He might have said so of "literary" and "history" too. We all know about the West's enchantment with Japan since Marco Polo called it "the land of gold" and Jonathan Swift a "flying island." More contemporary voices would have us believe Japan is the first nation to make it to the finish line of history. My claims for Japan will be exceptionalist because they are not; *The Rise and Fall of Modern Japanese Literature* is my motion to forge the four words "modern, Japanese, literary, history" into something ordinary but compelling as the constellation moves forward in our own time to surprise us, all over again, with the yet unimagined novelty of modern Japanese literature after its rise, fall and now what is arriving to take its place.

1

Bird-Chasing Omatsu

It is 1868, before the boy-emperor Mutsuhito's new patrons have moved his throne from Kyoto but after rebel troops fighting in his name have occupied the shogun's seat in Edo. The civil war will not be over until the middle of the following year, but the Tokugawa military's tent administration (*Bakufu*), in and around Edo Castle since 1603, has already been renamed the Eastern Capital in anticipation of the emperor's arrival. The local population is unsure whether to pronounce the new name "Tōkyō" or "Tōkei," and they wouldn't be entirely certain until the turn of the following century, but that is only one sign of the confusion that reigns in former Edo. Soldiers are encamped in the streets of what would later be called Ginza but with none of its department stores yet, just freak shows (*misemono*), street merchants, fortune tellers, town criers (*yomiuri*), and gambling parlors (*tekkaba*). There, a young woman, beautiful but of the untouchable caste (*hinin*), sings songs from door to door for small coins in a form of begging euphemistically known as "bird-chasing" (*torioi*), referring to the practice of dispersing harmful birds from fields with noise. Bird-chasing, along with so much street activity (such as hawking newspapers and cross-dressing in public), would be outlawed by the new government by the end of the first decade of the Meiji period.

This young woman, Omatsu (a name with all the plebian airs of "Molly"), never earns much but her good looks attract admirers. A soldier, Hamada, falls in love only to be swindled out of two hundred silver coins by Omatsu, who is still seeing another lover, fellow untouchable Ōsaka Kichi. Next to fall victim is clothing store clerk Chūzō. Infatuated with Omatsu, he is cheated out of money—actually, his employer's—by Omatsu in cahoots with her mother and Kichi.

More intrigue follows when Omatsu and Kichi head west to Kichi's hometown of Osaka, worried that the authorities are in pursuit. When a fellow criminal betrays them, Kichi is captured just outside Tokyo and imprisoned. But Omatsu escapes only to run into Chūzō, who, fearing his employer's wrath, has fled Tokyo meaning to commit suicide. Omatsu sees her opportunity. She says she deserves to die as well, and that it must be fate that has brought them together for a double suicide (*shinjū*). But, Omatsu adds, what's the hurry? You still have some money left, so why not live as husband and wife? At least for a few months, until the cash runs out? Chūzō pledges his love to Omatsu. Fleeing further west to skirt the civil war, Chūzō falls ill. Omatsu nurses him, but their money is pilfered and they have to depend upon the kindness of a merchant, Sadajirō. Sadajirō suggests to Omatsu that she could earn a good living if she came to work for him as a geisha. Omatsu sees another opportunity. Dumping the ailing Chūzo, she follows Sadajirō only to realize that she has sold herself into virtual sexual slavery. Sadajirō confesses that he had been trailing her and Chūzō, and that it was he who stole the last of their money. He is in fact the notorious criminal Sakuzō, and he means to keep Omatsu for himself. Resisting him, Omatsu tumbles into the sea and is lost beneath the waves.

Until, that is, a passing steamer rescues her. Making her way to the home of Chūzō's father, Omatsu pretends to be his legal daughter-in-law who therefore is entitled to financial support. Worried that Chūzō will show up and expose her charade, she feigns illness until she judges the coast clear, and only then tells Chūzō's parents that, alas, their son is dead. Buddhist pieties pour out of her. Surely now, she says to the father, you can have no doubts my story is true. Chūzō's family is convinced until Hamada storms into the house. He calls Omatsu a liar and declares her a *dokufu* (literally a "poison woman," but more broadly, murderess) and tells the parents the real story in lieu of the false one they've heard from their pretend daughter-in-law. Soldiers arrive and take

Omatsu away, not to prison but to Hamada's own house, where, still smitten, he devotes himself to her despite her low birth. "We are all brothers," he lectures her. Since they parted, Hamada has risen in the world, achieved all his worldly ambitions, and even wed the daughter of a powerful provincial lord. But his success is incomplete without Omatsu by his side. It may be wrong for a samurai to love a criminal, and an untouchable one at that, but love is *shian no hoka*—"blind."[1]

Omatsu sees more opportunity. Yes, she says, I have always desired you, too. More than two years of bliss follow, with Omatsu more beautiful than ever and looking as if *mushi mo korosazaru*—she wouldn't kill a flea.[2] Karma intervenes again, however, and Kichi, after his release from jail, is hired as a servant by Hamada and so crosses paths with his former accomplice. I have always, Omatsu tells the resurfaced Kichi, desired *you*. They hatch a plot against Hamada's legal wife, after whose departure the two lovers are free to lead a life of debauchery under Hamada's roof. Eventually, complications from their plot against Hamada's wife wrongly implicate Hamada himself. After he is hauled off to jail and commits suicide there, Omatsu and Kichi take his household valuables and head for Tokyo, where they hope to dwell undetected. But karma dictates otherwise. On their way east to the capital, they run into Sakuzō, who declares his intention to take Omatsu back from Kichi. When Kichi is killed in the ensuing struggle, Omatsu sees still more opportunity and goes to live with Sakuzō. She takes advantage of an unattended hunting rifle one day and tries to shoot him, but his angry pursuit of her is halted when a large bear eats him. The animal turns toward Omatsu. She runs and falls into a ravine, where an itinerant priest rescues her. Impressed by providence, she resolves to follow the Way of the Buddha and becomes the priest's disciple. Convinced that her beauty has been the cause of her downfall, she deliberately disfigures herself with tongs drawn from a fire.

For years she studies the holy sutras in a remote mountain village. But once a poison woman, always a poison woman. Longing for the big city, one night Omatsu sneaks into the priest's quarters intending to pocket enough money to return to Tokyo. When the priest awakes she pretends to be there to satisfy her carnal desires with him. The offended priest orders Omatsu out of the village, whose people beat her savagely as she leaves. Penniless, and with a face whose deliberate scars are festering and swollen, Omatsu turns to petty crime, resulting in her arrest and punishment all over again. Resolved to find her mother, she is caught in a terrible blizzard while making her way to Tokyo. As luck would have it, she runs into a now healthy and prosperous Chūzō. He gives her a little money as an act of compassion, enough to return her to the city and her mother, and even to pay for some medicine, but to no avail: her condition worsens, and on 9 February 1878, she dies, "running wildly like a mad dog," a fate in keeping with what is declared "the beastly nature of a beautiful woman" (*bijo no jushin*).[3]

This is a true story, though truth, its definitions, and antonyms are what I explore in this chapter. My reading will be less interested in Omatsu as a female criminal at the start of Japanese literary modernity than it will be in the negotiation of the actual versus the imaginary in early Meiji. The account I start with here is distilled from a wildly successful woodblock book printed by entrepreneur Ōkura Magobei in 1878 in his relatively new publishing operation, Kin'eidō, the same year that fountain pens and orchids as well as poison women were all the rage in Japan.[4] The story might be absurd, but so is Henry Fielding's picaresque *Tom Jones*. Technically the format was that of a *gōkan*: an illustrated, woodblock-printed *kusazōshi* (picture book) but bound in smaller format. Once denigrated by writer Tamenaga Shunsui (1790–1844) as playthings (*gangu*) for women and children,[5] they served as a vehicle for popular fiction in the late Tokugawa period, often incorporating what we would consider "news." First written in *kana* syllabary, later with Sino-Japanese graphs glossed phonetically for reading by women and children, *gōkan* were soon the most widespread of *gesaku* writing and in time built the mainstay readership of modern fiction. Their success was not without resistance, however: famed male writer Uchida Roan (1868–1929) commented in 1912 on how uncomfortable the sight of women reading still made him.[6]

The appearance of *Torioi Omatsu kaijō shinwa* (The New Maritime Tales of Bird-Chasing Omatsu) sparked a major revival of the genre, producing "the first best-seller made by a newspaper."[7] *Shinwa* was written in three volumes over approximately forty days by dramatist and *gesaku* writer Kubota Hikosaku (1846–98), who had been born into the family of a shogunal vassal (*bakushin*) only to slide down the social register after the Meiji Revolution. He worked various jobs: as a bureaucrat, assistant to kabuki dramatists, a hack journalist, a *machiai* (brothel) proprietor and finally, a tea ceremony devoteé and tutor.[8] His *Shinwa* was overseen, however, by Kanagaki Robun (1829–94), a *gesaku* writer of humble origins who rose rather than fell in life, from being the son of a fishmonger to reach in time the upper echelon of the cultural establishment through ambition and hard work. *Shinwa* was illustrated by Yōshū Chikanobu and after it went on sale on 20 February 1878, sold an impressive eight thousand copies.[9] It was sold without proper binding just to keep up with demand.[10] It cost a little over twelve *sen*, roughly the price of a good *gyūnabe* (beef bowl)—a relatively high price in part because of the expense of woodblock printing, which cost one yen per ten lines at the time.[11] In the following years, dozens more *gōkan* attempted to replicate *Shinwa*'s success, and many did quite well, especially once the use of metal type after the early 1880s brought costs and prices down.

Shinwa was noteworthy in other ways. It was based, more or less, on a series of fourteen newspaper installments. No article had ever been serialized at such great length. Two or three parts had been the rule. They ran from 10 December 1877, to 11 January 1878 under the working title *Torioi Omatsu no den* (The Account of Bird-Chasing Omatsu) and with only one anonymous illustration. Unlike the *gōkan*, the newspaper version was meant to be *read* rather than viewed,[12] and for that reason it has been lauded as epochal (*kakkiteki*) in literary history.[13] It was the first time a newspaper led readers to a novel, if we may use the term loosely. Close examination reveals that *Shinwa* is already unusual for a *gōkan*. Sino-Japanese characters are provided with phonetic glosses to ease reading, and the illustrations and the text do not always match up. It may seem odd that Omatsu's exploits were reported as news, upstaging the 1877 Seinan War (also known as the Satsuma Rebellion), but that is what weekly news magazines still do.

The history of Japan's newspapers, per se, is not long, if we follow Albert Altman's definition of the medium as a "periodical in publication, mechanical in reduplication, available to all readers willing to pay the price, miscellaneous in content, timely in material, and published by a going concern."[14] Preceded in the early seventeenth century by *kawaraban* (handbills that "effortlessly crossed the fluid borders of science, magic, astrology, folk belief, political/moral ideology, literature, poetry, and religion"[15]), its proper history begins with the modern arrival of foreigners in Japan, who had their own periodicals in their restricted settlements. The *Nagasaki Shipping List and Advertiser* commenced in 1861; and in his 1881 book, *Young Japan*, foreign journalist John Reddie Black tells the story of explaining to a storeowner in 1872 that he needed to stock newspapers every day; the proprietor did not realize the news constantly changed,[16] though in hindsight we might say he had a point.

Initially the press was an interest of the state and soon its arm. As early as 1857, Emperor Kōmei was listed as a subscriber to the *Illustrated London News*.[17] The first Japanese-language newspaper was the *Kanhan Batabia shinbun*, a translation of a Dutch paper published in Java and sponsored by the Bakufu six years before the revolution. The first paper to use metal type was the 1869 *Yokohama mainichi shinbun*, a project underwritten by the Kanagawa prefectural governor. The *Tōkyō nichinichi shinbun* had most of its print run purchased by the treasury (Ōkurashō),[18] just as the Foreign Ministry subsidizes today's *Japan Times*. But the newspapers did not lack for readers. When train service started in 1872, newspapers were there for sale in the stations. Passengers were soon reading them on board. By 1873, there was a boom in newspaper publishing when the government counted seventy-nine nationwide. Newspapers around the world were key in the development of national modernity, not only because they began to make transparent the heretofore invisible workings of government, but because "the temporal distance between reader and event is bridged by the technology of instantaneous dispersal of news—which makes possible a relatively small temporal gap between reader and event."[19] The development of a national postal system started in 1871, and newspapers enjoyed free delivery for a decade. Local libraries, which prohibited reading aloud along with smoking and conversation, were built and reading rooms (*shinbun jūransho*) were set aside for newspapers, even in the prisons for the rising numbers of inmates who could read. This and the rationalization of publishing costs helped the Japanese, already highly literate, constitute a national readership united by the distribution of news and magazines. Newspapers, along with the telegraph, railroads, and steamships, meant that the face-to-face communications of the Tokugawa period were rapidly replaced with media that spread and accelerated contact between individuals and groups. Newspapers soon replaced the Tokugawa period's for-profit lending libraries (*kashihon'ya*) as the source of reading materials for the public. With the start of subscription home delivery in 1877, "the public acquired the habit of reading a fixed amount of printed material each day."[20] The proliferation of newspapers in early the Meiji period, coupled with the introduction of inexpensive one-yen *enbon* editions of books at the start of the Shōwa period (1926–89), was the signature event in the creation of a national readership for fiction in Japan.

The audience for Kubota's *Torioi Omatsu no den* and the later *Shinwa* may have constituted the first modern readership in Japan by virtue of its scale,[21] and it is not so far-fetched to think Omatsu's wide-ranging travels had something to do with the marketing of the newspaper outside Tokyo. That *Shinwa* appeared first in the newspapers and only later as a book points to how differently a story would be received as a collective news experience in lieu of a private literary one. "As the book page yields the inside story of the author's mental adventures," noted Marshall McLuhan, "so the press page yields the inside story of the community in action and interaction."[22]

Serialized reports, each approximately two columns in length and in time run for as long as six months, were an early form of media narrative dubbed *tsuzukimono* or *tsuzukibanashi* (continuing stories). They were defined by Nakamura Mitsuo as "writings in a documentary vein in a fictional form," indicating a telling generic confusion,[23] or what Michael McKeon, speaking of seventeenth-century England, called the "double epistemological charge" of news to be historically objective yet "demystified as a 'romance' convention in disguise."[24] Despite the fact that these *tsuzukimono* have to be regarded as news journalism (*kiji*) common at the time—the *Omatsu no den* installments were the same length as more unambiguous news items—these are held to be the precursors to the newspaper fiction (*shinbun shōsetsu*) securely in place by the end of the nineteenth century. Like Omatsu's, the most popular were soon reissued as books that sold as genre hybrids (from our point of view) of news and entertainment. *Shinwa*, for example, retains the precise details of time, amounts of money, and people's ages but is also replete with the sorts of punning and other wordplay associated with *gesaku* and not news. In 1885, an essay published in the *Yomiuri shinbun* by journalist Katō Hyōko under his penname Renga Kanjin already noted the debt that fiction owed to newspapers' problematic precedent of publishing *tsuzukimono* in a medium dedicated to news:

> A newsman would be ashamed to publish tawdry or lewd *tsuzukibanashi*. He can only take what is interesting or meritorious from what his reporters [*tanbōsha* (poorly educated, underpaid menials)[25]] have managed to learn and, venturing into neither libel [*hiki*] nor obscenity, turn it into fiction or light frivolity, and hardly earn accolades from readers. As one person has said, these long stories resembling fiction are better published in reserved literary sections of the newspaper, than mixed with articles in the miscellany pages [*zappō ran*]. . . . But since our *Yomiuri shinbun* cannot print fiction as news, in the coming year we will create a separate section for it.[26]

But no sooner than 1886 the *Yomiuri* stopped publishing *tsuzukimono* and replaced them with the generically secure *shinbun shōsetsu*, making the transitional genre a brief one.

Fiction in newspapers is first attributed to the *roman-feuilleton* found in the

Parisian press in the first half of the nineteenth century. By the 1860s, it had reached the Anglo-Saxon world, where the press was largely regional rather than national as in France and Japan. In any case, the practice did not last long there. But it has continued to the present day in Japan. It is debated whether *Shinwa* should be called Japan's first *shinbun shōsetsu*—*Iwata Yasohachi no hanashi* (The Story of Iwata Yasohachi, 1875) and *Kinnosuke no hanashi* (The Story of Kinnosuke, 1878) are also mentioned as possibilities. But *Iwata* was written in an old-fashioned, early-nineteenth-century style and serialized in only two parts, while one contemporary observer judged *Kinnosuke* to be "seventy percent fiction, thirty percent fact"[27]—so much fiction making needed, perhaps, to drive home the point that moral didacticism was still required. Literary history reflexively awards the title of first *shinbun shōsetsu* to the somewhat later *Konjiki yasha* (The Gold Demon, 1897–1902) by Ozaki Kōyō (1868–1903), even while opinion concedes that *shinbun shōsetsu* is the original "foundation of our national literature" (*kokumin bungakuteki kiban*).[28] But histories of modern Japanese literature never begin the development of the modern novel in Japan here, in 1885, with the relegation of the fictional to its own newspaper pages. That landmark development has to wait until Futabatei Shimei's *Ukigumo* two years later, when generalizations such as Edward Seidensticker's that the "obsessively, gnawingly intellectual" "single theme" of modern Japanese literature is the "identification of modernism with individualism" might ring true.[29] As Ozaki Hotsuki notes, the standard narrative of modern Japanese literary history starts with Shimei because there it locates the germination of the *kindai jiga* (modern self). But in doing so, that history is "chased into a dead-end alley" and rendered a history of "the superfluous man" (*yokeisha*).[30] Mainstream literary history in Japan has only in recent decades looked at newspapers and their readership, but no subsequent single theme in Seidensticker's estimation would have been possible without them.

Tsuzukimono were long disparaged as reading fit only for "cats and foxes," a euphemism for "geishas and prostitutes."[31] Literary historians might categorize *Shinwa* as Tokugawa-period, not modern, literature on the basis of a convoluted plot. But they overlook the interest of the state and media in just how the work circulated as fiction or not fiction. In part this may be the consequence of the fact that reports of unambiguous news—details of the Seinan War, for instance, and ominous developments on the Korean peninsula—had appeared in newspapers in serialized formats of similar size and design. An emphasis on war reportage may have retarded the development of newspaper fiction in Japan.[32] In any case, most literary historians take the appearance in the mid-1880s of experimental fiction penned by a new elite trained in Western languages and literatures as the origin of Japanese literary modernity. Impressed by the colloquial and mimetic nature of European fiction, the intelligentsia more or less adapted it for their own language and milieu. The *tsuzukimono* and the tales of murderesses they so often related led some to define the genre as synonymous with female criminality and were sometimes judged too journalistic to be serious literature. They tended to report names, dates, and locations precisely rather than veil them to avoid shogunal censure, as was the practice in earlier times. Alternatively, they were judged too plainly holdovers of late Tokugawa, premodern *gesaku*. While literary historian Honma Hisao, for example, praised *Shinwa* as somewhat better than other early Meiji accounts of *dokufu*, it too, like others, "was nothing more than the unique product of an amateurish [*sarushibaiteki*] and transitional time."[33] It was the much later literary historian, Kamei Hideo, who saw the *tsuzukimono* had a different topology and chronology than had Tokugawa-period literature, replete with the accuracy of detail part of the disciplinary discursive regimes Japanese modernity would impose.[34] Like newspapers in the West, they provided a metonym for what modern life was and aspired to be. The fact newspapers matter so little to us today registers not only the rise of digital media, but raises the question of whether we still live in modernity.

Omatsu's adventures, told not only in newspapers and books but on the stage, in popular ballads (*kudoki*), and woodblock prints, is where modern literary history arguably begins, counter the claims of scholars like Kitagawa Tetsuo that the *Shinwa* "is far from what modern literature would be."[35] Rinbara Sumio has argued that *tsuzukimono* debuted in the popular press (*koshinbun*; small newspapers) as "the first self-consciously literary works after the revolution that had as their background an awareness of the new age."[36] My *Shinwa* précis contains a few references to a rapidly changing, modernizing, early Meiji Japan, such as steamships and new medicines. There are more, specifically in the area of changing law, with references to the 1868 Charter Oath of Five Articles (*Gokajō no goseimon*) that acknowledged some rights for commoners. Drafted to quell potential opposition to the new government, the Charter Oath declared that "all absurd customs of olden times shall be abandoned," including social and class prejudice,[37] and its force then and in subsequent Japanese law has made it vaguely comparable to the English *Magna Carta*.[38] Much is made in *Shinwa* of the legal emancipation of the untouchable caste in 1871, permitting someone like Omatsu to marry into the samurai class; to the reformed criminal code of

1868 that treats Kichi far more lightly in the age of *bunmei kaika* (civilization and enlightenment) by replacing the hot-water ordeals (*kugadachi; yugishō*) and judgments by fire (*higishō*) with more benign punishments; to the overnight success of entrepreneurs like Chūzō, free to practice an entrepreneurial capitalism discouraged under neo-Confucianism; and to the lowering of travel restrictions to allow the movement up and down the archipelago that Omatsu and company enjoyed.

But despite the opportunities a modern, liberal Japan offers Omatsu, she avails herself of few. Time and again she reverts to her nature (*sujō*) as an untouchable member of her criminal caste. Here, as in the early English novel, questions of truth are aligned with questions of virtue or its lack. The didactic reversal of Omatsu's evil (*aku*) is part of a broader dialectical reversal because the formalistic requirements of fiction contest the genre's privilege to represent the world. "The novel has a definitional volatility," according to Michael McKeon, "a tendency to dissolve into its antithesis, which encapsulates the dialectical nature of historical process itself at a critical moment in the emergence of the modern world." A novel has to explain and solve problems at the same time, and while the story of Omatsu is certainly not the first work in Japanese literary history to do so, it is the first to do so amid a modern state's anxiety over the attempt. Frankly, it fails in the attempt—no problems are really solved—in part because it is only awkwardly that "dynamic model of conflict"[39] with an unstable and shifting border between the true and the false, that novels are held to be. Mimesis in fiction is historically a social relation, and in *Shinwa* it is facilitated through the instrumentality of textual features.

Earlier *gesaku* made explicit reference to contemporary events, but just because those events are modern ones does not make the genre itself modern in the sense we might use that word. In Tsubouchi Shōyō's 1885 *Shōsetsu shinzui*, traditionally taken as the manifesto for modern Japanese literature, the author makes an interesting parenthetical remark. He suggests that the written language of the *kusazōshi*, if properly reformed, could constitute the basis of a modern Japanese novelistic idiom. Shōyō notes, almost incidentally, that Japan's easily legible *koshinbun* had in recent years begun serializing "miscellaneous reports" (*zappō*) called *tsuzukimono* that approach what a modern fiction style for Japan might be. He notes approvingly that the *tsuzukimono* used Tokyo diction to describe things that, though fanciful, also "deal with matters in, for the most part, a factual manner" and so qualify as realistic—Shōyō's most desired goal. Theories that have sought to account for the emergence of modern Japanese fiction in the mid-1880s posit a parallel binarism: one of continuity and change and the other native versus foreign, both borrowed from the larger discourse of Western Orientalism and Japanese historical-area studies. We are told, for example, that Japanese long before the modern era were writing novels, that the psychological insights of Murasaki Shikibu (973?–1014?) or the social consciousness of Ihara Saikaku (1642–93) had evolved, even teleologically, into prose genres cognate with those of early modern and modern Europe. The flip side of this argument is that modern Japanese literature traces its nature to an eager encounter with the West and its novels. Historical surveys of the makers of modern Japanese fiction are filled with anecdotes of youthful discoveries of Fielding, Turgenev, Balzac and von Hoffman, as native genius sought selfhood, realism and individuality. In this narrative, the cultural achievements of the West forcibly impose themselves on a culture more or less primed for such ideas. That this binary is devoid of any dialectical or materialist analysis belies the fact that an Orientalist essentialism insinuates itself into modern Japanese literary history, regardless of approach.

At the same time, these arguments are not entirely wrong. One American scholar of modern Japanese literature declared that in the late Tokugawa and early Meiji periods, "virtually nothing happened to women who did not reside in the few square miles encompassed by the licensed quarter of Japan's major cities."[40] Japanese scholarship has never been this myopic, but where it has attempted to accommodate Omatsu within an account of literary modernity, it has done so on the basis of her highly gendered, errant behavior.[41] The early Meiji period is remarkable for its many celebrated female thieves and murderers in accounts collectively known as *dokufumono*, the poison women stories, whose origins are variously traced back to late Qing detective fiction, or in Japan, Saikaku, Takizawa Bakin (1767–1848), Tsuruya Nanboku IV (1755–1829), or Tamenaga Shunsui (1790–1844), in whose *Shunshoku umekoyomi* (*Imitations of Spring: The Plum Calendar*, 1832–33) the word *dokufu* finally appears.[42] The list could go on since the taxonomy of *akujo* (evil women), *tōfu* (jealous wives), and *kijo* (ogresses) in Japanese literature and theater can and have been serially cited as precedents. In the early and mid-Tokugawa period, there were popular tales of a female bandit, Omatsu, but her exploits were not treated as news. In the Meiji period, the *dokufu*'s heyday was the late 1870s, but her influence continued into the twentieth century. Writing on nineteenth-century *dokufu* Takahashi Oden, Matsumoto Kappei noted in 1981 that it was currently popular for women to kill their children by stuffing them into coin lockers at train stations.[43] It was with Omatsu that the definition of *dokufu* was fixed for the modern period; novels by later authors such as Kunikida Doppo (1871–1908), Nagai Kafū (1879–1959), Tanizaki Jun'ichirō (1886–1965), Shiga Naoya (1883–1971), and today's Murakami Ryū (1952–) would star them. As Honma Hisao put it, Meiji *dokufumono* were read "in every harbor and inlet [*tsuzu-uraura*]"[44] and surely contributed to the spread of newspapers across the archipelago and thus to the imagined community of modern Japanese nationhood. But at the same time, the popularity of newspapers presented the new Japanese state with a pressing crisis in the management of information. If, as Habermas has argued, modernity is initiated by the advent of a widened public sphere, and if the press is "the public sphere's preeminent institution," then Japan's modernity as well as its newspapers owes a debt to Omatsu.[45]

Literature before 1868 was thickly populated with stories of crimes and criminals, of course. There are examples in the eighth-century *Nihongi* (Chronicles of Japan) and the *Kojiki* (Records of Ancient Matters). But the precise types and venues of crime in the Meiji period are significant in a history of modern Japanese literature. Crime, for one thing, was suddenly more common in early Meiji if only because the new government's new laws criminalized heretofore unregulated behavior, such as Omatsu's bird-chasing begging. Comprehensive, uniform national law supplanted local legislation. Although travel restrictions were lifted at the start of the Meiji period, the promulgation of the Household Registry Law in 1872—and with it the requirement that all citizens return to their birthplaces to register—meant that the regime's efforts to restore social order in the wake of the revolution sent many people, like Omatsu, scurrying the length of the archipelago. When Meiji writers such as Narushima Ryūhoku (1837–84) at the era's beginning and Kasai Zenzō (1887–1928) nearer the end called themselves outlaws, they were appropriating as metaphor the precarity of segments of the population liberated in some regards but newly contained in others.

The most notorious poison woman was Takahashi Oden, who was convicted in 1879 after a three-year trial for the premeditated murder of a lover. Twenty-nine years of age and beautiful, we are told, Oden had wandered the streets of Tokyo with the bloody murder weapon, earning her the extraordinary sentence, for a woman, of a public beheading. An autopsy on her body reported the source of her villainy to have resided in her oversized genitals, rumored to be where Oden hid the (modern) gold watches she was fond of pilfering. Those genitals were detached, preserved and stored at the Osaka Imperial University Medical School until they were destroyed in a 1945 air raid. By 1879, the year of her conviction, torture had been abolished in Japanese law, but it had been replaced by the pseudoscientific technology of a pathologizing state.

Oden, which is to say the journalistic, fictional, theatrical, and visual depiction of Oden—Robun's 1879 *Takahashi Oden yasha monogatari* (The Tale of Takahashi Oden the She-Devil) is the most famous—was dismissed by Sir George Sansom as a "sordid story" "of no particular interest" to students of her period.[46] But since Sansom, she has been cited as a modern figure because of how she exercised her rights as a juridical subject during her trial. There was nothing old-fashioned about her as she used everything *new* about the Meiji period to her advantage. Historians saw her as a perverse example of the period's ideology of the self-made man, a Horatio Alger in reverse who pulled herself up by her own efforts to attain fame and fortune. Beginning, not coincidentally, with the U.S.–Japan Security Treaty (popularly referred to as *Anpo*) protests in the 1950s and 1960s, literary historians sympathetic to the defeated political Left characterized Oden and other *dokufu* as eruptions of a negative energy (*fu no enerugi*) emanating from the lower urban classes betrayed or disappointed by the promises of the Meiji Revolution.[47] Omatsu has been read as having no sense that she was a criminal. She is held to have been motivated by a just desire for revenge against the samurai and urban merchant-class strata then reforming themselves. The government liberated her untouchable caste, *de jure*, in 1871 when it issued the Emancipation Edict as part of the ongoing modifications of the national criminal code. These legal changes are abundantly referenced in the *Shinwa*, and it is important to note that the Omatsu of *Shinwa* is far less evil but more conventionally criminal than the Omatsu of the serialized original. She and her sisters *were* what they *did*, and thus modern if we define that term as "any attempt . . . to become subjects as well as objects . . . to get a grip on the modern world and make themselves at home in it."[48]

Marxist historians of the novel such as György Lukács and Lucien Goldman maintain that the genre necessarily has "a dialectical nature [deriving] from the fundamental community of the hero and of the world presupposed by all epic forms and, on the other hand, from their insurmountable rupture." In *Theory of the Novel* Lukács writes that the genre is characterized by the problematic hero who searches for authentic values in a degraded world; hence, Goldman points out, the hero can appear before us a madman or a criminal.[49] They may have been thinking of Cervantes, and there is hardly anything picaresque about Omatsu. Still, opinion is divided. Some scholars see in *dokufu* transgressions a reaffirmation of the social order and its strictures, and thus in the *dokufumono* a narrative in keeping with the late Tokugawa Confucian ideology of *kanzen chōaku* (promote the good, castigate the evil). D. A. Miller puts the case more generally: "Modern social organization has made even 'scandal' a systematic function of its routine self-maintenance."[50] Literary historian Maeda Ai is quick to see Robun's defense of the social order in his interlinear comments in the *Shinwa*.[51] No Japanese *dokufu* deeds go unpunished, be it by the heavens or the state. Others point out that the female criminal is a stock character in Japanese culture from the late eighteenth century, and more telling of that era's famed decadence than of any social struggle. There were letters to the press that decried the Omatsu reportage for the damage it would do to the progressive cause of women's social—read modern—improvement, though in another twist it is precisely these doubts about the nature of the properly modern that constitutes a necessarily self-critical modernity.[52]

My story of literary modernity in Japan is indifferent to these debates. I am interested instead in where the *dokufu* accounts were published and under what rubric rather than for any implications of their antisocial crimes for modern citizenship. We can crudely map where a space opened up between the false and true for things not quite either. *Dokufumono*, writes Hirata Yumi, "took actual events perpetrated by women as their core, and traversed the thin line between the true and false."[53] The reading public learned of Omatsu via the newspapers, but newspapers were new at the time. Despite the fact that the Tokugawa period had official journals called *gosata-chō* (government orders) and *goyuhitsu nikki* (official clerks' diaries) to record government actions, orders, notices, appointments, and dismissals on a monthly subscription basis,[54] newspapers in our sense of the word appeared only during the Meiji civil war in order to satisfy curiosity about a government at war with an armed opposition. They grew quickly. In 1870, there was only one newspaper in Japan using metal type. Two years later, there were seventy-three, and the real boom in newspaper publishing had only just begun—a boom contemporary with that of the *dokufu* "scandals," the word itself censorious and so an exercise in social control. The Meiji government inherited a body of Tokugawa-period law that strictly controlled publications dating back to the Kyōhō Reforms (*Kyōhō no kaikaku*) of the first half of the eighteenth century, but none governed newspapers, since none existed. After the revolution newspapers proliferated in two categories that persisted until the early 1880s (again coterminal with the end of the *dokufu* boom). The *ōshinbun* ("big newspapers," so named because they used larger sheets of paper) used a language dense with difficult Sinitic compounds and reported on government affairs. The *koshinbun* (with a larger circulation than *ōshinbun*) were, with their earthier vocabulary, illustrations, and, as one fan wrote, *zokudan heiwa* (talk of everyday life), far easier to read.[55] For readers of the *koshinbun*, a few years of rudimentary education were sufficient. They also sold more copies because they reported on matters of more popular interest. While the *ōshinbun*, for example, told readers that government ministers were appealing matters of policy directly to the throne, the *koshinbun* let readers know, for instance, that yesterday morning a horse ran into a Mr. Ono Yoshizo's house and made a real mess of things. One of the *koshinbun*'s *ōshinbun* competitors accurately defined the "little newspapers" as "nothing but reports of fraud, larceny, love suicides, elopements, brawls, homicides, and rape." The first issue of the *koshinbun Yomiuri*, for example, printed

> several stories on filial behavior; a report on a farmer's wife who, according to rumor, recovered the use of her paralyzed arms through faith in the *kami* (deities); the number of silkworm cards destroyed by fire in Yokohama; the number of passengers and the volume of freight carried from October 19 to 26 on the railway leaving Yokohama station, as well as the revenue earned; news about a fire in Nagasaki; and a story about 48 persons bitten by mad dogs near Kuwayama, this last being a transparent advertisement for a nostrum recommended for such complaints.[56]

The original account of bird-chasing Omatsu also appeared in a *koshinbun*. The *Kanayomi shinbun*, the "Syllabary-Reading Newspaper," so named because it provided phonetic glosses for its Sino-Japanese graphs, was founded in 1875 by Kanagaki Robun, a former *gesaku* writer who turned to journalism in 1872 when he announced in a letter to the Ministry of Education that the Japanese people had come "to despise vulgar novels as falsehoods and delusions."[57] The mood of the time was serious—Japanese officialdom was debating whether to invade Korea—and Robun joined the rush to march in step with the Meiji state's emphasis on the practical and useful over the literary and the frivolous, though early journalism was certainly literary with the infusion of rhetorical figures (*engo*), puns (*kakekotoba*), and didactic narration.[58] In all likelihood, Robun and his *gesaku* peers thought of their newspapers as means to enlighten readers, the duty with which Confucianism charged them. Reports on and after the revolution were certainly meant to edify, not just inform, readers. At the same time, the new media had to attract readers, and *gesaku* writers proved useful. The rise of journalism in Japan provided employment for legions of professional writers, but in Japan as elsewhere in the modern world it was at the price of imposing certain constraints on what they would be paid to write. Attractively priced at only eight *ri* (later rising to one *sen*), and with a circulation of five thousand, the *Kanayomi* was an important vehicle for the writers and journalists who formed more or less a de facto opposition faction to the government, a stance which only increased circulation until the paper's demise in 1880.

Some habits die hard. Robun, praised in an 1894 eulogy for *mantenka o baka ni shitaru* (having poked fun at the universe),[59] was the author of the Omatsu series of articles and the overseeing editor (*bun'etsu*) of the subsequent *Shinwa*. The *Kanayomi*, like other *koshinbun*, was divided into a number of sections: *ofure* (notices), *shinbun* (news), and *yosefumi* (letters to the editor). Added later were *mankokubanashi* (stories from abroad), *kanayomi chinbun* (the *Kanayomi*'s weirdest), and lastly the *myomyo kibun* ("The Kitty-Kat Kolumn") which reported gossip about geisha and other denizens of the licensed quarters. These Kitty-Kat Kolumns were what probably led John Reddie Black to decry Japanese newspapers. "Their columns were always defaced with such filthy paragraphs as to render them worse than contemptible."[60]

The Omatsu articles, however, were printed in the *zappō ran* (catchall miscellany) section of the *Kanayomi*. The term *zappō* dates back to 1875, when in September the *koshinbun Hiragana e'iri*, just founded, used it to mark a section in which a Japanese piecemeal rendition of *Hamlet* was being serialized. But intellectuals like Narushima Ryūhoku (1837–84) considered *zappō* the basest pages of the *koshinbun*. The placement of Omatsu's news story there may indicate some difficulty on the editor's part deciding just what kind of story hers was. One definition of *tsuzukimono*, if tautological, held that "as literature [*bungaku*], they speak of the real [*jitsu*]. They are found in newspapers' miscellany [*zappō*], and thus are the so-called literature of miscellany."[61] But modern Japanese literature becomes imaginable precisely in that gray and inchoate area. "Ambivalence is the foundation for the double or reflexive nature of the novelistic discourse," writes Lennard Davis. "This ambivalence is a precondition for the simulacrum theory which both denies the novel's true nature and its mode of production by substituting a false explanation for the novel's existence."[62] In Japan that precondition was satisfied with the assignment of realist fiction making to a middle category between the strictly true and the patently false: *shōsetsu*.

In reaction to the pressure of Western imperialism and in recognition of

Japan's technological gap with Europe, the Meiji state ruled from its inception that the slogan for all spheres of national life would be *jitsugaku sonchō* (esteem for the practical). In 1872, the Ministry of Education issued three dicta (*sanjō no kyōken*), including one mandating that "the rules of heaven and the ways of men" (*tenri jindō*) should be "made evident" (*akiraka ni subeki koto*), doubtlessly a warning to writers such as Robun that "frivolous writing" would not find official favor.[63] Such admonitions drove some *gesaku* writers into journalism, but their problems only followed them. Newspapers in early Meiji Japan did report factual news. But, at the same time under government pressure to be didactic, as well as competitive pressure to entertain readers whose former supply of *gesaku* fiction had been curtailed by that same government, newspapers found the literary potential of *tsuzukimono* like Omatsu's irresistible. Such reportage was in keeping with Meiji enlightenment notions insofar as they detailed everyday real life, but its emphasis was thoroughly social, not historical. It ran counter to the state's moralistic aims when Omatsu and her wayward sisters had unexpected, widespread charismatic appeal. If modernity is a process of creative destruction of residual social conventions, then it should not be unexpected that delinquency accompanied modernization. But *tsuzukimono* articulated other contradictions animating Japanese modernity. As they grew more literary and less journalistic, they were at the point where modern Japanese literature was guaranteed a role distinct from, while interpolated with, purely material modernization.

I can illustrate this by returning to the initial fourteen-part serialization of the Omatsu saga in the pages of the *Kanayomi*. Earlier I stated that her story appeared in print through 11 January 1878, but that is when the serialization was abruptly interrupted, not smoothly *concluded*. In the last installment Robun informed readers Omatsu's saga had gone longer than anyone had expected (*zongai nagaku nari*) and had surely now bored (*taikutsu*) everyone.[64] Readers of the newspaper serialization never learned of Omatsu's miserable death, despite the fact that Robun's *Omatsu no den* installments had created an unprecedented suspense among readers denied any foreshadowing of plot.[65] Those readers were reassured by Robun that a complete account of Omatsu would soon appear in book form, and it did. In his preface to *Shinwa*, Robun explained the decision to terminate the newspaper serialization. Despite gratitude for readers' enthusiasm for his newspaper's bird-chasing Omatsu, such a lengthy narrative (*nagamonogatari*) was "fully incompatible with the nature of a newspaper" (*sukoburu shinshi no hoi ni tagaeba*). Such incompatibility risked violations of its own, insofar as serialization was infringing on the explicit rules and implicit conventions of Japanese publishing then coalescing, while also a burgeoning complex and organized form of commodity production. With no small amount of irony, a genre of writing, monitored and regulated by the government with an anxious concern for truth, found favor among readers for its tales of law breaking. This made the *Kanayomi* and other "small newspapers" distinct from the more respectable larger ones. "From the point of view of the *koshinbun*," writes Rinbara Sumio, "the government and the *ōshinbun* were the same thing [*dōshitsu*]."[66] To ask how modern literature in Japan was from the start incongruent but related to enlightenment thought (*keimō shisō*) is to ask how the *koshinbun* established the literary as something simultaneously true and false.

The issue with Omatsu's *Kanayomi* story was not its length but its incommensurate narrative. The government's 1872 press regulations dictated that imaginative writing was prohibited from making fabrication appear true, and it was surely Robun's recognition that the literariness of the Omatsu articles had become more prominent than their newsworthiness that led to his decision to drop further publication of them in his newspaper. But literary historians often decline to take up *tsuzukimono* such as Omatsu's because they are not literary *enough*. In his same apology Robun praises the Omatsu saga with august language lifted from Confucius's *Great Learning*, calling it an *onko-chishin no dai jitsuroku*, a "great and true story from the past that illuminates the present." *Jitsuroku* (factual records) were writings (often handwritten to avoid censorship) disseminated via lending libraries dating back to the Tokugawa period but especially popular during and after the 1868 Meiji Revolution. Yet *jitsuroku* were prohibited from reporting current events and circulated as histories (*rekishi*) or tales (*monogatari*).[67] They mixed fact and fiction and served as newspapers to the extent they reported happenings more or less promptly and over large geographical areas. "The *jitsuroku* did not aim to criticize the Establishment or the status quo in Tokugawa Japan," writes Peter Kornicki, "but they did seek to appeal to an interest in current events, however adulterated the news they presented may have been, and in doing so they were . . . in defiance of the law" and clearly meant to circulate beyond the cities to the nation as a whole.[68] Meiji-period literary historian Okitsu Kaname (who did not much care for Meiji-period literature) will say that the news content of *Shinwa* when compared with the newspaper serialization was "essentially zero" (*hōdōsei wa zero ni hitoshi*), but is still redolent of *jitsuroku*, as were many of the late Tokugawa *kusazōshi* that still circulated in the first decade of the new era. Okitsu concedes that the *gōkan* versions of serialized stories retained a "respect for factuality" (*jijitsusei sonchō*).[69] Out of them eventually developed such twentieth-century genres as detective and mystery novels, in which criminals are replaced by their close cousins, the police.[70] The endless debate over Omatsu and other *dokufumono* or *tsuzukimono*—are they literature, or news?—is not only inde-terminate, it is misdirected. *Jitsuroku* were never wholly factual, but had already mixed the fictional with the actual. In all early Meiji newspapers it was impos-sible to distinguish clearly between news and what was frequently fudged as "documentary mixed with falsehood" (*uso-majiri no jitsuroku*).[71]

When I stand in line at the supermarket and read in tabloid headlines that Hillary Clinton has adopted a baby from an alien species, as the *Weekly World News* ran in 1993, do I ask if this is true or false?[72] A tabloid does not demand or even invite that question. That is a question posed only when information is deemed fundamental to an individual's social subjecthood as a citizen, voter, investor, consumer, or so on—when the modern state exercises its authority in the interest of, and responsibility for, inoculating that information from the false. What is exempt from such intervention is the modern discourse of the literary, which is to say the fictive, and that divorce is just what we witness when we see Kanagaki Robun move Omatsu out of his newspaper and put her in his preternatural incarnation of the modern Japanese novel. This history begins with Omatsu, because with her we detect the start of a decisive break between discourses of the true and the false, leaving a state-sanctioned place in between for the modern fictional, a discourse that must be truthful but allowed to be not strictly true. I can establish this by placing the history of the *koshinbun* and the *tsuzukimono* against that of the legal offenses of slander and libel in Japan, the first of the contexts I use in this literary history. I choose this one, hardly controversial, because the law has long sought to rule what writers can and can-not say. In 1673, the government, which was highly suspicious of any treatment of current events in books or on the stage, prohibited (if not very effectively) current events in books or the *kawaraban* broadsides. The fourth Tokugawa Shogun, Ietsuna, "required writers to secure permission from the city magistrate (*machi bugyō*) before discussing public matters, reporting unusual happenings, or writing about anything likely to be embarrassing"—precisely the techniques still used by authoritarian states today. As in those states, seventeenth-century Japanese still found ways to circumvent such prohibitions. Profit is a power-ful motivator and there was money to be made in marketing the news. The *kawaraban* were the precursors of modern newspapers, full of "news of fires and assassinations, sightings of ghosts, double-love suicides, pictures of festivals and sporting events, stories about the birth of triplets, tales of volcanic eruptions and mermaid spottings."[73] "No event, not even a thunderclap, was too insignificant" for literary treatment in a *kawaraban*.[74] *Kawaraban* had a history of two and a half centuries before Meiji, but despite their regulation by a sweeping 1722 code outlawing any "strange hearsay" (*isetsu*) by requiring all publications to carry the real names of authors and publishers, in 1854 a million copies of five separate *kawaraban* were circulated in what was soon to be renamed Tokyo.[75]

The modern period witnessed a rapid evolution in the state's consensus over what could be published and under what conditions, and in its policies concerning mass media we can best see how state control operated generally.[76] In 1869, the same year that the government made approval by the authorities a prerequisite for newspaper publishing, the government ruled that "accusing a person of misconduct is strictly forbidden" (*hito no tsumi o bukoku suru koto gonkin nari*), but no reference is made as to whether those transgressions need be *false* in order to be prohibited.[77] In 1870, the revised legal code specified that verbal abuse (*bari*) against an official carried a penalty of being caned ninety times; against a commoner, it was ten lashes with a whip. Regulations in 1871 defined a newspaper as "the authentic records of the time" forbidden "to turn falsehood into truth."[78] Although statutes at this time in Japan were still more influenced by China's Ming Code than by Western principles, [79] all punishments were converted to terms of imprisonment. Still, the words for libel and slander do not appear. But regulations prohibited the defamation of foreign countries and all baseless reporting (*mukon no gen*).[80] Though never promulgated, draft regulations in 1874 would have allowed for damages to be claimed on the offense of *bari* (abusive language), or what we would recognize today as libel and slander minus the establishment of falsehood. Subsequently, the 1875 Law of Libel and Slander, replacing the term *bari* with the more exacting terms *zanbō* (libel) and *hibō* (slander), made clear the state's aim of suppressing popular movements by curtailing all negative publicity of the state.[81] The differentiation of fact from fiction is a spurious byproduct with important consequences. Article I states, "Any statement, whether it be based on the fact or not, which tends to injure the honor of the individual is a libel. Any statement which tends to give him a bad reputation and not to deal only with his behavior itself is a slander." We might also detect here an acknowledgment that behavior is something that can be reported upon objectively. The Newspaper Press Law of the same year made libel or slander in a newspaper the responsibility first of the editor and then the writer as an accessory.[82] In 1879, for example, a newspaper publisher was imprisoned for casting aspersions on a government bureaucrat.[83]

This Law of Libel and Slander, enacted by the Council of State in June 1875, distinguished between two kinds of libel:

> One kind consisted in the publicizing of an individual's activities, whether true or not, that were injurious to the individual's reputation; and the other consisted in the act of publicizing disreputable remarks about an individual without any reference to specific activities of the individual. . . . The seriousness of the offense depended on whether the libelous activities were directed against the 1) Emperor, 2) the Imperial Family, 3) the duties of government officials, or 4) peers, ex-samurai, and commoners. . . . It need hardly be said that this *Libel Law* together with the *Newspaper Press Law*, which was enacted on the same day, were quite positive instruments in the suppression of the liberal right advocates.[84]

That a tabloid could defame Hillary Clinton by accusing her of harboring an extraterrestrial lies in the fact that such publications lie outside the strict application of standards of fact versus falsehood. They are literary and allowed imaginative speculation, and so we can understand why the story of Omatsu, popular during the same time the Law of Libel and Slander was in effect, was part of an early moment in Japanese modernity relatively unbothered with distinctions between literary and documentary, factual and fictional. Instead, only the security of public figures endangered equally by true or false statements made about them mattered immediately to the authorities.

By the 1880s, the *koshinbun* had largely merged with the *ōshinbun*, and the *tsuzukimono* had mutated into something recognizably fictional with the appearance of *shinbun shōsetsu*. In the 1880s, when newspapers began identifying *shinbun shōsetsu* authors by name, Japanese law regulating the press and defining libel was rewritten. The intent of an author accused of making a demonstrably false (as opposed to simply defamatory) statement about a public figure was made part of establishing culpability. Literary history should pay attention to this. By the end of 1887 and with the issuance of the Press Regulations and the Publication Regulations, the state made complete its differentiated treatment of truth in newspapers versus books; a new libel act promulgated in 1876 increased the risk to journalists of prosecution.[85] In March 1882, journalist Maeda

Kōsetsu, writing under a penname in the *Tōkyō e'iri shinbun*, admonished his fellow reporters to distinguish between fact and fiction, and an editorial the following year in the *Yomiuri* sounded the same alarm.[86]

In *Discipline and Punish*, Foucault writes that among the questions for modern societies are: "How can one extinguish the dubious glory of the criminal?" "How can one silence the adventures of the great criminals celebrated in the almanacs, broadsheets and popular tales?"[87] In modern Japan the tales of poison women were exiled from the newspapers no sooner than they begin to undermine the social order. But while they were exculpated from the daily press by the mid-1880s, their continuing presence in fiction could still question the social order and at the same time buttress it. The enlightened Hamada Shōji in Kubota's *Shinwa* could have come right out of Fukuzawa Yukichi's polemics on modern citizenship. Rather than read *dokufumono* thematically, reading them against their place in media yields a different insight: that the order disturbed was that of a discourse of truth generically policed from a discourse of falsehood, with a space quarantined for the ambivalent literary in between. Omatsu died scurrying about like a crazed dog. If "madness," according to Foucault, "begins where the relation of man to truth is disturbed and darkened," we may know why she did. Everywhere her story hints at high stakes in that relation, certainly each time the plot turns upon the problem of contested believability. Whenever Omatsu related her past to a man, lies (*tsukurigoto*) were mixed with truth (*makoto*), and when those lies are initially uncovered by Hamada is when she is labeled a *dokufu*. She might just as well have been called a modern novelist. At one point, all that Omatsu has ever said is declared "the utterings of a poison woman, lies that appear true but allow her to escape."[88] Her speech is as slick as her actions. The novelistic scene is one of contested believability, and it doesn't end there. Speech, its relation to truth and fiction, is parallel with social conduct and its relationship with the legal and illegal.

Novelist Nagai Kafū once wrote that Meiji-period *dokufu* were a literary phenomenon despite the fact that those years saw more than their share of actual "tattooed female pickpockets." Kafū faulted the confusion of life with art on the stage for this, since theater used real life for its dramas and those dramas governed what audiences believed. The result, he wrote, was a confusion of the real and the fictive.[89] Moreover, the evil (*aku*) one saw in *dokufu* kabuki plays, for instance, reminded Kafū of Baudelaire's 1857 *Les fleurs du mal*, the literary work that Foucault in his own time cited as the epitome of modernity. It is less the ethical category of evil and more the confusion of the real and fictive that makes works such as *Omatsu* candidates for mention in literary history: their indeterminacy marks the epistemological limits after the clash of history with the imagination.

Is this true of the novel generally? In *The Origins of the English Novel* Michael McKeon argues, "The first sort of instability with which the novel is concerned has to do with generic categories; the second, with social categories."

> Questions of truth and questions of virtue concern different realms of human experience, and they are likely to be raised in different contexts. Yet in one central respect they are closely analogous. Both pose problems of signification: What kind of authority or evidence is required of narrative to permit it to signify truth to its readers? What kind of social existence or behavior signifies an individual's virtue to others?[90]

These are questions Omatsu's story posed for Japan, just as *Moll Flanders*, *Robinson Crusoe*, and *Tom Jones* did for England. The *dokufu* fundament of modern Japanese fiction is cognate with McKeon's insight that the novel manages modernity's stake in epistemology and the ethico-political, as well as in literary history's attestation that the criminal and the insane are literary figures that embody paradigmatically that interest; early Meiji fiction was precariously wayward in its themes and its implications for social knowledge. It is tempting to think along with McKeon that, as with popular criminal biographies after England's own revolution, Japan's *dokufumono* and its "delinquent folk hero . . . is compelling enough in his pursuit of freedom to suggest that the common way of 'error' may in fact be the road of individual truth."[91]

Omatsu has the last word. Every celebrated poison woman after Omatsu is historically attested by police and court records and, in the case of Oden, there was even a jar of pickled body parts. Omatsu's is a true story, but I have to qualify that. No one has established that Omatsu ever really existed, despite the believable detail with which her exploits were told in the *Kanayomi*. Maybe she did exist, maybe she didn't; and maybe the White House really does have a nursery for baby extraterrestrials. That we don't worry *too* much about things suggests that some of the stories we enjoy telling each other don't really matter, at least so much that Kanagaki Robun and Rupert Murdoch need to be sanctioned for every liberty they take with the facts. The larger and more interesting question is why modern societies not only tolerate but may require texts that parade as true but are manifestly false. It is, as James Fujii has put it, the "paradoxical fictional imperative to pursue the truth"[92] that will animate and vex the Japanese state's efforts to govern metaphors throughout the modern period. The production of the *imagined* real may have something to do with how modernity reinvents itself, or with how human creativity and our appetite for play must be indulged even as it is commodified. With the founding of the *Asahi shinbun* in 1879, the distinction between the *ōshinbun* and the *koshinbun* became moot. The *Asahi* combined both. In 1907, Natsume Sōseki joined its staff as a full-time novelist. "The nexus between news and novels," Davis observes, "is a powerful one because it allows us to see that fictional narratives, by participating in a journalistic discourse, are also part of an information disseminating system that is by definition social,"[93] even for a misanthrope such as Sōseki. In Japan Kōno Kensuke makes a similar point: "Fiction serialized in the newspapers . . . constructed its narrative on the basis of miscellaneous news reports of society, and shared with journalistic media its discursive panorama,"[94] creating a loaded sense of time encompassing past, present and future over the course of the serialization, be it long or short.

If it took the Meiji state over twenty years to build its initial set of institutions—from the overthrow of the Bakufu in 1867–68 to the convocation of the first constitutional Diet in 1890—the press was leading among those institutions. "No single institution," writes James Huffman, "did more to create a modern citizenry than did the Meiji newspaper press."[95] But so did modern fiction, which had been expelled and then quarantined within just that institution. By 1900, there were complaints from readers that there was too much to read.[96] Books were already losing their aura. There was pleasure in consuming news as well as fiction, but the state endeavored to make sure that readers knew which was which. In time, *tsuzukimono* were absorbed into and assimilated by the *ōshinbun*, minus much scandal; it became the much-vaunted political novel (*seiji shōsetsu*) by the start of the 1880s. But newspapers continued to replace "the 'world' in which events arise with the 'world' in which events are narrativized, accepting the real to be the world of words,"[97] recalling Wolfgang Iser's definition of the fictive "as an operational mode of consciousness that makes inroads into existing versions of the world."[98] In doing so, fiction mimicked the foreground of the modern nation in a cacophony of languages and styles, from the journalistic to the fantastic to the polemic. As noted of early American novels, the genre did not wait for a "favorable context in which it could flourish, but instead immediately embarked on a program of cultivating the very social context it required,"[99] which is why speaking of the rise of the modern Japanese novel makes no more sense that claiming that a few years later the Japanese people "awakened" to their rights. The arena for modern fiction was created by works such as *Shinwa* hardly because it accompanied the "growth of the bourgeoisie" or any other apology for the genre. It was "the outcome of a *relationship of forces* between the 'modern' social classes—one in which the nation is a *stake* for the various classes."[100] One searches in vain in the Omatsu stories for the modern self (*kindai jiga*) long deemed the *sine qua non* of modern fiction in Japan. What we find instead is a plethora of talk of people's rights and new entitlements: that is to say, traces of a class struggle about to be squashed in political events. The doubt that *tsuzukimono* cast on Westernization and modernization in the wake of the failure of class enfranchisement "renders them part of the realm of modern literature" (*kindai bungaku no ryōiki ni zoku suru mono*).[101]

By the middle of the Meiji period, criminality in fiction was rivaled by a resurgence of the ever-popular theme of "young men and women meeting by chance or fate" and caught up in "anxious romantic feelings."[102] As we see next, those feelings lead us back to shifting class boundaries in Japan and new social protocols between the genders. Ginza's beggar Omatsu will find a younger sister in apprentice courtesan Midori, whose tragic fate will unfold in the 1890s as a securely literary narrative. As a consequence, we readers will be "obliged by the very form to take sides."[103] The side that we take will be modern, liberal, and wholly in the interests of the mature Meiji state.

2

Midori's Choice

Literature in the early Tokugawa period held that *shinjū*, or the double suicide of a man and woman celebrated in Saikaku's stories and Chikamatsu's plays, was "the ultimate gesture of love."[1] But by the time of courtesan Hanaogi III's failed *shinjū* attempt of 1785, the public, which was once scandalized and affected by such demonstrations of frustrated love, was now merely scandalized. Edoites were newly unsentimental about the fate of courtesans, professional women whose unmet personal desires no longer seemed tragic, only clichéd and rehearsed, even self-indulgent. The late Tokugawa may have still feared ghosts, but it was jaded to hackneyed appeals to emotion, including from beautiful women trapped within the quarter while yearning for a lover outside.

Yet a hundred years later, audiences were again ready to lend the courtesan their sympathies. Higuchi Ichiyō (1872–96) lived in the capital's Ryūsenji neighborhood in 1893–94 and saw prostitution firsthand in the adjacent Yoshiwara. She published her novella *Takekurabe* ("Child's Play") in 1896, the story of the adolescent Midori on the verge of her induction as a prostitute into Tokyo's most famed and notorious licensed quarter. It won the spontaneous praise of many readers, including influential critics. Despite her early death, Ichiyō, largely on the strength of this one work, became the only woman writer of the Meiji period canonized among the progenitors of modern Japanese fiction. One reason is the nostalgia readers may have felt for a work and a writer whose idiom was so thoroughly antiquarian in its style, syntax, and rhetoric. *Takekurabe* is often cited as the most—even only—neoclassical (*kotenteki*) work of modern Japanese literature. The title refers to the Heian-period *Ise monogatari* (*Tales of Ise*), and Maeda Ai sees in it a melancholy parody of other works of classical literature.[2] It impressed contemporary readers with its command of older literary styles and its nuanced descriptions of its unlikely people: children who lived on the outskirts of Yoshiwara, where families hoped to prosper but just survived. Today *Takekurabe* is still hailed as the *zesshō* (poetic masterpiece) of Ichiyō's works,[3] "the beautiful story of a young girl,"[4] still receiving the "highest compliments" from Ichiyō's fellow writers now as well as during her lifetime.[5] It details the entry of two young boys and a girl into adulthood over the course of one summer into winter: Nobu, the son of a Buddhist priest; Shōta, the son of a pawnbroker; and Midori, destined for a career as a courtesan. Once easy playmates, puberty introduces new emotions into their friendship, which is frustrated by the futures prescribed them. Midori, Ichiyō's principal point of view, knows the affection she and Nobu share can lead nowhere; the novella concludes with her tomboyishness forcibly turned into the timidity of a female groomed for sex work. Nobu is equally constrained to follow in his father's footsteps, first at seminary and then the temple.

Mori Ōgai (1862–1922), Ichiyō's greatest fan, praised *Takekurabe* for its "real, human, individuals."[6] Each of them may be positioned differently vis-à-vis the money economy of the quarter, but it was Midori above all whose fate struck readers. Taken from childhood in order to join her older sister Omaki as a prostitute once she reached puberty, Midori's "tragic [*aware*] fate makes the reader feel her misery," in words of one of Ichiyō's male colleagues.[7] It is the presence of this reader, and the absence of anyone similarly sympathetic in the novella itself, that makes *Takekurabe* a work of modern literature. When novelist and critic Sata Ineko (1904–98) points out that Midori's mother feels no "hesitation, regret, compassion or sadness" at having sold both her daughters into prostitution, her icy persona stands diametrically opposite the contemporary reader who, we are told, feels precisely, if vicariously, just those emotions.[8] The novella opens during a festival and ends with another, when the gates to

Yoshiwara are opened to the public and which one foreign observer called "red-letter days for brothels and their inmates . . . . The women are on display in the cages seen in the daytime"[9] in a demonstration of the total absorption of Yoshiwara into the world of money, work riddled with commerce if not modern manufacture.[10]

Jonathan Zwicker observes that the contradiction "between the reality of a money economy and the social myth of a world in which money did not exist, was becoming, over the course of the nineteenth century, increasingly untenable."[11] Still, in its day *Takekurabe* was read less as social critique and more as a confession (*zangeroku*).[12] Its English translators describe Ichiyō's work as pathos, a characterization that continues the tradition of emptying *Takekurabe* of its potential as a class and gender snapshot of late-nineteenth-century Japan. Robert Danly cites as Ichiyō's "essential themes" "the fundamental loneliness of modern man, the illusionary nature of friendship, society's oppression of those who do not dwell in the mainstream, the inevitable disappointment that life brings, the generational sense of abandonment and yearning." A generation later, Timothy Van Compernolle went further and identified "Ichiyō's ceaseless gestures toward classical literature" as part of the dialogic encounter that actively produced literary modernity.[13] But just where did the modern interlocutor in that dialogue come from? And why was that interlocutor's most explicitly modern mention in the novella that of venereal disease examination stations (*kensaba*), excised without explanation from all English translations of *Takekurabe*, including Danly's?

In the tradition of Tokugawa literature to which Ichiyō is said to belong, Saikaku, Ichiyō's distal literary mentor, used the courtesan as a foil for what he in fact valued: sincerity (*seijitsu*), though always corrupted by money. Saikaku's ideal of the genuine heroine has its opposite in the low-class prostitute given to deceit; the world of money that created her quarter was also the world that put her morally at fault. By the end of the nineteenth century, Saikaku's moral certitude was replaced with something much less secure. If Ichiyō's stories are full of young men and women whose lives go astray, the reason lies outside the licensed quarters and in something larger. There is now a calculus for judging moral action and human behavior by a new set of rules whose origin is located somewhere more worldly than elegant red-light districts. If our fondness today for Ichiyō's novella is based on its singular evocation of an age now gone, it is also true that modern literature *in toto* is, as Gerald Graff once put it, "determined by a logic of agoraphobia: literature is anything and everything that the marketplace is *not*—disinterested, autonomous, a communicative mode that does not 'mean' but simply 'is.'"[14] A fear of the market is predicated on a market that is pervasive and powerful, and in the case of Higuchi Ichiyō, whose adult life might be called a search for capital, a necessary quest at odds with another logic in retreat but not fully evacuated.

When Parisian photographer Hugues Krafft visited the Yoshiwara in the early 1880s, he called its women "artists" who "preserve and promulgate the melodies and lyrics of their country," in a setting Sir Henry Norman described a decade later "as quietly and orderly as Mayfair or Fifth Avenue."[15] A casual reading of *Takekurabe* can still give the impression that Yoshiwara was an elegant setting for licensed prostitution. In part due to Ichiyō's famous novella, we now think of Yoshiwara as part of the old downtown of Tokyo, but in her day it was only recently so. In the early Meiji period the vicinity was rustic and surrounded by rice fields. But a growing city changed all that. For some time it *was* sophisticated, though as would be true of its decline, its heyday was the result of a number of contingent historical factors, despite attempts in the twentieth century to recuperate the style of the quarters (*iki*; bordello chic) as somehow ineffably Japanese.

As a Western observer noted in his account of Yoshiwara shortly after *Takekurabe*, the earliest history of brothel quarters in Edo was that of the state's extension of the rule of self-interested law into the arena of prostitution. As early as 1528, the Muromachi Bakufu established a state bureaucracy to administer and tax prostitution. It was Hideyoshi who opened Japan's first *kuruwa* (gay quarter) in 1589. But it was during the Tokugawa period when the state began to, in Maeda Ai's words, "effectively manage the sexual energy" of the licensed quarters through strict regulation.[16] In 1612, Shōji Jin'emon petitioned the government for permission to set up a neighborhood dedicated to the sale of sexual labor. "Strict enquiries will be made as to the matter of kidnaping and as to the engagement of adopted children, and should any cases occur in which such reprehensible acts are attempted, information will be immediately given to the authorities."[17] But in fact the law that came to rule with Shōji's permission to establish Yoshiwara was that of surplus money seeking a conspicuous display of consumption. What was consumed was women: but *which* women was something from the start governed in part by what we can call brand merchandising. "Any event that had the least bit of potential for publicity was made into an instant 'tradition.' As time passed, this impulse had an unfortunate effect, as more and more the quarter became transformed into a site for glittering spectacles." Unfortunate or not, from its start Yoshiwara was a place about more than sex: it was where an open competition otherwise proscribed in Tokugawa society was, occasional sumptuary laws notwithstanding, allowed. "The single arena in which ordinary merchants could strive for status and realize their potential was business. . . . There was no better place to display their economic prowess than at the Yoshiwara."[18]

"In officially designated *akusho*—literally, 'places of odium'—where an official Confucian version of order and propriety no longer held sway," elaborates Japan historian Leslie Pincus, "Edo townspeople celebrated an efflorescence of real wealth and unrealized aspiration in new and widely disseminating cultural forms."[19] "What was called the 'world of prostitution,'" concludes a Japanese colleague, "was in fact the world of the one freedom allowed in a feudal society." But by the latter half of the eighteenth century when Edo was the center of cultural production, literature, save staid *yomihon* historical novels, had made Yoshiwara and the emerging unlicensed quarters that competed with it a source of inspiration. "Tokugawa literature was Yoshiwara literature."[20] But the success of Yoshiwara was pyrrhic by this time. The name of the place itself, a synonym for prostitution, hid the fact that by the early 1800s Yoshiwara's illegal competitors were experiencing an unprecedented prosperity that far surpassed that of old-hat Yoshiwara. Worsening rural poverty led families to sell their daughters in increasing numbers, resulting in a flood of private prostitution (*shishō*) by the late Tokugawa period.

By 1896 and *Takekurabe*, Yoshiwara had been in fiscal decline for a century as new "special areas," in Fukuzawa Yukichi's phrase, throughout the city were allowed to house sex work.[21] But in 1899, it was estimated that three thousand prostitutes still worked in Yoshiwara,[22] and a 1900 prefectural court ruling declared their treatment hardly different from "that accorded to convicts."[23] Its physical decline came with a devastating fire in 1911, then a U.S. air raid in 1945, and finally, it was bulldozed on the eve of the 1964 Olympics. Despite attempts to modernize Yoshiwara after the Meiji Revolution—street lamps, Western-style buildings, and the *kensaba* for "gay quarter diseases" (*karyūbyō*)—the changed economic and ideological landscape of the Meiji period guaranteed the end of Yoshiwara's earlier, spectacular function. In 1896, when Ichiyō published *Takekurabe*, the most popular hobby in Japan was stamp collecting, not courtesan collecting.[24]

Fires and the opening of the railroad in 1872 were the occasion for the development of the Ginza district five miles distant from Yoshiwara. It came to life in the mid-1880s and gave rise to the leisure-time pursuit of *ginbura*, or strolling in this neighborhood of the nouveau riche. They had a new place for conspicuous consumption: not behind gates and secured by a moat but in the open, as the state encouraged what had been long repressed: personal initiative and ambition rewarded with material possessions. "All up and down Ginza were Horatio Algers," notes Edward Seidensticker.[25] Seiko watches and Shiseido cosmetics were born there; eventually the first cafés would appear in Ginza, too. This was at the expense of the licensed quarters. Baudelaire's poetry describes the street, the scene of the *flâneur*, as the site of French bourgeois modernity in the mid-nineteenth century. "From this moment on, the boulevard will be as vital as the boudoir in the making of modern love," writes Marshall Berman, as well as the making of modern money.[26] In Japan, where the rise of Ginza is a historical analogue, this modernity was not met with universal approval. As leisure in the Meiji period came to mean things other than dallying with women, the availability of whom became, to Nagai Kafū's chagrin, "city-wide."[27] The pleasure quarter no longer functioned as the quarantined zone dedicated to the celebration of the sexual, but instead, its shameful discharge. Ichiyō writes in *Takekurabe*:

> In the evening they rush into the quarter, at dawn they leave less cheerfully. It's a lonely ride home, with only dreams of the night before to keep a man company. Getaways are under cover. A hat pulled low, a towel around the face. More than one of these gentlemen would rather that you didn't look. To watch will only make you feel uneasy. That smirk of theirs—not half-pleased with themselves as the sting of their lady's farewell slap sinks in. After all she wouldn't want him to forget her.[28]

Certainly not, if her livelihood depended upon him returning. This marks a signature shift in the Meiji period: at the same time that entrepreneurial capitalism was given open license, a kindred spirit of modernity—accompanied by embarrassment over foreign attention—prompted the government to emancipate Yoshiwara prostitutes in late 1872 in the aftermath of the Maria Luz incident, when Japan freed Chinese laborers after a Peruvian ship transporting slaves to South America docked en route in Yokohama. The *Shōfu kaihōrei*, popularly referred to as the "Cattle Release Act" because human sex workers were compared to farm animals, made all prostitution voluntary and was hailed as a *bunmeiteki hōrei* (civilized law).[29] This could be called the advent of civilization and enlightenment in the licensed quarters, buttressed by the arguments of forward thinkers such as Fukuzawa Yukichi, who argued prostitution quarters were necessary "for a thousand and one reasons" to accommodate male "animal urges" and thus preserve orderly, peaceful society. This unexamined axiom of wanton male sexuality and its costs to women's health in particular justified the state's incursion into the organization of sex work and then, by extension, into that of other gendered labor practices, not just that of café waitresses (*jokyū*) and, in time, comfort women (*ianfu*) but, as we will see, in the industrial workplace too. Women were, in short, the first necessary currency of exchange for the purchase of civilization.[30] The Cattle Release Act was also a preliminary and not terribly well-thought-out response to what Bernard Silberman called Japan's central problem of the nineteenth and twentieth centuries, "the governability of society."[31] Any feminist reading of modern Japanese history would recognize female sex work as an index of this governability. One overly optimistic report in 1906 said only 5 to 10 percent of prostitutes suffered from a "lack of freedom";[32] but *jiyū haigyō*, or "free cessation," from sexual bondage was more hypothetical than real.[33] What is certain is that the logic of rationalization applied to sex work helped destroy what lingering romance attended Yoshiwara and the other brothel neighborhoods. Maeda Ai writes, "The world of the licensed quarters, the *akusho* which along with the theaters was one of the sources of Edo aesthetics, was abruptly turned into a pedestrian [*sanbunteki*] marketplace for money and sexuality."[34]

A consensus emerged that sex work was a necessary evil rather than a point of pride. "I consider it wise for Japanese men to hide their behavior," writes Fukuzawa Yukichi. "The reason is that we, too, seek to progress in the stream of civilization and we endeavor to quickly assume the appearance of modernity and thus to become a modern nation. There is a difference of heaven and hell between hiding and exposing our moral behavior."[35] As with much in modernity (death, excrement, punishment), sexual commerce had to be made invisible. "With liberation, the old brothels became *kashizashiki*, literally 'rooms for rent,' and the crisis passed," writes Edward Seidensticker. "The old trade was permitted under a new jargon, the ladies now in theory being free agents. They were permitted to do business in the rented rooms, so long as they were licensed."[36] What is missing here is any recognition of how ambivalently women must have regarded the state's efforts to rescue and protect them. "'Modernization,'" writes Kazuko Tsurumi, "curtailed rather than augmented an earlier freedom and equality for women and men."[37] Prostitutes, even the young Midori, could be nominal entrepreneurs no longer indentured in law but no less constrained by the vagaries of incomes and expenses. No longer property owned by the brothels (whose social capital was spent down after the Meiji Revolution), they were now sex workers, to use an anachronism, who exploited their own labor in the newly enfranchised cause of ethicized self-interest.

Brothel owners typically rented rooms to sex workers for three yen a month, and written agreements (a practice pioneered in the equally female textile industry) replaced oral, informal ones. Many of these changes were lauded as embodying the spirit of Meiji progress. Still, the start of venereal disease examination stations in Yoshiwara in 1875 (following the first in Yokohama set up by an English physician in 1868) marked the imposition of new governmental control. Requiring sex workers to submit to examination once a week, Yoshiwara took on the air of, in the words of visitor Pierre Loti, a zoo.[38] Symbolized by the Western-style clock tower erected in Yoshiwara to tell time, sex work was regulated and rationalized by the state, as it is today by the police under such euphemisms as "soap lands." At the same time, as a cash-strapped government authorized the opening of licensed quarters in other Tokyo neighborhoods, sex work in Yoshiwara became subject to rationalization of free market competition even if its labor force was not really free at all. As Komori Yōichi has argued, the *kensaba* were the best proof of the Japanese state's dismantling of the licensed quarters as *akusho* and then reconstructing them as highly disciplined workplaces within the modernizing nation-state.[39] *Takekurabe*, praised for its lyricism, was also a virtual log of Meiji-period economic reorganization along the lines of classic economic liberalism.

Ronald Dore long ago documented how, outside of samurai education, which emphasized individual achievement, Tokugawa-period Japan seldom stimulated an atmosphere of competition, worried over unleashing an ethos of "impure motives."[40] When Fukuzawa Yukichi was translating English treatises on economics into Japanese, he came across the word "competition," and, finding no Japanese equivalent, coined the now standard word *kyōsō* (race-fight).[41] Fukuzawa also deployed the word *jiyū* to translate "freedom" in his influential work *Seiyō jijō* (Things Western, 1866–70), which was then adopted by Nakamura Keiu in his 1871–72 translation of Mill's *On Liberty* (*Jiyū no ri*). By the end of the 1870s, the Japanese were treated to freedom pills, freedom candy, freedom water, freedom walks, and eventually freedom marriage.[42] But as Fukuzawa made clear in *Gakumon no susume* (*An Encouragement of Learning*,

1872–76), individual freedom and sovereignty were principles because the freedom and sovereignty of individual *nations* was what was really at stake. "When the people of a nation do not have the spirit of individual independence, the corresponding right of national independence cannot be realized."[43]

The Meiji period saw the importation of many ideologies: French humanism, American Christianity, and German nationalism, for example. But nothing was more influential than British classical liberalism. The works of over a dozen major proponents of economic liberalism were translated into Japanese in the first two decades of Meiji, and Japanese theorists such as Kanda Takahira, Fukuzawa Yukichi, and Taguchi Ukichi soon wrote their own. Aware of the possibly unsettling effects of freedom, these Japanese nonetheless endorsed the unseen hand of laissez-faire capitalism to guarantee an efficient and fair equilibrium. Liberals such as Taguchi, who studied the Manchester school, saw no need for government regulation. He believed that workers, if unhappy, should simply quit and seek work elsewhere, or form a union—let the freedom to migrate from employer to employer solve all problems. A future president of Waseda University, Amano Tameyuki, popularized J. S. Mill's theories across Japan with his 1886 *Keizai genron* (Foundations of Economics) and made it near-standard reading in higher education of the time.[44]

But the ascendancy of the capitalist ethos meant the mystique of Yoshiwara was a casualty. The only references in *Takekurabe* to Yoshiwara's bordello chic, once its hallmark, is in the mimicry of young boys outside the quarter and its logic. Osanai Kaoru (1881–1928), pioneer of modern Japanese theater, described the Yoshiwara customer as likely "a numbers man in a visor cap, or a wandering singer of Osaka balladry who does the outskirts of town. No one could think of Yoshiwara as in the slightest degree a romantic setting."[45] What stands in the place of a romantic setting are the brutal marks of the market. In 1899, J. E. De Becker might have defended the proprieties of Yoshiwara when he protested, "The best houses do not exhibit the women in cages,"[46] but it was a more ardent foreign fan of the quarter, Sir Henry Norman, who commented on the topic of the "enrolment of recruits" when he wrote he "could not help being reminded of the automatic pig-killing at the stockyards of Chicago."[47]

Here is what happened. The unsavory aspects of prostitution, like those of making money, were now openly displayed and approbated by a Meiji-period ethos of material acquisition in the national interest. Sex workers were emancipated but not liberated. The labor required to enact that ethos was transparent. Higuchi Ichiyō may have decried her whole, brief, and impoverished life the absurd and cruel lengths people went to in her day over money, but her celebrated stories are nonetheless doggedly precise about that money and its pursuit. And it is Meiji-period money, not Tokugawa-period money. The men who want to purchase her sister Omaki's favors are the newly rich and powerful: bankers and members of the Diet, for example. "What fools people make of themselves over money!" Ichiyō exclaims in her diary, but in *Takekurabe* the lives of some very sympathetic characters, too, seem to revolve around it.[48] We see this obsession in women's lives elsewhere in Meiji-period Japan. Japan in the mid- to late nineteenth century, like other non-Western parts of the world facing encroachment by Euro-American imperialism, had the problem of developing an industrialized, capitalist economy with neither a sufficient industrial labor force nor the capital to expand it. As in other countries trying to secure both, the initial response was to exploit the cheapest labor in light industry so as to reap the greatest profits — profits that could then be redeployed in more highly skilled and ultimately more profitable enterprises. The first modern silk filature in Japan was opened in Satsuma in 1868, and the first under state patronage opened in 1870, the same year Japanese concubines were awarded the same rights as wives. In 1877, the state opened a large-scale modern textile factory in Hiroshima with thousands of mechanical looms imported from England. But the real boom in the textile industry began in 1896, the year of *Takekurabe*.

If Japan can be said to have had an industrial revolution, it began with mechanization and a factory labor system in textiles, a revolution that many economic historians of Japan date from the time of the first Sino-Japanese War (1894–95), just when Ichiyō was drafting *Takekurabe*.[49] By 1899, textiles employed 62.8 percent of all factory workers in Japan, and Thomas Smith declared it the "first triumph" of Japan's industrialization.[50] The workforce in the mills was almost entirely female, though Smith never mentioned it. Higuchi Ichiyō's singular status as a leading woman writer contrasts with the dominance of her gender in the factories of her era. In this, Japanese labor was at one with the world. "One of the enduring images of industrialization, created by contemporaries and transmitted by historians, is of the female factory worker," write Louise Tilly and Joan Scott of Britain. "She is the prototype of the wage-earning woman."[51] In Japan, female textile workers were often, like Ichiyō herself, the daughters of impoverished samurai, and long into the history of Japan's industrialization its labor *remained* female. Koji Taira observes, "For a long time, Japan's economic and technological advances were supported by the backwardness of the industrial labor force numerically dominated by women and girls."[52] Nowhere was this more true than in the textile industry. "At the turn of the century," according to Jon Halliday, "of the 422,019 people employed in the 7,284 factories in Japan, 257,307 were female."[53] And as Thomas Smith pointed out, all factory workers at this time in Japanese history were treated as near outcasts.[54]

In her history of women textile workers in Japan, Patricia Tsurumi writes, "During the 1880s and 1890s the proud, confident reeler from an ex-samurai or well-to-do commoner family was replaced by a silk worker with a different background, the daughter of marginally independent cultivators or tenant farmers."[55] As Ichiyō writes in *Takekurabe* apropos of prostitutes but relevant to factory workers as well, "There are times when daughters are more valuable than sons."[56] These female workers were the heirs to the late Tokugawa women who left home to take employment in the cities. "By the late 1880s the poor districts were becoming crowded with hired laborers, peddlers, porters, and others who formed the nucleus of a proletariat."[57] This proletariat did not form itself discreetly. The working conditions of Japan's industrial labor, and especially that of the female textile workers, was noted and deplored. They were always bad, but historians have argued they worsened over time and one named them "slave-like."[58] These conditions, as documented eventually in such studies as Hosoi Wakizō's *Jokō aishi* (A Tragic History of Female Factory Workers, 1925), were frightful, though just how much worse, if at all, than rural labor remains debatable. After sketching the history and recruiting methods of the mills, Hosoi describes how the initial thrill of leaving villages and moving to the cities to work in modern industries gave way to deteriorating work environments once the *jiyū kyōsō* (free competition) and *sōdatsu* (scramble) for female employees began and mobility for women was restricted rather than their compensation augmented. Modern contracts were trumped by traditional management techniques redolent of feudalism.

Jokō aishi made a significant impression on the Japanese reading public, and not just because it described lesbianism among the workers and their use of the floor equipment as dildos.[59] "The unfortunate irony," writes Gail Bernstein, "is that each new mechanical or organizational innovation to rationalize production had a detrimental effect on the [female textile] factory workers."[60] By 1899, the wages of a female worker were less than one-third of what they were in 1873 in terms of purchasable rice quantity, and less than that of a housemaid. With Midori and her sister Omaki in *Takekurabe*, the loan or advance both factory and brothel employment provided was conflated with traditional exhortations to dedicate oneself, particularly if one were female, to acts of filial piety. When prime minister Itō Hirobumi was asked in 1896 what he thought of Japan's system of public prostitution, he replied that "it was a splendid arrangement which, among other things, enabled filial daughters to help their poverty-stricken parents."[61]

The social view of the industrial labor force has been linked to traditional, that is, pre-Meiji inclinations to differentiate the citizenry along rigid class lines. Andrew Gordon writes, "By 1900, the new order of supposed equality was several decades old, yet many workers felt they were in fact part of a despised underclass."[62] He suggests an active and persistent contradiction: the Meiji period nominally "leveled" class distinctions, yet there was "the persistence of semi-outcast status for many [industrial] workers." It is not clear why this should be a remarkable fact. If the persistence of such distinctions helps to depress the cost of labor, it is surely as logical as many contradictions are. If the state fostered a near cult of women's productivity in the last two decades of the Meiji period, and it did, it happened at the cost of its professed rhetoric of a beneficent modernity for its people. By the turn of the century, even the Japanese government was expressing concern for the working and living conditions of labor. In the Ministry of Agriculture and Commerce's five-volume *Shokkō jijō* (Conditions of Factory Workers, 1903), one finds frequent expressions of censure for management's indifferent at best, brutal at worst, treatment of its employees. This sympathy on the part of the authors of *Shokkō jijō* is similar to the reactions that critics of *Takekurabe*, such as Ōgai and fellow writer Kōda Rohan (1867–1947), had for Midori, Ichiyō's young courtesan in vocational training. Could these shared reactions be linked if not to a common humanism then by a common sense itself of quite recent invention? That sympathy should be shown for factory workers as well as prostitutes suggests something new in play, given a tradition in Japan of thinking that people's lot in life was more a matter of birth and fate than of individual choice, or social contingencies.

In Ichiyō's story "Yuki no hi" (A Snowy Day, 1893) a young girl desires to leave the countryside and go to the city in the company of a man who represents the urban, the sophisticated, the modern: the eroticized object. But the story has a somber ending:

> My regrets come too late, and my illusions have all fled. I have tried to sustain a melody I never knew; the man I have been faithful to has disappointed me. Indeed, there is truth to Murasaki's poem: "The first snow falls on a world of rising sorrows." Again this year it comes, oblivious to all the sadness it brings,

so proud of itself for decorating, even for the moment, a broken, ruined fence. There was a time when I loved it, the first snow, but I was younger then.[63]

Could such a story have reminded readers of one of the many rural girls who, seduced literally or figuratively by a mill's broker, goes with him to Osaka or Tokyo only, once again, to be disappointed? Are Ichiyō's stories, if not about the industrial labor force of early Japanese capitalism, nonetheless made sensible by the social forces at work in creating a modern Japanese working class?

Karl Marx writes in "Theses on Feuerbach IX" that "the highest point reached by contemplative materialism, that is, materialism which does not comprehend sensuousness as practical activity, is the contemplation of single individuals and of civil society."[64] Perhaps this means that our modern societies, composed of individuals in contractual relationships with each other, have to reject sensuousness as the basis for any production. It would be difficult to describe Japan at the time of the Meiji Revolution as such a society, given the importance of Tokugawa "pleasures" for the kinds of surplus knowledge and values that urban merchant wealth was creating. One of the five articles proclaimed in the Meiji government's 1868 Charter Oath read: "The common people, no less than the civil and military officials, shall each be allowed to pursue their own calling so that there may be no discontent."[65] This was in no way a recognition of *individual* rights, only collective class ones. Notions of politically, socially, and economically autonomous, enfranchised individuals are attributed to the influence of the works of Mill, Locke, and Smith into Japanese; Rousseau's ideas were introduced to Japan via Takahashi Tatsurō's book *Jiyū shinron* (On Liberty) in 1871. Nakamura Keiu soon undertook a translation of Samuel Smiles's 1859 treatise on great men, *Self-Help*, and argued in his preface to it that the West's strength derived not from military might but from its "spirit of liberty."[66] Hattori Toku translated part of *The Social Contract* in 1876–77, which was followed by a complete translation in 1882 by Nakae Chōmin. By 1885, Fukuzawa Yukichi had naturalized the logic of the social contract when he opined, "That freedom and pleasure ought to be common possessions of both men and women is a concept that cannot be refuted. When something in limited quantity belongs to two parties, if one party takes a larger share, the other party's share will decrease." In 1875, Fukuzawa noted with approval that he had witnessed a modern contract marriage between Mori Arinori (who had argued that same year for consensual marriage in the pages of the *Meiroku zasshi*) and Hirose Otsume. "We are in an age," Fukuzawa wrote a decade later, "when a couple, a man and a wife, should be able to establish a home of their own without the backing of a house."[67] The invocation of contracts is significant since, as Ueno Chizuko has pointed out, the Meiji period came to refine and exploit marriage as a *keizai kōi*—an economic act congruent with the bureaucratization (*todokeide-shugi*) of everyday life in Meiji Japan.[68] "If sufficient money is offered" for a prospective bride, wrote Fukuzawa, "the marriage takes place; if not, then there is no marriage. Such transactions reduce marriage to buying and selling arrangements."[69] The majority of women born in the Meiji period had their husbands chosen for them by their parents, most often their fathers, on just such a basis. But those who did choose their own mates did so without parental approval, and in many cases those women were employed and living away from home[70]—precisely the category associated with female textile workers and female sex workers working as *kashizashiki* entrepreneurs.

But this history of modern liberal ideas of the individual linked to his fellow individuals via networks of mutual interdependence made possible through an inalienable subjecthood might also be given a more materialist and certainly less contingent history. After Foucault, we understand that governmentality, most prominently in the form of the nation-state, requires us to be free so that we bear regulatory control ourselves. A somewhat less depressing account, and one specifically addressed to Japan, is Bernard Silberman's contention that it is possible to speculate that herein lies the essential importance in Japan of the emergence of a capitalist mode of organizing resources. It was not that it created a class that sought to pursue its interests logically toward the formation of an appropriate political structure. Rather, the development of commercial capitalism produced so powerful a constraint that a new leadership had to view society's interests in terms of individual wants, that is, it had to accept the conception that society's interests were somehow bound to the right of the individual to hold property, and had to transform this concept into various abstract forms.[71]

I return to this point to argue that for women, the only property one might conceivably be granted ownership was one's own body, and the labor it could use (sell) in its own interests. But I want to note first that the history of the Meiji period is a history of a move toward these various abstract forms in controversial fits and starts. For example, newspapers ran a number of Confucian-based editorials opposing market speculation as a form of gambling—and a threat to national morality—when a modern commodities exchange was established in Tokyo in 1876.[72] Initially founded to retire public debt though private purchases in the wake of the revolution's civil war costs, private and semiprivate concerns such as railroads and shipping firms soon raised much capital on these and subsequent exchanges, but the government remained of two minds about any joint-stock system and its ethical implications. Finally, the state allowed stock exchanges in 1878 in Tokyo and Osaka modeled after the London Stock Exchange, with the textile industry instrumental in their founding.[73] The government subsequently enacted its Law of Exchanges, enabling joint-stock exchanges and bourse systems in 1893, after which there followed a boom. Ichiyō's *Takekurabe* is serialized in seven parts in the literary journal *Bungakukai* from 1895 to 1896, just as the boom was peaking. (In 1896, future novelist Masamune Hakuchō debated whether to become an author or a commodities trader, recognizing that creative writing was its own variety of speculation.[74]) But liberal economic ideas, especially ones involving competitions with no recourse to appeal, are not always attractive. Maruyama Masao observed that free competition was "something far from the idea of a game in which the participants compete under accepted rules in the spirit of fair play. Rather, the use of the term conjures up scenes of train rush hours — the world of *yūshō reppai* (the survival of the fittest) that knows only the rule of the jungle."[75] Competition is embedded in the narrative of *Takekurabe*, from the discreet rivalry of courtesans for patrons to raucous gangs of young men competing for turf when the quarter is open on its festival days. In "The Culture Industry," Adorno and Horkheimer complained:

> Every bourgeois characteristic, in spite of its deviation and indeed because
> of it, expressed the same thing: the harshness of the competitive society. The
> individual who supported society bore its disfiguring mark; seemingly free,
> he was actually the product of its economic and social apparatus. Power based
> itself on the prevailing conditions of power when it sought the approval of
> persons affected by it. As it progressed bourgeois society did also develop
> the individual. Against the will of its leaders, technology has changed human
> beings from children into persons.[76]

We are almost back to Midori's fate, and the contemporary reaction to it, in light of the historical and necessary conflicts at play in Japan over the individual and her rights and obligations under industrial capitalism in a bourgeois society. But there is one more piece of the puzzle to put in place: the liberal ideology of the Meiji marketplace and its antagonists, and the second of the contexts about which I structure this literary history. A recurrent problem in the Meiji period was a shortage of labor, despite the fact that the labor market grew slowly in Japan due to "a deep-seated antipathy to paid employment as a way of life."[77] As early as 1866, the Yokosuka Naval Dockyard was forced to raise wages to prevent workers from quitting.[78] In 1880, the Ministry of Finance was worried about the number of laborers accepting offers of work from rival employers and not fulfilling the terms of their existing contracts.[79] The problems accelerated during that decade with the proliferation of urban *yoseba* (exchanges) to keep up with the growing demands for day labor power,[80] and the collusion of managements to prevent the mobility of labor with regulations in 1886. By the time of Ichiyō's *Takekurabe*, labor disputes were increasing dramatically. There were strikes and walkouts by female textile workers in 1885 and 1886. The year 1897 is traditionally cited as the start of modern labor unions in Japan, though collective action and bargaining in Japanese industry were a feature since the time of the Tenma Cotton-Spinning Company strike in 1889.

Keeping workers in place was the greatest problem for capital. Male workers moved from job to job because that was the tradition of the Tokugawa-period journeyman. In 1885, Fukuzawa wrote with approbation that "in this age, men act with complete freedom."[81] Andrew Gordon points out, "Inducements to stay failed in part because most workers did not move from job to job merely in search of higher wages. Mobility was a central part of the 'proper' worker career. The custom of 'traveling' predated the high demand for skilled labor of the late nineteenth century." This, despite the fact Gordon also indicates that the "key feature of jobs in the factory is rather the ability of regular men *to remain if they so choose*."[82] Ardath Burks writes:

> There was a period in the earliest stages of the Meiji era when political thought and a series of reforms did indeed reflect assumptions of economic determinism. These early assumptions were not, however, Marxist but were closely affiliated with imported doctrines of laissez-faire. There was indeed an "age of translation," when versions of classical economics brightened the hopes of countless Japanese. There was also a widespread belief in liberation, a faith that in a different sense the economy would be master and politics its handmaiden.[83]

But choice is a false consciousness we should interrogate. Theories of economic liberalism imported into Meiji Japan expressed freedom as a key feature not only of markets but of labor as well. Adam Smith's *Wealth of Nations* spoke to the Japanese of "the free circulation of labor." This free circulation (while recalling that we have no freedom not to work if we wish to survive) was a principle that informed political and social thinking as well as industrial. But for female workers in the textile industry, choice was only partially and imperfectly offered. Sumiya Mikio quotes from contemporary sources: "Factory girls are all free laborers and they cannot be under any restraint to be imposed by their employers. They can move freely from one factory to another."[84] But according to Gordon, "The 'mobility' of textile workers, usually teenage girls committed for only a short time to factory work, often took the form of escape from a heavily guarded dormitory."[85]

In 1888, the Spinning Industry Association adopted a convention prohibiting the migration of workers as well as the unfair treatment of workers. It required any new employer to obtain the acquiescence of the former employer in an effort to reduce mobility.[86] Women workers were the object of special ideological appeals as well as special physical obstacles to their willful departure. While Japanese business consistently argued that management-labor relations in Japan were governed by warm family (*katei*, a construction of Meiji-period civil law) values and not by the mechanism of an exchange of labor and money as in Western countries,[87] paternalism toward women allowed such strategies to be applied more thoroughly and ruthlessly. The relationship of the female worker to her job environment "was rationalized in terms of the '*ie*,'"[88] as was the relationship of the female sex worker to her job environment. State discouragement of prostitution focused on sex workers who, according to an official in Tokyo's Bureau of Social Affairs, "personally *desired* to be a prostitute."[89] Underlying this was the assumption that women were naturally "mothers, and unnaturally waged labour . . . Masculine sexuality by comparison is relatively free from alliance constraints just as male labour is waged, public, alienated, and free."[90]

Yet there was a countervailing discourse of economic freedom overlapping with that of social and political freedom that was also important to the construction of Meiji modernity. When John Whitney Hall enumerated the features of modernization at the Hakone Conference, under economic modernization, he cited "a widening of the range of personal choice, and sooner or later a reduction in the range of economic and social inequalities"—a reduction accomplished through "the spread of wage labor, a mechanism which according to liberal economic theory equalizes the net advantages of different occupations throughout the economic system."[91] As Jürgen Habermas put it:

[Civil] society solely governed by the laws of the free market presented itself not only as a sphere free from domination but as one free from any kind of coercion; the economic power of each commodity owner was conceived quantitatively to be of an order precluding it from having an influence upon the price mechanism, and thus from ever providing direct power over the other owners of commodities. Such a society remained subordinate to the market's nonviolent decisions, being the anonymous and, in a certain way, autonomous outcome of the exchange process.[92]

Women were bound for periods of usually three years to work in a mill by an apparatus of contracts that, even if signed by a legal guardian, was still a recognition of a new kind of social relation. The former world was transformed into the new as status was replaced by contract. The Japanese state, defined as a community of citizens to be the counterweight to the social differentiation that results from modernization itself, was organizing its modernity along the concept of free individuals bound together collectively through conventions and contracts entered into freely. French sociologist Alain Touraine observed generally that "capitalist society is based upon the twin dichotomies between, on the one hand, a bourgeoisie motivated by acquisitive desires and workers subject to discipline, and, on the other, economic activity, which is public and therefore dominated by competition or money, and private life, which is where we learn to obey laws, rules and conventions. . . . [I]nstincts are set free in public life, and it is in private life that the weight of the law makes itself felt."[93]

Habermas argued the political complement to these dichotomies when he said, "The peculiar character of the modern state first comes into view, however, when the principle of civil society is conceived as a principle of market-like—and that means *nonstate-like*—association."[94] Ichiyō, to return to her, charts this character and its collateral effects. In her short story "Yamiyo" (Encounters on a Dark Night, 1894), two males, one poor and true, the other rich but fickle, compete over Oran, an orphaned waif whose life choices are governed by poverty. Oran asks poor Naojirō to murder her more affluent suitor, reminding him of a modern truism: "The competition is severe, Naojirō. Failure is quite common. . . . Things don't always go smoothly. Success is not automatic." This is a lesson Naojirō masters promptly when he only wounds his rival. "Once again, Naojirō had failed in a world where others were more cunning." But Naojirō *had* the chance to compete, just as traders in the rice exchange had the chance to both make money and lose it. Ichiyō ends her story with a terse passage about the fate of Oran's house once her two erstwhile lovers were gone: "Within three months, the pavement round the front gate had been handsomely repaired. Each day the gardeners and carpenters were busy there. It seemed that someone new was living in the house. . . . It's a wide world, after all. These days the trains run everywhere."[95] No one, and certainly not Ichiyō, could have written "These days the trains run everywhere" without a deep appreciation of how modernization was changing everyday life, including the family. Someone else had won, it seems, and while no one we know gained happiness, all ended according to the logic of the game. Marx describes it this way: "The bourgeoisie has resolved all personal honor and dignity into exchange-value; and in place of all the freedoms that men have fought for, it has put one unprincipled freedom—free trade."[96] It is time to look again at *Takekurabe* and what was at stake in Ichiyō's novella about the loss of childhood innocence matched with induction into the semi-feudal capitalism of Meiji Japan.

Patricia Tsurumi presents the brothel as an alternative to the loom, but that is not quite accurate. First of all, "alternative" implies substantial and meaningful difference between options, and as Tsurumi also points out, mills, like Yoshiwara, could have had moats built around them. De Becker writes of Yoshiwara that the courtesan's "freedom is so curtailed by circumstances that she cannot even sleep and eat independently,"[97] and the lives of the factory workers, kept captive in crowded dormitories, might not have offered any meaningful improvement. Second, Tsurumi reveals that some 30 percent of licensed prostitutes in the 1920s cited "cotton-spinning operative" as their previous profession, indicating that these alternatives might more properly be characterized as a career trajectory. The women who went into prostitution, as a rule, would not have been terribly different from those who went to the textile mills—so many were surplus daughters, not needed in rural agricultural work or more profitably employed elsewhere. One part of Tsurumi's project is to put factory and brothel work in a similar frame, as when she writes, "Not only were the girls and women used as money-making machines; factory women, apprentices, and prostitutes were also commodities used as private sexual objects by the men who controlled them." "Respectable people," she goes on to say, "looked down upon the daughters of the poor; in the popular mind, being 'sold' to a textile mill was akin to being 'sold' to a brothel."[98]

But is this enough to say? Does it explain Midori and the reading public's reaction to her? It is quite possible that widespread concern about the treatment of factory workers in the 1890s led to a heightened sensitivity over the fate of all females then being routinely exploited in the economy. But for a Mori Ōgai to sympathize with Midori, there has to be a sense of a shared fate, of a social contract that she, too, might be expected to enjoy. Remember that Midori is the one child in the neighborhood expected to really succeed in terms of Meiji *risshin shusse* (rising in the world) because she can move with her family upward in terms of class, from rural peasantry to purveyors of women. She will succeed not by becoming a commodity herself but by becoming a *worker* who sells her body, or more precisely, her labor. One hundred years earlier it might have been more appropriate to describe Yoshiwara courtesans as things whose value, whose preciousness, lay inherently in them. But as in the European nineteenth century, when according to Foucault "value ceased to be sign, it is a product,"[99] the Japanese courtesan's worth by 1896 was based on a system of circulation and exchange which, even if she was not wholly a part of, held she *should* be. Preciousness is no longer inherent. It is relational, active, unstable. It behaves, in a word, like capital.

Sir Henry Norman noted the quasi-modern nature of Yoshiwara when he wrote, "The whole system is based upon the theory of a civil contract."[100] The nature of the work is contractual, true, but the status is not insofar as it is, from the girl's point of view, quite involuntary. At this point in time, the doctrine of possessive individualism—the belief that the individual exists independent of her social relations, that is, she exists in and for herself, fully in command of her personal characteristics and ends—had not fully emerged in Japan, certainly not for women. For that to occur, social acceptance of a new alternative mode of appropriation would prove necessary, a development which only became possible with the conceptual severance, and the discrete annexation of human labor power in place of the appropriation of human beings. At this penultimate moment, Midori, a child indentured by her family but as a quasi-modern worker, makes *Takekurabe* the quasi-modern work seen today as half *monogatari* (where character is fixed, i.e., not relational) and half *shōsetsu* (where relations are crucial).[101]

There is a specifically feminist take on this particularly murky moment of modernity that Midori can be said to inhabit. "Hegel," according to Habermas, "describes market commerce as an ethically neutralized realm for the strategic pursuit of private, 'selfish' interests, whereby this realm grounds 'a system of complete interdependence,'"[102] but others, such as political theorist Carole Pateman, are suspicious. "The social contract is a story of freedom; the sexual contract is a story of subjection. . . . [T]he character of civil freedom cannot

Figure 2.1. A five-thousand-yen bill featuring Higuchi Ichiyō

be understood without the missing half of the story that reveals how man's patriarchal right over women is established through contract." This helps us understand how important *Takekurabe* has been to the ideological work of Japanese literary modernity. If "The employment contract and . . . the prostitution contract, both of which are entered into in the public, capitalist market, uphold men's right as firmly as the marriage contract,"[103] we can think of how Midori, as both worker and prostitute at the Daikokuya brothel in Yoshiwara, is subject to distinctly modern forms of patriarchy as well as of capitalism.

Fukazawa Yukichi was complimented for his progressive tracts on the status of women in the Meiji period, but his views ought to be understood within the general framework of rationalization and modernization. When he witnessed that unprecedented marriage between Mori Arinori and Hirose Otsume, he saw in it a social innovation meant to rework marriage as a contract entered into by two equals. The social contract has to be one, according to Fukazawa, entered into autonomously. This is Hegelian: the legally sanctioned and free choice of a mate and the subsequent formation of a self-determined inner life of a family is one means by which participants in civil society are wed to the modern liberal state as well as to each other. Fukazawa's motivation was not purely humanitarian. He also says, "It will be a great advantage for men to train women to be fully capable, because that will increase the 'manpower' of each household, and for the country it will mean increasing its work force twofold."[104] It would not be until the 1946 postwar constitution that marriage would be defined as a mutual consent between a man and a woman.

In Ichiyō's "Wakaremichi" (Separate Ways, 1896), a friendship between a boy and a girl ends when the latter becomes someone's mistress. The story is modern for the same reason as *Takekurabe*. Midori might prefer to fall in love with Nobuyuki and grow up to marry him. But her family and employer have other plans for her. The appeal of both works lies in the fact that by 1896, the contractual right—as well as obligation—extended to women included, in the minds of modern critics such as Ōgai and Rohan, the right to choose a mate much as a worker might choose her job: choosing a mate is tantamount to choosing a job. This is the era in which *ryōsai kenbo* (good wife, wise mother) is advertised by the state as the modern destiny of women. Higuchi Ichiyō, single and childless, could hardly be a model for her gender until, more than a century later, the Bank of Japan saw fit to put her portrait on its five-thousand-yen note, updating her heroine's nineteenth-century use-value for our twentieth-century exchange-value trade. Natsume Sōseki, the writer I will explore in the next chapter, will be worth only one thousand. If modern societies—unlike today's, when capitalism and the nation are at war with each other and the nation is losing—were produced in part by the exercise of rational legal authority over a market economy, then the story of criminal bird-chasing Omatsu is joined a quarter of a century later by that of legitimate sex worker Midori. Neither of their stories is sanguine. The enduring fantasy that Midori had a happy family was always just that in modern Japanese literature, where there are very few cheery households under any circumstances. Once we do find some, literature may no longer be modern, and paper currency, whoever adorns it, won't matter much anymore.

3

Sōseki Kills a Cat

Despite the frequent assignment of his 1914 novel *Kokoro* to American undergraduates, Natsume Sōseki's most canonical work is in fact *Wagahai wa neko de aru* (*I Am a Cat*, 1905–6). It may be an odd choice. Edwin McClellan, *Kokoro*'s translator, dismissed *Neko* as not serious literature.[1] In Japan, literary historian Itō Sei judged it shallow and full of failed attempts at humor (*shippai shita dajare*). Another authority, Yamamoto Kenkichi, called it not only eccentric (*fūgawari*) but "an odd blunder without precedent, or repeated, in Japanese literary history."[2] Nonetheless, it was Sōseki's first work to sell well. His wife reported it earned enough for her to splurge on a hat.[3] In fact, with no little irony it went on to become, as one Japanese scholar put it, *wagakuni no kokumin bungaku*, or, "the national literature of our country."[4] Children are still assigned it in middle school, and one scholar has just declared its spin-offs across media an archive for literary history.[5] As Komori Yōichi says, "Everyone knows it."[6]

But its place in Sōseki's oeuvre and literary history is anomalous. Narrated by a cat, not much more happens in it aside from some vague human discussions of a marriage, and without the skilled handling of its principal human character, Professor Kushami, the novel would certainly be judged a failure by even more critics. Most gave it a cold reception when it was published. In our own time, Yoshimoto Takaaki admitted *Neko* was a popular hit in its day and still well known, but criticized its contents as not all that interesting and doubted many readers ever finish it.[7] It belongs to the early "humorous phase" of Sōseki's career, and he himself called it a satire (*fūshi*) in a letter to a friend.[8] Some think the work a riff on the 1904–5 Russo-Japanese War (in the fifth chapter, the cat fights with a mouse), though that is hard to see; wars are seldom easy to make fun of.[9] It is dismissed as the one funny (*omoshiroi*, *kokkei*) novel Sōseki ever wrote. Journalist Hasegawa Nyozekan saw *Neko* as a retreat half a century into Japan's pre-Meiji past.[10] Read as a mockery of Sōseki and his circle of self-important late Meiji intellectuals, *Neko* suggests little of the broadly construed national experience of modernity that works embedded in a school curriculum usually do. Just why *Neko* remains such an important work to modern Japanese literature and its history, despite the novel's quirks, is the question I pose in this chapter.

Neko is narrated throughout by the house cat belonging to Professor Kushami ("sneeze"), and it is his sardonic observations of human—but especially Meiji intellectuals'—foibles that have made it a perennial favorite. Its title, so redolent of the Meiji innovation of *enzetsu* (speechmaking) invented by Fukuzawa Yukichi in 1874 as a means for enlightening the unenlightened,[11] was a knowing reference to the penchant of then–prime minister Ōkuma Shigenobu for deploying the presumptuous first-person singular pronoun *wagahai* at the start of his illocutions and ending his sentences with the equally pompous copula *de aru n de aru*. Sōseki's ridicule of *enzetsu* speechmaking is found throughout the novel. By its conclusion, when the nameless cat-narrator falls into a barrel and drowns, *Neko* is a massive, meandering, amusing and pedantic send-up not only of Meiji-period social manners but of the cacophony of contemporary media. In 1905, Sōseki was writing something not quite prose (*sanbun*), not quite poetry (*haikai*), not quite writing (*bun*). He ran, as one of his interpreters, Karatani Kōjin, has said, against the grain of his era. *Neko* is a hodgepodge of writing styles and discourses, culminating in what Karatani calls "carnivalesque,"[12] hardly a contribution to the modern Japanese literature of the time as much as a statement of disagreements with it. But in a testament to Sōseki's success, Karatani also allows that *Neko* still reads as satire today.[13]

Unlike Sōseki's carefully crafted later novels, *Neko*, which started out life as a short story intended for the amusement of friends, has no plot structure or character development. It is, in Sōseki's own words and those he also used to describe Lawrence Sterne's *Tristam Shandy*, writing "without a head or a tail, a creature like a sea slug."[14] Part of the reason must be that Sōseki constructed his novel with the older Tokugawa culture he grew up amid—*Neko*'s cadences as well as its anecdotes recall traditional storytelling—and with all the new things that modernity was bringing Japan, things he noted but was not obsessed with. "In the process of his writing the story," writes one Japanese cultural historian, "we can see his unconscious grasp of the relationships of media to human beings."[15] That grasp remains invisible to many critics, even as they pore over its text to prove it part of what Sōseki stands for literary and national history: Japan.

Sōseki remains an odd—but wholly appropriate—token of Japan's fitful modernity. As novelist Mizumura Minae (1951–) says of him, "When a national language is formed there emerges, almost magically, a national figure who singlehandedly comes to embody that historical process."[16] If Professor Kushami is discouraged with the bourgeois world he inhabits, it may be because, as historian Tetsuo Najita put it, "Sōseki, reflecting on the modernization of Japan, did not see it as the actualization of human expectations in which modern man is happier than his ancient ancestors, but rather as a cruel exploitative march leading toward total nervous exhaustion."[17] Sōseki expressed his cynicism by writing a series of novels that, while none but one autobiographical, nonetheless drew upon experiences akin to those of his social and intellectual cohort. The first line of his 1908 *Nowaki* (Autumn Wind) reads, "Shirai Doya is a writer [*bungakusha*]," which means Shirai is a teacher, writer, and preacher—but above all a *failure*, given what Sōseki considered modern Japan's indifference to its intelligentsia. That such novels are popular may have to do with, as Jay Rubin puts it, "the indelible imagery with which [Sōseki] conveys his view of the world,"[18] but just how and why Japan's putatively greatest modern writer could be so while steadfastly critical is also in question here.

Sōseki's sarcasm has seldom been interpreted as ideological. While he took public stands that might have had political import—such as declining a Doctor of Letters from the Ministry of Education or protesting the government's establishment of an official committee on literature—it is said that Sōseki did such things out of personal integrity, not political intent. Sōseki was doubtlessly irritated by (as he was by many things) the jingoism of his day. In his lecture "Watakushi no kojinshugi" ("My Individualism," 1914) he famously quipped that few Japanese citizens sell their bean curd for the sake of the nation. There is some truth to Katō Shūichi's banality that while Ōgai collaborated with the state, and Uchimura Kanzō criticized it, and Nagai Kafū fled from it, "Natsume Sōseki minimized it."[19] But if it is the nature of the modern capitalist state to appear minimized, then Sōseki and his sour ironies do appear out of sync. Irony, though often cited as subversive, was part of Japanese modernity no less than the West's, where the complicity between modernist irony and an indifference to issues of power is well noted. In considering Sōseki we might keep in mind that novels often speak to us from outside the ruling elite but inside the nation. Despite the incessant work of critics intent on proving that every feature and contour of Sōseki's work is traceable to his own ill-ease (even dis-ease), the fact that modernity means a move away from the public to the private may also mean that the fetish of a recalcitrant Sōseki is a cover for what may be more properly thought of as ideological work. In 1905, the Naturalist school (*shizen-shugiha*) that would so rile Sōseki was hardly in place, but its linguistic idiom was, and Sōseki was already at war with it. Unlike the narrator of Shimazaki Tōson's *Hakai* (*The Broken Commandment*, 1906), who is submerged in its main character, Sōseki's narrator stays with us and remains uncommitted fully to his story. How does he do this? Karatani would say: by resisting the narrative past tense Futabatei Shimei pioneered for modern Japanese fiction, and thus "resisting the narrative mode of modern fiction." *Neko*, like other early Sōseki works, is narrated largely in the unusual first person and often in the nonpast tense. But Sōseki's *Neko* is not, however much we may wish, all about some kind of resistance. Only with great and counterproductive irony did Sōseki cling to the already recherché *kokkeibon, yomihon, haikai,* and *kanshi* (Sino-Japanese poetry) in his twentieth-century writing, the extinction of which, writes Karatani, "was tantamount to the establishment of modern 'literature.'"[20]

Higuchi Ichiyō is not the only impecunious modern writer who is now celebrated on Bank of Japan notes. One of the more recent ironies associated with Sōseki has been his face put on the one-thousand-yen bill by the state in 1984, despite Sōseki's distaste for the government's honoring intellectuals and his impatience with money overall. *Neko*, like many Sōseki novels, is interpreted as hostile to modernity because of the author's annoyance with wealth, of which he had none. (Kushami's family name, Kaneda, translates as "money field.") But what work in literary modernity unambiguously embraces it? Sōseki, who valued his privacy and made private the very stuff of Japanese literary modernity, has his face circulating as an icon on the national currency. But could there be collusion here, not insult? Alain Touraine argues, "The history of modernity is the history of the emergence of social and cultural actors who," like Sōseki, "increasingly lost their belief that modernity was the first concrete definition of the good."[21] But Sōseki's astute reader, Etō Jun, asserted that, far from being antagonistic, "Sōseki came to regard the Meiji nation-state as his own."[22] Who is right?

Neko was originally no more than its first chapter. It was quickly written by Sōseki as a piece to be recited aloud for the entertainment of the other members of the Yamakai reading group in early 1904. The Yamakai was a small group of intellectuals and literati that gathered around the central figure of Takahama Kyoshi (1874–1959), who once ruled prose with *yama*, or a climax, to be bad prose. Kyoshi recalled the day Sōseki read his piece. "It was so different from anything else I had heard at the Yamakai that I didn't know quite what to make of it, but because it was so humorous I was really in favor of it. . . . I put it in the January issue of *Hototogisu* the following year. It made him instantly famous."[23] The setting was a *rōdokukai*, a "reading-aloud club," then a popular pastime mentioned offhandedly by the young poet Tōfū in *Neko* and, according to Takahashi Yasuo, a remnant of "voice culture at the time of print culture."[24] Such clubs exist today, if only for poetry. Orally delivered prose is reserved for radio, compact discs, podcasts, and other digital media. The performative nature of *Neko* might be seen in that its opening pages are in meter: it was designed to be read aloud at the Yamakai, with Sōseki in the position of a raconteur (*hanashika*) and fellow writers as his audience. Speaking and its dissonance with writing was a theme of Sōseki's all his career, and the Yamakai's theatricality is important for the significance of *Neko* to Japanese literary history. But theatricality, as we will see, was important elsewhere in 1904 Tokyo.

The mid-1880s, often referred to as the Rokumeikan era, were the height of passion in Japan for reform. *Kairyō* (improvement) was a fashion that was applied to seemingly everything, including theater. The Society for the Reform of Theater (Engeki kairyō kai) was established in the summer of 1886 by prime minister Itō Hirobumi's son-in-law Suematsu Norizumi, recently returned from England. Itō was a founding member, as were Inoue Kaoru, Hozumi Nobushige, Toyama Masakazu, and Fukuchi Ouchi (Gen'ichirō). From the start, theater meant kabuki, and in October of that year Suematsu outlined in a speech what the ten goals of reformed kabuki were, and they included government regulation of copyright and performance rights. Not all his reforms were accomplished, but that one was. From the start, important voices for the modern theater, such as Ōgai and Shōyō (whose translation of *Julius Caesar* was composed in the metered style of *jōruri* ballad dramas), opposed the society for what they viewed as unwise restrictions on artists. It was the notion that collusion between artists and the government could produce meaningful culture which was suspect, but that was precisely what the state had in mind. Ozaki Hotsuki noted that in time, even *rōkyoku* (musical ballads) and *kōdan* (historical tales) came to "reek of national prestige" (*kokui sen'yō to itta nioi*).[25]

The greatest accomplishment of the society was the official recuperation of kabuki in 1887, when the emperor saw it for the first time. As Edward Seidensticker phrased it, this quasi-official *tenran* (imperial viewing), one of many during the Meiji period, "bestowed the ultimate cachet."[26] Ichikawa Danjūrō IX, Onoe Kikugorō V, and Ichikawa Sadanji performed in a palace garden before the emperor, aristocrats, high officials, and members of elite society who otherwise would have never set foot in an actual theater. The actors did no vulgar *sewamono* (popular pieces), only dance and a historical drama, *Kanjinchō* (*The Subscription List*) by Namiki Gohei III, based on the utterly respectable noh play *Ataka*. The intent was to give official approval to a model reformed kabuki, a kabuki devoid of contemporary reference. This was part of the move, beginning with the emperor's 1876 *tenran* of noh, to spark a revival of the comatose classical theater and make performance part of the newly formed nation-state. *Kōdan*, which would come to bear much of the work of nationalist pedagogy, was performed before the emperor a decade later.[27]

Ironically, imperial patronage of kabuki, like other performing arts, in effect meant there was no urgent need to reform it further. Its classic form was now part of the national heritage. The fortunes of the Society for the Reform of Theater fell along with those of the Itō government, but kabuki had been officially licensed. Once the repertoire had been canonized, one of the prime functions of Tokugawa-period kabuki—namely the dissemination of current events—was eliminated. Okitsu Kaname, despite his prejudice against early Meiji literature, correctly pointed out that the history of Japanese fiction, as it moved into *kindai* (the modern), includes its relation to theater. If the modern English novel evolved in part out of the ballad, the Japanese did so out of the stage. But theater did not usually include such *yose engei* as *kōdan* and *rakugo*.[28] *Rakugo*, translated "public storytelling"[29] and defined as "a short humorous story ending in punch line,"[30] was likely thought too crude to be literature. There is little redolent of modern literature in *rakugo*: no self-absorbed narrator, no anguished superfluous men. In fact, the opposite: the narrator is just that, never a character himself, and his stories come from the public baths, the streets, even the toilets, not his own mind—and certainly not from the universities. Shōyō did not have the more plebeian forms of *yose* performance in mind when he argued for the need for a national theater (*kokugeki*). Nonetheless, the more popular forms of theater were likewise inspired to reform themselves in line with the national spirit of *bunmei kaika*. *Yose,* something akin to vaudeville, came to Edo from Osaka at the end of the eighteenth century, traditionally dated from 1798 when Okamoto Mansaku from Osaka began performing at a straw store in Edo's Kanda neighborhood. It evolved, says Andrew Markus in his essay on Tokugawa-period *misemono*, from "humble narrative performances in market places and alleys."[31] Gerald Figal writes, "Popular performers and the crowds they attracted were effectively taken off the open streets (historically the place of revolutionary action) and contained within a controlled economy of structures. It seems fitting that the word for the variety halls called *yose* signifies 'a place that brings in the crowds.'"[32]

Consequently, the number of *yose* halls exploded in the early Meiji period during the first stage of the ghettoization (under the slogan of *bunmei kaika*) of public expressions of sentiment. Despite government measures aimed at their suppression, by 1855 there were nearly four hundred *yose* halls in the city, and admission was inexpensive, still only three or four *sen* well into the middle of Meiji.[33] Along with the *kawaraban* discussed in the first chapter, oral performances, especially *kōdan*, were the dominant means for spreading news of current events in late Tokugawa, and the state meant to control them. All manner of public performances were still prohibited in the early years of Meiji, and the reason was clear. Any assemblage was liable, as the newspapers reported, to disruption by *ranbōmono* (the rabble), and any crowd's speech was unpredictable. Typical of late Tokugawa performance, write Heinz Morioka and Miyoko Sasaki, "is a group of characters who extend the objects of their jokes and pranks to include the established social order."[34] And not just jokes and pranks: the authorities found explosives in the summer of 1867 in a *yose* theater, placed there by an Aizu domain sympathizer who was also the father-in-law of the *rakugo* artist Karaku IV. More than a century later, a day laborer quoted in Edward Fowler's ethnography of Tokyo's San'ya *yoseba*, told him that *rakugo* was "the best literature of protest we had. Thanks to *rakugo* the common people could voice their resistance to authority."[35]

But this was not true in the first years of the twentieth century. When Sōseki speaks alternately through his cat and Professor Kushami, he resembles nothing more than the traditional *rakugo* storyteller, though unlike a *hanashika*, Sōseki presumably did not improvise in front of his audience. (Kyoshi thought *Neko* odd for its cat, though there are many *rakugo* with animals.)[36] It is said that Sōseki's ardor for *rakugo* was at its height at this time.[37] Mizukawa Takao suggests that he had resumed attending *yose* in 1904,[38] and his wife Kyōko confirms it in her memoirs.[39] But Sōseki had grown up with *rakugo*, attending performances at the Isemoto Hall in Nihonbashi as a boy. Still, he notes in his semiautobiographical *Michikusa* (*Grass on the Wayside*, 1915), which describes his life during the two years he wrote *Neko*, an ambivalence toward Tokugawa culture that helps explain the ideological work *Neko* undertook.

By 1877, the number of *yose* in Tokyo had declined dramatically. Although eventually *kōdan* and *rakugo* would modestly revive, all *yose* made concessions to modernity. The improvisational capacity of *rakugo* became the preserve of *manzai*, and even there it is largely gone today. In the early years of the Meiji period, Matsurintei Hakuen II gave up his celebrated *shiranamimono* (stories of banditry) in order to curry favor—which is to say, survive—by turning to *kaika kōdan*, or "Enlightenment historical stories," such as that of Christopher Columbus. During the newspaper boom of the mid-1870s, San'yūtei Enchō (1839–1900), the most iconoclastic performer of the Meiji period, would perform *rakugo* based on articles that had appeared in print that day. Inouye Jukichi, an observer of everyday life in Tokyo at the end of the nineteenth century, pointed out just how important *yose* still was at that time. "The influence of these halls on Tokyo life cannot be overlooked. Newspapers are, it is true, now leavening the whole society; but it is still from the halls that the artisan to-day gets all his knowledge, meager as it is, and to the same source may be traced his familiarity with the notable events and heroes in the history of his country. In its educating influence, the story-teller's profession is an important one."[40]

In 1888, the emperor attended a performance of *kōdan* by Momokawa Jōen, whose work *Hyakumyōden* (The Tale of a Hundred Cats) may have inspired Sōseki. Enchō claimed the emperor attended *rakugo* three years later, but official court records contain no mention of this. *Rakugo*, unlike other *yose*, eventually decided to remain "classic" (i.e., focused on stories of love, parents and children, wives, gangsters, ghosts, lords and retainers, samurai, and so forth) but not without some innovations first. When Sōseki was growing up, his was a neighborhood and household steeped in *yose*. In "Garasudo no uchi" (*Inside My Glass Doors*, 1915) he recalls hearing a raconteur renowned for his stories of military exploits at the neighborhood hall. Those frequent trips to the Isemoto meant he heard famous *kōdan hanashika*, and he continued going to the *yose* halls more or less his entire life. In an 1888 letter to his mentor, the poet Masaoka Shiki (1867–1902), whose friendship was in part based on a shared fondness for *yose*, Sōseki writes about going to see San'yūtei En'yū perform and being so entertained that he temporarily forgot his chronic stomach troubles.

En'yū was renowned for his *suteteko* dance, first performed in 1880 and most popular when Sōseki was an adolescent and young man. A reference to it found its way into *Neko* later. It did not originate with En'yū—like break dancing, it came from the streets, in this case said to be Yoshiwara, or possibly Shizuoka province. One night at the Asakusa Namikitei *yose* hall, En'yū suddenly rose from his cushion, lifted his kimono, and tucked it into his obi. Exposing his thighs, he stuck out his shins, sang a song mocking himself, and feigned tearing off his famously large nose while dancing an odd jig across the stage to the shocked applause of the audience. Okitsu Kaname considered this event "the prologue to a new era's popular arts."[41] Until this, dancing in *rakugo* had been restricted to the movement of the upper body while sitting on the stage, and Okitsu Kaname says the crowd at the Namikitei broke out into a near-riot.[42] En'yū was immensely popular in postrevolutionary Tokyo, where audiences gathered from all over the country. Other dynamic movements in *yose* followed, such as the *hera-hera* dance of Mankitsu (a *magodeshi* of En'yū's), which he would perform half-naked. Some theatergoers wanted the police to put an end to such antics, but En'yū and his successors defended their art as in the spirit, naturally, of modernization. If Enchō perfected Tokugawa-period *rakugo*, En'yū was the father of modern *rakugo*.

It is often said such antics in *rakugo* were required to attract audiences of Tokyo newcomers not very familiar with the standard repertoire, but there may have been something else going on. If the shift from oral communication to written text in the Meiji period was a shift from sound to visual space, it did so only through stages. Physical motion on the stage may be important in hindsight for its downgrading of speech more than for its literally spectacular novelty. In doing so it creates, intentionally or not, an immediacy prelingual and thus precognitive. "The gesture," writes Tsurumi Shunsuke, is personal and spontaneous, "as disposable as a paper cup."[43] "Though words are grounded in oral speech," Walter Ong thinks in a view similar to Sōseki's, "writing tyrannically locks them into a visual field forever."[44] It has been suggested that what attracted Sōseki to *rakugo* included its *kyōdōtaiteki na fun'iki*, which is to say its collective, communal setting,[45] a setting emphasized when En'yū and Yanagiya

Ko-san III made *rakugo* increasingly comic. En'yū's innovations, if not precisely modernizing *rakugo*, did revitalize it for new audiences. Okitsu Kaname called En'yū "the popular poet of Enlightenment and Civilization."[46] But at the same time, another scholar suggests that Sōseki preferred *rakugo* to the more modern *shinpa* and *kōdan* because in performance the latter were less natural, which would seem to mean spontaneous. In Sōseki's novel *Sanshirō* (1908), one character remarks how lucky he is to be living at the same time as Ko-san, and in his diary Sōseki compared a pantomime he saw in Kensington with En'yū's performances. His own public lectures were not without *rakugo*-esque elements of performance.[47] When he delivered his lecture on individualism in front of university students, he retold at length the *rakugo* story of the "Meguro mackerel" (*Meguro no sanma*), likening himself to a boned fish to apologize for taking to so long before accepting an invitation to speak at their school.[48] Sōseki's attachment to *rakugo* was already conspicuous in *Neko*—he gives Kushami's wife a nose as large as En'yū's. But other things happened in the interim to make this connection complicated and far from benign.

Stenography had a special appeal to Japanese when it arrived in the Meiji period. For a range of reasons related to modernization, the Japanese were eager for a means of precisely transcribing speech as quickly as it was enunciated. Once Takusari Kōki adapted Issac Pitman, Graham-style phonetic stenography for Japanese by 1882, it was put to immediate use. Takusari claimed *sokkibon* could be easily used to record "all manner of reports, arguments, conversations, and plain speech."[49] As one exuberant supporter predicted that year, Japanese stenography would make possible "the direct transcription of, including other things, 'assemblies, street corner disquisitions, and parodies of Buddhist scripture.'"[50] Takusari even harbored hopes his stenography would replace Japanese orthography altogether, and the Diet adopted this new technology only eight years later in order to officially record its proceedings. But the first professional Japanese stenographers went to work at *anti*government political assemblies, a newer Meiji public space. The Meiji constitution, according to Andrew Gordon, had given an important new legitimacy to political rallies and speech meetings (*enzetsu kai*), speaking tours (*yūzetsu*), and, later, demonstrations. "By the late nineteenth century, hundreds of legal, open political rallies were convened each year in Tokyo alone,"[51] and stenography facilitated the distribution of the words spoken and heard at those assemblies to supporters of the People's Rights Movement nationwide.

A student of Takusari, Wakabayashi Kanzō, opened a stenography study group (*sokkibon kenkyūkai*) in his home to propagate the technology. One way to do so was to produce transcriptions of popular storytellers' texts for sale to the public. In 1884, after paying a preliminary courtesy call on San'yūtei Enchō at home, Wakabayashi and fellow stenography enthusiast Sakai Shōzō attended Enchō's hit revival of *Kaidan botandōrō* (The Peony Lantern, A Ghost Story) for fifteen days, and then published the text, whose marketing made much of the innovative method of its transcription. It was published in 1885, the same year as Shōyō's *Shōsetsu shinzui* and against the backdrop of a burgeoning movement to reform the written language for modern ends. Wakabayashi's preface to *Botandōrō* made much of stenography's contributions to modern society, including to the organs of state—transcription, he immodestly claimed, would be a great linguistic boon to the "improvement of our nature in the future."[52] It was the first of many *sokkibon* that would follow and prove quite popular. Okitsu Kaname suggests that *Botandōrō*'s ghost story about a poor family combined with the astute psychological description of a murderer was perfect for audiences mindful of modernization. An 1884 printing of the work refers explicitly to Wakabayashi's *gengo chokusha*, the direct representation of language, as having achieved great success in transcribing such signs of modernity as "the Diet, speeches, conferences, and the like." Wakabayashi boasted that he thought Japanese transcription would be a great boon to the enhancement of "our nation in the future." So accurate a transcription of colloquial Japanese, *Botandōrō* was used as a textbook for teaching the Japanese language abroad. Wakabayashi transcribed *Botandōrō* to give form (*keitai, sugata*) to speech (*hanashi*),[53] but the irony was that as oral culture was rendered text, the missing voice was installed as prior to the book, as *bun* became *bungaku*.[54] Transcribed *yose* proved inspirational for the authors soon to be credited with establishing modern Japanese literature's standard idiom. The opening lines of Japan's much-touted "first novel," *Ukigumo*, were influenced by Enchō's mode of oral delivery. But unlike Enchō's *Botandōrō*, in which all problems in the story are solved, in Shimei's masterpiece none were.

At the same time, stenography precipitated changes in popular culture and its consumption. Enchō's improvised performances became fixed texts. "These were well-received," writes Nanette Twine in her account of the development of modern written Japanese. "They enabled people to read the words of the famous storyteller exactly as he had delivered them, without leaving home."[55] But Enchō remained a storyteller who many thought worth leaving the house to hear. Born in 1839 in the downtown Edo neighborhood of Yujima, Enchō first performed at the age of seven while studying under Enshō. Early training in art is said to have given him the inspiration for the introduction of the many props and musical instruments that made his early performances so singularly creative and popular. Enchō's popularity not only restored the fortunes of the San'yūtei lineage, at that time eclipsed by the Yanagiya, but also revived *rakugo* overall, particularly after the catastrophe for theaters after the Ansei earthquake in 1855. Even after he abandoned his more florid performance style for the single prop of the handheld fan that became his trademark, *rakugo* would be evermore theatrical after him. One of his most popular types of performance was *sandai-banashi*, in which the *rakugo* raconteur would ask the audience to shout out three topics that he would then weave into a single, seamless story. We know that Enchō first joined in the fun in 1863, when he spun a story out of "spring rain," "lovesickness," and "a pepper tree pestle" (*surikogi*).[56] Despite Andrew Gordon's contention that "unlike Kabuki, variety theater, sumo wrestling, or moving picture shows, rallies offered the prospect of audience participation,"[57] and while we must rely on secondhand accounts of his performances by contemporary observers, we can imagine the atmosphere of the *yose* hall when a performer of Enchō's popularity was present as anything but passive. Enchō came to respond to the spirit of the times (as had En'yū with his tale of Christopher Columbus) by performing works inspired by European writers such as Maupassant. He was not entirely taken in by fashion. When his first original work, *Shinkei Kasanegafuchi* (A Spine-Chiller in Kasanegafuchi) was transcribed in 1884, he took advantage of the homonym *shinkei* (nerves) for *shinkei* (true views) in order to make the *kaika senseigata* (professors of Enlightenment), in a word, nervous.[58]

The success of *Botandōrō* boosted the popularity of *sokkibon*. Seven hundred and fifty had been published by 1900.[59] In *Neko*'s third chapter, Kangetsu mentions the popular magazine *Bungei kurabu*, which published stenographed versions of *rakugo*.[60] But much earlier in the Meiji period Enchō had performed and published his most important and popular work, *Shiohara Tasuke ichidai ki* (The Life of Shiohara Tasuke, 1878). In the *jitsugaku* (practical learning) spirit of Meiji, Enchō joined other storytellers like *kōdan* raconteur Shōrin Hakuen II in going to rural locations for research and to conduct interviews that would culminate in *jitsuroku ninjōbanashi*, or real-life accounts of everyday life. *Shiohara* was one such work. Enchō started his research for it in 1876, and with *Botandōrō* they were the most important popular theatrical influences on the development of modern Japanese fiction, in part because they abandoned tired talk of Buddhist karma and Confucianist *kanzen chōaku*. A real Meiji success story, the tale of a coal merchant making his fortune against the odds, *Shiohara* marked a departure for *rakugo*. If still didactic, it is by example rather than by dictate. Its influence was pervasive. It sold at least 120,000 copies, and perhaps as many as 200,000. Young women of good families were overheard incorporating its colloquialisms into their banter.[61] Selections from it were put in ethics textbooks for the public schools, and it was this work that Enchō claimed to have performed before the Meiji emperor in 1891.

Shiohara is acknowledged as one of the pioneering works upon which *genbun'itchi*, the modern vernacularized literary language, was constructed. Transcribed by stenography not in a *yose* theater but in the more restrained environment of a teahouse with geisha as an audience,[62] the published version became an important primer for young writers. Futabatei Shimei, credited with the pioneering use of *genbun'itchi* in *Ukigumo*, had been urged by his Shōyō to read *Shiohara*.[63] There is a contradiction here. A modern language standardized *and* colloquial—how can it be both? Modernity would prefer that language, like so much else, be rationalized, that is, made uniform, but it must also remain *popular*, which means it never will achieve uniformity. What is required is an illusion. "To imagine a language," Ludwig Wittgenstein claimed, "is to imagine a form of life,"[64] and in Japan, linguist Kindaichi Haruhiko similarly observed, "A national language is something that is made."[65] By whom and for whom? Bakhtin wrote, "But everywhere and always 'literary language' has as its arena of activity the conversational language of a literarily educated circle."[66] The *genbun'itchi* movement of the first two decades of the Meiji period pivoted around debates over the notion of the *demos*, the citizenry, and the problem of class inherent in prior forms of language and scripts. The government put it this plainly: *gengo wa kokka no genki*—language is the lifeblood of the nation-state.[67]

In the 1870s, the statesman Ōki Takatō successfully introduced into the schools *kotobazukai*, a pedagogic program to teach all students in all regions of the country a standard colloquial Japanese. But by the end of that same decade the colloquial style in textbooks, magazines, and newspapers was on the verge of disappearing—it was the transcribed performances of Enchō that revived its popularity.[68] Eventually orthographic reforms were ceded to the state. By the time Sōseki was writing *Neko* in 1903–5, the Japanese language had clearly become a concern of the government, as was what the public read. Increasing the citizenry's literacy may have been part of catching up with the West, but sexuality and socialism were not to be among the assignments.

James Fujii has argued that the polyphony of a work like *Neko* has to be interpreted as *resistance* to what he calls the monologic subject of a state-sponsored
linguistic project.[69] There is, however, a more nuanced and historically accurate
way of describing the dissonance between the Sōseki text and the trend of a
modern language. Apropos another language standardized at a comparatively
late stage, Italian, Antonio Gramsci said, "Every time the question of the language surfaces, in one way or another, it means that a series of other problems
are coming to the fore: the formation and enlargement of the governing class,
the need to establish more and intimate and secure relationships between the
governing groups and the national-popular mass, in other words to reorganize
the cultural hegemony."[70] Rather than cast Sōseki and his *Neko* as challenges to
the state, it is more useful to think of them as players in this ongoing negotiation
of competing hegemonies. In 1892, prophetess Deguchi Nao wrote down the
words of the gods in *kana*, the Japanese syllabary. When these words were later
rescripted, with Sino-Japanese characters where the transcriptions of sounds
once stood, she had them burnt.[71] Deguchi thought the use of "ideographic"
kanji "injurious to the nation."[72] Throughout the Meiji period, but especially
in its last years, various forms of orality were being converted into text. In the
third decade of Meiji—the decade that cuts the Meiji period in two halves, the
first still dominated by oral delivery and the second by print—newspapers,
responding to the commercial success of the *sokkibon*, began carrying *rakugo*
and *rōkyoku* in their pages. By the end of the Meiji period, the practice of *kakai*,
where Japanese poems were recited aloud to audiences and fellow participants,
had given way to the now modern practice of reading poetry silently rather than
listening to it.[73] The text becomes ontological. "When language, as spoken and
scattered words, becomes an object of knowledge," according to Foucault "we
see it reappearing in a strictly opposite modality: a silent, cautious disposition
of the word upon the whiteness of a piece of paper, where it can possess neither
sound nor interlocutor, where it has nothing to say but itself, nothing to do but
shine, in the brightness of its being."[74]

The storyteller on his platform had once been the preeminent trope of urban
Japanese culture. Kamei Hideo has labeled Enchō's recitations *shūgōteki* (collective), emphasizing the presence of the crowd. There, Kamei suggests, even an
autonomous self "can be viewed as existing collectively while it is transformed
in everyday life into a multiformed self."[75] Ochi Haruo has suggested that Enchō
was "the face of the storyteller before the fact of the novel . . . someone who
approaches in nature what Walter Benjamin termed his storyteller [*Erzähler*],"

part of a collective experience that modernity would alter, if not eliminate.[76] Increasingly, Enchō's texts, fetishized, replaced him. In 1886, Enchō began to serialize, using stenography, his *rakugo* in the newly founded *Yamato shinbun*, prompting his competition to do the same.[77] But this was a shortsighted strategy. Eventually the genre of transcribed oral performances would be killed off in the first decade of the twentieth century by *kaki-kōdan*, works never performed but printed from the start. In time, some *rakugo* as well would be written before publication and never performed live in front of an audience; they were edited for erotic content and marketed to the *katei no chanoma*, the family room of the household, and heralded a new form of fiction.[78] "The incarnation of the spoken word as printed text," writes J. Scott Miller, "allowed it to be viewed as a commodity rather than as an art form. Storytelling had been a group experience of immense, even ritualistic, vitality, but the act of reading, beginning as it does with the acquisition of a book, led to a different narrative experience."[79] *Rakugo* live began with the raconteur's *maeoki* (informal introduction), including thanks to the audience for coming, which linguist Nomura Masaaki says "constructed a shared lingual space between the performer and the listener," but no transcribed *rakugo* included any of them. In the controlled environments in which *rakugo* artists performed for transcription, there were no real audiences and thus no need for any theatrical bond.[80]

Sōseki's *Neko* preserves traces of an orality not found in textual culture— Sōseki wrote about how his grandfather lived in an utterly oral culture bereft of print[81]—and it casts a shadow on the new material culture of publishing. Ishihara Chiaki suggests that *Neko* "resides entirely with [Japan's] many oral cultures" as it is only the voice of the cat that constitutes *Neko* as a unified literary work.[82] It would be the loss of that collective experience and the production of the text that would be *Neko*'s success. Benedict Anderson finds it useful to quote Benjamin in looking at the work performed by the modern novel:

> What differentiates the novel from all other forms of prose literature—
> the fairy tale, the legend, even the novella—is that it neither comes from
> oral tradition nor goes into it . . . The *Erzähler* takes what he tells from
> experience—his own or that reported by others. And he in turn makes it the
> experience of those who are listening to his tale. The novelist has isolated
> himself. The birthplace of the novel is the individual in his solitude, who is
> no longer able to express in an exemplary manner his weightiest concerns, is
> himself uncounselled, and cannot counsel others. To write a novel is to carry

the incommensurable to extremes in the representation of human life. In the midst of life's fullness, and through the representation of this fullness, the novel gives evidence of the profound perplexity of the living.[83]

Not all forms of orality are evacuated from modernity, however. They come and go. One can see almost any day on America's CSPAN a lone congressperson delivering a speech before an empty House or Senate chamber, save for a stenographer (who retextualizes the teleprompter) who is recording his or her words. Why doesn't the congressperson simply *hand* his text over to the stenographer? Why this performance? One might as well ask: what is the relationship between orality and textuality in modernity, and how is that relationship related to governmentality, or more precisely for us here, between Sōseki's reading aloud of the first chapter of *Neko* at the Yamakai and its subsequent publication in *Hototogisu*?

Maeda Ai suggested that the greatest impression that *Neko* gives its reader is that everyone is talking all the time.[84] The Tokugawa cultural influences on *Neko* are many. Commentator after commentator has explored the relation of the novel to *kokkeibon* such as Jippensha Ikku's *Tōkaidōchū hizakurige* (Shank's Mare, 1802–22), for example. When *Neko* was published it was described as a *bunmeiteki* (civilized) *Hizakurige*.[85] But nothing is taken as so influential on this novel as *rakugo*. *Neko* is certainly not the only founding work of modern Japanese literature in which traditional forms of theater figure. Shimei's *Ukigumo*, for instance, is often said to be indebted to *jōruri*.[86] But *Neko* is a high-water mark. Senuma Shigeki sees signs in its second chapter of the *rakugo* "Jugemu" (Limitless Longevity), and in the fifth chapter, of "Hanairo-momen" (Light Blue Cotton).[87] Chapter 2 mentions explicitly En'yū's trademark *suteteko* dancing, Meitei's uncle is a character who could have come right out of an En'yū story, and the conversation between Kushami and his wife about Roman kings in chapter 3 resembles En'yū's disciple Enzō's work. When Blackie the Cat talks about New Year's "congratulations" (*omedetē*), he sounds like Hachi-san and Kuma-san, two of classic *rakugo*'s most familiar characters. But the *rakugo*-like content and style of *Neko* were not guaranteed to endear it to the authorities, who had chosen to rescue only dry, historical *kōdan* among storytelling traditions. Writers themselves had ambivalent views on the *rakugo* legacy. When Uno Kōji (1891–1961) heard that Kikuchi Kan had dismissed a story of his as simply "Osaka *rakugo*," Uno retorted unkindly that Kikuchi's fiction was *kōdan*.[88] But it is important to note that while some of the formal features of *rakugo* (such as its liberal use of onomatopoeia) were incorporated into modern fiction, the same cannot be said of its themes, and much to its detriment according to social critics such as Ozaki Hotsuki, who bemoaned the loss of popular themes and the raw energy in them.[89]

Others had a different opinion of *kōdan*. Okuma Shigenobu, the prime minister lampooned by Sōseki in *Neko*'s title, once claimed that "*kōdan* are what cause the Japanese people to win wars."[90] "So completely were *kōdan* identified with the good old values of loyalty and patriotism," writes Jay Rubin, "that, in 1911, the Ministry of Education actually formulated a policy of promoting their production."[91] These were *kōdan* no longer delivered orally and in real time but via such modern media as magazines. In his memoirs, the founder of Kōdansha, Noma Seiji, boasted that his magazine *Kōdan kurabu* (Kōdan club) converted the masses (*minshū*) not just into national citizens (*kokumin*) but ideal citizens (*risōteki kokumin*). To do so, he argued, oral *kōdan* had to be converted first into legible texts (*yomimono*).[92] The *rakugo* used to great effect by Sōseki in *Neko* to satirize may not be so much an opposite, counterhegemonic move against the state's appropriation and control of the printed word, but one part of that process.

Yose was in serious decline by the time of *Neko*'s publication. "The great masters of Meiji Yose," says Edward Seidensticker, "are said to have striven for small, intimate audiences. A hundred was the ideal size."[93] By the early years of the twentieth century, mass culture was targeting larger groups, while its consumption was occurring in newly atomized locations. *Sokkibon* were a crucial stage in this evolution. They made reading "a familiar, rather than alienating, activity and thereby served to promote and sustain mass literacy, bridging the gap that separated participating as an indulged member of a *yose* audience from playing the reader's role before an open book."[94] In the second chapter of *Neko*, Kushami and his wife discuss the possibility of an excursion to the theater for a performance of *gidayū*. I quote it at length because it says much about *Neko*'s stance toward oral culture. Kushami tells his friend Meitei that:

> My wife had earlier asked me, as a year's end present to herself, to take her to hear Settsu Daijō. I'd replied that I wouldn't say no, and asked her the nature of the program for that day. She consulted the newspapers and answered that it was one of Chikamatsu's suicide dramas, *Unagidani*. "Let's not go today; I don't like *Unagidani*," said I. So we did not go on that day. Next day, my wife, bringing out the newspaper again, said "Today he's doing the *Monkey Man at*

Horikawa; so, let's go." I said let's not, because *Horikawa* was so frivolous, just *samisen*-playing with no meat in it. My wife went away looking discontented. The following day, she stated almost as a demand, "Today's program is *The Temple With Thirty-Three Pillars*. You may dislike the *Temple* quite as strongly as you disliked all the others; but since the treat is intended for me, surely you won't object to taking me there." "If you've set your heart on it so firmly, then we'll go: but since the performance has been announced as Settsu's farewell appearance on the stage, the house is bound to be packed full and since we haven't booked in advance, it will obviously be impossible to get in. To start with, in order to attend such performances there's an established procedure to be observed. It would be hopeless to try going about it in the wrong way. You just can't dodge this proper procedure. So, sorry though I am, we simply cannot go today."[95]

To Kushami's private joy and his wife's more obvious disappointment, the couple is finally unable to go to the theater at all. This exchange sketches the modern Japanese intellectual's relationship not just to older forms of oral popular culture but to his or her literal place. Kushami, one such modern intellectual, cannot and will not go out in the public, certainly not to a *yose* hall where the crowd rules. It is not far-fetched to say that early in his most canonical novel, Sōseki kills off oral culture. Life takes place at home and nowhere else. Habermas observes of this shift: "The sphere of the public arose in the broader strata of the bourgeoisie as an expansion and at the same time completion of the intimate sphere of the conjugal family. Living room and *salon* were under the same roof ... conjoined in literature that had become 'fiction.'"[96]

But Professor Kushami's home is not all that intimate. It is the site, unlike Japanese homes today, of an incessant traffic in visitors. The "completion of the intimate sphere of the conjugal family" was underway but not yet fully accomplished. Meanwhile, in *Neko*'s chronological setting of 1904–5, life was taking place in some very public places. Despite the fact that a police order issued in 1887 severely limited public political gatherings,[97] the years 1905–18 have been dubbed Japan's "era of popular violence." Of the six major riots in those years that left at least twenty dead, the Hibiya riot of 5 September 1905, was the most insurrectionary. What was revolutionary here, as indicated by Yoshino Sakuzō, was that this was "indeed the first time that the crowd acted as a political force." That crowd, and those that followed for another decade and a half, had something of the carnival to them: "The theatrical quality of the events, the parody and the inversion of symbols, and the echoes of festival celebration seen in the use of traditional drums to build atmosphere at a rally and the coincidence of riot and holiday would have been familiar to a Tokugawa peasant or town-dweller."

In 1914, an eighteen-year-old lumberyard worker by the name of Tanaka went to an *enzetsu kai*, or speech rally, that erupted into a riot. Tanaka thought them "entertaining" (*omoshiroi*). These same years, says Andrew Gordon, Tanaka also went to Nihonbashi to join in stone throwing.[98] After 1918, no more city riots took place. The crowd was effectively dispersed into the myriad privatized realms that constitute modern life, away from the spontaneous, improvisational speech assembly or *yoseba* that was a threat to the policing of modern social groups. On 5 September 1905, the Hibiya Park rally against the terms of the Russo-Japanese peace treaty ended with some of the crowd marching to the Shintomi-za theater to hold another public meeting. The Shintomi-za had been used for rallies before. As Gordon points out, *enzetsukai* along with outdoor rallies and even riots were considered "inexpensive forms of popular entertainment."[99] On 15 August 1881, there was an *enzetsukai* to oppose government developmental policies for Hokkaidō.[100] This time, however, the theater's management, seeing the crowd, tried to renege on the deal and summoned the police. On a day when the temperature neared one hundred degrees, the two thousand protesters inside the theater and many more outside began to riot once the authorities ordered everyone to disperse. By late afternoon a thousand rioters had attacked and damaged Tokutomi Sohō's *Kokumin shinbun* offices.[101] The line between the public assembly (including within theaters) and public sovereignty was a frayed one.

Traditional storytellers often got into trouble if their stories were implicated in antisocial behaviors. In 1842, the Edo magistrate restricted *yose* to four themes and only four: the Japanese gods (*shindō kōshaku*), Confucianism (*shingaku*), military exploits (*gunshō kōdan*), and tales of old (*mukashibanashi*).[102] Performers soon found ways around this, prompting further restrictions. At the start of the Meiji period, the 1842 rules added that no women or musical instruments were to be on the stage. Hinotani Teruhiko noted that the Japanese press reported police surveillance of *rakugo* and Enchō's worries over addressing political topics in his performances.[103] Baba Bunkō had been executed in 1758 for, among other infringements, criticizing Tokugawa officials on stage.[104] By 1882, punishments were less severe. Bakahayashi Don'ō I was sentenced to three months' hard labor and a fine of twenty yen for saying that "His Majesty the

Emperor sits quietly on his throne squeezing out taxes from the people."[105] If pressure on *yose* halls eased in subsequent years, it was possibly because there were fewer of them.

But the damage was done, and the audiences for criticism delivered openly in theaters were handled differently than readers in private. Balzac once called the cabaret "the parliament of the people,"[106] but without the cabaret's Japanese equivalent, the *yoseba*, such political assemblage was occluded. By 1872, the state was encouraging *yose hanashika* to promote "the spirit of the 'Imperial Way' (*kōdō*)" in their programs and refrain from criticizing government officials and their actions,[107] but that proved less efficacious then trying to get raconteurs to stay silent on any potentially controversial themes. What are the advantages to the suppression of oral discourse to the state? There are many. Speech is spontaneous, improvisational, uncontrollable. It cannot be commodified, only experienced. It requires a collectivity, not an individual. Modern novels are written only to be printed and consumed individually, not sung or read aloud or performed. That makes a difference. "The fact that novels are not written for performance," says Patrick Parrinder, "has profound implications for their relationship to the state and civil authority."[108] In 1908, two days after the trial of Naturalist writer Ikuta Kizan (1876–1945) for obscenity, a Police Bureau official complained that Naturalists wrote things "so obscene they can't be read aloud to the family."[109] But novels were *not* being read aloud to families in 1908, just a few years after the intensely oral *Neko*. Once works deemed indecent or subversive were banned—and many were— then the decline and domestication of *yose* meant that control of the crowd was nearly complete.

Sōseki once criticized the unruly, rude behavior of drunken spectators at En'yū's performances.[110] Notorious for his misanthropy, Sōseki did not care for crowds or their tastes. "If you go and visit the vaudeville houses and other entertainments favored by our own lower classes," Sōseki wrote, "you will sometimes find the strangest things winning applause. You would find it strange because the parts that earn the most applause are the parts that would cause any ordinary person to furrow his brow. If Mr. Zola and his ilk were to come to Japan and appear in our vaudeville houses, I am certain they would pack the house."[111] That *Neko* would be so full of *rakugo* is not a nostalgic retrieval of the Tokugawa collectivity, as Nagai Kafū's work might have been. (Kafū toyed with the idea of becoming a *rakugo* artist, going so far as to take the stage name of San'yūtei Yumenosuke.) It is a mimicry that objectifies, and therefore empties, the crowd's potential energy. "It was the *novel*," writes Timothy Brennan, "that historically accompanied the rise of nations by objectifying the 'one, yet many' of national life, and by mimicking the structure of the nation, a clearly bordered jumble of languages and styles."[112] Or as Bakhtin put it, "The novel senses itself on the border between the completed, dominant literary language and the extraliterary languages that know heteroglossia."[113] The polyphony of *Neko* has to be seen not as any move against a totalizing, monologic, standard-Japanese-speaking subject, but as a bold instance of the exchange that can occur between literature and other institutions competing for a share of power.

In Stephen Greenblatt's example of Shakespeare and his references to exorcism at a time when all Papist rites were outlawed, he puts it this way: "*King Lear*'s relation to [Samuel] Harsnett's book [on exorcism], then, is essentially one of reiteration, a reiteration that signals a deeper and unexpressed institutional exchange. The official church dismantles and cedes to the players the powerful mechanisms of an unwanted and dangerous charisma; in return, the players confirm the change that those mechanisms are theatrical and hence illusory."[114] What would be the similar exchange in *Neko*? Sōseki celebrates the carnivalesque potential of oral performance, but by putting it into a text—a modern text—that same orality is extinguished. Sōseki was not the first Japanese writer to struggle with this. "The critical place that the spoken voice of the storyteller has been accorded within the history of the modern Japanese novel," points out Jonathan Zwicker, "also needs to be seen within the context of a dense and intimate interaction between print and oral storytelling that extends back into the early years of the [nineteenth] century."[115] *Neko* was a great experiment in how to represent speech in modern prose, and it did unusual things. A letter is read aloud rather than silently, for example. Yoshimoto Takaaki goes so far as to say the merit of this novel lies in its use of dialogue (*kaiwa*), and dialogue reminiscent of *rakugo*, at that. "To put it simply," he says, "*Neko* is a work of humorous fiction [*kokkei shōsetsu*] of highbrow, intellectual *rakugo*, and as such occupies a rare place in Japan's modern literature,"[116] perhaps forgetting that Futabatei Shimei had been advised by Tsubouchi Shōyō twenty years earlier to write his signature *Ukigumo* "in the style of Enchō" (*Enchō no rakugo-dori*).[117]

But there were costs. "Our writings," Diderot said, "can impact only a certain class of citizens, our speech on all."[118] In the early twentieth century, Japan arrived at the state Goethe noted of eighteenth-century Europe: everyone was reading "silently to one's self," "a sorry substitute for speech."[119] As Nanette Twine points out, *Neko* is "studded with question marks, quotation marks, dashes, and lines of dots to indicate fragmented speech, in addition to the standard commas and full stops. Paragraphs are indented. In some sections dialogue and narrative are separated, with dialogue beginning a new line; in others, Sōseki reverts to the older practice of leaving dialogue in the body of the narrative, separated only by quotation marks."[120]

Sōseki was struggling with the problem of managing orality *within* textuality. His cat, observes Seth Jacobowitz, "employs several strategies for representing speech," including a stammer.[121] Kōno Kensuke argues that Sōseki's practice in *Neko* of putting all punctuation in the same manuscript page box as the graph initially made reading the novel more difficult. But at the same time, in suggesting to readers an affinity between his fiction and writing in Chinese, he revived the "paragraph-less text." When *Neko* was published as a book in 1905, it attracted attention not just for its contents but for its materiality as an object. It cost a relatively high ninety *sen* because it was designed and illustrated by a number of accomplished artists retained at Sōseki's request. The punctuation, the spacing, the length of it—all were different from previous books. The effect, according to Kōno, was that "the realism and breath in reading was marred, but it produced the visual effect of having looked upon a Chinese text." [122] The other effect, of course, was that it was a book full of talking but without a voice.

Orality never really disappears from modern life. The print-centric culture of Sōseki's adulthood was firmly established in the third decade of the Meiji period as silence was enforced in designated reading spaces: not just libraries, but also prisons and trains.[123] This would be upended by the end of Meiji and throughout the subsequent Taishō period (1912–26) by the marketing of the phonographic record—once predicted to replace books entirely[124]—and then by the debut of wireless broadcasting on 22 March 1925, and the return of sound to public space. (The actor Tokugawa Musei performed a funny scene from *Neko*'s eleventh chapter on NHK radio.[125]) This is what Walter Ong referred to as secondary orality: telephones, radio, and television.[126] Like primary orality, Ong's secondary orality produces audiences, and they are immense. But sound is not the same as speech, which labors under particular suspicion in modern nation-states. "Terror is the normal state of any oral society," wrote Marshall McLuhan, "for in it everything affects everything all the time."[127] This would be a different orality, as the real innovation was radio in the household. People did not need to go to *yose* theaters; the radio brought voice into the home. More and more, private spaces such as Professor Kushami's living room had come to replace the open spaces to which people traveled to assemble, but the voices they heard in those privatized spaces were those regulated by state broadcasting. NHK began transmitting in 1928; a 1932 survey of listeners found the most popular programs were *naniwabushi*, *kōdan*, and *rakugo*.[128] Moreover, radio brought voice that everyone with access to it heard simultaneously. As media historian Takeyama Akiko put it, *jikan* (time) became *jikaku* (precise moment in time), as home listeners who tuned in to radio were aware not only of minutes but seconds, something not possible when the hour was signaled by temple bells or cannons going off at noon, more or less, at Edo Castle.[129]

Neko mocks Meiji society, but Sōseki's face adorns the money. Just what is being celebrated? Professor Kushami is an English teacher, a language the Japanese can read but cannot speak. Could it mark, in *Neko* and his other works, the crucial shift away from the public and to the private that modern literature enables? If Sōseki is Japan's greatest modern writer, if it is his "voice" that is now held to speak for Japan's intellectual modernity, is it more than a coincidence that this happens just as literal voices matter less and less? "How can one reduce the great peril, the great danger with which fiction threatens our world?" asked Foucault. "The answer is: one can reduce it with the author."[130]

On 21 March 1905, half a year after Sōseki finished *Neko*, the first meeting of the Rakugo kenkyūkai (*Rakugo* Study Group) convened in Nihonbashi, prompted by the fear that *rakugo* was losing the battle with other entertainments. Meetings continued until the earthquake in 1923. Sōseki attended the first and often thereafter, which is surely ironic. The cat that Sōseki kills in *Neko* was just the beginning. The relationship of the Meiji state to literature was not just the former's intervention in the latter. The two theories and practices of governmentality and how we write and read about it are inconceivable without each other. The notion of a collective state does not come into being without our social differentiation into individuals, and literature is one means by which modern nations interpolate us as such.

The context for late Meiji literature I offer in this chapter has been the shifting stakes of orality and literacy in a developing modern nation-state. Those stakes do not stop moving. By the last decade of the nineteenth century, Japanese had started complaining about the din other people made reading aloud, and in the last full year of Meiji others bemoaned the loss of the Benjaminian aura of the woodblock printed book and its replacement by the book as commodity (*shōhin*).[131] An emperor did not deign to see *rakugo* performed until 1973, and only sixteen years later the last dedicated variety hall in Japan, the Motomakitei in Ueno, went out of business. If people watch *rakugo* today, it is usually on television in the privacy of their own homes. Theater in Japan evolved from "a participatory experience that involves multiple senses, to theater as a text to be read aloud on stage and heard in silence by [the] audience";[132] now we multitask while watching shows on personal devices. Literacy and orality are continually challenged but survive because both are resourceful, as we will see. When the real cat in Sōseki's home died, the family buried it along with the dogs and the goldfish in the backyard. It looked, records his wife, like an animal cemetery.[133] Sōseki's fictional pet was not so lucky. Animals in contemporary Japanese literature often talk, read, and write; and they will be prepared, in turn, to bury us. But in the interim, the history of modern Japanese literature will be told by a mute cat who died to be born again, a hundred times and more, in printed reincarnations.[134]

4

Narcissus in Taishō

For literary historians the Taishō period is the years 1910 to 1927, from the start of the arts and literature coterie journal *Shirakaba* (White birch) to the suicide of Akutagawa Ryūnosuke (1892–1927). But literary historiography has only recently granted this span the distinct status as a historical problem.[1] It was long the habit to characterize Taishō as an extension of the late Meiji period or the precursor to early Shōwa. If modern Japanese historiography conventionally starts from one of two points, the Meiji Revolution in 1868 or the imposition of fascism after the China Incident in 1931, then in either case the Taishō period risks dropping out completely.

But what gives Taishō its mass and centrality in literary history is its ongoing association with *shi-shōsetsu*, the Japanese I-novel, and that genre's notoriety for a stubborn egocentricity. Its very claim to being literature is suspect. Postwar author Furui Yoshikichi (1937–) thinks that a literary form in which "the narrator converses with himself" "inevitably approaches an oral telling."[2] Unwelcome, it is derided as tenaciously and tediously common by many. "Writers will go on studying themselves, their unpleasant childhoods, and their unhappy love affairs," writes Howard Hibbett: "Narcissistic, self-lacerating, nostalgic, bitter."[3] If this is true, it was certainly so in the 1910s and 1920s when, as Edward Fowler puts it, "The *shishōsetsu* so dominated the Taishō literary world that the phrase 'Taishō literature' now connotes its heyday."[4] Whether this is to the credit of Japanese literature or its detriment is still debated, as if the stakes are preternaturally high, and high for matters other than the purely literary. Today the characteristics of Japanese I-novels remain one of the more important issues in determining the morphology and ethics of modern Japanese literature *in toto*. Hirano Ken went on record saying the tradition of *shi-shōsetsu* is the *only* tradition of which modern Japanese literature can boast; Miyoshi Yukio rejoined that "Whether one cares for *shi-shōsetsu* or not, it lies at the center of Japan's literary tradition, and is its very archetype [*genkei*]."[5]

This apparent consensus does not mean that the *shi-shōsetsu* is *the* representative form of modern Japanese literature, or even that of a newly reevaluated Taishō period. As any number of scholars today have pointed out, the emergence of *shi-shōsetsu* occurred as popular fiction (*taishū bungaku*), an extension of the development and expansion of literary journalism, gained popularity along with the detective novel, the mystery novel, and literature of the occult and the fantastic. These are genres where there is little, if any, of the narrow perspective, plotless organization, and distrust of invention said to be typical not only of the I-novel but modern Japanese prose literature in general. That said, *shi-shōsetsu*, the alleged Japanese propensity for it, its origins, and its import remain many critics' obsession. Since the 1970s, critics Karatani Kōjin and Hasumi Shigemitsu have had a lot to say about it, as has novelist Mizumura Minae. No other topic in modern Japanese literary history has attracted such attention. Outside Japan we have not only Fowler's important monograph on the subject but Irmela Hijiya-Kirschnereit's and Tomi Suzuki's work as well. Briefly, I can reduce Fowler's argument as one of linguistic determinism. "One cannot narrate the experience of another person in Japanese without fictionalizing or 'lying'—that is, without assuming a pose of omniscience that allows access to the minds of others."[6] Therefore Japanese fiction favors what Fowler says is the free direct, monologic style associated with narration in *shi-shōsetsu*. Hijiya-Kirschnereit, in her attempt to deduce scientifically the *shi-shōsetsu*'s literary morphology, posits a structural model that necessarily embodies factuality, a focus figure, the narrative perspective, the temporal structure, level of plot, and lastly philosophy as the genre's constituent parts. It is a model I worry tells us too much in an attempt to be historically comprehensive, and yet too little in that she hardly suggests *why* this constellation of features should have obtained, precisely the question that developmental literary history seeks to answer. Tomi Suzuki abandons the attempt to define the genre of *shi-shōsetsu* and asks instead why critics, starting in the late Taishō period, suddenly discovered earlier fiction to be in hindsight all about the "self," a troublesome term for which I will borrow and reserve for amendment later, William James's definition as "everything that can be called me or mine."[7] This is a development, Suzuki suggests, linked to the larger intellectual contexts that the Taishō intelligentsia inhabited, such as "Taishō Democracy," reiterating the familiar argument that the Taishō period raised its curtain with what is called the "awareness of the self." In doing so, however, Suzuki shifts what Fowler and Hijiya-Kirschnereit considered to be the inherent features from the I-novel to readers of the I-novel, a move that displaces but does not resolve the broader issues literary historians might want to explore.

The larger problem of Taishō and its culture — one that historians have long analyzed in terms of popular as well as elite groups — remains unsettled and even unaddressed, and so too the controversy of the I-novel. I would like to revisit the assumptions we have followed in our attempts to arrive at the root of what constitutes the "I" of the Japanese I-novel, and more ambitiously, the why. The matter of *shi-shōsetsu* is in ways a stalking horse for the issue of the self, a word that appears in many Japanese guises in the vocabulary of the Taishō period but one which is certainly modern and specifically, though not exclusively, Taishō. In his well-regarded book *Taishō bungakushi* (Taishō literary history, 1963), Usui Yoshimi defined Taishō literature against that of Meiji exactly in terms of its "development through the assertion of a self [*jiko shuchō*] based upon various private, subjective [*kosei*] tastes and interpretations." Like others, he ruled the *kindai jiga* (modern self) the unequivocal *sine qua non* of modern Japanese literature.[8]

Nonetheless, few critics, past or present, pondering the problem of the self in modern Japanese literature have proceeded armed with tools even remotely psychoanalytical. This is curious, not least of all because Taishō-period essays on *shi-shōsetsu*, such as those by Kume Masao and Uno Kōji, reveal more interest in the I-novel's properties of *shinkyō* (mental states) than in its debatable merits as putative autobiography. Yet we decline to look at the I-novel outside a narrowly defined narrative or intellectual context. Despite Fowler's tentative concession that "the *shishōsetsu* is more a cultural than a literary phenomenon,"[9] scholarship has not much contemplated other high and low Taishō cultural practices and discourses that just might shed light upon *shi-shōsetsu*-ness, which, adapting a definition of autobiography by Paul de Man, we can say with irony is any prose or picture "in which the author declares himself the subject of his own understanding."[10]

In the first chapter of Sōseki's *Neko*, Professor Kushami takes up watercolors, at the time something of a fad among the Japanese. He imagines himself an Italian master and paints a portrait of his cat. "And there he was," the cat-narrator tells us, "fairly killing himself at being Andrea del Sarto." The efforts are wasted. The cat reports indignantly that his dilettantish master's portrait in no way resembles him. But Kushami's poor talent for verisimilitude has a counterpoint at the start of *Neko*'s second chapter, when the master receives a New Year's card from a professional painter acquaintance of his. When the cat catches a glimpse of it, he is surprised—but just how much?—to notice that "there could be no shadow of a doubt: it was a portrait of myself. I do not suppose that the painter considered himself an Andrea del Sarto, as did my master; but, being a painter, what he had painted, both in respect of form and of color, was perfectly harmonious."[11] Del Sarto in real life may or may not have done one self-portrait. Art historians debate whether the subject in *Portrait of a Young Man* (ca. 1517–18) is holding a piece of molding clay, a block of marble or a brick—apparently the question depends on this answer.[12] Similarly, whether the truth in *Neko*'s postcard is contrasted with the falseness of the portrait on account not of any success or failure in capturing the "inner" anything of the cat. Rather, it is all decided by the rules of painting that govern our apprehension of an image as real or not—"form and color" must be "perfectly harmonious" in ways that presumably do and yet do not correspond with what would be, say, photographic realism. There is an important point here. Sōseki is not concerned, at this stage of his satirical novel, with his late Meiji period's budding obsession with immanent reality, but instead with a learned mimeticism. In the second chapter the cat, watching Kushami write in his diary, says his master's "human mentality" is completely obscure to him. "Is he feeling angry or light-hearted, or simply seeking solace in the scribblings of some dead philosopher?" Unlike human beings, cats would never keep diaries because they have no inner lives: "Among cats both our four main occupations (walking, standing, sitting, and lying down) and such incidental activities as excreting waste are pursued quite openly. We live our diaries, and consequently have no need to keep a daily record as a means of maintaining our real characters."[13] Together these passages set the stage for what I will say about Taishō-period writing against this chapter's chosen context, namely, that brief time in modern Japan when the artistic and the literary worlds were intimately allied in the pursuit of an ideal narcissism. Be it either world, that project touched on theories of representation alternately transcendental and immanent. More concretely, they suggest that we are taught how things should *appear* versus the way they are only subjectively known and then represented. What will unite these alternatives will be a shared attention to the evolving concept of a self in a modern liberal nation-state. In his history of modern Japanese literature, Karatani Kōjin, always attentive to the political stakes, quotes Paul Valéry on the early twentieth century: "Everyone began to paint."[14]

Jürgen Habermas has pointed out how important European art was to modernity, as religion ceded its authority to it alongside science and morality.[15] But J. Thomas Rimer has said of Japan that "little attention has been paid to that provocative period from about 1905 through the early 1930s, when so many movements were launched in the visual arts."[16] Some techniques of Western painting were introduced by the Jesuits to Japanese Christian converts in the late sixteenth century, and painter Shiba Kōkan, a student of *rangaku* (Dutch learning) in the late eighteenth and early nineteenth centuries, deployed what H. D. Harootunian terms an "empirical investigation based on the plurality of perspectives in viewing an object."[17] In 1855, the pre-Meiji state established the Bureau of Western Studies, and painting was one of the technologies it investigated. In 1876, the government founded the Technical Art School to introduce Western art, where a number of talented European artists taught.[18] The post-Meiji state began to develop an official government system for the visual arts in 1907, when it staged its first show, the *Bunten* (Fine Arts Exhibition). Soon the Taishō period, in addition to being the heyday of *shi-shōsetsu*, marked the point after which Japanese *yōga* (Western-style) painters created their own works rather than imitate Western masters. It was also the most productive period for Japanese self-portraiture. Shortly after the Tokyo Fine Arts Academy was founded in 1896, it made a self-portrait a requirement for graduation, an "epochal event" in Japanese cultural history.[19] What makes this interesting is that self-portraiture in Japan, compared with that in the West, does not enjoy a long history, unlike portraiture, which Arthur Waley noted the Japanese excelled at.[20] In Europe, self-portraiture came into its own between the late Middle Ages and the seventeenth century, when the glass mirror was perfected, and quickly developed into an art meant to disclose the inward state of its subjects.[21]

Self-portraiture in Japan traditionally never attempted this, just as autobiography was rare despite the handful of exceptions such as those by Arai Hakuseki and Fukuzawa Yukichi. Tsurumi Shunsuke claims there are comic self-portraits done by the transcribers of sutras in the Nara period,[22] and the practice of self-portraiture in Japan might be dated back to the late twelfth century with Fujiwara Nobuzane, though no premodern self-portraiture stages the drama of a divided self in dialogue with itself. We need to wait until contact with European painting to find self-conscious self-portraiture in Japan, such as Shiba Kōkan's painting of himself in the early nineteenth century. But this example is so rare that we cannot claim a genre of self-portraiture for the Tokugawa period. Meiji was different. If the genre of self-portraiture in the West is associated with the Renaissance, either because that was when there was an awakening of self-consciousness of the individual that prompted painters to portray themselves,[23] or because new technology—the glass mirror—was suddenly available,[24] then Japan in the last third of the nineteenth century seems analogous. Haga Tōru, in his study of Western-style painting in the Meiji period, concentrates on Takahashi Yuichi, a samurai of the Sano domain born in Edo in 1828 who was ordered by the Bakufu to study Western painting as a technology the state wished to acquire. His 1866–67 self-portrait was the first done in oils in Japan. Haga says that self-portraiture in Japan flows not from the predicament of an artist lacking commissions or the means to hire models, but specifically in Takahashi's case from a rite of passage to "confirm his existence."[25] Takahashi himself said that oil painting did not depict the form of things as much as "it reveals their implicit meanings."[26] Kuwabara Sumio similarly argues that Meiji-period self-portraiture is linked to a rising awareness of the political and social self (*jiga*), but then goes on to suggest that photography subsequently came into Japan so quickly that self-portraiture in painting never performed the singular mimetic function that it had in the West.[27] Just as photography in the West altered painting, literary modernity in Japan altered *bungaku*. It no longer needed to *tell*—other institutionalized discourses (*gaku*) now were charged with that—it was free to *express*.

All this talk of awareness and confirmation of existence may be ontologically suspicious, but the upshot was that Japanese self-portraiture was, from very early on, a self-reflective practice. It was therefore a preeminent example of what a Japanese modernity, as both modern and on the periphery of the West, might look like. Ishiko Junzō observed much later that "the self-portrait is for us more the 'modernity of art' than 'the art of modernity.'"[28]

In the twentieth century, self-portraiture is an important part of almost every *yōga* artist's oeuvre. But just as *shi-shōsetsu* dominated Taishō, so was the self-portrait arguably the most modern genre of oil painting during the same period. Kuroda Seiki, Yorozu Tetsugorō, Umehara Ryūsaburō, Takamura Kōtarō: we could go on naming the prominent Taishō-period painters who painted pictures of themselves. It has been suggested that it was a 1910 debate on the mission of painting, involving writers as well as artists, that intellectually inaugurated the Taishō period. Honda Shūgo marks this "Conventions of Painting Debate" (*Kaiga no yakusoku ronsō*) as the moment that decisively ended the objectivism of Meiji writing and painting,[29] once Mushanokoji Saneatsu (1885–1976) and Yanagi Sōetsu among others argued that what is key in painting is neither its ability to affect viewers nor its intrinsic personality, but rather its *jiko chūjitsu* (fidelity of self), a major tenet of the *shi-shōsetsu* genre to come.

Art history contributes to literary history here not only because art theoreticians are utilizing the same vocabulary as literary critics—that had been true at least since Tsubouchi Shōyō in the 1880s, who relied on a vocabulary of landscape (*fūkei*) copying (*mosha*) in developing a parallel ocular realism to his literary one—but also because the specific shared terminology is concentrated on issues of selfhood, representation, and the relationship between the two. The spirit of realism trumpeted in Shōyō's manifesto *Shōsetsu shinzui* would have an impact on one of the most prominent, Asai Chū.[30] The issue would be "how to make language copy (represent) the visually constituted word against the temporality implied in the linear flow of language."[31] Leo Tolstoy's 1893 *What is Art?* was widely read in Japan. At the turn of the twentieth century, Masaoka Shiki's *shaseibun* school of poetry wanted to borrow painter Asai Chū's *yōga* techniques for its literary practice.[32] In 1909, Tokuda Shūsei (1871–1943) was talking about color and shadow in literary prose;[33] Shimazaki Tōson and Kunikida Doppo learned techniques from the *plein aire* sketches of the Impressionists. Mori Ōgai, friends with artist Harada Naojirō his whole career, defended *yōga* when it came under attack from ultranationalists. Kishida Ryūsei's theory of art inspired Kajii Motojirō (1901–32), and he taught Mushanokoji to appreciate Dürer; Nagayo Yoshirō (1888–1961) wrote a novella with Ryūsei as its hero; Akutagawa Ryūnosuke acknowledged his debt to Cezanne repeatedly. Readers of Sōseki, himself a painter whose novels *Sanshirō* (dubbed by Haga a *kaiga shōsetsu*, or "painting novel")[34] and *Kusamakura* meditate on painting, found descriptions of nature in his works "so evocative, so 'immediate' that they have actually occasioned a number of paintings."[35] In the Meiji period the Japanese encountered Goethe

Figure 4.1. Kishida Ryūsei, *Jigazō* (self-portrait; 1914)

and Blake, both artists and writers, and in Taishō they celebrated the work of Van Gogh and Munch, who advanced the use of self-portraiture to display what we now call subjectivity. Van Gogh, who in his youth was interested in literature as well as art, alone did thirty-seven self-portraits in oils, several with Japanese woodblock prints in the background. By late Meiji, Japanese literary Naturalism had rejected the putative objectivity of Zola and replaced it with an insistence on authorial subjectivity. Soon thereafter self-portraiture (*jigazō*), conceived as "self-confession rhetoricized," was aligned with *shi-shōsetsu*.[36] For many in the Taishō period, confession was a ritualized discourse in which the speaking subject was also the subject of the statement or enunciation. In the chapter on Van Gogh in his *Kindai kaiga* (Modern painting, 1958), Kobayashi Hideo called his subject's letters "confessional literature" (*kokuhaku bungaku*).[37] He viewed Van Gogh's paintings the way he read Dostoevsky and Japanese *shi-shōsetsu*: as self-confession (*jiko kokuhaku*).[38] The relationship between self-portraiture and autobiography has been noted since Rembrandt, whose seventeenth century was as interested in all sorts of autobiographical narratives—many of them in the confessional mode—as it was in his ninety-odd self-portraits.[39] The Impressionists, whose impact on modern Japanese painting is legendary, were explicit on this point. "I have painted many self-portraits in my life, corresponding to the changes in my state of mind," wrote Courbet. "In a word, I have written my autobiography."[40] The Taishō period discloses ways self-portraits and I-novels converged to suggest a shared etiology.

The figure opposite is an early self-portrait by Kishida Ryūsei, an artist hailed as the very emblem of Taishō-period art.[41] Born in Ginza in 1891 into a family descended from early pioneers of modern journalism, he studied art under Kuroda Seiki. His own career as a painter started as the Taishō period began. He was exhibiting by the age of twenty and continued to do so until his premature death. Two of his paintings were designated official Important Cultural Treasures in 1971, and another of his paintings fetched a record price at auction in 2000. But nearly all art historians agree that it is Ryūsei's self-portraits that made his reputation as an artist and which now serve as a logo of the period in which they were painted. Ryūsei did more self-portraits than any other Japanese painter, a project he commenced at age seventeen and continued up to the time of his death. Ryūsei's many self-portraits are not only the key to all his work but, it is claimed, the key "to a broader understanding of Taishō culture."[42]

If Ryūsei is key, he was especially so in early Taishō. In 1913–14, he did almost thirty self-portraits, not counting the many more numerous drawings, portraits declared unparalleled not only for their number but, in the words of one of his biographers, their continuity, the strength of their self-affirmation (*jiko sankō no tsuyosa*), and their power of self-examination (*jiko tankyū*).[43] Just why this should have been so is an issue for art history. Novels presumably have to be about people, but painters can depict anything, so the choice of the self as a subject must be all the more deliberate. Ryūsei, like many of his contemporaries, was a student of Dürer as well as Rembrandt, the Eyck brothers, Cezanne, and Van Gogh (one of whose self-portraits is said to have inspired one of Ryūsei's own).[44] The influence of the German Renaissance on him is plain. Like many of his generation's intelligentsia, Ryūsei was drawn to Christianity, and it is in the Christian pursuit of the soul's redemption through individual action that some have perceived the source of Ryūsei's obsession with the self once he renounced a belief in God for the conviction that art offers a road to personal salvation. Others have been more secularly existentialist in their analysis. "His obsession for using the human face for a subject is thought to confirm his own existence as he vacillated between moods of self-assertion and loneliness."⁴⁵ But nearly everyone has concluded that Ryūsei was committed to the solitary exploration of self that so characterizes the modern Japanese intellectual's agenda, and never more so than in the Taishō period. Of Ryūsei's 1914 self-portrait *Kuroki bōshi* (Black Hat), Haga Tōru says he was seeking, in a phrase lifted from poet and sculptor Takamura Kōtarō (1883–1956), *uchi kara kakutoku* (possession from within): "Kishida Ryūsei was a Shirakaba school painter who continually, and at times excessively, exhausted himself attempting to forge as one the aesthetics of painting with the interiority of his 'spirit of the self' or, as he would put it in his own idiom, his *jibun*."⁴⁶ Kishida noted in his signature essay, "Uchi naru bi" (Beauty Within, 1918), that beauty does not exist objectively in the world but is the result of a human subject who perceives it. "'Beauty,'" he wrote, "exists within the human species [*jinrui no naimen*]."⁴⁷ That subject in the context of Taishō art and literature is one's own self and never anyone else's, at which point it is reasonable to ask if this context is best described as starkly narcissistic.

Narcissism here is more than another way of saying self-absorption, but not quite the naming of a specific neurosis with a clinical profile associated with grandiosity, exhibitionism, the need for constant attention and admiration, emotional shallowness, hostility or indifference to the feelings for others, and severe disturbance in interpersonal relations. Still, these characteristics occur everywhere and certainly in many modern novels. Perhaps modern artists are party to an extreme narcissism on account of the power of a reinforcement both intrapsychic and intrapersonal. Lionel Trilling called neurosis a gift for creativity.⁴⁸ But if we find the *shi-shōsetsu* interesting precisely because it dramatizes narcissistically the dynamics of a fragile self, then writer Kuroi Senji, in an essay of Modigliani's self-portraiture, may hint why in terms more modernist than medical:

> Self-portraiture is perilous. It is an expression of the self's awareness, an act of searching for the links between the self and the outer world. It is an enterprise of realizing pride in existence that communes with narcissism. Self-portraiture must be called above all dangerous painting from the point of view of its subject. It exposes the self to the outside. At the same time, the subject can be

none but a dangerous human being. Perhaps the person who delves in his self also delves into the other, and delves into the world.[49]

Another Taishō-period writer, Sigmund Freud, published his essay "On Narcissism: An Introduction" in 1914, just as self-portraiture and *shi-shōsetsu* in Japan were gathering strength. In Freud's narrative, the newborn's psyche is unstructured and his libido stands in an undifferentiated ego-id relationship of autoeroticism. The infant does not relate to the world around him, because he *is* the world. With the differentiation of an ego—the "narcissistic wound" once the infant realizes his mother, not he, can grant or withhold certain pleasures—the libido cathects the ego, which is to say, the self. This is what is called primary narcissism, and much of its energy is later invested in object-love. But in secondary narcissism, that found in adults, the libido is withdrawn from the external world and reinvested in the self, which is why the long-standing psychoanalytical definition of narcissism is simply the libidinal cathexis of self, the self's libidinal involvement with itself, its mode of investing energy in developmental functions, which means that the growth of our identity is necessarily narcissistic in the broadest sense. In post-Meiji self-portraiture, narcissism cast a strong shadow in portraits done by younger painters. Narcissism nested not in their paintings' style, but in the frustrated desires, anxieties, impatience, and loneliness leading to narcissism, and made their paintings to some critics closed off and confined.

Part of this complaint does seem applicable to Ryūsei. Narcissism in Japanese self-portraiture was less the byproduct of painterly technique than of something more profound: the insecurity and frustration of young Japanese artists of the time and their resulting withdrawal from the world, a point amply made about other Japanese intellectuals who were not artists. But Ryūsei was exceptional in this regard. The self (*jiko*) was Ryūsei's most important theme throughout his life, and it was a life not particularly happy. "The 'self' for Ryūsei was never a stable object," writes one art historian, and it was "a problem fraught with risk for him."[50] Whether narcissism in Ryūsei, that is, narcissism during the Taishō period, is the problem addressed or the solution proposed to something is a question that requires our attention. Ryūsei was a writer in addition to being a painter—his collected works run to ten volumes—and his many essays on aesthetics as well as his extensive diaries give us an opportunity to hear him directly. In "Uchi naru bi," Ryūsei offered a definition of beauty: "It is both instinctual and intentional. Beauty can be said to exist objectively in this world only in this internal sense."⁵¹ This is baldly narcissistic insofar as no work of art for Ryūsei exists without a subject—his self as he most often called it—that creates and appreciates it. In "Jiko no geijutsu" (The Art of the Self, 1914) he wrote, "I want to stare at the paintings I paint all by myself. In fact, there is no alternative to oneself [*jibun jishin*] for anyone who understands oneself [*jibun*] best, who lends support most to oneself."⁵² Ryūsei's redundancy is wholly subsumed in his project of selfhood. In "Jiko no sekai" (The World of the Self, 1913) he ruled that "a person without a 'world of the self' cannot grow .... Without a world of the self he cannot achieve selfhood. ... I believe that there is no such thing as a 'self' without this love."⁵³

Ryūsei's almost delirious incantation of his selfhood is part and parcel of the cult of narcissism attached to the Taishō-period Shirakaba school of writers and painters in which he participated and who introduced to Japan Western artists from Da Vinci to Picasso. Their journal, *Shirakaba*, was published precisely around the dilemma of a self not wholly idiomatic in the Japan of this time. Ryūsei was the intellectual protégé of Mushanokoji, the Shirakaba's chief ideologue and the author of what might be modern Japanese literature's most narcissistically invested work of fiction, "Omedetaki hito" (A Dim-witted Man, 1910). Ryūsei in turn exerted more influence on the Shirakaba than any other visual artist linked with it. In his essay "Jiko no tame no geijutsu" (Art for Oneself, 1911), Mushanokoji echoes Ryūsei when he commanded, "Be true to oneself [*jiko*]. Labor for the sake of the self [*jiga*]. It is fine to kill oneself for the sake of selfhood."⁵⁴ Elsewhere he wrote, "I love my Self, because I want to develop my Self, and want to give life to my Self.... I will not sacrifice my Self for anything. Instead, I am willing to sacrifice everything for my Self."⁵⁵ All this is cognate with the Shirakaba school's tenet that both the ethical objective of mankind and the aesthetic objective of the artist is *jiga jitsugen* (realization of selfhood). It is also what drove the Taishō period's conspicuous devotion to *images* of the self. In an essay published in the January 1912 issue of *Shirakaba*, Yanagi Sōetsu asserted that the very purpose of art is for the benefit of the self (*jiko no tame*) and that its goal lies in how the self is expressed, *not* in beauty. His examples are all artists: Cezanne, Van Gogh, Gauguin, and Matisse.⁵⁶

Mushanokoji and Ryūsei were the first Japanese to champion the work of Dürer, whom H. W. Janson declared to be "the first artist to be fascinated with his own image" as a consequence of a Christian humanism unleashed by Martin Luther.⁵⁷ Shirakaba humanism also has its own Christian roots, principally via

Tolstoy. It might seem difficult to link humanism—love for others—with narcissism, but in fact that is precisely what psychoanalytic theory insists upon. In what Theodor Adorno hailed as "among Freud's most magnificent discoveries," Freud wrote in his 1921 "Group Psychology and the Analysis of the Ego" that "narcissism could be an almost insuperable barrier to the formation of groups,"[58] but once members of a group share a common ego ideal, their narcissistic self-love is redirected toward this ideal and so binds the members together. Freud had more to say about this ego ideal in his 1914 essay, where it "is now the target of self-love which was enjoyed in childhood by the actual ego. The subject's narcissism makes its appearance displaced on to this new ideal ego, which, like the infantile ego, finds itself possessed of every perfection that is of value. . . . What he projects before him as his ideal is the substitute for the lost narcissism of his childhood in which he was his own ideal."[59] This logic of the psyche permits us to link the Taishō period's *jindōshugi* (humanism)—which in Freudian terms we might interpret as the Shirakaba school's superego—and new democratic ideologies and such utopian projects as the Shirakaba school's New Village movement, with such narcissistic statements as Mushanokoji's proclamation in his journal that, "For me there is no greater authority than myself. . . . I only love myself."[60]

But if the process leading to a narcissism both positive and negative is akin to what Freud predicted, one of the places we can turn to investigate that hypothesis is Taishō-period fiction. "A kindly nature," Freud wrote in his study of Leonardo da Vinci, "has bestowed upon the artist the capacity to express in artistic productions his most secret psychic feelings hidden even from himself, which powerfully grips outsiders, strangers to the artist, without knowing whence this emotivity comes from."[61] Taishō literary culture was self-obsessed: not only in fiction but in the painting of the time, attesting to the view that the *shi-shōsetsu*, commonly traced back to the peculiar form Naturalist writing took in early-twentieth-century Japan, is in fact a Shirakaba school product derived from the premise that the self equals the universal. Put another way, without the narcissistic identification that a libidinal investment in a concept such as "universal" connotes, there would have been no I-novel.

This is not necessarily regretted. Hijiya-Kirschnereit, for whom the term *shi-shōsetsu* had to have been coined with ironic intent, notes the genre's "exaggerated narcissism both of the heroes and the writers themselves. The shamelessness and exhibitionist ambition, the masochistic delight in relating personal disasters that confront the reader would all be unthinkable without the high degree of eccentricity that is a result of the isolation of the subject. To become aware of this narcissism one need merely open any shishōsetsu."[62] Hijiya-Kirschnereit's pejorative use of the word "narcissistic" depends upon what is a "narcissistic understanding of narcissism," that is, that a project of self is *covering up* another image, the image that exists out there in the realm of the putative real. This idea is certainly the legacy of Freud, since he emphasized the subjective force of distortion. He thought all artists were narcissistic. Hijiya-Kirschnereit, in the spirit of Freud, infantilizes the artist insofar as she believes the work of art a substitution for the renunciation of an instinctual gratification.

One can apply this idea to Japanese literature in the Taishō period. Shiga Naoya's diary declares, in a perfect display of the artist's defensive narcissism, "I have come to truly love my own face. . . . I now believe that there could hardly be anyone as marvelous as myself,"[63] and he gave us *An'ya Kōro* (*A Dark Night's Passage*, 1921–37), a novel whose narcissistic investment is literally spectacular. Shiga's novel was built around what might be derided as a psychopathology. The novel's hero, Tokito Kensaku, is initially repulsed by sex with adult women. "It is rather from watching a pretty young mother shower 'little Japanese-style kisses' on her baby that he derives his most unequivocal sensual pleasure at this stage."[64] At the heart of Freud's analysis of Da Vinci lies his so-called vulture fantasy, where the alleged memory of a dream in which a vulture whips its tail repeatedly against the lips of infant Leonardo "emphasizes the intensity of the erotic relations between the mother and the child."[65] Elsewhere Kensaku's desire to revisit the infantile narcissism of the child's unity with the mother is why, while he cannot be sure just why he is so drawn to a geisha's breast, he is sure that "at the moment they stood for the one precious thing that could fill the void."[66] That void is surely Kensaku's need to love and be loved. But as Freud intuited, "The sexual instincts are at the outset attached to the satisfaction of the ego-instincts; only later do they become independent of these."[67] We can argue whether Kensaku's adult sexuality is afflicted by an excessive narcissism. Such judgments have to be cultural and therefore relative, but let us recognize that narcissism *is* Shiga's theme. "If *An'ya Kōro* is 'a novel of love,'" William Sibley concludes, "it is more precisely a novel about self-love . . . the painful and dubious project of achieving a mature love of self that is rooted in healthy infantile narcissism and tends toward eventual fulfillment in death."[68] Heinz Kohut argued that a child will replace the perfection of its mother once it discovers her to be imperfect by "establishing a grandiose and exhibitionist image of the self" and then "by giving over the previous perfection to an admired, omnipotent (transitional) self-object: *the idealized parent image*."[69] These reactions are amply evident in Shiga's novel. But so too are they everywhere in the Shirakaba school and the era which it dominated. Another novel that easily comes to mind is Satō Haruo's (1892–1964) *Den'en no yūutsu* (The Melancholy of the Country, 1914), a work hailed as yet another icon of Taishō.[70] The story of an intellectual's solitary decline into melancholia (ruled by Freud a narcissistic disorder), by the end of the novel Satō's hero has abandoned any hope of finding the peace of mind he sought by isolating himself in the countryside. He goes out to the well in the yard behind his rented country house and reenacts Ovid's tale: "The water in the well was brimming round and still as it does in the morning. His face was reflected there. A blighted leaf from the persimmon tree fluttered, dropped, and floated, solitary. Round ripples spread silently across the surface from its gentle touch. The water quivered and then returned to its former stillness: stillness that was stillness—limitless stillness."[71] Satō's forlorn hero cannot ever retrieve the object he so desires, his Freudian lost love-object. Here is the narcissistic identification of the melancholic Freud described in his essay "Mourning and Melancholia," where "hate is expended upon this new substitute-object, railing at, deprecating it, making it suffer and deriving sadistic gratification from its suffering."[72]

Satō published his short story "Enkō" (Halo) in 1914. Subtitled "An Essay on Love and Art," it suggests the importance of psychoanalysis's libidinal cathexis of self to Satō's writings. An unnamed painter is surrounded by happiness when he moves both his art and his beautiful new wife to an atelier on the bucolic edge of the city. He decorates their new home with sketches of the sea he did on their recent honeymoon and thinks to himself: She is perfect. As is he himself, when he receives a letter he assumes is a generous commission. "I really have become a great painter."[73] But the letter brings a disturbing request; a former lover of his wife wants a portrait of her. The painter confronts his wife and she admits, yes, I did love him—just as I love everyone, especially anyone who says he loves me, and you most of all. Oddly cheered by these words, the artist sets about to paint his wife. Giving such a portrait away will prove his magnanimity and confirm his own perfection as a person; it will give him all the more plea-sure. Like God with the world, he starts the portrait on a Monday and finishes it six days later. The portrait pleases him. He thinks it his own *bunshin*, his own self in another, and while he is sad to part with the painting, he honors his promise and dispatches it to the letter writer once the oils have dried and he has placed it in a magnificent frame.

Three days later another letter arrives. Not a thank-you note, but an explanation of why the letter writer must return the portrait. At first the work angered him, then made him suspicious and finally frightened. Surely this cannot be a painting of your wife, it must be of someone else. The letter writer thinks it was meant to resemble Sandro Botticelli's fifteenth-century *Madonna of Magnificat.* In time the letter writer sees a halo in the new painting. Did you mean it to be there? If not, he writes, then your sin is very deep, the result of your *geijutsujō no byūken* (artistic misunderstanding). The painting must be rejected. Satō's piece on art and love concludes when the painter, throwing the half-read letter away, asks his wife if this former admirer of hers is a poet. No, she answers in a clear voice from the adjoining room. "I'm sure he was a critic."[74]

Wry, to be sure, but also meant to say something about the narcissistic artist versus the rest of us. Remembering Freud's take on narcissism, the painter and his wife live in a remote world wholly of their own: self-involved, perfect, womblike. The joy the painter derives from his isolation is narcissistic. It is a setting for his art and for a wife whose portrait is tantamount to a self-portrait, so invested is he in both her and her image. That the letter-writer-critic sees in the canvas not the wife—his former object-love—but a famous painting of the mother of God suggests several things. First of all, the painter seeks in his work to depict what was the original source of his bodily pleasure, his mother's body, as well as himself at the moment when he, an infant, was not in the world so much as all of it. Such a moment, when discovered in a Taishō-period I-novel, recaptures the potential of narcissism to generate self-knowledge, not self-obsession. Second, when the correspondent speaks of an "artistic misunderstanding" in *not* painting what is plainly there for all to see—the halo—perhaps we are meant to think, as did Freud's Da Vinci, that the artist's introversion makes him or her both creative and blind to the story that creativity is charged with telling.

I may have given aid and comfort to critics who never cared for *shi-shōsetsu* by associating it with the unpleasant pathologies we think of in clinical narcissism. But since early Freud, narcissism has been viewed in an ambiguous light, if only because he saw that narcissism is part of our healthy development as well as a constant threat to it. We know that the narcissist seeks individuality at all costs but cannot live outside a continuing state of fusion in trying to recapture that joy at his mother's breast so touchingly noted by Shiga. Christopher Lasch, no friend of modern cultural narcissism, conceded, "Narcissism appears realistically to represent the best way of coping with the tensions and anxieties of modern life, and the prevailing social conditions therefore tend to bring out narcissistic traits that are present, in varying degrees, in everyone."[75] I put forward the hypothesis that this paradox parallels the paradox of the modern, defined by the simple irony that in modernity we are all individuals but also all interrelated. If the narcissist is forever engaged in the impossible mission to reexperience the pleasure he knew when he was yet to distinguish his own body from that of his mother, then the modern person is equally at a loss to recapture the moment before our alienation from the faiths, religious or social, of earlier times, either those of our societies or those of our childhoods. Kuroi Senji, in his essay on Modigliani, says, "In self-portraiture the artist exists completely alone. Before him is the mirror, and he himself is present only in its reflection. That is to say, he is made to stand before his virtual image rather than before humanity."[76]

Narcissism can motivate us to do many admirable things. Narcissus is the enduring figure in the West of self-reflection, and therefore one of the sources of the modernist sense of self. But this can be misleading. It was the earlier, Romantic Narcissus who was a hero who symbolized the virtues of self-observation and the powers inherent in the self, a Narcissus to be clearly distinguished from the modernist Narcissus to whom we are more directly heir today and who is concentrated upon his sterility. Self-portraiture is a process through which one arrives at greater self-knowledge, but that is already a kind of knowledge that in modernity is approached via self-love. Narcissism is a quest for wholeness or perfection, a quest that goes in no direction guaranteed to be either salutatory or regressive.

While our narcissism is never wholly overcome, only rechanneled because it represents a complete and profound mode of gratification, different cultures at different times may choose to celebrate this neurosis over others. Natsume Sōseki complained that Meiji-period Japanese were suffering from nervous exhaustion due to the stress of Westernization. But none of the Shirakaba school, come Taishō, seemed to suffer from it. Indeed, they inhabited a time that was spectacularly rife with narcissism. These were the years of a cult of feminine beauty and of famous convicts, as well as autobiographical fiction and self-portraiture—Freud added criminals and women to artists among his categories of natural narcissists. These were also the years when wall mirrors appeared in new, modern Japanese homes, replacing the more discreet *kyōdai* and giving modern home dwellers the means and the incentive to remain frequently aware of their surroundings and their looks. The best-known description in literature of such a house is that in which Jōji and Naomi dwell in Tanizaki Jun'ichirō's novel, *Chijin no ai* (A fool's love, 1924), a novel thoroughly driven by narcissism.[77] The Taishō period was witness to a cult of gender ambivalence clearly narcissistic. It was when urban Japan saw the rise of a modern and mass consumer culture based on narcissistic identification and gratification, celebrated by the opening of the Marunouchi Mitsukoshi department store in 1919; when the Japanese cinema came into its own, and with it the rise of movie stars such as Onoe Matsunosuke and audiences' narcissistic investment in them; and when proponents of Taishō Democracy found their ideals popular in part because of the narcissistic appeal of a concept of *minshū* (the masses) that empowered everyone. In terms of intellectual life, one could argue that the rise of the Taishō-period *Nihonjinron*—treatises on the merits of the Japanese and their culture—also represents a self-focused narcissism. In the late 1920s and early 1930s, more than a few Japanese intellectuals began to speculate and promote the uniqueness of Japanese culture. In Tanizaki Jun'ichirō's essay "In'ei raisan" (In Praise of Shadows, 1933), Japanese domestic architecture is praised for its mimetic extension of the Japanese body and its comportment: miniature, colored, reserved.

Ryūsei's portraits were of close friends and relatives, so they are in a real sense pictures of *his* relationships and, by extension, himself.[78] As portraits of his daughter replaced self-portraits—the first of her was *in utero*, via the 1913 nude of his pregnant wife Shigeru—Ryūsei was painting himself in the guise of Reiko.[79] No resemblance is necessary for reference, only a kind of modern knowledge to relate object (person) to representation. In his major theoretical statement, *Bi no hontai* (The Essence of Beauty, 1920), Ryūsei said that the value of a portrait does not depend upon any resemblance to its subject.[80] Nearer our own time Jacques Derrida echoed that the "act of naming should allow or *entitle* me to call just about anything a self-portrait, not just any drawing ('portrait' or not) but anything that happens to me, anything by which I can be affected or let myself be affected."[81]

There is a painting by Ryūsei entitled *The Two Reikos* (*Futari Reiko kazari-gami zu*), but in real life Ryūsei had only one daughter by that name, whom he painted repeatedly. They are portraits that, as one art historian has it, "everyone keeps imprinted in a corner of their mind."[82] In this one work Reiko is portrayed on the canvas twice, three times if we count the presumed reflection in the handheld mirror. Bernard Denvir, in his book on Van Gogh, defined the self-portrait as "a self seeing a self seeing a self," and this Taishō painting is an explicit example of such multiple representation.[83] The kneeling Reiko

Figure 4.2. Kishida Ryūsei, *Futari Reiko kazarigami zu* (The Two Reikos; 1922)

arranges the hair of the sitting Reiko, and the two of them are in a room devoid of anything but themselves and their personal accessories. If this was the first painting Ryūsei ever did entirely from his own imagination, then with Freud's tribute to the insight of artists in mind, his state of mind might be on display. The sitting Reiko has a bit more of a smile than the kneeling Reiko, on account of a specular image that, Narcissus-like, pleases her while the kneeling Reiko, also gazing upon "herself," wears an enigmatic smile. Perhaps Ryūsei refused to think of the Reiko paintings, which he began around 1917, as any sort of turn away from his previous obsession with self-portraiture in the earlier years of Taishō, but rather a continuation of the self-portrait project albeit through a different subject, a reversal consistent with Freud's observation that parental love "is a revival and reproduction of their own narcissism."[84] *The Two Reikos*, whether Ryūsei's displaced self-portrait or not, seems indicative of larger forces at work in Taishō that encouraged both self-portraiture and *shi-shōsetsu*, forces that shaped a production of modern selfhood predicated on the quasi-libidinal powers of self-reflection and thereby self-knowledge.

The emergence of the modern subject in the West is often linked with the rise of subjective self-consciousness promoted as reason. The later struggle to develop modern concepts of identity and selfhood in Japan took place in various and not always complementary areas—law, politics, philosophy, the marketplace—but with Western precedents before them. In the Taishō-period arts, a productive narcissism was put to the task of modern subject making. The Japanese I-novel is criticized for its renunciation of the greater realm of the social, but this obsession with the private, the inner, the self could have been inspired by an insight akin to Max Weber's, when he declared modernity is built upon our disenchantment with the world. Gazing at one's own reflection, whether in Ryūsei's painting of his daughter, or in the surface of Satō Haruo's well at the conclusion of *Den'en no yūutsu*, might be one Japanese attempt to produce a homegrown modern subjectivity that is not only related but con-stituted by an affect of inwardness. One can still ask whether these Japanese narcissisms are indulgent self-adorations or commendably moral because they are self-reflections. The difference is that in the former, "one is lured by the merely accidental appearance of the world," whereas in the latter, "conversely, one glimpses the objectivity of the enworlded being."[85]

In some instances it is surely the latter. I want to speculate why the Japanese construction of a modern self would experiment, quite self-consciously, with extended forms of narcissism. We know that portraiture is a performative prac-tice. Painters have often inserted themselves into their works. Michelangelo is Saint Bartholomew the Martyr in the *Last Judgment*; Caravaggio put his own face on the severed head of Goliath.[86] In Japan, Asai Chū insinuated his own features onto his human subjects. The same can be said of the *shi-shōsetsu*, which Edward Fowler says "is less the vehicle for personal affirmation . . . than a theater where the hero acts out his ambivalence toward the self."[87] The narcissistic per-formative might be recast as a modernist reflexive. The Taishō obsession with selfhood may be what Japanese modernity had to have been since early Meiji:

a necessary contemplative, which is to say interrogative, mediation of what arrived from abroad. As much as Freud may have admired artists, he did not want to give them credit for knowing what they were doing. Taishō I-novelists and self-portrait painters may have, however. The Taishō laboratory of narcissistic culture can be seen as part of the fabric of a culture stranded on the Eurocentric periphery, where focus on oneself was forced upon an intelligentsia where selfhood was plagued by doubts over its claims not only to legitimacy but to any workable agency whatsoever. In hindsight, narcissism appears not only expedient but effective and inevitable. "The problem of form-giving in the modern (post-epic) world may be resolved in two different ways," writes Anthony Cascardi, "through the representation of a world that is objective, rational, and real; and through the creation of a free and autonomous individual and independent self. But in a deeper respect these solutions are versions of but one, for the represented world is the subject's world."[88] If the "represented world is the subject's world," then it is an option for the artist and the writer to make his or her world *the* world, in lieu of returning to our pre-oedipal lives, and this is what Taishō *shi-shōsetsu* and the self-portrait finally share. As André Gide says, there is all the difference between "the unworthy narcissism of self-adoration and the moral narcissism of self-reflection."[89] For Taishō-period writers and painters, Narcissus may have been the tool not so much to create the self but to articulate their own edition of modernist artistic creativity.

If the West's metaphors for representation are visual—the mirror and the lamp—then Japan's are the mirror and the sun, and from the start associated with the power of the state. As told in the *Kojiki*, the Sun Goddess and mother to future emperors Amaterasu is tricked out of her cave through the use of one, and that fact has rendered the mirror, along with the jewel and the sword, the preeminent symbols of Japanese sovereignty as the imperial regalia. But Japan's encounter with modernity, the mirror and narcissistic construction of the modern subject tell part of the story of how Japanese national being is reflected rather than sovereign. In an oft-quoted paragraph from the end of Shiga's *An'ya kōrō*,

> [Tokito Kensaku] felt his exhaustion turn into a strange state of rapture. He could feel his mind and his body both gradually merging into this great nature that surrounded him. It was not nature that was visible to the eyes; rather it was like a limitless body of air that wrapped itself around him, this tiny creature no larger than a poppy seed. To be gently drawn into it, and there be

restored, was a pleasure beyond the power of words to describe. The sensation was a little like that of the moment when, tired and without a single worry, one was about to fall into a deep sleep. He had experienced this feeling of being absorbed into nature before; but this was the first time that it was accompanied by such rapture. In previous instances, the feeling perhaps had been more that of being sucked in by nature than that of merging with it; and though there had been some pleasure attached to it, he had at the same time tried instinctively to resist it, and on finding such resistance difficult, he had felt a distinct uneasiness. But this time, he had not the slightest will to resist; and contently, without a trace of the old uneasiness, he accepted nature's embrace.[90]

This famous passage has been called many things. A Zen-like epiphany, a very Japanese intersubjective reunion with nature, or the state of mind in a man as he slips from life into death. It has certainly struck many readers as sexual, the libido-fueled nostalgia of a child dreaming of returning to the body of his mother who was once not only the source of rapture but of his very own body. Freud would have it that artistic narcissism is an identification with the mother, and that is why his Da Vinci came to see the world's manifold beauties as a reflex of his earliest internalization of how his mother regarded him. Artists do have imaginations, and Shiga is less recalling a perfect unity before a divided self and its other doomed for disappointment than he is elegantly inventing it for us.

In Ovid's poem there is also a description of nature, of a pool. "Grass grew around it, by the water fed / And trees to shield it from the warming sun."[91] It is there that Narcissus, like Tokito Kensaku, discovers his image at the end of his life. Julia Kristeva has called Narcissus a modern character, one who "turns sight into origin and seeks the other opposite himself, as product of his own sight. He then discovers that the reflection is no other but represents himself, that the other is the presentation of the self. Thus, in his own way, Narcissus discovers in sorrow and death the alienation that is the constituent of his own image."[92] Tokito Kensaku, too, makes a discovery of selfhood on the side of a mountain as he lay dying, that very much in a world inseparable from the narcissistic image he projects himself into a moment of rhapsody: self-reflection, I think, not self-adoration. Writing of Conrad, Marshall Alcorn noted that his use of "identification, empathy, idealization" "are best understood as 'narcissistic variables,'" which an idealizing and reflective endeavor of fiction explores and makes use of.[93] I do not mean to reduce narcissism and the part it played in Taishō culture and society to psychobiography. It is via the conscious cultivation of the natural narcissism human beings know as infants born of parents that Taishō writers and painters strove to install a selfhood in equal parts intuitive and resonant with Western examples of self-reflection from Dürer through the Impressionists and into the age of mass media. If so, then the genre of *shi-shōsetsu* begins to dissolve away to start to become part of something much bigger—not just the sordid, confessional novels of a Chikamatsu Shūkō (1876–1994) or a Kasai Zenzō (1887–1928), but the poetry of a Satō Haruo, the masochism of a Tanizaki Jun'ichirō, and the Whitmanesque lore of an Arishima Takeo (1878–1923). It becomes the tenor of an age, dubbed Taishō by a feeble emperor, and therefore something that, like the air, we can hardly measure because we are so perfectly, comfortably, surrounded by it. The self is finally reduced here to our intuition of the interrelatedness of all our experiences.

By the twentieth century much art, visual and literary, came to be seen as self-referential and thus, whatever the putative theme, metaphorically self-portraiture. Gadamer argued that that a portrait's claim to significance lies in its intended reference,[94] just as Japanese literary theorists of Taishō selfhood argued that a similar intention had to lie not only behind the *shi-shōsetsu* but all genuine (*honkaku*) literature. At the same time the primacy of the modern nation-state and its interests resulted in the widespread condemnation of narcissism. In Greek myth, Narcissus rejected the love of men and women and so invited vilification. The same is true of *shi-shōsetsu* in Japanese literary criticism and historiography, where it has been excoriated since Uno Kōji's attack in 1925, intensifying with time. "Authoritarian institutions have tried to install self-hatred rather than self-love in their subjects,"[95] and with the rise of militarism in the 1930s, Japan's own highly narcissistic emperor (-system) succeeded in just this. Portraits of the emperor hung in all classrooms. But if *shi-shōsetsu* failed us somehow, it was because it was self-reflexive, intransitive, without a predicate. The solution for writers was to see the author produced in whatever he or she wrote. His or her style became the ineffable presence on the page. And there it stayed, until history brought the world to war. Yanagi Sōetsu declared in 1912 that Japan's murder of tens of thousands of Chinese, Koreans, and Russians in its colonies were "incomparably tiny things" when compared to the three Rodin sculptures the Shirakaba school acquired.[96] Surely that theory of aesthetics is what failed, not one word of literature. By the start of the Shōwa period, his paintings of Reiko now more famous than he himself was, Ryūsei largely abandoned human portraiture and returned to his Japanese roots by painting landscapes in China's Sung dynasty style.

5

Imperial Japan's Worst Writer

"Korea will never produce a great literature," opined Arishima Takeo at the start of the twentieth century, "because it is not a nation."[1] It hardly had a chance. Japanese hegemony in Korea commenced with the end of the Russo-Japanese War in 1905, just as Japan's discourse of a *kokumin bungaku* (national literature) was also beginning. The same year cultural historians cite as the start of the Taishō period, 1910, was also the year that the Great Han Empire, renamed Chōsen, was formally annexed as part of the Empire of Japan. Karatani Kōjin cites the development of Japanese imperialism in distinguishing between the Meiji and Taishō periods,[2] and that development is leveraged in the rise and subsequent fall of the Japanese language in Korea and what was written in it, the theme of this chapter. Colonial writers writing in Japanese—though not Japanese themselves—would test the perimeters of modern Japanese literature, inseparable from the modern Japanese nation-state, and its writers would be tested themselves.

Historians have long agreed that the history of modern Japan cannot be written without the history of Korea. George Akita stated that "the split in the ranks of the Meiji government in October 1873 over the question of sending an expedition to Korea" is the one single event most responsible for the establishment of a parliamentary government in Tokyo.[3] From the time of the Bakufu's belated drive to modernize, one of the biggest political battles in Japan was the *seikanron*—the debates over whether to invade, again, the Korean peninsula. The reasons had to do with more than national vanity or access to resources. The notion of a *kindai kokka* (modern nation) was worked out in Japan with important reference to the place of what was not Japanese but still Japan's. The history of Japanese modernity requires the history of Korea for reasons not just geopolitical but structural; Japan's notion of itself as modern necessitated the discursive production of an underdeveloped Korea. It was a prize acquisition, with twice the land area and five times the population of Taiwan, which had been acquired at the end of the nineteenth century. An important strategic segue into Manchuria, it was the largest of all Japanese colonies. "India," wrote Samuel Smiles in his influential book *Self-Help*, "has been a great field for the display of British energy";[4] for Japan, so too would be what was euphemistically referred to as the *hantō* (peninsula).

After Emperor Taishō died in 1926 and the Shōwa era began with the accession of his son Hirohito, the history of Japanese literature is commonly told as a tragedy that culminates with the end of the Second World War. Kawabata Yasunari (1899–1972) and a host of other modernist writers, many of them women, are always cited among the literary stars of the time. But otherwise we are told that *shi-shōsetsu* ran its course and a left-wing literature dedicated to the chronicling of the proletarian class briefly flourished only to collapse in the early 1930s under the combined weight of state suppression and its own mediocrity. The war years were roughly fifteen if one counts from the Manchurian Incident in 1931, eight if one thinks of the China Incident of 1937, three and a half if we mean the War in the Pacific initiated by Pearl Harbor at the end of 1941. These years are colored by writers' collaboration with the war effort, most spectacularly in the case of former left-wing apostates, by the stoic silence of a few of the more prominent literary figures, and by the general decline in the quality and quantity of literature production all around, given the material and ideological demands of the war.

Less often mentioned is what transpired in Japan's overseas possessions, colonies, and protectorates during these years, despite the fact Higuchi Ichiyō's mentor Nakarai Tōsui (1860–1926) wrote a novel as early as 1891 featuring a hero of mixed Japanese and Korean parentage set in the peninsula.[5] More broadly, scholars such as Haga Tōru have insisted that modern Japanese literature's *cas de conscience* is just how writers regarded Korea.[6] Certainly a postwar national shame over a legacy of imperialism is one reason. Another and more cogent one is the dilemma implicit in the term Japanese literature (*Nihon bungaku*), where "Japanese" is unproblematically understood as an ethnic, racial, or simply geographic attributive. Colonial Japanese literature, literature outside those islands labeled strictly Japanese, is unimaginable from the perspective of a nation that has only once in its history (the first half of the twentieth century) thought of itself, its language, and its literature as international and cosmopolitan. This is the same fifty years when the metropole of the West was momentarily displaced by the logic and rhetoric of an empire in which Tokyo stood at the center and cities like Keijō (Seoul) and Taihoku (Taipei) were situated first at the far periphery, then evermore proximate as the empire stretched from Siberia down to the waters of Australia and the borders of India. Japanese de facto rule in Korea after the Russo-Japanese War began just as the concept of a national literature (*kokumin bungaku*) in Japanese was being fully mobilized for deployment abroad as well as at home.

In much of East Asia, Japan introduced modern institutions (education systems, post offices, hospitals, transportation, police, etc.) via the instrument of the Japanese language.[7] The notion, too, of a modern literature is one that, in Korea and China, is irrevocably linked to the ideologically purposed notion of a Japanese precedent. But it is also true that the notion of a modern Japanese literature is irrevocably linked with Korea and China. Tsurumi Shunsuke inaccurately claimed that that one of the defining characteristics of modern Japanese literature until the end of war in 1945 is the absence of works set in Korea.[8] In fact, Shōwa literature, that published between 1925 and 1945, cannot be recounted without reference to Japan's overseas possessions and writers' discourse on them. Many Japanese writers—Futabatei, Doppo, Ōgai, Sōseki, and Yokomitsu Riichi among them—were intrigued by the continent (*tairiku*) or the South Seas (*Nan'yō*) and published travelogues of their visits to them. The reputation of Japanese literature in early Shōwa, writ large, is one of Japanese writers still enchanted with the West. Yet in this same period Japanese business, labor, the military, and the government bureaucracy were one step ahead. *Datsu-A* (Out of Asia) was a slogan already replaced by *Kō-A* (Develop Asia).

In literary circles the relationship between Japan and the colonies (*shoku-minchi*) was both subtle and significant. Speaking of Manshūkoku, the Japanese puppet state in northwest China from 1932 to the end of the war, Kawamura Minato declared its coloniality central to Japan's Shōwa-period modernity.[9] He argued that modern Japanese literature's encounter with Asia—specifically Korea—relativized Japanese literature's dogmatic assertions of its uniqueness and autonomy.[10] These are views that, if approaching the status of a truism in recent scholarship, nonetheless fly in the face of a tradition of cultural historiography that has treated the development of Japanese modernity with scant reference to overseas possessions and their relations with metropolitan Japan. In the early Shōwa period those relations were not inconspicuous to the Japanese themselves. "A great many," Kawamura adds, "believed that it was the historic fate of Shōwa Japan to exchange Meiji and Taishō ideals of Westernization and economic prosperity for the extension of hegemony [hakkō ichiu] over all of Asia, and for the establishment everywhere on the continent of what slogans such as 'Peaceful Rule Through the Imperial Way' [Ōdo rakudo] portended."[11] One part of this expansion was to be accomplished via literature. Not limited to travelogues, Shōwa literature assisted in the development of the colonies via its return to what, thematically, Japanese had surrendered at the onset of their modernity and the resultant turn to the dilemma of the urbanized intellectual: the glory of land, the farmer and his struggles, the local citizenry as a whole. Shōwa-period literature was to be as much a challenge to modernity as the period's politics were. The first Akutagawa Prize was awarded in 1935, for example, to the initial part of Ishikawa Tatsuzō's (1905–85) novel Sōbō (Emigrants), the story of Japanese in Brazil, demonstrating that literature in the second decade of Shōwa was cognizant of the global dispersal of Japan's people. But at the same time, extending its purview to the empire's furthest territories, Japanese literature was to achieve a modernity that, once preoccupied with the nation's insularity, had eluded it. Were Japanese literature—Japanese-language literature—to exist not only at home and the near colonies of Korea and Taiwan but as far away as Singapore, Manila, and Shanghai, then the previous opposition of Japan versus the West would be replaced by an internal diversity (Malay Japanese literature, Philippine Japanese literature, Chinese Japanese literature) that would nonetheless be whole due to its linguistic unity.

Edward Said notes this kind of literary, and at the same time imperial, modernity in Culture and Imperialism. "Many of the most prominent characteristics of modernist culture," he writes, "which we have tended to derive from purely internal dynamics in Western society and culture, include a response to the external pressures on culture from the imperium." His examples are largely English novels that look purely English, but are so because of the ideological work they perform as, "a domestic accompaniment to the imperial project for presence and control abroad."[12] Japanese literature and its relationship to imperialism for many reasons (not least that it was an anti-imperial imperialism) expressed itself in ways unencountered in *Clarris* or *Mansfield Park*, but it was there in the Shōwa period and its messy aftermath. In this chapter I focus on Korea and its circle of writers, Japanese and Korean, who were centered in Seoul, at the time renamed Keijō and the center of the peninsula's cultural life. Korea, with its large population, produced copious amounts of literature in Japanese, particularly when a generation schooled in the language from childhood came of age. Moreover, Korea was the object of a sustained campaign not only to produce literacy in Japanese—true to some extent from Burma to the Kurils—but to eliminate its indigenous language. And not just that: to eliminate Korean culture and national identity *in toto*.

One might argue that a Japanese and a Korean more easily assimilate than, say, a Frenchman and a Senegalese. After all, both cultures share a long, intertwined history, including Sinification and mutual cultural (not to mention genetic and linguistic) exchanges. But most important for the modern literary history of Japan would be the spread of the Japanese language, the foundation upon which Japanese imperial rule would rest, and with it the elimination of Korean. The process of the imposition of the Japanese language was gradual, and marked with important debates within the Japanese government in Seoul and Tokyo, but relentless. For most of the colonial period, Korean—already the object of intense modernization in the final years of the Chosŏn dynasty (1392–1910)—was a required subject in elementary schools up and down the peninsula, but more significantly, Japanese, also a required subject, had more classroom time and resources devoted to it. In 1938, Korean was reduced to an elective course of study and eliminated entirely from the curriculum in 1941, a shift that paralleled the colonial regime's winnowing of Korean-language publications at the same time. The results, while not as impressive as those obtained in Taiwan, with its smaller but more literate population, raised the percentage of Koreans able to speak Japanese to over 22 percent in 1943 from only a bit over 12 percent five years earlier.[13] The figures for elites were of course much higher.

The key—if contested—slogan of the Japanization campaign was *Naisen ittai*: the unity of Japan and Korea, a catchphrase defined curtly by Governor General Minami Jirō as "turning the peninsular population into loyal imperial subjects."[14] This term that replaced the earlier *Nissen'yū* (Japanese Korean fusion), marked an intensification of Japanese imperialism. *Naisen ittai* was not so much a policy as it was the formalization of the violence waged against Korean nationalist aspirations from 1910 onward. But while many Koreans rightly saw nefarious ambitions behind *Naisen ittai* and so argued against cooperation with it, others optimistically heralded it as a liberal move on the part of the empire to suppress racial discrimination. In Japan proper, these years saw an unprecedented boom in interest in many things Korean. Never were more works of classical and modern Korean literature translated into Japanese. In Korea itself, even nationalists, given what seemed to be the hopelessness of their cause by the late 1930s, came to see *Naisen ittai* as the best deal they could hope for, and from among those nationalists emerged what we could call collaborationists. In contrast to collaborators, who sought their own material advantage, collaborationists sought to ameliorate colonial subjection by cooperating with the colonizer when ultimately national aims might be served. It was from among these collaborationists—as well as a number of rank collaborators—that the Japanese selected their Korean spokesmen for *Naisen ittai*.

While collaboration in colonial Korea is understudied because of ongoing and unresolved political issues, historians have made progress in the study of political and economic elites in Korea who participated in the modernization of the peninsula's infrastructure under the Japanese. Carter Eckert, for instance, has written of the Korean bourgeoisie's gradual assimilation into the structures of the Japanese colonial system once hopes for a genuine Korean nationalism were crushed by the end of the first decade post-annexation. Among the reasons cited for this assimilation were the bourgeoisie's need, given the weaker state of the Korean economy, to enjoy access to Japan's more advanced resources, not to mention expanding markets in the newly acquired possessions and colonies. This explains, in Eckert's view, why the bourgeoisie could be even more enthusiastic about *Naisen ittai* than some of its colonial masters.[15] Koreans had been eager witnesses to Japan's modern development from its inception, after all. News of the Meiji Revolution summoned Koreans to Japan who hoped to bring lessons home. In ways that would have lasting if not always salutary effects, the Korean introduction to Western ideas was largely through Japan.[16] Progressive reformer Kim Ok-kyun studied with Fukuzawa Yukichi, whose Keiō Gijuku would be the first university in Japan to bestow a modern education on a Korean. While subsequent Japanese interventions across the peninsula disillusioned many "pro-Japanese nationalist" Koreans about the ultimate benefits of a modern Japan (if not modernity itself), the appointment in 1905 of Itō Hirobumi to Seoul as the first Resident General, atop his function as an advocate for Japan's parochial interests, was not a wholly disingenuous mission to bring to Korea the benefits of modernity. When a patriot assassinated Itō in late 1909, Natsume Sōseki made a quick study of it for his next year's novel, *Mon* (*The Gate*).

The rise and fall in the number of Koreans moving to Japan for study made clear the objectives of the empire. While the number of scholarships granted to Koreans decreased after 1910 as Japanese-style institutions of higher learning were established in the peninsula itself, the numbers dramatically rose after 1919 — from 448 to 1,192 — in the wake of the March First Korean revolt against the Japanese occupation.[17] Throughout the colonial period, the numbers of Koreans traveling to Japan for study on private, family funds generally increased until the 1930s, when the collapse of the rural economy impoverished many families. In part this was due to the limited access to universities in Korea (state schools limited most enrollment to Japanese nationals), but also because of the allure of an advanced Japanese technological and cultural milieu. Waseda University was a particularly attractive destination for young Korean intellectuals. Poet Ch'oe Nam-sŏn (1890–1957) and novelist Yi Kwang-su (1892–1950?) were among the pioneers of modern Korean literature who attended Waseda. But in a recurring pattern, many leading intellectuals who received their tutelage in modern ideas in Japanese institutions would find their credibility undermined back home in Korea when they attempted to introduce those same ideas. It was, for instance, Kim Ok-kyun's reliance on Japanese ideology as well as actual support that "undermined his patriotic justification" for his attempted 1884 coup against the Korean crown.[18] As the colonial period progressed, and with the introduction of the *kōminka* (imperial subjectification) and *Naisen ittai* policies, the predicament of the Japan-trained, if not always Japan-sympathetic, Korean intelligentsia grew acute. This was especially so for Korean writers, for whom the ideals of art learned in Japan came into conflict with the demands of a colonial regime at home. Many intellectuals in Korea evinced the dual attitude that, even if they were to make a patriotic contribution through their actions, it was difficult to move forward with cultural work informed with that ideology.[19] We can see that the *bundan* in Seoul was at the nexus of a particular conflict between literary and artistic theories of Japanese modernity and the exigencies of the modern Japanese state, and for nearly half a century the Japanese empire. The Tokyo *bundan* — the central *bundan*, be one a writer in Niigata or Nagoya or Seoul — matured in the Taishō period as an integrated institution superintending literary production in the rapidly expanding market for fiction. The *bundan* in Seoul was not only much smaller but positioned quite differently within the colony than was the Tokyo *bundan* in the home islands.

When Korean writers began publishing in Japanese and reaching metropolitan audiences, Japan's consensus over its literature faced a crisis. Chang Hyŏk-chu's (1905–97) short story "Gakidō" (The Realm of Hungry Ghosts), published in *Kaizō* in 1932, occasioned the following postscript from that journal's editors: Chang "is surely the first Korean writer to make such a spectacular debut in our literary society [*wagakuni no bundan*], and it makes clear to the world everywhere that such writers do exist."[20] Chang had come along at just the right time as left-leaning journals such as *Kaizō* were scrambling for new material in the wake of the repression of Proletarian literature at home. Being a Korean writer at this juncture was a distinct advantage and accounts for some part of Kim Sa-ryang's (1914–50?) subsequent success as a finalist for the Akutagawa Prize in 1940 for his 1939 story "Hikari no naka ni" ("Into the Light"), written in a Seoul boarding house just as the debate in that city over what language writers should use was at its height. Both men provoked the Japanese *bundan* in a language forced upon them. But ironically they rendered a valuable service to Japan. Chang would go on to become one of the most notorious collaborators with the Japanese, while Kim eventually joined the Communist resistance in China, but both embodied through their often highly introspective use of the colonial language the inherent conundrum of literature in Korea under Japanese rule.

The existence of Japanese-language authors in Korea could not be easily redeemed. In a 1936 roundtable discussion entitled "Chōsen bunka no shōrai" (The future of Korean culture) published in the journal *Bungakukai*, Korean poet Im Hwa (1908–53) estimated that all of Korea had approximately 80 writers, only 50 of whom were actually earning a living as writers—this, in contrast to Hayashi Fusao's (1903–75) estimate of Japan's number at 2,200. Part of the reason was that Korea had fewer outlets in which writers could publish. More importantly, the Seoul *bundan* was mostly a coterie of Japan-educated intellectuals writing largely in Japanese and therefore for a small audience at home.[21] The lingua franca of the literary establishment was Japanese. Expatriate Japanese writers were few in number, and their names are seldom familiar to us today. The most prominent was Tanaka Hidemitsu (1913–49), who lived in Korea from 1935 to 1938, then again from 1940 to 1942. He had a day job with the Yokohama Rubber Company, but otherwise he wrote to support the war effort.

Flattering himself as half Korean (*nakaba hantōjin*),[22] he insisted that wartime writing was important for the sake of the nation (*okuni*), and that the former creed of "art's for art's sake was a 'Judacism,'" views in line with his views on literature in Nazi Germany.[23] Tsurumi Shunsuke mistakenly summarized his novel *Yoidorebune* (The Drunken Boat, 1949) as "the tale of a middle-aged man who knows not how to love."[24] It is in fact thoroughly political. Many of his Japanese characters are apologist faculty at the imperial university or bureaucrats in the colonial administration. They embody the supervisory examples of a Japanese tutelage that had superintended the history and development of a modern Korean literature. The most prominent Korean writer in the Seoul *bundan* was Yi Kwang-su, also known by his Japanese name Kayama Mitsurō; like others, he had strong pro-Japanese (*shinnichi*) propensities for which he would be vilified after the 1945 Liberation.

A colonial literary establishment such as the Seoul *bundan* is a worldwide feature of modern imperialism: French in Tunis, English in Port of Spain, Spanish in Manila. In each we find literary language and style linked inseparably with issues usually coupled in the metropole as aesthetics and nationalism. Korean students who went to Japan to study modernization soon wrote of their experiences. In the first decade of the Meiji period, their language of choice was *kanbun*, a form of Sinitic common to Japan and Korea. But from 1880 to 1920—when a generation of Koreans educated under the Japanese began to write in Japanese—works in various forms of Korean (which was evolving into a *kukŏ* [national language]) were common. Korean Japanese literary scholar Im Chŏn-hye has stated that Yi Su-chŏng, who taught Korean in Tokyo from 1883 to 1886 while studying agriculture, was the first Korean to write in modern Japanese as both a religious proselytizer and an aspiring literatus.[25] In 1919, Korean students in Tokyo founded the coterie literary journal *Ch'angcho* (Creation), the first such enterprise in Korean literary history. Read mostly in Korea, it introduced literary ideas from Europe (via Japanese translations) and Japan itself. Despite its brief run—it lasted only nine issues—it is credited with providing a key stimulus to the development of *kundae munhak* (modern [colonial] literature) in the Korean language. Works of literature in Japanese by Korean residents of Japan during this same period steadily increased and exploded in number with the Proletarian literature movement in the mid-1920s. On the one hand the internationalist orientation of the movement in Japan meant that its Japanese-language journals such as *Tane o maku hito*, *Senki*, and *Puroretaria bunka* sought out and published Koreans, while on the other hand

Koreans themselves were looking to publish in a language—Japanese—that might reach a larger and international audience. The postwar *zainichi* (resident Korean) writer Kim Tal-su has pointed out that nearly all the Korean characters in Japanese literature are found in the Proletarian works of this period, when the enemy of both the domestic working class and the colonies was one and the same: Japanese imperialism.[26]

The Proletarian movement came to an effective end under government pressure in 1932, shortly after the Mukden Incident. Japanese editors and readers on the Left found their appetite for socially critical literature satisfied by stories of the travails of rural life in the colonies. Japanese magazines as big as *Kaizō* or as important as *Bungei shuto* published not only Chang Hyŏk-chu and fellow Korean writers but writers from Taiwan and Manchuria. For his part, Chang saw publishing in Japanese as a way to move beyond the smaller confines of the Korean language and convey his theme of Korean life to a larger public. The problem was that without a coherent national entity, the concept of a Korean national literature was something of a non sequitur. In its place was installed, if problematically, the Korean *language* as the firmament of a national literature. "The establishment of an independent and unique Korean literature," writes Nayoung Aimee Kwon, "was itself an impossibility" at the time.[27] In less than a decade, Chang's and others' announced ambition to use the Japanese language to propagate what could then still be called a Korean literature would mutate into a tool of the colonial regime to further its *kōminka* and *Naisen ittai* aims. The years 1941 to 1945 are referred to in Korean history as the "dark period" (*amhŭkki*), the historical "blank" of a Korea on the brink of absorption into the Japanese polity and cultural sphere. The use of Korean, despite a peninsular population overwhelmingly illiterate in Japanese, was effectively impossible. *Kukŏ* (Korean) was now *kokugo* (Japanese), and Korean writers were at best "peninsular writers" (*hantō sakka*), at worst "Greater East Asia Co-Prosperity Sphere writers" (*Tōa Kyōei Ken bungakusha*). Korean literary history holds inviolable the judgment, in the words of Paek Ch'ŏl (1908–85), that "the five years from 1941 through 1945 were the darkest and most shameful in the history of Korean literature: a blank period that ought to remain a white sheet of paper for literary history."[28]

The changing stakes of literary language, once an issue that some Korean intellectuals might have convinced themselves was innocent of Japanese imperial ambitions, were made painfully clear in the 1936 "Future of Korean Culture" roundtable discussion between Korean and Japanese writers. It began in response to Hayashi Fusao's disingenuous remark that Japan (*naichi*) knew nothing of Korea. Kim Mun-jip (1909–??) then complained that with the rising price of paper and colonial policies, Korean writers were less and less capable of finding places to publish that would presumably educate Japan about Korea. A Japanese participant suggested that Korean writers publish in Japanese (*naichigo*) in order to achieve financial viability. Akita Ujaku (1883–1962) chimed in, saying that it was the hope of not only Japanese writers but the Japanese masses to have Koreans write in Japanese for them. The mood of the conversation grew more strained when Hayashi bluntly asked that Koreans write all their literary works in Japanese (*naichigo de yatte moraitai*) following one Korean writer's timid proposal that they might write in both languages. Turning up the heat, playwright Murayama Tomoyoshi (1901–77) ruled it a plainly "political problem" for any Korean fluent in Japanese to choose to write in Korean. To this a Korean writer insisted that Korean culture must express itself via the Korean language: to write of it in Japanese was to Japanize it (*naichika*). Others agreed. "Korean literature, written in anything but Korean," Yu Chin-o (1906–87) added, "cannot be called literature." When Hayashi told these Korean writers that they *would* write in Japanese, he was challenged rhetorically: "Will that be for the sake of Japanese culture? Or for the sake of Korean culture?" Hayashi's answer, which in an earlier decade might have meant something more cosmopolitan and less imperial, answered, "For the sake of world culture" (*sekai bunka no tame*).[29]

The importance of the Japanese language to the ideology of Japanese colonialism can hardly be overstated. One can trace the linkage of the Japanese language to Japanese national identity and Japanese imperialism in, for example, the Meiji-period writings of Ueda Kazutoshi, who in 1894 called a nation's language its "very blood"[30] and "the bulwark of the Imperial Household."[31] His students made the establishment of a standard Japanese language (*hyōjungo*) important for the ease of spreading it to new territories and possessions. In 1895, Japanese had already been proposed as the East Asian common language for reasons of scholarship and commerce. But later ideologues, after the 1910 annexation, equated *Nihongo* (Japanese) with *Nihon seishin* (the Japanese spirit). It was impossible, as critic An Ushiku put it, to remain silent in colonial Korea,[32] so important was it to Japan that the assimilation (*dōka*) of the Korean people be built upon the use of Japanese language. As a corollary, use of other languages—in the 1930s and 1940s Korean, but in earlier stages of Japanese national consolidation Ryukyuan and Ainu—was tantamount to subversion.

An editorial in the *Tōkyō nichinichi shinbun* as early as September 1910 called for the mandatory imposition of Japanese upon the Korean people and the annihilation of the Korean language. Although colonial policy was famously mercurial, Japanese was mandated for sole use in the public realm and ambitiously mandated for the private realm as well by the late 1930s. By the end of the Meiji period, the Korean and Japanese words for "national language" (*kukŏ, kokugo*) referred solely to Japanese. With the outbreak of an expanded war in China in 1937, the use of Japanese throughout the peninsula was increasingly encouraged. A Korean's use of his or her mother tongue in many public venues was, if not treasonable by the last years of the war, dangerously political.

Why did Korean writers bother to write? The answer lies, as it does in other places at this time in history, in the complicated and morally ambiguous conundrum of collaboration. In the unjaundiced sense of simply "working together," collaboration has a long tradition in modern Japan and Korea. The hopeful attention that Korean intellectuals paid Japanese modernization from the early Meiji period naturally resulted in tutelage under their Japanese counterparts. Kim Mun-jip, for example, claimed he was a disciple of Yokomitsu Riichi and a friend of Kobayashi Hideo. Yi Kwang-su's classmate at Meiji Gakuin, Yamazaki Toshio (1891–1979), was an important literary influence upon him, as was Kinoshita Naoe (1869–1937) and Kobayashi. Nakano Shigeharu (1902–79) had several close Korean colleagues, and avant-garde poet Yi Sang (1910–37) was apprenticed, albeit from a distance, to Japan's modernist poets and their movements, such as Dadaism, Formalism, Futurism and Surrealism. By the 1920s, literary ideas, imported from the West or original, would appear in the Japanese colonies almost concurrently with their debut at home. This was not what we see in Pound and Eliot, or Gauguin and Van Gogh. Korean and Japanese collaborations were cross-straits partnerships; they were still unequal. The common language of collaboration was Japanese, and therefore even the most informal or well-meaning encounter of Japanese writers with their Korean admirers was inevitably a process of identification. Even when the exposure to Japanese ideals of modernity and nationalism resulted in the transfer of ideas that were inspirations for Korean rebellion—Yi Kwang-su was one of the signatories of the 1919 Declaration of Independence—those ideals were articulated in a Japanese linguistic and intellectual idiom and signaled an ironic allegiance. As industrialized nations penetrated agrarian ones around the world, the allure of what was offered to local elites proved irresistible. Ronald Paulson phrased it in general terms: "From the standpoint of the collaborators or mediators the invaders imported an alternative source of wealth and power which, if it could not be excluded, had to be exploited in order to preserve or improve the standing of indigenous elites in the traditional order."[33]

One of Paulson's "alternative source[s] of wealth and power" was the language of the colonizer. As Korean writers sought to build a modern Korean literature with attention to Japanese precedent, they did so in the Japanese language. They bonded with a colonial establishment and at the same time grew alienated from a Korean lived experience that was, in comparison to that of Japan, underdeveloped. Japan and the Japanese language made for Koreans a world larger than their own, and that cosmopolitanism produced an opportune nationalism, insofar as it demanded Koreans enjoy the same freedoms as Japanese as the benefit of membership in the Japanese intellectual world. The irony here is not wholly on the Korean side. Colonial authorities, while in a position to exert power over the colonized, could not do so without the mediation of elites within the colony. Modern Korean history repeats such ironies frequently. In 1924 and in the wake of the defeat of the nationalist uprising in 1919, Yi Kwang-su spoke for many intellectuals when he called for a cultural nationalism that could exist and even thrive in Korea despite a political imperialism that engulfed the country. This seeming accommodation with Japanese colonialism inspired charges of pernicious collaboration. Such compromises spoke of Korean national rights only within the context of Japanese sovereignty over the peninsula, and at the pleasure of Japanese officialdom. The Korean Japanese writer Kim Sŏk-pŏm (1925–), later one of Yi's most vociferous critics, stated the case with some sympathy: "The issue before the Korean intelligentsia was the Japan empire, the sole example of successful Asian modernization; and the backwardness of their own country, together with its modernization via the intercession of Japan. . . . This historical situation is what gave birth to collaboration with Japan."[34]

Writers such as Yi had often been sincere nationalists. That he and others would come to be judged, fairly or not, as collaborationists had to do with their acceptance of a certain truism in modernity that backfired on them. Western rationalism, an ideal introduced via Japan, held that it was logical for one race to dominate inferior ones, if only in order to improve the conditions of those subjugated nations. The reasoning of modernity boomeranged and convinced a class of modernizers of the impossibility of a nation both modern and Korean. Korea political scientist Bruce Cumings wrote:

This dilemma of a Janus-faced Japanese colonialism was particularly poignant for the cultural nationalists, who saw their efforts in the 1920's come to naught. Because many of them had become accustomed to gradualism and lacked the steely determination of more radical resisters, a number of them became collaborators. The great nationalist writer Yi Kwang-su, and the nationalist activist and ideologue Ch'oe Nam-sŏn come to mind as typical of this group. Had things developed as they had hoped, such people might in the 1950's and 1960's have been the self-confident, legitimate leaders of a post-colonial Korea. But in the last decade of colonial rule the upper stratum of a whole generation was turned into a collaborationist elite.[35]

Not every Korean writer would collaborate, of course. Some died in prison. But sufficient numbers did. Because of the disappointed hopes for Korean independence in the 1920s, the "Korea problem" for intellectuals was translated into the problem of how to interpret and adopt *Naisen ittai*, and just for that reason the binary of collaboration and resistance within the history of the Japanese empire has been grossly oversimplified. For someone such as Hyŏn Yŏng-sŏp (1906–?), the author of "Chōsenjin no susumu beki michi" (The Road Ahead for Koreans, 1938), the 1910 annexation was his country's practical equivalent of Japan's Meiji Revolution, accomplishing the same task of discarding older, feudal ideals and practices and replacing them with progressive, modern ones. This, he argued, sealed Korea's fate, and now there was nothing to do but forge ahead and do away with all things Korean. When, after the war, Korean national hero Kim Ku said, "Practically everyone in Korea is a collaborator,"[36] he certainly did not mean to exempt writers, out of whose ranks emerged spokesmen for assimilation with Japan, some of whom appeared more eager for absorption into the empire than were the Japanese colonial authorities themselves.

Many writers spoke out publically and repeatedly for assimilation with Japan in the last decade of the colonial period. This was the Korean equivalent of *tenkō* in Japan, the term for the political apostasy of left-wing Japanese writers under the threat of imprisonment and even death. Of the five thousand persons in Japan convicted of violating the Peace Preservation Law for Communist Party activity, fewer than two dozen remained in prison until the end of the war without having made a *tenkō*. (It is estimated that an equal number perished in prison.) We have no reason to believe that Korean activists and intellectuals were any more stalwart in their convictions than their Japanese comrades—in 1938, the colonial government reported that more than 60 percent of Korean "thought criminals" in jail had performed *tenkō*—despite the considerable mythmaking of a Korean resistance after Liberation. It is not an exact equivalent. If the Japanese apostates were meant to realize that, as part of the Japanese people, they were natural extensions of the emperor, the same could not be said of the Koreans, their masses as colonial subjects, or the intelligentsia who had to understand more logically that their very modern destiny was to lie in adaptation to—and absorption into—an advanced Japan. Just as one might argue that a left-wing literature in Japan could flip-flop with unexpected ease into a quasi-fascist literature—both were ideologically and propagandistically "mass"—so too, and perhaps even more easily, could a Korean literature that had once been nationalist become Japan-imperialist if it preserved the hope of an improved fate for the whole of the (formerly) Korean people? Hyŏn, for instance, was so committed in his support for assimilation that he told the older nationalist generation they should commit collective suicide, and lectured all Koreans that they should become more Japanese than the Japanese. Assimilation was the means of advancing the destiny of the Korean people. *Naisen ittai* would end discrimination against Koreans, a discrimination he believed was based not on any Japanese contempt for Koreans, *per se*, but rather easily eradicated "differences in lifestyles."[37] Hyŏn's pro-Japanese sentiments were so extreme as to have cowed even some Japanese, as did the pro-Japanese statements of other Korean intellectuals. As prominent a Korean as Yi Kwang-su, largely untouchable by the Japanese authorities, wrote prose described by Kim Sŏk-pŏm as "the language of a slave" to a Kobayashi Hideo embarrassed by Yi's sycophantic writings.[38] That such behavior would be possible from intelligent and dignified writers is indicative of the extreme situation, in Sartrean terms, in which the Korean intellectual was placed in the final years of the colonial period, and nowhere more dramatically and tragically than in the story of one of Korea's leading literary critics and most reviled collaborators. Kim Mun-jip's sad story symbolizes the complex, strange ties between Japan and Korea and, at the same time, the failure of modern Japanese literature to be anything more than a parochial national literature.

Kim Mun-jip is not one of the Japanese language's better-known writers, or Japanese literature's better-known fictional characters, but he is both. The reasons his name is not well known are many. His origins are obscure, though he would claim he was a descendant of Silla royalty rendered penniless and driven to Japan where he lived "the life of a beggar."[39] His career, equally melodramatic, was short, his reputation scandalous, and, not least of all, his names many. He wrote not only under the name Kim Mun-jip, but under its Japanese render-ing, Kin Bunshū; a Sino-Korean penname Hwadon ("Flower-Pig"); a Japanese name, Ōe Ryūnosuke; and in a joking reference to his fondness for alcohol, Ōe "No Drink" Ryūmujunosuke. He even took the name Inukuso Kurae, literally "Eat dog shit," a name for which he was called in by the colonial police and reprimanded.[40] His unbridled narcissism repeatedly landed him in trouble. He was guilty of a boastful mendacity that made him notorious and his life difficult, both during and after the war. We know that he attended Waseda Middle School in Tokyo, but his claims to have graduated from Matsuyama Higher School and the Tokyo Imperial University likely were not quite true in the first instance, and were plainly not in the second. Also telling of his character was his brag that he was a protégé of leading Japanese modernist Yokomitsu Riichi and a friend of Kobayashi Hideo. Nowhere in Yokomitsu's collected works is there even a single mention of Kim, and Yokomitsu was a writer famous for his promotion of *gaichi* (colonial) writers. Kobayashi, as we will learn presently, only wrote of Kim once, and certainly not in language we would associate with friendship. Kim's boasts to compatriots back in Seoul that he had achieved real fame in Japan were categorically false.

No one can say for sure, but a good guess would be that Kim, not an aristo-crat and not of *yangban* (land-owning) lineage, was instead a person of modest means from the sort of family that Changsoo Lee and George De Vos, in their study *Koreans in Japan*, describe this way:

> Among those [families] who were not so wealthy but who, by some means, were able to obtain an education, most tended to stay in Japan. They became part of an intellectual contingent of Koreans who found it more possible to express interest in the arts and social sciences in Japan than in a more stringently controlled and traditional Korean society at home. They found a type of minority niche within the more bohemian and dissident segments of Japanese society, some of them exercising a type of creativity that permitted some communality with their Japanese counterparts.[41]

There is every reason to suspect that Kim belonged to just this stratum of Japan-educated Koreans. He might not have returned to the peninsula in 1935 had he not made multiple inappropriate advances toward women from elevator girls to the wives and sisters of prominent Japanese. In his memoirs, Tamura Taijirō (1911–83) described Kim as a short, solidly built man with near perfect

Japanese but an unmistakably Korean face behind wire-rimmed eyeglasses, and as a man with an uncontrollable libido. Tamura tells us that Kim once chased his rival Hori Tatsuo (1904–53) with a knife and embarrassed himself repeatedly.[42] Kim made a sufficient scandal of himself in Japan that even the subaltern status in Japanese bohemia outlined by Lee and De Vos became impossible for him. He returned to Korea and its small *bundan* where in short order he earned a reputation as, in Kim Chong-guk's words, a "poison-tongued critic."[43] A 1936 gossip column in the colonial newspaper *Keijō nippō* labeled Kim a suspect criminal, a degenerate, and a half-crazed alcoholic.[44]

Kim published one very short story in Seoul but soon turned to criticism, and with that he earned his considerable if short-circuited fame. Writing in one of the two major Korean-language newspapers of the day, the *Dong-A ilbo*, Kim was one of the pioneers of modern Korean literary criticism, starting with his first article for the press, "Dentō to gikō mondai" (The Problem of Tradition and Technique, 1935). Many of his articles (under the heading "Hwadon's Column") were devoted to attacking other Koreans, but he also drew up an outline for modern literary criticism in his homeland. His magnum opus, *Pip'yŏng munhak* (Critical Literature, 1938) was composed of those newspaper essays and is possibly the single most important work of pre-Liberation Korean literary criticism, but its argument can be reduced to the simple equation of Korean literature to what is written in the Korean language. If it is true that modern Korean literary criticism owes its impetus to modern Japanese precedents, then *Pip'yŏng munhak* is the Korean expression of what was called in Japan *kōdōshugi* (actionism), the reaction against the perceived nihilism of Dada, Surrealism, and other European avant-garde-isms espoused by such writers as Funabashi Seiichi (1904–76) and Abe Tomoji (1903–73). In colonial Korea this resistance had a context different from Japan's. Korean literature was preoccupied with its survival under the Japanese occupation, and so issues of realism and language commanded attention. Metropolitan debates on modernism and aestheticism, while present in Korea, were inextricably linked with the demands of a native *minjŏkchŭi* (nationalism). The agenda that Kim and others of his day faced was, what *is* Korean literature, given the country's peripheral status in the imperium? Kim Mun-jip's answer was thus: Korean literature is none other than the Korean language, or as Kim phrased it, the *minjŏkŏ* (national language). This assertion may strike us as naïve, simplistic, or banal, but it was fresh in its day. Buttressed with Kim's credentials as a recent returnee from Tokyo, his position made him popular for a time, as he placed himself precisely in that small space allowed the

Korean intelligentsia before the aggressive *Naisen ittai* campaigns of assimilation.

Kim is an exaggerated example of the capability of the empire's movement to absorb Korea. Upon the publication of *Pip'yŏng munhak*, Kim's views swung half-circle. He became a Japanese sycophant in Seoul's claustrophobic literary circles. In a 1936 attack on Chang Hyŏk-chu and his upstart success, he ruled that "his writings are no better than a middle school student's composition." He gratuitously prefaced his assault with a blanket dismissal of Korean literature as lacking any worthy classics. The revered seventeenth-century *Chunhyangchŏn* (Tale of Chunhyang), he insisted, started out as a piece of Chinese literature. "Whatever one might say about Korean literature, it lacks art [*gei*]."[45] By 1938, the year Kim was honored to meet Governor General Minami Jirō in person, he wrote in the collaborationist journal *Sanzenri* that the best way to guarantee the survival of the Korean people was not only to cooperate with, but to welcome the amalgamation of the Japanese and Korean peoples. "Even if," he wrote in his 1937 essay "Bundan saiken ron" (On the Reconstruction of the Korean Literary Establishment), "the Korean people were eliminated and fully absorbed into the Yamato," that would not be "the end but, on the contrary, the expansion of our Korean blood. Complete *Naisen ittai* requires the co-mingling of both our lineages."[46] Not long afterward Kim abandoned any sympathy for even that dubious survival. In his 1939 "Chōsen minzoku no hattenteki kaishōron josetsu" (Preface to a Proposal for the Evolutionary Extinction of the Korean People) and "Shinmin no sho" (Our Loyal Subjecthood), two of the most infamous pro-Japanese tracts published during the colonial period, he argued that becoming Japanese was both his people's fate and his own fervent hope. "It is not enough," he wrote in the former, "for the Koreans to become loyal subjects of the emperor by wearing wooden sandals or eating their bland radish pickles. . . . What is necessary is the total evisceration of our spiritual innards. We must vomit out every last bit of our rotten, stinking guts from the top of our bodies; take enemas to cleanse all our lower bodies; and make our midsections clean."[47]

The crude language that Kim used in this essay is telling. His one collection of Japanese-language fiction, *Arirantōge* (The Arirang Ridge, 1938) is such an odd compendium of sexual and scatological fetishes, frankly described, that Kobayashi Hideo declared in a scathing review that sick writers (*byōteki na sakka*) produce sick writing.[48] Difficult to see as anything but a carnivalized expropriation of Japanese *ero-guro-nansensu* (erotic-grotesque-nonsense) passing as modernism, *Arirantōge* describes in a series of more-or-less linked stories a man's fetish for women's body hair, sadism, masochism, misogyny, mother complexes, and masturbation and homosexuality. Set in the 1920s (it references the Great Kantō Earthquake at its start and Akutagawa's suicide at its end), the Korean narrator starts out as a bartender in Seoul, a city that in Kim's rendition is suddenly and ahistorically cosmopolitan. It is populated with not only Koreans and Japanese but Indians and even one sophisticated Somalian jazz saxophonist who is a *habitué* at the White Russian–owned Grand Bohemian Hotel. This fantasy is in keeping with the expected links between the modern city and modernism, precisely Kim's overly ambitious project. The narrator travels—"flees" (*dassō*)—to Tokyo, "the huge, bottomless city." There, he stalks the better part of ten thousand Japanese women. He eventually becomes a barber in order to facilitate his fetish, one that he dubs *keimōshō*, or "stolen-hair syndrome."[49] "I am truly," he boasts, "a Hair Man [*ke-otoko*] proudly convicted of his crimes" (16). Along the way he praises various other fetishes. *Arirantōge* lingers over shoes (one lengthy piece in the anthology is entitled "Women's Sandals and My Youth"), urine ("Piss Women and Eternity"), lice, physical disabilities requiring sex on all fours, bed-wetting, and dirt. But the narrator claims women's hair as his own, unique pursuit. "Hair on the head. Hair on the body. I say it over and over again, a mysterious forest scattered all over the earth kneading together the joys of both heaven and hell" (33). "What is called 'hair' is like a cruel woman's personal capital. . . . Perhaps it is the cross that women, all women, bear" (19). The Korean narrator prays to Jesus at one point for more hair; elsewhere, he terms his passion a "religion" (26) and he does not "doubt there is a God of hair, a Buddha of hair" (26). Kim's narrator approves of Marx's view of the relationship between capitalist profit and warfare, but in the same paragraph manages to slip in mention of vaginas, rape, sexual intercourse, perversion, and only finally justice (*seigi*) (32). Women's hair (he favors armpits) is constantly given value (*neuchi*), and he reduces the worth of women to just how much they have of it. His collected booty fills trunks. He likes it long, thick and lustrous, but only on Japanese women. Korean females are reserved for scorn, while "Japan is the land of women" (*Nihon wa nyonin no kuni*), especially if they are young and pregnant. "Women in Japan were born for just one thing," Kim writes, "and that is sex [*koi*]" (149, 151).

This, I state polemically, might well be the worst work of Japanese literature published between the early 1930s and the end of the empire in 1945. I say so not on account of its record of perversions, which I can sometimes appreciate, but its celebration of abjection (by the end, our narrator is consigned to being a barber's assistant entrusted with tidying up Japanese women's pubic hair) combined with a failed pseudomodernist style. Kim Mun-jip combines in *Arirantōge*, written in a contorted, extended, truncated, at times even grammar-compromised Japanese language that nearly defies comprehension, all the exaggerated features of the literary modernism he observed in Japanese writers but did not absorb. If Tokyo is his ideal of the modern city (27), then Seoul is the Futurist city with Kim's invocation of its nuclear-powered vessels and sleek air buses (47, 52), neither of which existed or ever would. Male sexual desire, directed toward Japanese womanhood but displaced onto the fetish, is proposed as the epitome of modern human sensibility. Boasting repeatedly that his Japanese is better than his Korean, the narrator flatters himself by thinking he passes as a native speaker, but his humiliation at being discovered Korean is evident. In his postwar afterword to *Arirantōge*, Kim refers to these stories as his self-portrait (207), and in its stories he recalls a sad and tortured childhood that willed him his adult personality.

His frequent lament—boast—that his own command of Korean was poor supplanted the defense of the Korean language once put forth in *Pip'yŏng munhak*. This turnaround was coupled with his ad hominem attacks on fellow Korean writers and what is rumored to be further trouble with the law over his encounters with women. Newspapers reported in April 1940 that he had been arrested for sexual molestation, including that of a hapless elevator girl. Literary historians debate whether he served a one-year sentence, or if Japanese friends succeeded in having it suspended, but in either case in 1942 he was removed to Japan and virtually disappeared from public life, never to be heard from again. Kim's celebrity in Korea lasted all of five years.

"Under colonialism," wrote critic Kim U-chang, "the writer is, so to speak, self-recruited into an alien culture; but the colonizing society has no need of him, while the colonized society is much less in need of him."[50] Just why Kim shifted so quickly from the quasi-nationalist of *Pip'yŏng munhak* to the apologist of "Shinmin no sho" in the space of months was a question asked of many of his peers. It has been attributed to a fatal flaw of personal character, but I think otherwise. It is plausible that the shrillness with which *Pip'yŏng munhak* promotes the Korean language was the result of Kim's other peripheral relationship, after years in Japan, to Korea. Here was a bright *bungaku seinen* (aspiring young writer) who received a modern education in Japan, was taught the primacy of the *kindaiteki jiga* (modern self), was surrounded by heady talk of literary and artistic modernism but who, upon his return to the peninsula, grew frustrated with a culture he found so feudal and Confucianist that his education abroad must have seemed for naught.

Kim Yun-sik believes that Kim Mun-jip had two fates—a martyr's fate and a theatrical fate—as a direct result of the linguistic and specifically colonial situation he inhabited. "Coerced by the authorities to write in Japanese rather than Korean, to write in one's native language is to choose martyrdom, while to write in Japanese is no more than a choice to perform on a stage. Kim Mun-jip's tragedy was having to choose between being an artist and an actor."[51] These fates, an extreme example of what Korean writers in the late colonial period faced, became the theme of a novella that was written about Kim at the time. Kim Sa-ryang wrote *Tenma* (Pegasus, 1940) while living in Japan, but it is unintelligible without knowing the state of the Korean *bundan*. Kim Sa-ryang was then the best-known Japanese-language Korean writer, given his candidacy for the 1940 Akutagawa Prize. Born the second son to a prosperous Pyongyang family and raised, unusually for the time, as a Christian, he led a rebellion among his classmates after the 1913 Kwangju Incident but later that same year resolved to get to Japan no matter what. (He was smuggled with the help of an older brother in Kyoto.) With no little irony, he believed Japan a place of refuge from his own country's turmoil, though like many other Koreans he was briefly taken into police custody twice while there.[52] Kim Sa-ryang is also an ambivalent figure in the history of the colonial Seoul *bundan*: someone who wrote largely in Japanese, he thought he could preserve his Korean identity within it but was never comfortable with that decision; someone who collaborated with but eventually took up arms against the Japanese; and someone who had the credentials for writing an equally sympathetic and critical portrait of Kim Mun-jip—though one critic argues Kim recreated Kim Mun-jip as antihero Hyŏl-lyong to be a foil to himself.[53]

The setting of *Tenma* is Seoul in 1940, on the eve of the colonial authorities' full-scale assault on the Korean language. The novella's Hyŏl-lyong is a hack writer who had spent fifteen years in Japan. He wakes up one morning with a hangover in a Sinchon brothel. A man without house, money, or girlfriend, the previous evening he had crashed a meeting of Korean writers convened at a restaurant to discuss how to respond to his and others' support for the colonial administration's plans for the final eradication of the Korean language from public life—a meeting at which Hyŏl-lyong ends up having dishes thrown at him. Hyŏl-lyong's fight is with a critic named Yi Myŏng-sik, through whom Kim Sa-ryang may be expressing his own views on the problem of language and literature. "Of course I'm not opposing the idea of writing in Japanese," Yi says. "I'm no linguistic chauvinist. We've got to put those of us who can write to work communicating as widely as possible our way of life, our art. We should endeavor, for the benefit of those who don't care to write in Japanese, and for the benefit of the art of those of us who can't, to take advantage of the support and assistance of knowledgeable Japanese intellectuals in having them translated. It's absurd that some say that those who can't write in Japanese shouldn't write at all."[54] Kim Sa-ryang expressed similar views in a 1939 essay:

> Anyone who would sacrifice everything to write in Japanese must, I believe, possess positive motives, such as communicating news of Korea's culture, life and people to as broad a readership in Japan [naichi] as possible; or of being a go-between for spreading Korean culture throughout East Asia and the world. Without such motives, where is the necessity of writing in Japanese, a difficult language, and throwing away one's own tongue as well as the many readers to whom one should be speaking?[55]

In *Tenma* Hyŏl-lyong's response to such opinions was simply to call the use of Korean, now that Japan was waging full-scale war, tantamount to treason. The next day, sobering up at a café, Hyŏl-lyong sees in the newspaper that a writer, Tanaka, whom he had known in Tokyo is currently at a Seoul hotel on his way back to Japan from Manchuria. Thinking this a chance to redeem himself, he races to the hotel and naps for hours on a lobby sofa waiting for his acquaintance to return. He needs to waylay Tanaka for this: Hyŏl-lyong had met a young French woman in Seoul and, trying to impress her, had placed in her purse a photograph of himself that had appeared in some cheap magazine. But when this Frenchwoman was subsequently arrested at the Soviet border on suspicion of espionage, Hyŏl-lyong too comes under suspicion. Only an influential bureaucrat and journal editor by the name of Ōmura was able to keep him out of jail. Hyŏl-lyong has few friends left. As his career and even his sanity have deteriorated since his early literary successes, he has become desperate for attention. He loudly calls for support of *Naisen ittai* and attacks fellow writers when they are not forthcoming with it. But Ōmura, realizing that a discredited Hyŏl-lyong is useless to the Japanese, has told him he would do better to retreat to a Buddhist temple, take the tonsure, and abandon worldly affairs. Desperate, Hyŏl-lyong hopes that Tanaka, an old classmate of Ōmura, can keep him out of forced internal exile.

That night Hyŏl-lyong searches for Tanaka in one bar after the next. He passes a peasant who is selling flowering peach branches and buys one. At the next bar he finds Tanaka in the company of a Japanese professor in Seoul named Tsunoi. Neither is pleased to have been discovered by Hyŏl-lyong. Tanaka regards all the Korean writers he has met on his trip, including Hyŏl-lyong, as rank amateurs. For his part, the arrogant Tsunoi thinks Hyŏl-lyong the perfect example of young Korean manhood, "a race of utter cowards afflicted with inferiority complexes, impudent and given to factiousness."[56] Kim Sa-ryang made it clear that neither of these Japanese is much to admire either, but for the moment, his Tanaka is pleased to have Tsunoi confirm his view of Hyŏl-lyong, who is just then telling them that he is Korea's Rimbaud and praising Ōmura's program for Japanization. Rebuffed by Ōmura himself when he shows up at the bar, an intoxicated Hyŏl-lyong steps out in an alleyway, places the peach branch between his legs and shouts, "I'm going up to heaven! Hyŏl-lyong is going to ride these peach blossoms up to heaven!" (161). Kim Yun-sik reads this scene as suggestive of Christ's crucifixion even as it confirms Hyŏl-lyong's vulgarity. As Hyŏl-lyong drops the branch, he turns to see Tanaka urinating in public. While the three Japanese hail a cab, Hyŏl-lyong begs Ōmura to have the order that he retreat to a Buddhist temple rescinded. The novella concludes with the following day, with a hungover Hyŏl-lyong aimlessly roaming the city in the rain and wishing he were dead. He ends up back in the sleazy back ways of Sinchon, searching for the same brothel he woke up in at the start of the novella. Frantic, he knocks on locked gates and shouts as a storm approaches, "Help this Japanese [naichijin]!" "Open up! Let this Japanese in! . . . I'm no damned Korean [yobo] anymore! I'm Gennoue Ryūnosuke! Ryūnosuke! Let Ryūnosuke in!" (167).

"In the end, Hyŏl-lyong was unable to ascend to heaven" (162), but at one point in the novella the narrator interrupts to let us know Hyŏl-lyong is not a bad person, just a weakling with limited literary talent. His despair is not entirely his own fault—it reflects Korea. Hyŏl-lyong's fifteen years in Tokyo were no better than a stray dog's life (143). Try as he might to pass as a Japanese, his Korean face and tattered wardrobe gave him away. To compensate he pretended to be descended from Silla royalty, and that he was a famous writer back home in Seoul. It made the daily indignities easier to bear, and it helped him seduce a woman or two. In time he began to believe the lies he told about himself. Now back in Korea, he's just a fool who doesn't know it.

This may seem a cruel novella for one Korean to have written about another, and perhaps it was, but Hyŏl-lyong was not meant to be representative of all Koreans, and Kim Sa-ryang did put some part of himself in his portrait of him. He almost immediately regretted how one or two critics in Japan chose to allegorize his portrait of Hyŏl-lyong.[57] Kim Sa-ryang owed his success to his entree into the Tokyo *bundan*, but at the same time he understood the theatricality of being a writer in a language that few other than his colonial masters could read. It was a problem that beleaguered Kim Sa-ryang his entire career. A colonial intellectual who wrote almost exclusively in Japanese—though *Tenma* is peppered with Korean, French, and German words—he nonetheless understood the risk of his use of Japanese being interpreted as collaboration, and he frequently defended the use of Korean. "In a country where those who are literate can read nothing but Korean," Kim Sa-ryang wrote, "it is no proof of a love for our culture that all our writers have suddenly decided to write in Japanese."[58]

Eventually Kim Sa-ryang's doubts led him to move away from further accommodation with Japan. After his arrest by the police in Kamakura in late 1941, he joined the armed resistance against the empire, and reportedly died in 1950 a citizen of the Democratic People's Republic of Korea, which had dispatched him to the new war's front as a journalist. In hindsight Kim Sa-ryang was able to accomplish something Kim Mun-jip was not, and that is some part of why he is regarded today as less a pro-Japanese collaborationist. "The moment of the most abject dependency," writes Neil Larsen in *Modernism and Hegemony*, "by seemingly offering no resistance to the rationalizing agency of the modern, colonizing culture, derives from this extreme uneasiness the strategic advantage of being able to trump the superior power."[59] Kim Sa-ryang did this in *Tenma*, just as Kim Mun-jip failed to do in his own fiction. By the end of the war, there were 900,000 Japanese in Korea and 2.4 million Koreans in Japan.[60] The tragic history of the Korean peninsula in the twentieth century, a history that made ambivalence a costly option for Korean intellectuals, is not only the tragic personal history of men such as Kim Mun-jip and Kim Sa-ryang, but some of why Japanese literature in the twentieth century is also tragic. Kim Yun-sik's description of Kim Mun-jip's "martyr's fate" and his "theatrical fate" in the same breath was the dilemma of this colonial bind, and for both those who were bound and those who did the binding.

"Even if Korean writers commit *tenkō*," Hayashi Fusao once said, "they have no fatherland to return to."[61] Arishima Takeo may have thought Korean literature an oxymoron, but Ishikawa Takuboku's (1886–1912) poem on the occasion of the 1910 annexation invoked the issue of nationhood with a different take, one darkened by Itō's assassination abroad and the start of political trials at home: "The Korean nation rendered in deep black ink on the map; I hear the winds of autumn" (*chizu no ue Chōsenkoku ni kuroguro to sumi o nuritsutsu aki-kaze o kiku*).[62] Takuboku might have had a premonition of what was in the offing. The point of a chapter on Korea in a history of modern Japanese literature is that while modern Japanese literature developed in tandem with the Japanese nation-state, when that nation-state embarked on expansion the parallelism broke down and produced writers, in the Japanese language but not Japanese themselves, as abject as Kim Mun-jip and as despondent as Kim Sa-ryang.

Meiji statesman Mori Arinori argued early in his career that Japanese was a weak, deficient, and isolated language.[63] Among the strategies he advocated to remedy this was the extension of the language throughout what would later be called the Greater East Asia Co-Prosperity Sphere. It would be strengthened and empowered through its encounters with the other languages of the empire, a theory Mori shared with Hayashi Fusao, who believed the Korean and Japanese languages were destined to converge.[64] This was a utopian creolization that, as we see in the next chapter, was only realized—minus the utopian part, and with other languages—once the Second World War was over and it was Japan's turn to be occupied. Eventually Kim Mun-jip's *Arirantōge*, the tale of a Korean man's abject love for Japanese women, will be retold after the war in a novel set thousands of years in the future and in a universe where the hierarchy of races will be quite different. I take this up in the conclusion, but we are not even halfway there yet, and there is more real history that has to happen first.

Creole Japan

On 22 September 1950, a bloodied employee of the accounting office at Nihon University ran to a central Tokyo police box, where he told officers that he and two other university employees had just had nearly two million yen of the university's payroll stolen from them. He identified the thief as Yamagiwa Hiroyuki, a nineteen-year-old driver also employed at Nihon University. Yamagiwa had shouted, "Hey, stop!" (*Hei sutappu*) to the car in which the accountants were conveying the payroll. They gave a ride to Yamagiwa, but he suddenly stabbed his fellow driver with a jackknife. Attacking another employee to get ahold of the cash, Yamagiwa ordered the three out of the car and, taking the wheel, sped off. Alerted by a tip, two days later the authorities apprehended him and his girlfriend, Fujimoto Sabumi, in her apartment where they had been hiding. When confronted by the police, Yamagiwa turned to Fujimoto and said, "Oh, mistake!" (*Ō, misuteku!*), lending his broken English to what became known as the "Oh, Mistake! Incident."

The media played up Yamagiwa, Fujimoto, and their lack of remorse as symptomatic of the *après guerre* (*apure*) mood of Japan's

Occupation period (1945–52). John Dower, in recounting this incident, tells us that the couple "had no apparent interests beyond material consumption and sexual pleasure," but there is more to the story.[1] When interrogated by the police, Yamagiwa insisted that his name was George (a name he later had tattooed on his arm) and that he was not Japanese, a claim he insisted upon in a mishmash of Japanese and American English. I cite Yamagiwa at the beginning of this chapter in order to set the stage for a discussion of the widespread and significant creolization of not only language but many realms of public discourse and culture, including literature, during the Occupation, when approximately four hundred thousand foreign troops were stationed at over seven hundred installations along the length of the Japanese archipelago.

The hybrid (*zasshūteki*) history of Japanese thought and culture has been recognized for centuries, long before the country's encounter with the West and going back to initial contacts with the Asian continent. In 1955, left-wing critic Katō Shūichi summed up the compound cultural history of Japan in the wake of a conservative, post-Occupation reaction against Americanization. "The problem of Japanese culture commences with the fact that is hybridized," wrote Katō, "and ends with the positive recognition of that fact."[2] But hybridization, however necessary as a preliminary step in the evolution of a creolized culture, is not the same thing as creolization, defined for my purposes as "an apt metaphor for the transformation that languages and cultures undergo when, far from their original heritage, they turn into new, recombinant formations."[3] Creolization, certainly, in the extended sense that term is now used, but also in that process an assault on the Japanese language as a medium of communication. While Yamagiwa might have deluded himself in thinking he could speak American argot, the result here and in other examples is a crisis of signification in the wake of the war and under the pressure of Japan's subsequent neocolonization until the signing of the Treaty of San Francisco on 28 April 1952. We need to keep in mind Derek Bickerton's insight that a speaker of a pidgin, like Yamagiwa, "is a man who has just begun to build his second house when some disaster destroys his first one."[4]

The breakdown of language in postwar Japan commenced at the moment of the nation's rout. Hirohito's 15 August broadcast to the empire, his *gyokuon hōsō*, left more than a few listeners mystified as to its message, not least of all because no Japanese word for defeat or surrender was mentioned in it. The emperor, never good at public speaking (his nickname, the "ah-so emperor," swept the nation),[5] compounded his problem with a prepared text that a court scholar of classical Chinese had purposefully larded with nearly unintelligible Sino-Japanese locutions. All this was prophetic, for as Tsurumi Shunsuke would point out, words were to be key in the Occupation period. His examples include the substitution of *shūsen* (war's end) for *haisen* (war's defeat), and *shinchū* (stationed) in lieu of the blunter *senryō* (occupied). But Tsurumi's observation is misleading, too, since words had been key to Japanese polity since the start of its empire, surely since philologist Ueda Kazutoshi returned from his Meiji-period sojourn to Germany and announced a project to create a standard Japanese not for the ease of communication within the home islands, but as a pedagogy for use in spreading Japanese — first as a lingua franca, but eventually as a national language — throughout a Japan-dominated East Asia.

The ban on English in the Japanese language during the war commenced in 1938 with the promulgation of the National Mobilization Law (*Kokka sōdōin hō*), when efforts to impose a pure Japanese language on occupied territories, in which more than one hundred languages were spoken, were already under way. Ambitions for the unity of Japan and Korea (*Naisen ittai*) and for Taiwan's imperial subjectification (*kōminka*) rested squarely upon this linguistic imaginary. A quasi-creolization project, it produced both a burdensome, multilingual high literature (Chang Hyŏk-chu's "Gakidō," for example) and the ad hoc pidgins (*Naisengo*) spoken in Kim Sa-ryang's depictions of working-class mixed marriages.[6] Had it been fully realized, the Greater East Asia Co-Prosperity Sphere would have ruled one-third of the world and half its population, a realm within which hundreds of vernaculars were spoken. The need for colonial language policies was paramount. A frequently announced goal of Japan's dominion was the stemming of the growth of Western languages in Asia and their replacement with *Nichigo*, the language emanating from the Tokyo-centered imperial metropole.

The result was a myth of a language so pure, so oddly incapable of saying so many things, that it would be blamed for Japan's defeat. "The story is told," writes Nanette Gottlieb, "of Matsusaka [Tadanori] . . . pointing out the window at the ruins of Tokyo and asserting that the devastation had come about because the people of Japan had not had the words to criticize the military."[7] There is also the irony, germane to postwar Japanese literature, that many writers after August 1945 would want to reform the Japanese language and some actually harm it in the quest to redress the tyranny that it represented (and was represented in) before the defeat. The history of postwar Japanese literature, that is to say literature published in the decade after the Japanese surrender to the Allies, is keen on characterizing it as Americanized, but in practice that usually means little more than it was chaotic, helter-skelter, simultaneously "degraded" and "liberated" in what is frankly a moral verdict. When Shiga Naoya's 1946 short story "Haiiro no tsuki" (An ashen moon) first appeared, there was a reference to an automobile's *zutō* that in 1947 became *heddoraito* (headlight). Later that year it went back to *zutō* and finally *heddoraito* again. Editors were busy domesticating English under a hardly consistent American rule.[8]

The Occupation has been characterized as a time when Japan's relations with other countries and cultures were severely circumscribed if not prohibited altogether. Robert Ward notes, "Japanese citizens, with rare exceptions, were forbidden to travel or live abroad. Foreigners, save for those employed or approved by SCAP [Supreme Commander for the Allied Powers], were forbidden to visit or reside in Japan." But Ward goes too far when he adds, "The subjects of SCAP's experiment were isolated and many, if not all, disturbing outside influences were excluded."[9] Journalist Mark Gayn, on the ground in those years, puts it right in his *Japan Diary*:

> We have introduced Arsene Lupin to Japanese moviegoers, and we have made *Gone with the Wind* a Japanese classic as well. We have inspired the radio industry of Japan to emulate the ebullience, and shallowness, and countless entertainment tricks of our own radio. We have introduced jitterbugging to the young people, and put the movie industry face to face with the crucial problem of "to kiss or not to kiss." . . . We have taught Japan's children the magic words of *jeep-u* and *gum-mu*, and, perhaps not too happily, we have introduced the opening word to her Anglo-American dictionary: A-bomb.[10]

We know this and are not surprised. Japanese may not have had permission to travel abroad, but Americans—hundreds of thousands of them—were all over Japan, and their copies of the *Reader's Digest* and Marvel comic books found their way to the black market and beyond. General Headquarters had no plans to supplant the Japanese language with English, but Japanese themselves seriously debated the merits of such a move. Shiga Naoya may have been the exception for thinking French the way to go, but the year 1946 was full of literati voices calling for the radical reform or wholesale replacement of Japanese if they were to become a truly cultural (*bunka*) nation. Part of the urgency may have been inspired by the fear that, lest the Japan do something themselves, it would be done for them. But some other part was a predictable backlash against jingoistic language policies everyone recalled from the war years. If schools teaching English conversation sprung up like mushrooms in the wake of defeat, and if church services where sermons delivered by foreign missionaries were suddenly more popular, it was in some measure a reaction to the ban on English in Japanese public life and discourse since the promulgation of the National Mobilization Law and the subsequent demonization of much that represented, accurately or not, Western modernity.

In the early days of the American interregnum, two things were faddish: a return to social dancing (encouraged by the Japan Communist Party) and English lessons.[11] First on the latter's bandwagon may have been Ogawa Kiku-matsu, president of a publishing company and who, only hours after hearing the emperor's surrender speech, decided to come out by mid-September 1945 with a book entitled *Nichibei kaiwa techō* (The Japanese-English conversation hand-book). At a slim thirty-two pages and attractively priced at eighty sen, it sold upward of four million copies within a few months, a record for the Japanese publishing world not broken until the 1980s.[12] Of more interest is the radio program *Kamu kamu eikaiwa!* (Come! Come! English conversation!), whose heyday commenced with the assumption on 1 February 1946 of Hirakawa Tadaichi, a Japanese graduate of the University of Washington, of the role as host. Forced to return to Japan in 1937 when his wife's U.S. visa expired, he found work with the international service of NHK during the war. *Kamu kamu eikaiwa!*, a hit program until its cancellation in March 1951, was broadcast every weekday from 6:00 to 6:15 p.m. Its goal was to teach English conversation skills. Its name derived from its theme song, which went, "Come come everybody; How do you do and how are you / Won't you have some candy, one and two and three, four, five / let's all sing a happy song tra la la." Each Friday the program featured a foreign, which is to say American, guest. But the program's real effec-tiveness was ideological rather than linguistic. Listeners were taught to compre-hend such English sentences as "Well, newspapers do tell the truth nowadays."[13]

It was this program, and not the print *Nichibei kaiwa techō*, that encouraged the fantasy that the Japanese would become an English-speaking nation, but it also prompted amalgamation of English with Japanese in mass culture. The show was popular across demographics, and by 1947 had spawned a thousand fan clubs across the country. Its glory days ended with the close of the formal Occupation, but its impact on the postwar generation was lasting. The *Cam-bridge History of Japan* tells us, "Hirakawa Tadaichi . . . may well have been the most effective advertiser and popularizer of linguistic as well as cultural and political 'Americanisms.'"[14] His characters Jack (James) and Betty (Smith), American icons known by future generations of Japanese schoolchildren, were introduced by Hirakawa in 1949, along with many English loanwords and such hybridized, unidiomatic Japanese sentences as "Kore wa ippon no enpitsu desu" (This is a one pencil). The irony is that while General Headquarters and Japanese officialdom were busy devising ways to simplify the Japanese language, the influx of English words into the language was making it incomprehensible.

The penetration of American culture cannot be reduced to a litany of amusing anecdotes of a nation barely coming to grips with its subordination to a new American world order at home and abroad. The importance of English — a trope, really, for something as geopolitical as lexical — is evident across the expanse of Japanese high and low culture, from the most sacrosanct halls of power (the English word "person" was used in postwar cabinet meetings as a euphemism for *Tennō heika*, "His Majesty")[15] to the most profane venues (prostitutes spoke in a slang known as *pangurishu*, a neologism coined from the loanwords for whore and English). After its defeat Japan became a place where two languages (*nijū no gengo*) coexisted (*heizon*),[16] though it took three borrowings from Chinese to say so. This sweeping intrusion/importation of once-vilified English can be illustrated with three examples from 1948 to 1950, the period of most intense Americanization: a hilarious novel, the new constitution, and some pop music.

From May to December 1950, novelist Shishi Bunroku (1893–1969) serialized in the *Asahi shinbun* an immensely popular work, *Jiyū gakkō*, or "Learning to be Free" in my loose translation of the title. A funny novel about a diverse handful of people after the war, each of whom in his or her own way tries to discover just what this new "freedom" in postwar Japan means, it was made into not one but two film versions the following year. The better of the two, made by Daiei Studios, starred Kyō Machiko and had Shindō Kaneto as its screen writer; the film and the novel it was based on went on to become icons of postwar Japan five years into its foreign occupation.

This novel may be the best example we have of how Japanese culture was being amalgamated with American, even as the United States used its supremacy to stem popular resistance to some aspects of it. In the year of its publication, demonstrations in Tokyo were prohibited; Communists were barred from holding public office; the party newspaper *Akahata* (Red Flag) was ordered to cease publication as the Red Purge began; Itō Sei's translation of *Lady Chatterley's Lover*—a novel some think *Jiyū gakkō* parodies—was confiscated; and, not least, the Korean War commenced. Americanization under these conditions was evident in what people wore, what they ate, and, most prominently, how they talked in a patois termed by Shishi the *shin Nihongo*, or "new Japanese" of the day. This new Japanese was evident everywhere. Tsurumi Shunsuke notes that high-level bureaucrats were developing a new vocabulary in Japanese and sometimes English, replacing words based on imperial proclamations with neologisms fashioned out of the vocabulary of liberal American democracy.[17] But the manufacture of a new Japanese occurred on the popular level just as conspicuously. In one scene from Shishi's novel, a well-to-do couple entertains guests at their weekend home, addressing their guests as *misesu* and *misutā*, offering them *kokutēru*, serving trout sautéed in olive oil, and abandoning their guests in short order to go enjoy a round of golf. "Everything," Shishi writes, "was American-style" (*subete ga, Beikoku-shiki datta*).[18] It is full of newly coined expressions, such as "tonde mo happun"—the *tonde mo* of *tonde mo nai* (preposterous) plus English "happen"—or, in another example, *nebā suki* (never like). This mixture of English with Japanese—called *konketsugo*, or literally, "mixed-blood language"—is a hallmark of this novel, and I speculate that it reprised the anxieties of what the imposition of the Japanese language on colonial Korea, Taiwan, and Manchuria had done with its own creolization.[19] This is why *Jiyū gakkō* retains a modest place in literary history, not the fact that it was the best-selling novel during the Occupation. Some of the English-Japanese pidgin in *Jiyū gakkō* reflects usage then current in Japan (thirty young employees at the *Asahi shinbun* supplied Shishi with three hundred slang words), and the rest was of Shishi's own coinage but went on to become common after the success of his book. Much of the novel's slang—*ikare-ponchi, kyandi bōi*—was transient and now lost to the language (my 1968 edition of the novel has footnotes to explain much of the vocabulary), but others have been retained to the present day.

One day early in the novel, Komako, a thirtyish woman who studied English literature at university before the war and now supports herself by translating (she is working on a collection of Eleanor Roosevelt's essays) overhears a Japanese couple ten years younger than her speaking a strange mixture of Japanese and foreign words—English, she is sure, but unlike any English she learned in school:

Komako wasn't sure what their argument was all about, but what really stumped her was her total inability to understand the language the two of them were using. If it were English, then she thought she'd know even the more difficult idioms; but what was coming out their mouths seemed utterly different from anything with which she was heretofore familiar. Just what country's language was this? Was this the birth of the new era's Japanese?[20]

The use of English in Japanese fiction was nothing new in 1950. It had been a mark of modern Japanese literature since the nineteenth century. But it was never a pidgin in the sense that the conversations in *Jiyū gakkō* are. That is a development that had to wait until the Occupation period. In his book on creoles and Japanese, linguist Tanaka Katsuhiko anecdotally analyzed a Japanese-English pidgin that developed first in the vicinities of the Allied military bases and then spread. He recalled as a high school student hearing a prostitute say to a GI, "Me *wa ne*, want money *na no yo*," and calls it typical of how a pidgin utilizing English vocabulary and Japanese syntax was common at the time.[21]

The Japanese-English pidgin of the Occupation period was a popular response to the extraordinary situation of a foreign military on Japanese territory and not the result of an educated elite appropriating select foreign words and deploying them in such high-cultural texts as novels and treatises, as did Meiji enthusiasms for *wakon yōsai* (Japanese spirit, Western technology). Yoshimi Shun'ya has insisted that the influence of military bases on the postwar Americanization of Japan cannot be ignored, and while Americanization in East Asia in the 1920s was a phenomenon starting in the large cities of Tokyo, Osaka, Seoul, and Shanghai, it did not reach rural communities as postwar media could.[22] That said, one might expect to find in Shishi's novel descriptions of encounters between Japanese working-class people and Americans, the very scenes where a pidgin might be convenient. But we do not. What is striking in *Jiyū gakkō*, a novel about the Americanization of Japan under the Occupation, is the utter *absence* of any foreigners; indeed, the steadfast refusal of the novel to ever take note of the fact that Japan is under foreign rule. "Jeeps, movies, and democracy all came together," writes historian Carol Gluck, "with the result that the definition of the modern swerved in a material and populist direction simultaneously. . . . To say that a nation under foreign occupation had little choice about the source of such influence does not belie the evident enthusiasm for American versions of material modernity in the postwar years."[23] The question of the impetus for such enthusiasm aside, the agency producing cultural hybridity on so many levels remains unarticulated. The hand behind the pid-ginization—in time, the creolization—of Japanese culture remains invisible. Like the postwar constitution and popular song lyrics, or the jokes and rumors rife under the Occupation, subjectivity would appear only in disguise.

There are plenty of references in *Jiyū gakkō* to the *shin-kenpō* (new constitution). It inspires and permits the novel's characters to variously pursue their newly granted freedom. But like the language used by the novel's younger characters, the language of the Shōwa constitution was equally unfamiliar to many. It "was remarkable not only for its content but also for the modernity of its language,"[24] a veritable "revolution in legal texts."[25] Those observations lead us to another. As Gayatri Spivak could see, the Shōwa constitution provided a "different set of manipulations of narratives of origin and end."[26] The story of how the Shōwa constitution was drafted in English and only subsequently translated into Japa-nese is well known and has been told by many. It is not so unusual a story. The Irish Republic's constitution was written in English and only after translated into Gaelic; constitutions that exist in officially multilingual nation-states, too, have been drafted in one language only to be recast in others. The Meiji constitution, though composed in Sino-Japanese ("the Latin of Japan"[27]), was redolent of En-glish as well: in *From Sea to Sea*, Rudyard Kipling has fun at the constitution's expense when he writes, "It is a terrible thing to study at close quarters, because it is so pitifully English. . . . All the Japanese officials from police upwards seem to be clad in Europe clothes, and never do those clothes fit. I think the Mikado made them at the same time as the Constitution."[28]

Dick Hebdige uses the term "versioning" to describe "an invocation of someone else's voice to help you say what you want to say."[29] Ventriloquism was not rare during the Occupation. The initial draft of Hirohito's 1 January 1946 speech renouncing his divinity (sort of) was drafted by Harold Henderson during his lunch break, while he was lying on his bed in the Daiichi Hotel.[30] More generally, of course, the history of modern Japan and its literature is in-conceivable without translation. The Japanese word *kenpō* is of Chinese lineage and was adopted to translate "constitution" in 1873. Both the earliest modern Japanese novelist, Futabatei Shimei, and the most popular, Murakami Haruki, allegedly wrote some of their fiction first in Russian or English, respectively, and only then translated it into Japanese. It is, in fact, a cliché to point out that somehow Japanese modernity is managed only through the intercession of a Western language. But whatever the philological histories, the constitutions of many twentieth-century nations were feigned to be written, to borrow one of our American phrases, "by the people and for the people," not "by us and for them." Always a utopian project (Fredric Jameson calls the drafting of imaginary constitutions a "hobby"),[31] the postwar Japanese constitution started out as the result of twenty-five Americans working furiously if often cluelessly in General Headquarters over the course of nine days in February 1946. (They rushed in the hope to have the Japanese announce "their" constitution on George Washington's birthday.) These Americans, despite their liberal sympathies (most were Roosevelt New Dealers), were members of an occupying force that allotted the Japanese a full fifteen minutes to look over their draft—written in a language not their own—on 19 February, codifying a document that Americans admitted was "alien."[32] What Edward Seidensticker hailed as "among the Sacred Books of the East,"[33] Dan Henderson described more profanely when he wrote, "The postwar birth of the new Constitution was necessarily a Caesarean operation attended by an alien midwife,"[34] and one continually undermined by the Japanese state beginning no later than the establishment of the Self-Defense Forces in the 1950s.

The English-language origins of the constitution were then and still hidden and denied if exposed, despite the fact, as Gayn wrote in his diary, "It is an alien constitution foisted on the Japanese government, and then represented as a native product, when any Japanese high school student simply by reading it can perceive its foreign origin."[35] John Dower notes that the media at the time pointed out how "awkward" and "strange" the Japanese of the new draft constitution was,[36] but the press never went so far as to print any assertion that the document had an alien origin. Linguist Kyoko Inoue, in her study of the constitution, notes that the National Diet Library in Tokyo still will not allow any but members of the Diet access to the important minutes of the legislature's 1946 subcommittee deliberations over the draft constitution. "The only reasonable explanation" for this, she reasons, is to conceal, even after Japan had regained its sovereignty, "the true origins of the Japanese Constitution."[37]

The putative authorship of any modern constitution is tricky, not least of all because the "we" in so many nation-states is supposed to be its subject in all senses of the word. Our own American constitution is no exception. Howard Ziff usefully contrasts the Declaration of Independence—whose authorship was clearly established by the signatures at its end—with the constitution eight years later written "by the people," its signatures technically not that of authors but only of representatives of the states, whose "people" are the true writers. Ziff sees that our constitution "was authored by no particular person but anchored in the fiction of the general made possible by print."[38] This is in contrast with the Meiji constitution, whose authorship was, according to George Akita, clearly attributed to the emperor in order to forestall public opposition to it.[39]

The tide of public opinion was of little concern to General Headquarters in 1946, but the effects of an American-imposed constitution have been long lasting. Katō Norihiro has argued the postwar period can never be considered over until the constitution, whose foreign authorship "lies at the core of Japan's defeat and experience of occupation," is submitted to a national referendum for approval or rejection.[40] Part of the problem for Katō and other historical revisionists lies in the stylistic hybridity of the Japanese version of the constitution. While many observers in Japan, such as Hayashi Shirō, have noted the *hon'yakukusai* (translationese) tenor of the constitution,[41] Kyoko Inoue has best argued that there was an illocutionary inconsistency in the English draft of the Shōwa constitution, one that arose from the divide between the Americans' intentions and their real-world actions. Illocution and illocutionary force, terms from speech act theory, can be explained this way: illocution is when language makes something happen. In the American constitution, illocutionary force is uniformly and consistently expressed through the use of the modal verb "shall." "All legislative powers," for instance, "shall be vested in a Congress": here we have the implied agency of "We, the People" commanding their government to establish said institution. Not surprisingly, there are many examples of this kind of construction in the English draft of the Shōwa constitution. Article 31, for example, begins, "No person shall be deprived of life or liberty." It is almost certain that the drafters meant this to mean in effect "We, the [Japanese] people," order (our) government to do such.

But Article 20 says, "Freedom of religion is guaranteed," not "shall be guaranteed." Whose freedom? And guaranteed by whom? Inoue argues that here we have a distinct shift in authorship. It is no longer the Japanese people instructing their government as to what they shall or shall not do, but the *real* American authors of the constitution *telling* the Japanese people what rights they have or don't. Inoue, citing more examples of such inconsistencies, holds that the authors of the Shōwa constitution were not always uncomfortable with imposing rights and obligations upon a people ostensibly entitled to decide such things for themselves.

How did Japanese officials react to this English-language draft, and what transpired during the process of its translation? Like America's, Japan's Meiji constitution was consistent in its deployment of linguistic constructions. In a series of uniformly simple, nonpast-tense sentences, the Meiji constitution's assertions "reinforce the historical reality that the government had assumed the responsibility of ruling on behalf of the nation, and granted the citizens such rights as it saw fit." But the Japanese translation of the English draft of the postwar constitution, with modalities such as the English "shall" unavailable to it, replaces illocutionary commands with plain assertions. Inoue argues that this was a subtle encoding on the part of the Japanese translators to take note of the historical reality; it was not the Japanese people instructing its servant, the government, over what it shall and shall not do, but instead the American Occupation informing the Japanese people what those conditions would be. Compounding this was the translation of English "agentless passive" sentences ("All the people shall be respected as individuals") with topic-comment constructions in Japanese,[42] strongly implying, since the topic marker wa establishes the nominal it follows as previously established in discourse, as something which already exists. In this sense a Meiji constitution bestowed by the emperor upon his subjects is not so different from a Shōwa constitution given them by General Headquarters. Here, Inoue demurs from the views expressed by earlier commentators, such as Robert Ward, who insisted, "The American-authored constitution of 1947 was in spirit and provisions almost a complete inversion of its predecessor, the Meiji constitution of 1889,"[43] and John Maki's equally categorical claim that the postwar constitution "was not only completely out of tune with the former constitutional style, but with its own society."[44] Inoue concludes, "While the sense of command [in the Japanese translation] is lost, the actual language is faithful to the historical context because it was not the Japanese people who were placing limits on the government."[45]

One could argue, then, that the Shōwa constitution is not a hybrid document but one that neatly transfers the citizenry's subjecthood from one imperial regime to another. But it is not that neat. As I explore in the next chapter, there are terms and phrases in the Shōwa constitution, such as shōchō (symbol), that are uninterpretable in Japanese without reference to their English antecedents. It continues to be a document troubled by unidiomatic phrasing. Again, this is not a problem unique to the Japanese constitution, but it is indicative of a postcolonial and creolized linguistic, cultural milieu. As Mori Arinori presciently said in 1873, "The laws of the state can never be preserved in the language of Japan."[46]

My third example is not just linguistic but musical. Western music was introduced to Japan in the nineteenth century via Japan's military and public schools, resulting in an amalgam termed *kokugaku* (national music), parallel to national literature, theater, language, and so forth, and which may be called a first stage in a process of creolization parallel with the myriad hybridizations forged during modernization.[47] No number of casual encounters between Japanese prostitutes and American service personnel would have left much of an impact on the language of the nation as a whole. It would take more than that. After the defeat, the first group of Japanese to accommodate GIs was, if not sex workers, then jazz musicians. As in Germany (the first American jeep to approach Dachau had "boogie-woogie" inscribed on it),[48] jazz swept Japan after its wartime demonization as decadent. Troops required entertainment on base and it was popular to bring in jazz bands. Japanese brokers, forerunners of today's production companies, rose to the challenge. In the first years of the Occupation they revived the prewar hybrid Japanese entertainer: Nancy Umemoto, Peggy Hayama, Frankie Sakai, Ai George, Frank Nagai, and others. These musicians, or rather their handlers, might have thought their Americanized nomenclature would make them more familiar. But instead these names were often a source of humor for soldiers, sailors, and airmen, in keeping with Derek Bickerton's insight that creoles are "naughty children" who refuse to do what their linguistic parents tell them to.[49] Who *was* impressed was apparently the Japanese public, who came to know postwar, Americanized jazz via radio broadcasts and, with Oscar Peterson's historic tour in 1953, live. By the outbreak of the Korean War, there were 150 jazz bands in Tokyo alone,[50] a consequence of the Occupation's policy to promote American music and suppress kabuki, *rōkyoku*, *kōdan*, and other Japanese performance arts deemed feudal and antidemocratic.

Modern popular music (known broadly as *ryūkōka*) in Japan, and the distribution of it via radio, has a history going back to the early Taishō period. Edward Seidensticker dates it to Matsui Sumako's 1913 hit "Katyusha's Song."[51] Later, modern popular music was the result of the nexus between the broadcasting and recording industries in the 1930s. But music's rapid Americanization accelerated after the Occupation took control of radio programming and emphasized light music and jazz via such programming as *Keiongaku no jikan* (Light Music Hour) and *Jazu no oie* (Jazz for Your Home) on NHK beginning in September 1945. Once Occupation radio station WVTR (later FEN) was up and running, urban Japan was inundated with English-language radio, but since the language itself was unintelligible to most, it was not surprising that musical programming attracted the most Japanese listeners.

Consequently, English began to infiltrate Japanese parlance in ways that included popular music. After 1945, its melodies, lyrics, and performances carried the burden of shifting from a wartime culture to a postwar one. The Japanese music industry catered to the revived preference for American popular music by creating a class of entertainers with not only hybrid names but hybridized music. Examples include "Nyū Tōkyō songu" and "Jiipu wa hashiru" in 1946, followed by others such as "Tsū yangu" and "Wuddo ai rabyū," all popular with listeners if deprecated by music critics who deplored what they considered the deliberate bastardization of Japanese music by General Headquarters intent on Americanizing Japanese national life. There was no stopping it, however. Entertainers such as Eri Chiemi and Yukimura Izumi were noted for pronouncing even Japanese lyrics as if they were English. Soon, just what was a Japanese lyric versus an English lyric became hard to tell. "Jiipu wa hashiru" goes:

> Smart *na kawaii* body
> *Mune mo suku yo na* handle *sabaki*
> *Machi no ninki o atsumete hashiru*
> Hello Hello
> Jeep *wa hashiru* Jeep *wa hashiru*[52]

If the icons in Japanese popular culture of the American soldier were chewing gum, Lucky Strikes, and caramel candies, the jeep was a symbol of American power. But it was not the only one. The song "Tamaran-bushi" from 1952 went: "Japan *Yokosuka* wonderful / Beer *mo* girl *mo* very nice / Cherry *hana saku ano oka* ni / Sweet home *o tsukuritai*." "Tamaran-bushi" was attacked for its vulgarity (*teizoku*) in the newspapers. The Yokosuka Chamber of Commerce, which had commissioned it for a tourism campaign, was harassed by the local teachers union for its "colonial complex." The lyrics were rewritten.[53]

By the time commercial radio programming began in 1953, personalities such as Tony Tani were entertaining the nation with a DJ's patois seamlessly hybridized, as in his opening "Ladies and gentlemen! And *ottsan, okkasan*." But the creolization of Japanese popular music proceeded at the level of its sound as well as words. Again, this phenomenon was not uniquely postwar. Japanized jazz in the prewar period was the product of music composed by Kaga Masao, music that was *erejii-chō* (elegiac), such as his 1931 hit "Sake wa namida ka tameiki ka"

(Is Saké a Teardrop or a Sigh?) and thus not wholly foreign to Japanese tastes. But the postwar's boogie-woogie rhythms were largely unprecedented in Japanese music. Popularized by Clarence "Pinetop" Smith in 1929, boogie-woogie had its start in the 1910s in the American South and Midwest. Musically it has been described as a "primitive" pianistic adjunct to blues music, characterized by a steady, repetitive *ostinato* figure in the left hand or bass, emphasis on the last beat. Eventually it was codified in three forms: the eight-bar pattern, the twelve-bar pattern, and the sixteen-bar pattern. It was not, to be sure, respectable music in middle-class African American homes. It was a countercultural practice within prewar African American culture, though by 1938 it was being performed at New York's Carnegie Hall. There were some attempts to import boogie-woogie rhythms to Japan before 1945. Hattori Ryōichi, modern Japan's most important popular composer, wrote songs in the 1930s that incorporated boogie-woogie rhythms of a complexity then unencountered in Japanese popular music. But it would not be until the Occupation, specifically the years 1947 through 1949, that boogie-woogie would sweep Japan and dominate popular music of that period, a result in part due to the influence of African American service personnel in occupied Japan—jazz after the war, unlike before, was distinctively African American in tenor—but also because of the fortuitous collaboration of Hattori and the singer who would become known as the Queen of Boogie-Woogie, Kasagi Shizuko. Her vocals were identified by Japanese music critics as part of the same primitivist modernism they located in Duke Ellington and Cab Calloway.[54]

Hattori was drafted during the war and served three years in China. He was repatriated on the first ship out of Shanghai in December 1945 and headed straight to Tokyo's Nichigeki Music Hall to resume work. In February 1947 he staged a production entitled "Jazz Carmen," an adaptation of the American hit "Carmen Jones" which was hailed in the newspapers as proof of postwar Japan's popular music revival. The newspapers also took note of who played Carmen, pregnant star Kasagi Shizuko. Kasagi was from Osaka, the adopted daughter of a charcoal maker. She debuted on stage in 1927 in a local Shōchiku Girls' Revue musical production, but met Hattori only in 1938 when she was living in Tokyo and performing swing music with the Shōchiku Revue at the Imperial Theater. By 1939, Kasagi typified swing in Japan. Stage critic Futaba Jūzaburō wrote at the time with hyperbole, "Her swing feeling is something that contemporary Japanese singers are unable to express. . . . We have been searching almost desperately for those feelings in our country. But Kasagi Shizuko turned our melancholy into hope and joy."[55] Kasagi and Hattori began to record hit music together in 1939 with "Bugle and a Girl," reminiscent of Benny Goodman with its call and response to a "malleable tripartite,"[56] quite innovative for its day. Hits such as the song "Hotto Chaina" (Hot China) about Shanghai soon followed. In his memoirs, Hattori hailed Kasagi as a born vaudevillian.[57] Their greatest collaboration would happen in September 1947 when she recorded his hit song, "Tokyo Boogie-Woogie," the most notable song of the Occupation period. With sales of only a hundred thousand records, it was not a true best seller at the time; its rhythm was held too new and strange.[58] But Hattori recalls how black and white American GIs crowded the recording studio to listen to Kasagi when the Japanese manager of the nearby NCO club brought them over. Hattori says they were a nuisance, but there was no way to get rid of them. "Nihon wa senryōka da," he recalled. "Japan was under occupation."[59]

The song was an eight-bar rhythm that Hattori claimed he was inspired to write after hearing an American boogie-woogie over WVTR, though he also told a more fanciful version of its origins, something having to do with watching the straps "swing" back and forth on a Chūō line train. Tōhō Studios put it in a film and Nichigeki staged a production of "Tokyo Boogie-Woogie," in March 1948, the year it soared to the top of the charts. A boogie-woogie boom followed. Hattori wrote thirty boogie-woogie songs and recorded them all, and he was not alone. To "Tokyo Boogie-Woogie" was added "Osaka Boogie," "Hokkaido Boogie" and "Hakata Boogie"; there was "Home Run Boogie," "Hey Hey Boogie," "Boogie-Woogie Age," "Sakura Boogie," "Oriental Boogie," "*Michi-yuki* Boogie," even "Samisen Boogie." Kasagi sang most of these. She had many fans, including the president of the University of Tokyo, writer Yoshikawa Eiji, painter Umehara Ryūsaburō, and director Kurosawa Akira, who wrote the lyrics to, and begged Kasagi to perform, the song "Jungle Boogie" featured in his 1948 film *Yoidore tenshi* (*Drunken Angel*).

Kasagi, Queen of Boogie, "an icon of Occupation-period culture,"[60] became the most Africanized of all Japanese popular entertainers. First there was her voice. In an aside in Shishi Bunroku's *Jiyū gakkō*, the voices of male transvestites in an Ueno bathhouse are described as "odd . . . hoarse and deep . . . like that of Kasagi Shizuko,"[61] qualities associated with African American jazz vocals. The music that she and Hattori put together was inevitably different from the American precedent, however. Their boogie-woogie lacked the syncopation of African American boogie-woogie, and Hattori applied certain conventional Japanese patterns of earlier popular music to his songs. But to Japanese of the

Figure 6.1. Kasagi Shizuko performing "Jungle Boogie." Still from Kurosawa Akira's film *Yoidore tenshi* (*Drunken Angel*; 1948)

time, this unusual music was clearly linked to American—specifically African American—popular culture, even if it failed on many counts to be recognizable to Americans as the boogie-woogie with which they were familiar. Hiraoka Masaaki, who considers Kasagi unparalleled in the history of Japanese jazz, writes, "The quality of her voice, its enunciation, its powerful volume, was without exaggeration that of an African [*kokujin*]. . . . Boogie-woogie was truly the music of Africa." Critics, pleased and distressed at the advent of such music, termed it wild (*yaseiteki*) and primitive (*genshiteki*). At the same time, Kasagi and her music were widely interpreted as what was both right and wrong about Japanese culture as a whole during the Occupation. Her fan Hiraoka again writes, "Kasagi Shizuko was part of the reality of a defeated Japan being turned into a colony of the United States. She was also a singer who, with her boogie-woogie, jazz-inspired howling on stage, ironically struck a blow for the destruction of old Japan. She was a singer who, amid the burnt-out, garbage-strewn jungle of postwar Japan, looked for liberation with her instinctive body moves."[62]

Her performances, more powerful on stage than in films or recordings, could be scenes of mass hysteria. Police had to be present to dispel crowds if necessary.[63] Her performances were total spectacle, attended in droves by the female sex workers who were among her most fervent fans.[64] Kasagi was a cult figure for those who idolized a woman who did as she pleased—Kasagi raised her daughter, as did many prostitutes, without the aid of a husband. Her popularity coincided with that of the new religions sweeping Japan at the time, often featuring their own brand of frenzy, such as Kitamura Sayo's "dancing religion" (*Odoru shukyō*). As a result, Kasagi and her music were, like the GI base culture with which they were associated, soon deemed too dangerous for young Japanese women. (It was said to risk exciting them too much at a time when many things were exciting people.) As "Tokyo Boogie-Woogie" was all the rage in Japan, it was also the time of the Tokyo War Crimes Tribunal, the strike at Tōhō Studios, the proliferation of strip joints, and the height of the semipornographic *kasutori* magazines. Some music historians in Japan account for Kasagi's boogie-woogie music as the result of a troubled population's mass hysteria produced by the experience of colonization, and they may have a point.[65] Michael Bourdaghs is not quite right when he says the lyrics of "Tokyo Boogie-Woogie" "stress the transnational, global success of boogie-woogie music,"[66] a claim made earlier by Isoda Kōichi. Rather, the once-imperial city (*teito*) of Tokyo under the "universal patriarch" Douglas MacArthur was reduced to being an American city (*Beito*), a region (*chihō*) under American authority. Only with some irony can boogie-woogie music be seen as a sign of Japan's new cosmopolitanism under such conditions.[67]

There were many in the music business who never cared for Kasagi, in fact. Shindō Ken found boogie-woogie too American for his tastes, just as East German officialdom considered the same music "degenerate" and proof of "American cultural barbarism."[68] Shindō quotes Yazawa Tamotsu's view that the music of the time was the product of a national trauma.[69] The reign of boogie-woogie in Japan was not long lived, though it continues to be performed today in a retro mode that indulges nostalgia. Gramsci observed that "what distinguishes a popular song within the context of a nation and its culture is neither its artistic aspect nor its historical origin, but the way in which it conceives the world and life, in contrast with official society."[70]

Kasagi's career went into decline after her 1950 hit "Kaimono bugi" (Shopping boogie). She retired from the music business in 1956. Many have pointed out, as proof of her music's alterity in Japan, that fans may remember the titles of Kasagi's songs but nearly no one can recall the tunes. That is not true. In 2015, I went into a Tokyo noodle shop not far from the café where Hattori claimed to have written "Tokyo Boogie-Woogie." I was curious because it was named "Kasagi Soba." When I asked the proprietor if his restaurant had any connection with the late Kasagi Shizuko, he laughed no—but the older male customers

along the counter, hearing my question, all broke out into their amateur rendi-
tions of her hits. In hindsight it makes sense that a singer already popular before
the defeat rather than a brand new celebrity would be the most prominent sign
of the postwar period's creolization. "While native audiences were bombarded,"
writes Uta Poiger about West Germany at the same time, "by a good deal of
wartime and postwar American culture with which they were unfamiliar, they
also had access to old-time favorites (movies, stars, music) and, in relatively
short order, new native products."[71] In his history of Shōwa-period music, Kata
Kōji notes that starting in 1948, the once-salutary word *apure* (après guerre)
began to take on a negative connotation. Older Japanese, he writes, "understood
the shallowness of young people to imitate Americans by mouthing words like
'okay,' 'mistake,' 'me' and 'you.'"[72] Inevitably Kasagi and her music, caught up in
this reaction, reeked of the colonial (*shokuminchiteki*). Early boogie-woogie in
the United States might have been a popular challenge to the dominant music
culture, but boogie-woogie in occupied Japan was the opposite: a slavish *imitation* of an American master culture. Jazz historian Sonobe Saburō put the case
strongly when he wrote, "Boogie-woogie held sway in all the cabarets and shows
that were outlets for the superiority and sensualness of Caucasians trumpeting
materialist culture. What was formerly solely the private, pure, primitive release
of African American people was turned into the exhibitionism of a modern evil
display of evil flowers, and soon enough became the madness of the strip shows
filling the nights."[73] Such views may be evidence of their own mass hysteria,
however. Hiraoka, who believes that if one wants to find examples of truly colonial popular music in Japan there are far better places to go, thinks Kasagi
was aware of, and felt ambivalent toward, the ironic predicament of performing American popular music in an America-ruled Japan.[74] Kasagi's music was
far more than a simple, awkward amalgam of African American and Japanese
popular music. Its layers of borrowing, reiteration, and parody go deeper than
that and are evident in what I consider her most important legacy, the 1950
song "Kaimono bugi." Kasagi and Hattori Ryoichi were originally from western
Japan, and the hybridity of their music owed a great deal to Japanese dialects
as well as to American rhythms. While attending a *yose* performance at Osaka's
Hōzenji temple, Hattori heard the *rakugo* piece "Naimonokai" (Nothing to
buy), and was inspired to compose a boogie-woogie song about shopping. The
result was a song that Kasagi complained was nearly impossible to sing, but her
attempt to do so is her best work. It was, exaggerating only slightly, Japanese rap
and, like its American equivalent, equally insolent. For that reason and others,

it is an unusual song in the history of postwar Japanese music. It was, according to Hiraoka, an *osorubeki uta*, a formidable song.[75] Its lyrics are longer than those of other postwar songs, and markedly unlyrical. Instead, it competes with complex sarcasm, self-scorn, and indiscretion. Its words do not tell us why the singer is so busy—Is there a funeral? A marriage? Is she moving?—although we can confidently guess we are listening not to the master or mistress of the household, but a servant, an unusual if not unheard of choice of perspective, as is her exuberant use of lively Kansai dialect. The song recalls Osaka *manzai* and the *rakugo* of San'yūtei Kashō in its preference for the volume of its sentiment rather than refinement. Noisy instead of elegiac, verbose instead of resonant, it is nonsensical and comic rather than plaintive or repetitive, as was so much else of the music of its time, or today's for that matter.

It is a song of extravagance, of memories for an older time when delicacies like canned salmon might actually have been available. But it is not completely nostalgic. This song, like others sung by Kasagi, focuses on everything Japanese music traditionally eschewed: regional dialect, African American jazz, volume, verbosity, the irreverent spirit. This is like authentic blues, unlike that popularized by other singers such as Awaya Noriko, in that it is richly paradoxical. Why would also this be so? Hiraoka suggests that 1945 turned everything upside down in Japan, making room for music like this to emerge into a limited space that disappeared when *enka* (ballad) singer Misora Hibari usurped Kasagi's place as top pop diva. Replacing Kasagi's racial ambiguity with gender ambiguity, Misora, who came to be considered a *kokumin kashu* (national singer)—an honor inconceivable for Kasagi—represented a domestication of boogie-woogie energy and possibility, a corrective re-Japanization of postwar culture. Misora's achievement was the synthesis of the mournful *enka* music of the postwar period (her "Ringo oiwake" alone sold seven hundred thousand records in 1952)[76] with boogie-woogie, both genres sung to launch her career but soon superseded by the post-Occupation popular music we now associate with her. While popular Japanese music tells of sadness, melancholy, memory, and desire (*akogare*), during the Occupation years it also spoke of Hawai'i, starvation, and prostitution.

Misora was an ambivalent figure herself, if only in the androgynous quality of her voice and mannerisms, as well as the persistent rumors of her mixed Japanese Korean ethnic background, perhaps inspired by the fact that the "pure" Japanese genre of *enka*, too, had murky Korean origins.[77] Ambivalent but important—so important that her debut in postwar Japan was an event on a par, according to Shindō Ken, with the advent of the journal *Kindai bungaku* (Modern Literature) and the political debates conducted in those years about *shutaisei*, translated as "subjectivity" but better served with the term "agency."[78] With Shindō's insight, I will speculate about what unites Shishi Bunroku, the postwar constitution, and popular music.

The *shutaisei* debates from 1946 to 1948 are regarded as one of the central intellectual events in postwar Japan. Andrew Barshay has summarized the issue at stake in democratization, or democratic revolution: "What was to be the historical *agency* involved in bringing it about?"[79] The answer to this question was "the masses" for those associated with the journal *Shin Nihon bungaku* (New Japanese Literature), and "the individual" for those associated with *Kindai bungaku*. Some might argue that this was a pointless debate, because neither the masses nor the individual brought about the democratization envisioned here. But if Japan after 1945 was Americanized, it was in ways where traces of agency of any sort can be obscure: in a novel where its slang is shaped by occupiers nowhere evident, by a constitution whose language makes imperfect sense without reference to an English draft that officially does not exist, and in popular songs whose ultimate composers are African American. Michel Foucault defined the author as the "figure by which one marks the manner in which we fear the proliferation of meaning."[80] Our custom of attributing a discourse to its producer curbs the tendency to generate endless significations. Literary histories are the stories not of books but of books and their authors. Still, I note how mass culture in postwar Japan, without which it is impossible to think of literary history, is a culture without authors and therefore, if Foucault was right, with no way for us to rein in its promiscuous meanings.

A creole Japanese literature makes sense not just at the level of a novel's language but in the mixed milieu it takes as its grounded theme. Poet Miyazawa Kenji's (1896–1933) work on the remote area of Tōhoku has long been seen as a creolized mixture of regional language with standard Japanese and a mixture of oral and literate storytelling. The history of the colonization of Tōhoku by central Honshu suggests parallels with the experience of the Caribbean,[81] but they are limited. The best example of a Japanese creole novel might well be Abe Kōbō's last, unfinished work, written in a language consistently Japanese but otherwise not Japanese at all. Found on a floppy disk after Abe's death, *Tobu otoko* (Flying Man) was first published in April 1993 and instigated a critical debate on Abe's contribution to Japanese literature since 1945.[82] Citing Miyazawa, literary scholar Nishi Masahiko argued a creole literature is not limited to literature written in a creole language; literature involved with the social real of multiple languages and multiple cultural practices satisfies the definition.[83] In this sense *Tobu otoko* stands opposed to the notion of an unadulterated Japanese literature. In a patois made up of highly technical, medical, and largely otherwise quasi-scientific vocabulary (nothing new for Abe), it strays into unintelligibility. Abe likely began it in the 1980s, the result of his lifelong interest in creoles in general and the possibility of writing Japanese as one, part of his oft-stated ambition of interrupting a national literary tradition toward which he was hostile. This ambition was linked to his long-standing impulse to take the idea of a Japanese literature and rip it apart. "From the start of his career," writes his daughter Neri, "he discarded former concepts of language that needed to be destroyed, and wrote his fiction with a new, unique linguistic perspective."[84]

Tobu otoko may be a novel from the late 1980s, but Abe himself was a product of wartime Japan and its subsequent American subjection. He grew up not in Japan proper, but in the Japanese puppet state of Manchuria (Manshūkoku), where as a boy he heard pidgin languages on the street used by a multinational, multiethnic population and presumably as much on the border of intelligibility as *Tobu otoko*. "I remember when I was growing up," Abe wrote near the end of his life, "how people in the Manchurian markets spoke a pidgin [*kongōgo*] of Japanese and Chinese with each other." But Abe was far more interested in creole languages than pidgins, because pidgins still maintained a relationship with recognizably national languages. As an adult he was an avid student of scholarship on creolization. He read Derek Bickerton carefully,[85] and he was drawn politically to the ideas of pidgins and creoles because they waged war not only on national languages (as if they exist before nations do), but of nationality itself, a concept to which the fictional nation of Manshūkoku made him antagonistic. His utopian hope was that a postwar Japanese culture would not be Japanese but, as his daughter put it, "a creole culture, a culture omnipresent among humankind."[86]

Tobu otoko is a fantastic story about a neurotic male high school teacher named Hone Osamu who receives a telephone call at four one morning from someone purporting to be his younger half-brother, whom he doesn't actually have. This alleged younger brother is just then flying in the air nearby and, after being winged by an air gun shot by Hone's neighbor Namiko, dives into his apartment through an open window. The Flying Man/younger brother tells Hone that he makes a living mentally bending spoons. Hardly begun by Abe at the time of his death, the novel descends into a claustrophobic exploration of Hone's and Namiko's quite miserable lives. The Flying Man recedes as a character, and Abe is dead before he can tell us more about him. But what is creolized about the novel is first its deracination. Hardly anything apart from Hone's name and home address marks the story as recognizably "Japan" in any way. It signals Abe's final and most complete renunciation of a monologic, national, Japanese *anything*, and in its place he installs an existential parable in distinct counterpoint to the state's fetish of a Japanese cultural particularity. "Creolity [*kureōrusei*]," writes Odagiri Takashi, "presses for the transformation of the traditions, customs and habits of an existing society. It confronts any return to what Abe Kōbō termed the 'original' [*genkei*] of a culture."[87] We know that a de-Japanized Japanese literature is ironically a particularized response to a particular twentieth-century Japanese history, in the wake of a world war and a massive American restructuring of post-1945 Japan, part of the same process of decolonization that is recorded in the creole literatures of Africa, the Caribbean and elsewhere.

In 1965, Imperial Prince Mikasa submitted the following for the court's annual New Year's poetry competition, which that year was on the announced theme of *tori* (birds): "The belt-conveyor [*beruto konbea*] which brings in the feed revolves and / thousands of young birds / cluster about it to eat."[88] The surprise, inelegant insertion of English "belt-conveyor" points to the cacophony of the Japanese language that Abe Kōbō foresaw and welcomed. In the mid-1970s there would be another explosion of English words imported and changed into the Japanese language, the effect of new mass-marketing techniques and the more general political economy of culture along the creolization continuum.[89] What unites both waves of a creolized Japanese language is their common proof that, within the world order of hegemonic American English, an Anglicized Japanese language works as one of its pidginized dialects (*hōgen*).[90]

Although postwar Japan had a tradition of intellectuals arguing for its hybridity, starting with Katō Shūichi and Maruyama Masao, creolization itself is a word not heard much in Japan outside linguistics until the early 1990s, and even then, rarely applied to the Occupation period. Japan, described by one scholar as "a zero degree creole" (*kureōrusei no reido*),[91] hardly shares a history with the Caribbean. At a conference in 1998, Haitian actor Jacky Dahomay expressed surprise that the Japanese would be interested in creolization, so remote Japan's experience seemed from his own.[92] But like Haiti's former master, France, Japan in the 1990s was diagnosing itself as afflicted with an exhausted, depleted national literature. The global project of national literatures seemed over in many places. The United States turned to minority writing—African American, Asian American, and so on—to invigorate itself. France and Japan, alternatively, turned to theory. Today in Japanese academia as well as the popular media, creolization is invoked as a tool in dismantling the tyranny of the cultural homogeneity of the Japanese nation-state. Just as the Cold War was ending and the Japanese economic bubble was bursting, the Japanese intelligentsia's interest in creole studies soared—as did, not coincidentally, interest in postcoloniality in Japan and its backyard. While seldom applied to a Japan occupied by the United States, "creolization" and "postcolonialism" became common discourses, albeit with an odd evacuation of actual history. The Japanese media were alarmed by the sudden (?) presence of foreign guest workers from former colonies in its midst, and of a globalization of capital and labor from which Japan somehow had seemed remote. The lesson drawn, if quietly, was that the modern nation-sate, Japan included, was built in many instances on the back of empire and colonial subjugation.

I argue that Japan's invocation of the creole in recent decades is itself a process of creolization. Against the postwar ideology of a monoracial, monocultural nation, creolization as metaphor in the 1990s may have served as euphemistic chatter on the question of Japan's postcoloniality, including the question of collaboration with an occupying power from 1945 to 1952 and beyond. The tension between these two claims of Japanese identity may constitute a dialectical process of dismantling Japanese national identity as a whole, a process that accelerates in the new millennium. One might speculate that Japan's celebratory talk of creolization is akin to America's of multiculturalism: the proliferation of difference in both countries curiously follows the contours of a capitalism evermore invested in its globalization across an uneven world. (In a wonderful mouthful, Slavoj Žižek speaks of "multiculturist ideological poetry embedded in today's global capitalism."[93]) So Japan talks nowadays about its hybridity (*zasshū bunka*) without really meaning it; the terms are more ideological than historical. At the same time, this is jargon for the creative invention that a culturally exhausted Japan wishes it had more of, and it is a dialectic in which the organs of the state play continue to play an ambivalent and even contradictory role. Swedish anthropologist Ulf Hannerz notes:

> We have seen that the state is both a large-scale importer of culture from the center and a guardian of either more or less authentic traditions from the

periphery. But in between, frequently, there is nothing, or not very much. Perhaps it is inevitable that the state, for the sake of its own legitimacy, is a promoter of un-creolized authenticity. Yet it is also possible that this is a rather quixotic struggle, a production of culture of dubious merit in the view of large parts of the citizenry whose minds are elsewhere. It may be a perverse proposal, but it could be that to play its part in cultural welfare, to cooperate with that citizenry in shaping intellectual and esthetic instruments which help people see where they are and who they are today, and decide where they want to go, the state has to be more self-consciously, but not self-deprecatingly, a participant in a mixed cultural economy, a creole state.[94]

Abe Kōbō anticipated this. He was drawn to the idea of the creole because it interrupted and even destroyed tradition, but *kureōru* (creole) today in Japan is manipulated to take apart the putative cultural homogeneity of the nation-state. Admittedly there is something programmatic and even utopian about this scenario of an oddly native creative creole, but that underlies much of the optimistic attention paid a global (but not really) phenomenon of creolization, whether we (more often "they") are addressing the Caribbean, Africa, or other sites of European colonization and its contact zones. This paradigm does its distinct ideological work amid Japan's decline as a nation-state, even if it remains a humanistic project because it puts the human talent for invention and creativity at the heart of culture. But it is important to remember that creolization is not simply hybridization. The former requires violence of one sort or another, and in the case of Japan that violence was its own brute history as colonizer, followed by seven years of colonial abjection at the hands of the United States. What happens in the next two decades of modern Japanese literature will be the nation's stuttering and inchoate redress.

7

Beheaded Emperors and Absent Figures

On the evening of 1 February 1961, a young man appeared at the door of the Tokyo home of Shimanaka Hōji, president of the Chūō kōron publishing company. He identified himself to Maruyama Kane, the family maid, as a member of the political right wing and said that he wanted to see the master of the house. When Maruyama replied that Shimanaka was not at home, the visitor forced his way inside and stabbed Shimanaka's wife, Masako. As the assailant fled, Masako was able to instruct her teenage son to call an ambulance before she passed out. Masako survived. But Maruyama, who again tried to stop the intruder, was wounded fatally in the heart.

The next day the assailant, Komori Kazutaka, turned himself in to the police and confessed that his intended target had been Shimanaka Hōji. Komori had until the day before been a member of Japan's most powerful aboveground radical right-wing organization, the Aikokutō (Great Japan Patriotic Party). He carried a handkerchief with the salutation "Tennō-heika banzai" and a *waka*, a traditional Japanese lyric. The *Japan Times* carried a prose translation of both. "Long live the Emperor! Who will hesitate to sacrifice his life for the sake of the

Emperor and his country since the life of man is as transient as a dew drop on a leaf of grass."[1] What inspired this act of terrorism was an editorial decision that had embroiled Chūō kōron in scandal for months. In November 1960, the firm's monthly journal *Chūō kōron* published, after some hesitation, a short story by Fukazawa Shichirō (1914–87) entitled "Fūryū mutan," (The Story of a Dream of Courtly Elegance); *fūryū* (including its alternate reading *furyū*) can suggest many things other than elegance, including parody and the spirit of the carnivalesque. In Fukazawa's own recounting, he had the erotic—"no, the extravagant"—atmosphere of a Chinese brothel in mind when he wrote the work.[2] It is a short story that American historian of Japan Marius Jansen criticized, saying it "aroused the nation with a fantasy of imperial executions."[3] But Fukazawa possessed a better sense of humor than Jansen. Fukazawa started out as a professional guitarist under the stage name of Jimmy Uekawa, and he was fond of Elvis Presley. He turned to serious fiction in 1956 with what would be his best-known work, the novella *Narayamabushi-kō* (The Oak Mountain Song), which evokes the practice of geronticide in rural Japan.

"Fūryū mutan" recounts a dream of a popular revolt that not only overthrows the Japanese government but in a festive frenzy executes the imperial family in a series of intimately described decapitations. Responses to the story ranged from indignant shock to gleeful approbation. But almost immediately critics predicted that Fukazawa's life would be endangered. The Imperial Household Agency instigated legal proceedings on the grounds of defamation of character and violation of human rights. An intimidated Chūō kōron, confronted by an Aikokutō delegation, attempted to minimize damage by issuing apologies. The controversy eventually reached the floor of the Diet,[4] but despite all the attention paid it, the story did not travel much. Translator Edward Seidensticker told the Japanese press in December 1960 that "Fūryū mutan" was in "bad taste" and warned that if the story were to appear in English there would be "quite a reaction in America, where a Japan without an emperor would be considered a Bolshevized Japan."[5]

The unappeased right wing took direct action. With *Chūō kōron* already in its sights for a mildly critical essay on the imperial household, the Aikokutō demonstrated loudly for permanent redress, insisting that the journal cease publication and that Fukazawa be exiled. These demands were reiterated publicly at a Hibiya Park rally in downtown Tokyo two days before Komori's attack, which became known as the Shimanaka Incident. After the murder of Maruyama, Fukazawa went into hiding on 13 November and stayed there for five years. But the continuing repercussion of this act of terrorism is the onus under which literary depictions of the emperor's person still labor, despite the fact that the imperial system writ large was "one of the central themes of postwar Japanese literature."[6] "'Fūryū mutan,'" noted a former editor at *Chūō kōron*, "is a difficult work to find."[7] Copies of the offending issue of the magazine are often missing from public libraries, and the story itself is not included in the otherwise complete edition of Fukazawa's works or in any anthology of modern fiction. In 1988, one writer spoke of how over the years he had shared his worn, scotch-taped copy of the story with dozens of people who could not obtain it.[8]

After the Shimanaka Incident the Chūō kōron publishing company, once proud of its history of defending freedom of expression, canceled a special issue on the emperor system another of its house magazines had planned. Many observers date the start of the so-called chrysanthemum taboo—a reference to the design of the imperial seal—against public debate over the postwar emperor from the Shimanaka Incident. In 1965, philosopher Kōsaka Masaaki wrote that "to venerate Japan as our ancestral land is identical with venerating the emperor."[9] But John Dower countered, "The emperor-system . . . represented neither an inevitable nor a popular feudal legacy to modern Japan, but rather the conscious, calculated and *belated* popularization by the early Meiji ruling group of a waning and *elite* tradition"[10] no earlier than the start of the 1880s.

The *Asahi shinbun*, then Japan's most liberal major newspaper, published an editorial shortly after the Shimanaka Incident that ominously warned writers not to repeat Fukazawa's mistake. "It is too much for a writer to exercise his freedom of presentation to the extent common sense is completely forgotten for the sake of art."[11] So while there is no shortage today of books by Japanese intellectuals that analyze the emperor system in the calculatedly impersonal terms of political science or anthropology, the long-standing absence of critical, and especially fictional, representations of the emperor remains absolute. Public debate about the emperor can be a matter of life and death. In 1990, a college president was shot at for suggesting that the accession ceremonies for Hirohito's son Akihito should not be financed with public funds, and the same year the mayor of Nagasaki was seriously wounded by gunfire after he raised the issue of Hirohito's responsibility for the Second World War. In 1993, the homes of two publishers were hit with bullets, "presumably from rightist groups that call for the restoration of the Emperor to his God-like role."[12]

The injunction against discussing the person of the emperor does not have a long history. "Fūryū mutan" may be the last work of Japanese literature to feature an emperor as a character, but it certainly was not the first. Although it is often remarked, for instance, that "the scarcity of political topics is, in fact, a characteristic of Japanese literature,"[13] emperors were not always political topics, nor were they even political figures, at least not the sort who were readily offended. In *Genji monogatari* (*The Tale of Genji*), for instance, a reigning emperor is cuckolded by his own son, and on the early modern kabuki stage, while the names of the Tokugawa shoguns (who actually governed) could not be uttered, emperors were depicted as "human personalities with the foibles of ordinary people . . . sometimes played comically."[14] Chikamatsu Monzaemon's (1653–1725) many plays about emperors treated the sovereign as what Mikhail Bakhtin would later label carnivalesque. But in the nineteenth century, when modern state apparatuses coalesced around the ideological figure of a transcendental supreme monarch after the constitution of 1889 established the emperor as "head of the Empire, combining in Himself the rights of sovereignty,"[15] sensitivities were more easily riled. Removed from public view, the emperor took on the attributes of a totem.[16] In 1889, Miyatake Gaikotsu, editor of the *Tonchi kyōkai zasshi* (Journal of the Society of Ready Wit), was sentenced to three years' imprisonment for his magazine's depiction of the emperor as a skeleton. By act of law in 1897 it became a crime "to debase the dignity of the imperial house."[17] Novelist Satō Haruo notes that the charge of "dangerous thinking" (*kiken shisō*), which was leveled against the work of many left-wing writers in the 1930s and 1940s, first occurred amid vociferous criticism of a 1904 Yosano Akiko (1878–1942) poem interpreted as suggesting that the Meiji emperor, Hirohito's grandfather, was cowardly in ordering others to die for him in the Russo-Japanese War.[18] By the 1920s, "so sacred did the imperial household become," notes one historian, "that to write on that subject was an open invitation to prohibition."[19] One irony of the modern emperor system is that it is why Japan was never truly fascist; as Karatani Kōjin put it, "There can be no fascism that worships a king."[20]

In the postwar period under the American-imposed constitution, physical violence against writers thought to be disrespectful to the emperor may have escalated once the emperor was no longer a sovereign but a national symbol (*shōchō*). He is still an instrument of manipulation through which authority is legitimated. Nakano Masao's (1908–94) story "Sannin no hōkasha" (Three arsonists, 1956) prompted an assault by fanatics who believed that the work insulted the empress, and right-wing activists harassed even Hirohito's brother, Prince Mikasa, after he publicly expressed doubts in the mid-1960s when the prewar holiday Empire Day (*Kigensetsu*) was resurrected as National Founding Day

(*Kenkoku kinen no hi*). A small number of writers before Fukazawa were able to publish fictional works critically citing the emperor without unleashing the fury that engulfed "Fūryū mutan," but after February 1961 the situation for writers became distinctly different. Critic Kuroko Kazuo has concluded in recent years that "the quarantine of anti-emperor discourse has been a complete success."[21]

What was so pivotal about Fukazawa's story? Why did this work induce such violent response, when nonfiction essays by Marxist writers, among others, arguing explicitly for the abolition of the institution did not? Answers to these questions may also explain why an effective censorship persists in postwar Japan and how that censorship may be implicated in its theories of political enfranchisement and popular sovereignty. Moreover, these answers suggest how such theories depend on a rhetoric that Fukazawa parodied to disarm, with unforeseen consequences not just for the Shimanaka household but for the freedom of Japanese writers.

Little in "Fūryū mutan" invites the reader to take the story too seriously. The first-person narrator dreams that while aboard a Tokyo commuter train one morning he hears a rumor that violence has erupted in the Imperial Palace grounds at the center of the city. While transferring to a bus he asks others around him, "Is it a revolution? The left-wingers [*sayoku*]?"[22] He is told that the lower ranks of the military and police are all on "our side" and that weapons are being provided to the rebels jointly by the Soviet Union, the United States, and South Korea. The palace is completely occupied. A reporter from a women's magazine brightly announces from her car that she is off to take photos of "Mitchy's"—Princess (today Empress) Michiko's—imminent execution (331–32). Military bands, also pledged to the revolution, march by playing Brazilian rumba and mambo music to the applause of onlookers. The crowded bus takes its passengers to the palace grounds. Vendors hawking festival foods such as noodles and cotton candy line the plaza, and pinwheels and balloons are for sale.

Nearby, Crown Prince Akihito and his young bride, Michiko, are lying face-up on the ground, about to be killed. When they are beheaded with an ordinary saw, their heads roll away making metallic sounds (transcribed in Japanese as *sutten-korokoro* and *sutten-korokoro karakarakara*), as if the skulls belonged to robots—which is exactly what assassin Komori Kazutaka would later tell the police the reigning emperor had become.[23] The narrator, learning that the emperor and empress are to be killed in another area of the grounds, pushes his way through the crowds. He arrives a moment too late. A policeman directs the flow of pedestrians in a one-way traffic pattern around two headless corpses attired in proper English clothing. Noticing a scrap of paper nearby, the narrator picks it up and finds an illegible handwritten message. A person who is referred to as the *rōshinshi* (senior gentleman) and who introduces himself as a longtime employee of the Imperial Household Agency, informs the narrator that the message is the emperor's *jisei*, or farewell death poem (333). Suddenly a woman in her sixties appears, and the boisterous crowd recognizes her as Shōken Kōtaigō, or Dowager Empress Shōken, as the grandmother of Hirohito was called after her death in 1914. Seeing her in an expensive two-piece English suit, the narrator leaps at her, calling her obscene names (*kusottarebabā*, literally "shit-dripping hag") for using working people's money to buy such finery (334).

The dowager empress counters this curse in an inelegant countrified Kōshū dialect with equally scatological language (she calls the narrator a "shit brat"), and they wrestle each other to the ground (335–36). Meanwhile, the senior gentleman reads aloud the death poem written by Empress Nagako. The narrator, continuing to struggle with the dowager, notices that she and he share the same sort of bald spot on their heads and experiences an odd moment of empathy with her: the two form a vulgar complement to the more refined couples just executed. As a military band goes by playing a song with the Italian refrain "amore, amore, amore mio," the senior gentleman busily strings together discarded *Bunka kunshō* medals, the Orders of Cultural Merit awarded by the postwar emperor, as part of his symbolic role, for outstanding contributions to the nation (337). The senior gentleman points to the ancient imperial regalia — the mirror, the sword, and the jewel — also tossed aside onto the ground. No one, the senior gentleman regrets, wishes to buy them. He again starts to recite death poems, this time those of Akihito and Michiko. Elsewhere on the palace grounds a makeshift stage is set up for such popular folk entertainments as comic dialogues (*manzai*) and circus arts (*kyokugei*). Fireworks, each with a name redolent of classical court culture, illuminate the sky. The narrator, so moved by the celebrations that he has no regrets about dying, composes and recites his own death poem only to have the senior gentleman complain that the poem is plagiarized from Japan's first poetic anthology, the eighth-century *Man'yōshū* (Ten Thousand Leaves). The narrator improvises another death poem and shoots himself in the head with a pistol. Just then the narrator's nephew Mitsuhito wakes him from his dream. Apparently the narrator was shouting his final death poem in his sleep: "Natsugusa ya tsuwamonodomo no yume no ato" (Summer grasses! All that remains after the dreams of warrior; 340) — a poem lifted from Matsuo Bashō's (1644–94) *Oku no hosomichi* (Narrow Roads to the Deep North). A wristwatch by his pillow, one that stops running whenever he sleeps, uncharacteristically shows the correct time. Pleased that the watch now works properly, the narrator puts it on his wrist, and "Fūryū mutan" concludes.

This outline should make clear why "Fūryū mutan" is often termed *kokkei shōsetsu*, or "comic fiction." Yoshimoto Takaaki, arguably postwar Japan's most important public intellectual, called the story "highbrow *rakugo*" (*kōkyū rakugo*) in a curious defense of it.[24] But the term "comic" can impute contempt as well as denote genre, and the story was defended and attacked by partisans across the political spectrum with little predictability. For example, ultranationalist writer Mishima Yukio recommended that *Chūō kōron* publish it alongside his own short story, "Yūkoku" (Patriotism, 1961).[25] While Shimanaka Masako was recuperating from her wounds in the hospital, Mishima and his wife went to pay a sympathy visit, as did other noteworthy authors.[26] Writer and future far-right governor of Tokyo, Ishihara Shintarō, praised "Fūryū mutan" for pointing out how useless the postwar emperor was.[27] Meanwhile, old-line leftists such as Nakano Shigeharu lambasted it for a parodic flippancy no doubt antithetical to the premises of the intellectual arguments commonly advanced in attacking the emperor system.[28] A young Etō Jun thought the story not revolutionary but instead nihilistic (*metsubō*), expressing not anti-emperor sentiment but rather a Japanese fear of revolution.[29] From the Left, Ōoka Shōhei (1909–88), a harsh critic of the story, said no single work of fiction had ever before or since summoned such a dramatic reaction. He added that the images of violence and revolution readers saw in "Fūryū mutan" were much the same in television's coverage of current political riots.[30] In the wake of the Shimanaka terrorist attack, such leading intellectuals on the Left as Takeuchi Yoshimi, Tsurumi Shunsuke, Nagai Michio, and Maruyama Masao issued a statement defending the freedom of speech in Japan.[31] Noma Hiroshi, at the time a member of the Japan Communist Party, praised it a dozen years later, but other important literary critics were still calling the story "irresponsible" (*musekinin*).[32]

Fukazawa was censured by ideological opposites for the frivolous way he had dealt with two serious and inflexible orthodoxies: the authoritarian insistence on the emperor and his institution as the validating apex of social control and order, and the equally entrenched democratic position that had to take the emperor system seriously in order to criticize the hierarchical social order. In his 1958 essay "Kenryoku to geijutsu" (Power and art), left-wing critic Takeuchi Yoshimi noted how progressive criticism of the emperor system (a system Takeuchi declared immanent in "every tree and every grass") was based on mistaken assumptions that ironically guaranteed its reproduction.[33] Hinuma Rintarō called "Fūryū mutan" "a nonsensical modern-day fairy tale . . . neither a work that advocates revolutionary thought nor a work that contains much anti-emperor ideology." No story, Hinuma claims, that "annuls both the emperor system and revolution, both authority and opposition to authority," is apt to be welcomed by an intellectual culture divided, and made humorless, by the politics of the day,[34] politics dominated by the explosive, violent national debate in Japan at the time over the renewal of the U.S.-Japan Security Treaty.

What unites the critical reactions to the story is a shared discomfort with its aggressive use of carnivalesque parody, a discomfort that discloses the ideological limitations inherent in the liberal norms dictated for an ostensibly unfettered postwar Japanese literature under constitutional protections for freedom of speech. The story is not simply a parody of an emperor system whose ideological hold depends on its self-sponsored inviolable aura. In addition to the Imperial Household Agency, the imperial regalia and the Orders of Cultural Merit, "Fūryū mutan" mocks the largely left-wing rhetoric of revolution and even the term "left-wing" (a word that Fukazawa has fun with in his story by punning). True to the spirit of carnival, the mob spares no one guilty of self-importance from ridicule. "This is no revolution," says one bystander in the story. "We've got to overthrow the government and build a better Japan." When the narrator complains that the word "Japan" irritates him, the bystander explains, "Look, don't get riled. We're only calling it that for now" (330). The Rabelaisian temper of "Fūryū mutan" may be further linked with the controversy and homicide that ensued. Fukazawa's perverse disposal of four imperial heads—metaphors for high-culture authority—at the hands of a low-culture public not only inspired the laughter Bakhtin says "degrades and materializes" but incited angry and all too serious rebuttal as well.[35]

Fukazawa's story parodies a fundamental property of the postwar emperor system, and this property is what Fukazawa started with in writing "Fūryū mutan": the imperial family's composition of *waka* death poems.[36] Modern Japanese literature may be faulted for its lack of "powerful poetic movements,"[37] but *jisei* go back to the earliest Japanese literature and mythology. Yamato Takeru, a hero in the first extant work of Japanese prose literature, the eighth-century *Kojiki*, is sometimes held to have written one, and the death poems of Princes Ōtsu and Arima, both of whom were executed for treason, established as early as the eighth century a link among authority, political turmoil, and the composition of a final *waka*. Infirm Zen priests throughout Japanese history commonly wrote death haiku, but the nineteenth century saw a major revival of the *waka* death poem delivered in the face of an unnatural rather than natural death. The composition of *jisei* became "a widespread practice" once ideologues such as Yoshida Shōin and Nogi Maresuke used the genre to express boldly nationalistic and emperor-worshiping sentiments.[38] War criminals composed death poems before their executions in the late 1940s. Komori's death poem was written prematurely. More typical is the death poem of Yamaguchi Otoya, the right-wing youth who assassinated Asanuma Inejirō, the chairman of the Japan Socialist Party, only a few months before Komori's crime. Yamaguchi composed a *waka* before committing suicide in his jail cell. Kenneth Rexroth would list death poems, alongside the songs of cicadas and assignations with clandestine lovers, among the limited themes of traditional Japanese poetry.[39]

The phenomenon of the modern death poem illustrates the political context of poetry in Japan. *Waka* in general has long had a certain cultural authority—it is also called *kokka* (national poetry)—and its codified practice, *kadō*, metonymically represents state-sanctioned Japanese high culture, with the compositions of the imperial family at the apex. "This work," Fukazawa explained of "Fūryū mutan," "is the result of my resistance to the idea of *waka*. The aristocratic elegance [*fūryū*] of *waka* is completely ridiculous, sentimental nonsense. . . . If I were going to make fun of *waka*, I thought it would be best to do it with the imperial family."[40] In essence, for Fukazawa to make fun of *waka* (literally, "Japanese song") was to attack the one literary practice most explicitly identified as uniquely Japanese.

The first death poem in "Fūryū mutan," that of Hirohito, is written in a hand that the narrator cannot read. The senior gentleman recites it aloud to him. Like all the poems in the story, this one must be decoded and made comprehensible by a bureaucrat professionally charged with mediating symbols for ordinary people.

> *Miyoshino no mine ni shidareru chidorigusa fuku yamakaze ni yururu o mireba.*
>
> The drooping plover grasses
> On the high peaks
> Of sacred Yoshino
> I watch them quiver
> In the mountain wind.

This poem, again like all the others in the story, makes generous use of *waka* cliché. Nonetheless the senior gentleman provides an interpretation. Everything, he says, up to the verb "quiver," is a *jo*, or prefatory guide phrase, for what must be taken as a reference to the nation in upheaval. The poem is then unimaginatively paraphrased, "My word, what a national disturbance!" (334). Empress Nagako's death poem appropriately begins with a nod to her husband's.

> *Iso chidori oki no aranami kakiwakete sendo itoshi tomoshibi nururu.*
> The shore plover
> On the stormy seas
> Making his way
> How sad the ferryman
> His lantern made wet.

The senior gentleman's exegesis is brief. Again, everything up to "wet" serves as a preface, and "wet," the narrator is told, is finally all that the poem means. "Wet? Just wet?" the narrator asks. "What gets wet, and how? Don't you have any idea?" The senior gentleman responds that it is the essence of poetry to say things not explicitly but obliquely. Were he forced to elaborate, he would say that wet is an allusion to tears, implying the empress's great sadness. His pedestrian paraphrase is "My word, what a sad affair" (335).

The reader, however, might see the empress's mention of wet (*nururu*, also "to become damp or moist") as an erotic rejoinder to Hirohito's verb "quiver" (*yururu*). (The term for a love scene in the kabuki theater or in modern pornographic films, *nureba*, "wet scene," contains the root of the verb *nururu*.) Such undignified play in death poems may be some of the fun Fukazawa said he meant to make of *waka*, but his plain-talking narrator stubbornly concludes that anything that is a riddle (*nazo-nazo*) is apparently poetic and that this poem is not meant to mean anything. The senior gentleman demurs, and subsequent discussion of the death poems written by Crown Prince Akihito and Princess Michiko only widens the breach between those for whom poems are formulaically symbolic and those for whom the symbols are opaque or irrelevant.

Waka is a cultural practice long associated with the imperial institution. Until the postwar period there was an Imperial Poetry Bureau within the Imperial Household Ministry. While the importance of poetry to court life is clear to any reader of Japan's classical literature, it is the explicitly political uses to which poetry was put in the nineteenth and twentieth centuries that are at stake in Fukazawa's story. The recuperation of the emperor in the Meiji period as a divine monarch embodying the national polity (*kokutai*, literally, "national body") and subsuming his subjects is not unrelated to his touted reputation as a poet or to Fukazawa's festive, grotesque dismembering of the emperor's body. Historian Irokawa Daikichi reports that the Meiji emperor, Mutsuhito, was reputed to have written more than ninety thousand verses in his lifetime, the best of which he wrote during the national mobilization for the Russo-Japanese War. "And those poems," notes Irokawa, "had a definite effect on the attitudes of the people at that time."[41]

Mutsuhito's empress Shōken Kōtaigō—the only aristocrat in "Fūryū mutan" given a speaking part—in real life enjoyed a much better reputation as a poet than her husband did. (She translated, to cite one example of the worldly purposes to which modern poetry was put, Benjamin Franklin's aphorisms into *waka*.[42]) Hirohito was also a poet, as all emperors need be. One historian observed, "Like Shinto, poetry is alive and thriving at the Palace. Waka flourishes among the members of the imperial family. Members of the imperial family and famous poets present monthly poems on fixed topics at court, with the emperor and empress present."[43] Attendance was presumably obligatory, since the imperial family's single duty by that time was to preserve so-called continuous essential Japanese cultural values. These cultural values arguably reproduced ideological and political ones. *Waka*, through its conservative unity of aesthetics that define Japanese national identity, was the privileged instrument by which social and political difference among individual Japanese is purportedly dissolved.

The lyric poem in the West, which once had a public, ceremonial function, long ago became a private vehicle for self-expression. The Japanese *waka*, however, retains its ceremonial use, and proof of the difference is televised nationally each January when the imperial family, a handful of professional poets, some carefully chosen private citizens and even an occasional foreigner gather in the palace for the New Year's poetry party. This event, known as the *utakai-hajime*, is the modern version of a court ceremony supposedly dating back to the midtenth century. It is in fact no older than 24 January 1869, the second year of the Meiji period, when the tradition was introduced as a corollary to Japan's political reorganization under a modern monarchy alongside other bogus traditions such as the care of rice seedlings. In 1901, Basil Hall Chamberlain wrote "The Palace itself, conservative in most things non-political, offers to the nation an example of fidelity to the national traditions in matters relating to poetry. . . . Once a year, too, in January, a theme is set, on which the Emperor, Empress, and other exalted personages compose each a thirty-one-syllable ode, and the whole nation is invited to compete."[44]

Today the *utakai-hajime* is held every January in the Matsunoma Hall of the Imperial Palace and telecast nationwide, if to declining audiences. By 1874, any Japanese subject could submit *waka* on the assigned theme, and in 1879 the best of those submissions were for the first time recited at the *utakai-hajime*, along with poems written by the imperial family. After the Second World War, subjects (now citizens) whose poems were selected for inclusion in the *utakai-hajime* could attend the ceremony. The history of the *utakai-hajime*, then, is a history of an increasingly public, evermore media-managed and democratic event, although only members of the imperial family or court-appointed professional poets may speak at the ceremony. The event's significance is not taken lightly. One historian calls it "that ceremony among all imperial ceremonies with the most profound ties to the people,"[45] and another echoes this description with a twist: "of all the many imperial functions, none has created so deep a bond between the imperial household and the people as the New Year's Poetry Party. . . . The New Year's Poetry Party thus serves . . . to bind together the Japanese people through *waka*."[46] Another apologist writes, "What is in fact bound here is not just the emperor to the people but also the people to one another, so that subjective difference is erased not only between state and citizenry but also among all individuals."[47] But as political theorist James Scott points out, "Nothing conveys the public transcript more as the dominant would like it to seem than the formal ceremonies they organize to celebrate and dramatize their rule."[48] Critics and scholars elsewhere on the Japanese political spectrum offer different characterizations of the *utakai-hajime* and of exactly what, if anything, is exchanged between the emperor and the people. Certainly political leaders and offices around the world use public or semipublic functions to advertise legitimacy—in Japan, poetry; in Britain, thoroughbred horse racing. Yet while at Ascot it may matter to bettors which horses win, the quality of poetry at the *utakai-hajime* is eclipsed by the social setting in which the poems are recited: a televised tableau from the picture gallery of modern Japanese polity. As Katayama Sadami states, "The ceremony of presenting poems at court has nearly nothing to do with any of the literary issues in *waka* today, but instead has much to do with political issues. . . . Those of us who have poems chosen for the ceremony are, through our works, supporting the emperor system."[49]

Since Plato the problem for the West has often been how to keep the poets out of the ideal state; in Japan it has been how to keep them in despite wars, revolutions, and foreign occupations. In *The Republic* poets mislead us by portraying the gods as undignified and immoral. Poetry is dangerous because it mimics the spiritual and subtly trivializes it. Plato did not have to account for poets who, like modern Japanese emperors, were gods themselves. What he was concerned about was the menace of the symbol as a simulacrum, a false copy, of the truth. It is not what the poet *says* that is subversive but the poetry itself, and the poetry attests to its own falsehood. Europe came to accommodate poetry with power by retrieving falsehood as creativity and then valorizing creativity as a species of truth, but poetics have evolved differently in Japan. After the war Hirohito was reconstructed as a purveyor of symbols, a poet who was to express a conservative social collectivism through symbolic ceremonies and language. At the same time, he had to be a symbol himself; the first article of the postwar constitution defines the emperor as "the symbol of Japan, the symbol of the unity of the people." This statement is not a description of how people perceived the emperor but an ambiguous prescriptive definition that preserves the institution while emptying it of its former political authority. Legal scholar and onetime cabinet minister Matsumoto Jōji was quite surprised when he encountered the word for "symbol" in the draft constitution: "I thought it was a very literary choice of words."[50] In an essay on the symbolic (*shōchō*) role of the sovereign, Sasaki Sōichi, a member of the House of Peers at the time of the constitution's promulgation, notes that the term *shōchō*, which appears in no earlier Japanese legal document, cannot be defined in any purely Japanese context, and the ideological slippage Sasaki detected has animated much controversy among intellectuals since.[51] But for most Japanese, the meaning of the emperor as a symbol of the nation and its citizenry has been made unambiguous through the partnership of the media and the government, especially the Imperial Household Agency. Ceremonies such as the *utakai-hajime* serve to establish the emperor as a symbol of an essential and ahistorical continuity. Insofar as the emperor operates as the metonymic embodiment of national culture, with *waka* its high-culture epitome, then standing as a passive postwar symbol may not be unlike reigning as an immanent prewar deity. The symbolic ceremonies that the postwar constitution authorizes the emperor to perform are rhetorically the same ceremonies buttressing ancient claims to temporal power, updated with television crews.

The Japanese emperor has been described as "a symbol without referent" or a "free-floating signifier."[52] This is an idea popularized by Roland Barthes's observation in *Empire of Signs* that the Imperial Palace, the empty center of Tokyo, represents a "sacred 'nothing.'"[53] "The postwar emperor," observes Karatani Kōjin, "is the zero sign. It doesn't matter if he is present or not—and that is how his presence enlists our allegiance without resort to force."[54] A "zero" emperor, it is argued, is impervious to interpretation, critique and political debate. He is hegemonic in the sense that he is wholly self-referential and never contingent. Such theorizing is not far from what assassin Komori Kazutaka insisted to the authorities the emperor is: *zettai*, or "absolute."[55] But such claims derive from the postwar political invisibility of Hirohito, whose wartime reign was controversial. Hirohito's son Emperor Akihito is different and not at all absent. Film Director Itō Daisuke complained that before the war he was prohibited from even filming a peasant near chrysanthemums, so taboo was anything associated with the imperial family[56]; today, you cannot avoid depictions of the emperor. Historian Takashi Fujitani has written of the modern emperor and his system as a panoptic regime, but the truth may be that the Japanese public looks much more at him than does he them.[57]

The imperial household now represents upper-middle-class culture. The constant if controlled information provided to the public about the members of the imperial family portrays them as a contented modern family whose lifestyle is congruent with the material aspirations of the average Japanese. This change was accomplished most effectively in a coordinated media campaign surrounding an event that occurred just before the publication of Fukazawa's short story. For the first time in Japanese history, a crown prince chose a commoner for his bride. Akihito's engagement to Shōda Michiko, announced to the public on the morning of 27 November 1958, after a "tennis court courtship" begun in the summer resort of Karuizawa. News of the engagement, it is estimated, reached 95 percent of the Japanese population within three hours due to the combined efforts of print and broadcast media. It sparked the "Mitchy boom" of the late 1950s and successfully familiarized the imperial house with their marriage on 10 April 1959. Over half a million people lined the wedding parade route, while the average Japanese at home was reported to have watched more than ten hours of the event on television.[58]

Television in Japan in the late 1950s was not inconsequential for fiction. The reaction to "Fūryū mutan" might have been much the same without television, but the story might never have been written in the first place. Television in Japan dates from state corporation NHK's experimental broadcast on 3 June 1951, and by 1952 television signals were available on all of the four main Japanese islands. By 1958, a million households were paying subscription fees to NHK; by 1962, ten million; and at the time of the 1964 Olympics, seventeen million.[59] In 1990, there were estimated to be over thirty-two million subscribers.[60] Programming in the 1950s was largely sports like baseball and pro wrestling, as well as American imports (*Lassie* was especially popular). Special attention was paid to Japanese musical talent, and Misora Hibari was hailed as the answer to the television's prayers (*mōshigo*).[61] Writer Takahashi Gen'ichirō (1951–) insists that no author raised on television like himself would think his or her fiction is unaffected by the medium, if for no reason other than the television brings virtual human beings into the home.[62] But television hardly started out entirely new. At first it linked to older forms of culture. Newscasters read newspapers aloud, for example. Yet in time, as Kiyomizu Ikutarō foresaw in 1958, new media not only supplement or eliminate previous ones, but change them along the way.[63] Watching television cannot help affect the way viewers consider print. Newspapers, once indispensable to television news, eventually find their function duplicated, then eliminated, by that same medium.

Television did not begin with consumption at home, and this attenuated the full import of its technology. It began in public rather than private spaces. *Gaitō terebi* (street TV), like its predecessor *gaitō rajio* in the 1920s, was centered around sets placed in train stations, restaurants, department stores, appliance stores, even inside temples and shrines. Viewing television in public quickly became part of everyday life and changed it. Print media can be read at any time, in any place; radio and television needed proximity to the device and subservience to a fixed broadcast schedule: *jikan* (time) became *jikoku* (timetable), and times were precise down to the second. More important, new media took on important functions for the state. Television, like radio before it, initially brought *crowds* together against trends that were atomizing and individuating modern life. "What was important about street television," argues Yoshimi Shun'ya, "was not just its ignition for the proliferation of television generally, but its particular ability early in the postwar period to tie television together with the popular imagination." Yoshimi cites as an example the super-popularity on early television of the Korea-born pro wrestler Rikidōzan, the "best known man short of the Emperor,"[64] who made the ring a "national symbolic theater" opposite the Americanized sphere of occupied Japan. Rikidōzan, says Yoshimi, "performed" the role of being a Japanese, which made "Japanese" more real.[65] As Andrew Painter points out in his work on Japanese television, the medium "is important not so much because of the symbolic potency of particular TV programs, but because of its more general role in transforming the representational dynamics of modern societies."[66]

For that reason, and at exactly the same time, contemporary observers of early television in Japan expressed concerns. In 1958, legal scholar Kainō Michitaka was already warning that the immense capital required for television broadcasting, coupled with government control of frequencies, meant that freedom of speech in Japan was facing new hurdles. Broadcast technology may improve, Kainō argued, but nothing can be done to ameliorate its control by monopoly capitalism.[67] Only a few months before "Fūryū mutan" appeared, critic Sasaki Kiichi bemoaned the state of television broadcasting not just for its disappointing, dumbed-down contents but for its ideological effects.[68] Years later Jean Baudrillard observed that "TV, by virtue of its mere presence, is a social control in itself. There is no need to imagine it as a state periscope spying on everyone's private life—the situation as it stands is more efficient than that: it is the *certainty that people are no longer speaking to each other*, that they are definitively isolated in the face of a speech without response."[69]

The political repercussions of television in Japan become clear around the time of the struggle over the renewal of the U.S.-Japan Security Treaty, circa 1959–60. For example, when some twenty thousand Japanese stormed the Diet building on 27 November 1959, TV broadcast it live—"raw" (*nama*)—bringing a visceral sense of national crisis into the confines of the home. NHK was also there with its cameras when, on 19 May of the following year, five hundred police protected the Liberal Democratic Party representatives who voted in the Diet to pass the treaty renewal. At the time, television had an unexpected impact on viewers: "Only once in its history did television accelerate resentment against the government. This was during the May and June protest of 1960, when people were informed of round-the-clock developments in parliament and left their supper tables to join the demonstrations."[70] Some commentators believed that television had much to do with the scale and pace of the *Anpo* (Security Treaty) struggle. The long, unedited transmissions of the protests gave viewers the vicarious experience of participating in them, which then some went out and did.[71] When protester Kanba Michiko, a University of Tokyo student, was trampled to death outside the Diet on 15 June 1960, some watching television at home are said to have rushed to the scene. The government quickly realized how it could harness the power of new media, and by 1961, NHK had programs such as "Meet the Prime Minister" to do so. Private broadcasters gave candidates time for campaign messages.[72] It was not simply a matter of content; the medium of television affected how politics were received. Marshall McLuhan thought that with television, Hitler would never have been elected chancellor; conversely, without television Nixon would have been elected president in 1960.[73]

The upshot in Japan, too, was a shift in the relationship between the population with access to television and national polity. Interrupting the second game of baseball's Japan Series, film critic Okada Susumu recalled when news of Asanuma's assassination flashed across the bottom of his screen. "Looking back on the experience, I understand how just what power the spatial and temporal simultaneity [*dōjisei*] television wields."[74] Later Japanese networks would broadcast live, and for hours on end, student assaults on the Yasuda Amphitheater at the University of Tokyo; the hijacking of a Japan Airlines passenger jet; the police storming of the Red Army Faction (*Sekigunha*) in its mountain hideaway Asama Sansō; and the prelude to Mishima's 1970 suicide within the precinct of an army garrison. Both state violence and violence against the state became "breaking news" and so our grim entertainment. While Hirohito would not speak on television until the eve of his state visit to the United States in 1975 (he appeared on NBC's *The Today Show*), the ultimate sanction of state power was omnipresent on television if only because it was now part of everyday life, producing an epistemological homogeneity along with temporal simultaneity. Of the nineteenth century, Carol Gluck could confidently say the "imperial presence seldom impinged on the rigors of daily experience,"[75] but television changed that. John Fiske has said, "Film presents itself as a record of what has happened, television presents itself as a relay of what is happening,"[76] and so the latter allows us to share in real time the literal moment of persons who are elsewhere but in our homes as well. This brings us not only ubiquity, but instantaneous ubiquity. "It was the funeral of President Kennedy," wrote Marshall McLuhan and Quentin Fiore, "that most strongly proved the power of television to invest an occasion with the character of corporate participation. It involves an entire population in a ritual process. . . . In television, images are projected at you. You are the screen. The images wrap around you. You are the vanishing point. This creates a sort of inwardness, a sort of reverse perspective which has much in common with Oriental art."[77]

Oriental art aside, McLuhan misses an important point. There is no screen without an audience for it, and that audience construes the message/massage in its own ways. With broadcasts of the Japanese imperial household beamed into millions of homes, the emperor and his kin were familiarized. Though the emperor was still a subject of veneration, coverage of his activities on TV and in the tabloids made the imperial family celebrities. In Fukazawa's time, Shōda Michiko was familiarized with the Americanizing nickname "Mitchy" and made life-size, along with her future in-laws. This had consequences, as Fukazawa discovered. Stars who are no larger or smaller than life-size inspire not just admiration but hatred and envy among their fans, and the imperial family in its elegant domesticity did both. Nothing made the stakes clearer than the marriage of Akihito to Michiko. It is commonly said that that the investiture of Charles as Prince of Wales and then his marriage to Diana were the first royal pageants to take full advantage of television and its audiences, but this is not true. It was the betrothal and union of Akihito and Michiko, which, rather than elevating anyone as in the case of Charles and Diana, had the opposite effect. It turned two members of a modern royal family (one born into it, the other conscripted) into individuals, and it did so via TV. Part of the lore still surrounding Akihito and Michiko holds that during their engagement they exchanged traditional poems written in beautiful calligraphy on the best handmade paper,[78] but it was more modern technologies that reported such conceits to the nation. After the royal wedding television would firmly supplant radio as the preeminent national medium. Starting on 1 April 1959, all of Japan's newspapers, as if on cue, reversed the hierarchy of daily radio and television listings and put the latter on top of the former. The royal wedding was the transitional moment when the daily lives of the Japanese shifted from being radio-centered to television-centered. The Japanese imperial family was not invited into households with TV sets so much as they marched right in and rearranged the furniture. The home television set up in the *chanoma* became a *kamidana* (altar for the gods), the emperor and his spawn being among them.[79] The boom in the coverage of the engaged couple, but especially commoner Michiko, followed on the heels of a TV-instigated mania for hula-hoops and started with live coverage of the engagement announcement on 27 November 1958.[80] The Japanese media were obsessed with the upcoming event. Tennis became more popular, dolls were redesigned to look more like the future empress, and television sales went through the roof, even the extravagantly priced color ones.[81]

On the day of the wedding, 10 April 1959, no members of the media were permitted entry into the palace proper, but the parade route was lined with them. One hundred and ten cameras, four helicopters and over one thousand five hundred personnel were stationed along or above the streets. This was the first time that Japanese television turned its equipment away from a stage and pointed it toward events in the streets. The audience at home watched over ten hours of continuous coverage, nuclear families (*katei*) viewing the manufacture by the state and media of another one: Mr. Crown Prince and Mrs. Crown Princess. Television reporters there that day, such as NTV's Watanabe Midori, would later write about it with the awed excitement American broadcasters used for the manned moon landing.[82] Electronic media were key in the ideological privileging of the nuclear family, so much so that cultural historians of that moment speak of a "technological national identity." By 1961, NHK had started its fifteen-minute morning broadcasts of serialized family dramas (*asadora*) beginning with Shishi Bunroku's best-selling *Musume to watashi* (My Daughter and I, 1953–56),[83] as national a program as exists in Japan. The irony was that television simultaneously united the family by summoning them to the set yet replaced the family by taking on ideological work once performed by parents in socializing their offspring. In a prescient essay published in 1958, sociologist Kiyomizu Ikutarō noted that television may bring the family together, but it also ends any conversation among family members as they watch it, and they watch a lot. Drawn from the dark of movie theaters to the light of the home, television viewers assembled in small numbers that Kiyomizu termed "publikum en miniature," with consequences.[84]

Semiofficial histories of Japanese broadcasting might hold that the live broadcast of the wedding fostered "loving affection for the Imperial Household throughout the entire nation," but it was not exactly so.[85] During the procession, for example, live cameras caught a young man approaching the imperial carriage bearing the newlyweds and throwing a rock at it, transmitting the scene nationwide in real time. That rock, hurled across screens in millions of homes, could have been the rock that inspired Fukazawa Shichirō to write his funny little story and change the course of modern Japanese literature. The imperial household and its careful iconography were now close enough to touch, and even murder.

The expansion in mass culture in the postwar period—new publications such as the weeklies, certainly, but more than anything television—changed the situation for fiction. Multiple studies have attested to the dramatic drop in leisure time spent reading once television broadcasts began. But television is not, as McLuhan put it, "merely a degraded form of print technology."[86] As options for leisure activities expanded, fiction had a host of new rivals. The influence of the intelligentsia in general declined in the 1950s and 1960s as popular culture, led by the spread of TV broadcasting, confronted high culture, including literature.[87] In 2002, statistics had the Japanese watching more television than the French and Americans, and reading proportionately less.[88] In this context, critics have seen Fukazawa's "Fūryū mutan" as a reaction to the previous year's electronic spectacle of an imperial wedding. Fukazawa himself has said that he was disappointed at television that day, looking at the images of the beautiful royal couple whose union he regretted.[89] In 1959, Fukazawa published a brief essay in which he sarcastically claimed to oppose the marriage of an heir to a commoner because he had been looking forward to continued inbreeding that would produce a royal family with small heads, bodies like wasps', limbs like those of hairless rabbits, and a need for thick eyeglasses. Only then, Fukazawa predicted, would the Japanese people realize what a truly special imperial family they had.[90] But to Fukazawa's disappointment the imperial family was not to be special any longer. It was mom and dad and the kids playing tennis during the day, watching television at night, and inviting the neighbors in once a year to hear their homemade poems. What is noteworthy is not *what* emotion Fukazawa felt watching the crown prince and princess on television, it was that he had any emotion at all. The medium of television, brought into the home and assigned a role in the family as mundane as any household activities (cleaning, cooking, napping, etc.), possessed a "bodily intimacy" (*shinhensei*) that made the faces of those on the cathode ray tube as familiar (and liked or disliked) as the viewers' family members. As Minami Hiroshi observed, watching Japan's politicians scuffle on the floor of the Diet made them a "human interest story" devoid of real implications for Japan's national governance.[91]

Media attention lavished on the imperial wedding eclipsed coverage of the revision of the Police Law and the turmoil over the revision of the U.S.-Japan Security Treaty. The prewar concept of the emperor as immanent deity was replaced with the synecdoche of him as nuclear family paterfamilias. Until the end of the Second World War it was a punishable offense even to stare at a photograph of the emperor. Now, because of the barrage of media coverage lavished on him and his family, it is impossible not to. As television would soon be, the emperor was everywhere. This about-face in the representation of the emperor, the immediate context of Fukazawa's parody, presumably accounts for the character of the reporter driving off to photograph the princess's last moments. "The winter of 1958–59 provided one of the rare occasions for the Japanese people to show their interest and enthusiasm for the imperial house: every detail in the life of Michiko-sama was reprinted in the popular press," claims one of Hirohito's biographers.[92] But there is something backward in such a statement, unless the Japanese people collectively exercised editorial prerogative over the popular press. In fact, this enthusiasm was produced by the "collaboration between palace officials and the mass media."[93] The crown prince's love marriage to a commoner did not so much make the imperial family part of the public as render the public members of the imperial family. On the eve of "Fūryū mutan," the symbolic emperor system was domesticated through alignment with middle- and working-class desires and values, and television was the principal tool. Shortly after the war the "Emperor's Cup" was established as a horseracing prize, and the "Empress's Cup" was created for amateur sports groups.[94] It is precisely this domestication of the imperial family that Fukazawa discloses, parodies, and takes to a ribald extreme in his short story. There is hardly anything sacred attending the family. They share the vices of their subjects: they swear, brawl, write bad poetry, slavishly follow fashion, and suffer from hair loss. Their debasement culminates in the rolling sounds, transcribed *sutten-korokoro*, that conjure up the carnival's noisy revelry of a crowd playfully abusing its king or cardinals. "A vulgar, shameless materialism of the body," says Terry Eagleton of the carnivalesque, "rides rampant over ruling class civilities."[95] But it is as misleading to call the parody in "Fūryū mutan" explicitly anti-imperial as it would be to call Gargantua's iconoclasm revolutionary. Carnivals are frenzied but brief, and Fukazawa has the narrator of "Fūryū mutan" woken from his anarchic dream by a concerned nephew whose name sounds like an emperor's. Fukazawa mocks the politics that alternately sustains and critiques Japan's modern emperor system, and such a repudiation could only be couched in terms distinct from the terms of that politics. "Laughter alone," observes Bakhtin of Rabelais's Europe, "remained uninfected by lies" because neither the church nor state had cause to condone it.[96] Likewise in modern Japan, neither the received aesthetics of the *waka* nor the equally sober postwar ideology of a symbolic emperor prepared readers for Fukazawa's riotous mirth.

On 1 January 1946, Hirohito publicly renounced his divinity in a statement that said in part, "I am one of the people like you, with the same interests as you, and I want to experience the same joys and sorrows." These unprecedented words debuted a new subjectivity for Hirohito and reasserted a familiar one: a "you" (*nanjira*) homogeneously addressed as the "people" (*kokumin*). Such a position, binding all Japanese in common "interests" and "joys and sorrows," is coordinate with the postwar reclamation of the emperor, once a transcendental signifier of a national polity (*kokutai*), as a symbol that collectivizes all Japanese.

"The wholeness [*zentaisei*] of the people is a subjective wholeness," wrote philosopher Watsuji Tetsurō, a stalwart absolutist before 1945 and afterward an apologist for the emperor's symbolic status. "It is not possible to understand it objectively. That is why it can be expressed only as a 'symbol.'"[97] This subjectivity of a universalized bourgeois identity is not to be analyzed, critiqued, or even understood, but only signified literarily as a symbol. Similarly, in "Fūryū mutan" Fukazawa takes Hirohito at his postdivine word and refuses to let him become the validating transcendental signifier of any political position. Fukazawa cavalierly treats Hirohito as befits a symbol, one whose being is dependent on what is symbolized and not the other way around. The death poems written in a literary language too obscure for the delegate of state power (the senior gentleman) and the audience for the exercise of that power (the narrator) make no sense, and so the vaunted aesthetic-political unity of the Japanese people becomes little more than a figure of speech. After Hirohito told Richard Nixon in September 1975 of his "fukaku kanashimi to suru ano sensō" (profound sadness over the Second World War), Japanese journalists asked Hirohito if this choice of phrasing meant he felt responsibility for the war. Hirohito replied, "I am not a student of literary matters and thus do not understand figures of speech."[98] Understanding figures of speech risks understanding their referents. To query the figure of the symbol, as Fukazawa interrogates the imperial family in his story, is to expose it as an awkward trope easily undone by parody, satire or irony. *Waka* are so prominent in "Fūryū mutan" because in poetry, the Japanese language's most privileged expression, the investments in the symbol run the highest.

The most rhythmic, original, and powerful language in "Fūryū mutan"—its real poetry—is to be found not in any of its dull or plagiarized *waka* but in a transliteration that made some readers laugh and drove one to murder: *suttenkorokoro*, the onomatopoeic and alliterative word for the sound of two heads rolling across the ground. Nagai Kafū once noted, with characteristic pique, that since the Meiji period the press reports in detail the imperial body, including the state of appetites and bowel movements.[99] When it came time in 1989 for Hirohito to die, the press was attentive to all matters pertaining to his colon. John Whitney Hall was mistaken when he wrote, "Stripped today of power and sovereignty, the emperor serves only in the most *disembodied* of the manifestations with which he was historically endowed."[100] But it is because of the words that Fukazawa chose that he had to flee for his life, and that Maruyama was killed.

Julia Kristeva, in her essay "The Ethics of Linguistics," writes, "Murder, death, and unchanging society represent precisely the inability to hear and understand the signifier as such—as ciphering, as rhythm, as a presence that precedes the signification of object or emotion. The poet is put to death because he wants to make language perceive what it doesn't want to say, provide it with its matter independently of the sign, and free it from denotation. For it is this eminently parodic gesture that changes the system."[101]

Fukazawa's grotesquely funny and infuriating *sutten-korokoro* similarly "makes language perceive what it doesn't want to say." It viscerally displays the fragile "constitution" of Japan's symbolic god-family. If this "eminently parodic gesture" did not change the system in quite the way Kristeva would hope, it certainly changed how writers could thereafter treat Japanese emperors. While one can write about the emperor system in rarified jargon, such immediately concrete and common language as spoken by the merry narrator in "Fūryū mutan" is apparently no longer available to writers. For years Fukazawa and his five dogs, like Salman Rushdie (whose Japanese translator, Igarashi Hitoshi, was murdered in the summer of 1991), moved from one safe house to another escorted by the police. Once the furor had subsided Fukazawa again took up parody, but no longer in literature. In 1965, he started a collective in Saitama prefecture called the *Rabu mii nōjō* (Love-Me Farm), where he dedicated himself to growing strawberries and making bean paste. He worked as a ticket scalper and a pimp, and wrote that he thought of becoming a porter or a traveling salesman.[102] By 1971, he was running a muffin stall grandly dubbed the Yumeya (Dream Shop) in a working-class neighborhood. One hardly expects such activities from a modern Japanese writer, but they seem typical of someone who sought to deflate the rhetoric of power, be it political or intellectual, with the popular parodic gesture. In accordance with Fukazawa's instructions, his 1987 Buddhist funeral featured recorded music by Rod Stewart ("Da Ya Think I'm Sexy?"). His real-life death poem was poetry written not in the idiom of traditional Japanese aesthetics but in the vulgar, popular, irreverent slang of a British rocker.

Not many Japanese authors have had careers as sensational as Fukazawa's, and few have so offended the political orthodoxies of progressive intellectuals and imperial absolutists alike. "No work in the history of postwar Japanese literature," wrote one critic, "so roiled society as 'Fūryū mutan.'"[103] Ōe Kenzaburō observed that not one of Fukazawa's fellow writers did anything concretely to aid him.[104] Fukazawa's career repaid the compliment. But at the same time, none save Fukazawa has so dramatically and tragically demonstrated what the effective limits of free speech and artistic license are in a society that can otherwise legitimately claim to be among the world's more tolerant. "Hirohito is dead and Akihito reigns in his stead," wrote Matsuura Sōzō in 2000, "but in Japan there is still no freedom to criticize the imperial institution."[105] A discouraged Kawamura Minato concludes that the literary establishment in Japan is far more accomplished in naming scapegoats than it is defending freedom of expression.[106]

In recent decades the Japanese press has continued to be harassed by the right wing and, under prime minister Abe Shinzō, the state itself. The Japanese media's right to speak, whether exercised by the oppositional media or the reigning sovereign—the current reigning emperor Akihito has been attacked for his comments on his country's wartime aggression—is a controversial and fragile privilege, even as the state now suffers its loss of hegemony over governing metaphors for Japan such as "the Yasukuni Shrine, the national flag, and the national anthem."[107] In 2012, fifty years after the Shimanaka Incident, one of Fukazawa's biographers said that Japan lacked full freedom of speech.[108] As I write this in 2016, the Japanese government is forcing the resignation of outspoken television newscasters, and NHK censored Emperor Akihito's televised speculation on his abdication.

Japan's resilient emperor system is relevant to how modern Japanese literature is modern, as well as Japanese. It is first among the central institutions of Japanese modernity about which literature might have something to say. But it is also a topic which resists fictional representation and thus marks the limits of representability. Every literary modernity has its boundaries—America's is pedophilia—but this is Japan's. A pop culture version of *utakai-hajime* is state television's annual year's end *Kōhaku uta gassen* (The Red and White Song Festival Contest), in which songs sung by celebrities—the males are white, the females red—battle each other, prompting Tsurumi Shunsuke to call it today's real poetry competition (*uta-awase*).[109] It draws more television viewers each year than any other musical program and is said to be enjoyed by the imperial family. Like the commoners' poems in the *utakai-hajime*, songs are chosen by a committee, not by public polling, but nowadays cell phones are used by viewers at home to participate in the voting over whether red or white wins. At the end of the show, all join in to sing a Japanized version of the Scottish "Auld Lang Syne," one verse of which says the Japanese people "single-mindedly serve the country" (*hitoe ni tsukase, kuni no tame*).

Fukazawa disapproved of television, if not quite. "You say you hate television," said one interviewer, "but I'm told you have three TV sets in your home." Fukazawa responded with a grudging "yeah."[110] "Television is such a universal presence," wrote historian Takashi Fujitani in 1992, "that a simple counting of the number of households that own television sets can no longer adequately describe its ubiquity."[111] From today's perspective we see that television was just a brief-lived, transitional technology that has given way to newer media, as smart phones minimize the need to assemble in groups the same way silent reading more than a century earlier had. Mass assemblies now are flash mobs summoned via texting. Thanks to the Internet, "Fūryū mutan" is no longer difficult to obtain. Anyone can buy the Kindle edition from Amazon.co.jp for 398 yen or with the right app get it for free. And in 2015, state television's broadcast of the *Kōhaku* song contest drew its lowest ratings in history.[112]

Reading Comics/Writing Graffiti

In the run up to the marriage of Crown Prince Akihito and Shōda Michiko, and amid growing protests over the renewal of the U.S.-Japan Security Treaty, both the imperial family and the bilateral pact were derided in the *manga* (graphic novels) increasingly read by university students alongside their Jean-Paul Sartre, Albert Camus, and homegrown existentialist novelist Ōe Kenzaburō.[1] These manga, no less than Fukazawa Shichirō's short story, were met with right-wing protests and government intervention ranging from harassment with megaphones to threats of official censorship under the law.

This chapter's theme is the cultural nexus in 1960s Japan of manga, graffiti, and radical students, a triple context united by a shared resistance to received literary, social, and political orthodoxies. The *gakusei undō* (student movement), which I studied as an undergraduate in 1970s Japan when it still cast a pall over university campuses, dates back much earlier. "The closing years of Meiji and the early years of Taishō," states historian Peter Duus, "were in some ways similar to the American sixties."[2] But it was with the 1948 founding of *Zengakuren*—an acronym for the All-Japan Federation of Student

Self-Governing Associations—that its most dramatic history unfolded in decidedly public view thanks to modern media, above all television. The circumstances of the late 1960s and early 1970s that led to the eventual collapse of the student movement—the internecine violence of the most extreme sects, the failure to prevent the Security Treaty from being renewed once again, spectacular terrorism around the world, so forth—are well known. Sociologist Patricia Steinhoff has studied the organizational structure of radical student groups, concluding that the Red Army Faction "robbed banks and hijacked airplanes the same way Sony researches and markets a new project."[3] Kazuko Tsurumi examined the class backgrounds of student radicals to discover that they often came from the ranks of small-scale farming families,[4] descendants of the same peasantry that rose in revolt (*ikki*) in previous eras. Student radicals in 1960s Japan have been portrayed as paradigmatic of, most modestly, the traditional breeding ground for modern popular revolts or, most grandly, Japanese society as a whole.

I approach them differently, not solely as a social or political phenomenon but as a pivotal cultural one. I turn to radical students not because, as Tsurumi discovered, they read Marx, Lenin, and Mao, but because they also read comics, workably defined by Roger Sabin as a "booklet, tabloid, magazine or book form that includes as a major feature the presence of one or more strips. . . . a narrative in the form of a sequence of pictures—usually, but not always, with text."[5] Japanese histories of postwar manga have placed them under the rubric of literature (*bungaku*) as mass culture increasingly blurred the line with the high.[6] With transcribed sound effects added to the narrative and dialogue found in traditional fiction, manga arguably comprise the preeminent form of popular literature in Japan from roughly the end of the Occupation to the near present, as new digital media cut into all print sales. "What happened behind the barricades was often no different than what happened in leisure time: The students spent their time reading comic books."[7] The relationship between university politics and manga was not quite that casual, of course. "If you look into the relationship between students and manga," wrote the left-wing weekly *Asahi jānaru* in retrospect, "what you find is the 'university laid waste.'"[8]

There are many parallels here with U.S. "underground comix" of the same period, when cartoonists such as Robert Crumb started their iconoclastic careers in or on the periphery of college campuses. Aside from some of Skip Williamson's work, edgy American comics/comix were not political—no more so than the hippie was political—but specialized in giving vent to male

heterosexist desire. Williamson pointed toward the problem when he speculated, "It may be a paradox to mix comics with revolutionary culture, because
comics deal with cliché situations created by decadent society."[9] As we see here
and in subsequent chapters, the issues for late-twentieth-century Japanese literature will overlap with those of the American literature, but never will be exactly
the same. I start by sketching some of the ways the radical student movement in
1960s Japan was implicated in popular culture: as the inspiration for it, as consumers of it, and as producers of it. If we understand manga of that time as the
preeminent pop of pop culture, then we can agree with Andreas Huyssen when
he wrote, "As an 'emancipation euphoria' spread, mainly among high school and
university students, pop in its broadest sense became amalgamated with the
public and political activities of the anti-authoritarian New Left."[10]

If it is also true that the student radical was, by 1970, "the most distinctive
indigenous cultural figure of the post war era,"[11] that was to the result of the
translation of student activism into what we anachronistically recognize as a
"lifestyle" marked by smart accessories. Radical students in the 1960s adopted a
look—helmets, towels wrapped about the neck or face, and the menacing poles
known as *gebabō* ("violence stick," from the German *Gewalt* and Sino-Japanese
bō). With the adoption of such a distinctive look, the radical students assumed
the status of a subculture in Japan independent not just from other groups of
students but from the established political Left. The government might have
dampened the appeal of radical student groups if it had been able to ban the
trendy apparel of those groups. But that is not what happened. After the student
revolt at the University of Tokyo (Tōdai) in 1968, its televised finale beamed
into homes across the country, that subculture was marketed with actors done
up as rebellious students in advertisements, comedy shows, soap operas and,
most to my purpose, manga.

How the student movement was implicated in 1960s popular culture can
be mapped by examining manga, their contents, authors, and readers. They
were, alongside Japanese pinball (*pachinko*), the two leisure activities of postwar adult popular culture earlier the preserve of children. What other country
in 1970 boasted a radical student group that took its name—the *Nyarome*
Corps—from the name of a cat in a popular comic book, Akatsuka Fujio's
Mōretsu Atarō (Fierce Atarō)?[12] In the late 1960s, writes former student radical and later manga critic Kure Tomofusa, one began to see references in the
press to the popularity of comics among university students and a rise in their
political content.[13] A 1965 survey of Kyoto University students revealed that

the manga magazine *Shōnen sundē* (Boy's Sunday) was the fourth most widely read weekly among all.[14] Commenting on a trend noted in the United States as well,[15] psychoanalyst Okonogi Keigo recalls that "from the mid-sixties through the height of the campus revolts, one would see piles of manga strewn about the haunts of young activists. Until then people had read manga in private, but in the sixties it had become a public activity even among adults. One could frequently see young people deep into their manga, even in university offices."[16] Okonogi goes on to remark that reading manga in the latter half of the 1960s was countercultural, much like wearing T-shirts and blue jeans or listening to folk music was. Reading manga, he claims, was *jiko shuchō* (self-expression). In a 1969 roundtable convened on the topic of contemporary manga, Ozaki Hotsuki said that nowadays younger people were choosing them to express their selfhood (*jiko o hyōgen suru*).[17] That was a selfhood older critics perceived when they attempted to make the countercultural recognizably modernist. But the real point was never what manga narrated. It was that students all along the political spectrum were reading them; indeed, it was that they were being *read*, period. They became a symbol of the everyday, not the extraordinary or cultish. "Manga amuse," wrote Takeuchi Osamu in his history of them. "Manga seduce. Manga scream. Manga break taboo."[18] But manga were omnipresent.

Most intriguing about Ozaki's observation is not that young people were expressing their selfhood, or whatever, via popular culture, but that they were doing so in public space: in classrooms, trains, anywhere enjoying without embarrassment a pastime long thought juvenile and best confined within the privacy of the home. Manga, or more precisely, their display, had become a public, even mass *action* outside secluded silent reading itself, and one akin to the action associated with the often violent demonstrations of a public and mass radical student movement. In his melancholy memoirs written after twenty years of imprisonment for his role in masterminding the hijacking of Japan Airlines Flight 351 in 1970, Red Army Faction leader Shiomi Takaya says he was fond of serious fiction as a boy. Sōseki's *Neko* was his favorite novel, and he also liked Twain's *The Adventures of Huckleberry Finn*, Luo Guanzhong's *The Romance of the Three Kingdoms* and Shi Nai'an's *Water Margin*. All are stories of youth battling an inhospitable world. Inspired to pursue literature at university rather than his father's choice of medicine, Shiomi especially identified with Sōseki as a fellow intellectual who sought to be both an individual and something more. But once Shiomi turned to radical politics and direct action, he found his comrades were reading something other than Dostoevsky or Lenin; they were reading manga. His close friend and hijacker of Flight 351, Tamiya Takamaro, who spent decades in involuntary North Korean exile, was especially fond of Kajiwara Ikki's (1936–87) *Ashita no Jō* (Tomorrow's Joe, 1968–73), the popular story of a working-class boxer. Shiomi says they were criticized by some comrades for spending too much of their revolutionary time reading comics; they truly were the "manga generation." In hindsight Shiomi concludes that stories such as *Ashita no Jō* were part and parcel of the infantile Left's romanticism of the time, and that the appeal of a youthful boxer sprung from the same naïve humanism that drew them to the Red Army Faction in the first place. Attending Tamiya's 1995 Pyongyang funeral, Shiomi noted that the spirit (*seishin*) in hijacking an airliner was the same spirit celebrated in *Ashita no Jō*.[19]

Japanese journalism was almost a decade late in picking up on manga's newfound popularity among university students and reported on it only after discovering young workers reading them at inexpensive rental libraries (*kashihon'ya*) that originally catered to children from lower rungs of the socioeconomic structure.[20] (In the late 1950s women's groups questioned just how sanitary these libraries were for their sons.) Tsurumi Shunsuke's students, conducting fieldwork in the early sixties, found two young men in Kobe, both working at a dry cleaners, who paid to borrow on average three manga a day. Their favorites were Shirato Sanpei's (1932–) violent manga.[21] Shirato, a middle-school dropout, had begun serializing his work *Ninja bugeichō* (Military Exploits of the Ninja Warriors) in the late 1950s, the story of peasant rebellions, class conflict, and popular millenarian movements (*yoarashi*) set in the tumultuous Sengoku period (1467–1603). *Ninja* was widely criticized at the time by many, including by the Japan Communist Party, for its graphic violence. Over a thousand people are killed in *Ninja*, eight-five of them by decapitation in scenes of grotesquery never depicted before in modern Japanese media. Some readers wrote letters decrying *Ninja* as no better than latrine graffiti (*benjō no rakugaki*).[22] But by the time Shirato finished his full seventeen volumes in 1962, it had sparked a boom in *gekiga*, "dramatic" manga. The impact of *Ninja bugeichō* and subsequent works by Shirato was considerable and long lasting. In 1966, Ōshima Nagisa, a director associated with the New Left, made a feature-length film based on *Ninja bugeichō* composed of Shirato's original drawings photographed from varying angles while voiceovers provided the narration.

Lengthier and more ponderous than what had come before, *gekiga* were an adult genre of Japanese comics. The term today simply denotes narrative manga targeted to younger (and not so young) males, but it was first used to describe

Figure 8.1. Still of Kagemaru from Ōshima Nagisa's film *Ninja bugeichō* (Military Exploits of the Ninja Warriors; 1966)

comics with greater realism, especially concerning contemporary events. The 1963 murder of a teenage girl (the Sayama Incident), for example, was made into a *gekiga*; one scholar called Fukazawa's "Fūryū mutan" the *gekiga* version of a revolution.[23] Yamaguchi Masao thought Fukazawa inhabited the adult world and Shirato the child's, but that they shared a common brutality (*zankoku*).[24] Moreover, *gekiga*'s use of such quasi-cinematic techniques as close-ups suggested its rise in popularity was linked to young people's new "television literacy."[25]

Shirato's comic about anonymous organizers behind famous figures in Japanese history such as Oda Nobunaga and Akechi Mitsuhide appealed to radical students, then being expelled from the rolls of the old Left Japan Communist Party. Shirato was not a political company man. He had participated in the bloody violence of the 1952 May Day protests but subsequently spent most of his time cloistered at a secret Chiba address to draw what he had seen rather than foment more of it. He located revolutionary action not in Leninist vanguard leadership but in subjective, individual action. Like students subsequently drawn to the New Left by the end of the 1950s, he was not fond of the positions the establishment Left took in legislative politics, and he reflected that antipathy in his graphic novels inspired by the failure of the 1960 *Anpo* struggle. In an early essay on Shirato by noted authority Fujikawa Jisui, *Ninja* was hailed as an epochal work that expressed the "anti-establishment energy" of its day.[26]

With *gekiga*, students became regular readers of manga,[27] and manga displaced a portion of Japanese popular fiction. A work such as Shishi Bunroku's *Jiyū gakkō*, had it been published a decade later, might have appeared as a graphic novel. In this same period, comics in the United States also began to attract young adult readers. The 1954 institution of a morals code for American comics, designed to shield children from baneful effects, meant that the industry had to find new audiences, hence the birth of the superhero new wave, such as *Fantastic Four*, *Spider-Man*, and *Thor*. Marvel's Stan Lee had Spider-Man's alter-ego Peter Parker pose before bookcases lined with existentialist texts.[28] But Japan's popular culture in the late fifties and early sixties was more overtly political in Japan than in the United States, and the comics read by university students reflected that difference. George Orwell, in his study of boy's weeklies in 1930s Britain, noted the stubbornly conservative basis of the genre and wondered "why is there no such thing as left-wing boys' paper?"[29] The answer was money. English publishing was already monopolistic by the 1930s. But Shirato worked for himself and for small entrepreneurs he knew personally. He was the son of prominent proletarian painter Okamoto Toki, but circumstances forced him to make a living after the war by turning to *kami-shibai* (street corner storytelling aided with paper drawings). Marilyn Ivy discloses that the artists who drew the props for *kami-shibai* performers—Tezuka Osamu (1928–89) was one example—went to work in manga as street performance was killed off by television.[30] Tsurumi Shunsuke compared the profession with that of being a ninja, a messy profession called "rhizomatic" since both engage in guerilla-like actions. (One writer has called *gekiga* "serialized *kami-shibai*."[31]) Shirato sketched from a perspective that appealed to radical students. Even as skeptical a critic as Satō Tadao stated, "It is an undeniable fact that Shirato's works are historically materialist," and Tsurumi thought Shirato's worldview Hegelian. "Out of the generation that loved his comics came brave combat squads of students marching bow-legged on account of their wooden staves [*gebabō*], their helmeted heads masked with towels."[32] As a popular quip had it at the time, radical students brandished "the left-wing *Asahi Journal* in the right hand, *Shōnen Magazine* in the left."[33]

Ninja bugeichō takes place in the late sixteenth century, from Nobunaga's first military victories to his last defeats. While Nobunaga was a historical figure, we do not have references to ninja in any archives about him. For Shirato to write about them, then, might have been tantamount to a declaration that the historical record is at least incomplete and possibly even false. An oppressed peasantry does battle with ruling elites made up of *daimyō* and conniving clerics, and sometimes they win. More than fifty major characters appear in *Ninja bugeichō*, but the central hero is Kagemaru, who struggles to lead his seven personal followers in revolt. Kagemaru became an icon for New Left students and their own struggles. In the post-*Anpo* context of a mass politics defeated by an ostensibly democratic state, *Ninja bugeichō*'s litany of agrarian revolts, urban millenarian movements, and violent class warfare proved popular among students considering direct action. Some university students might presumably miss girlfriends or mothers while in jail, but one of the leaders of the student movement at Tōdai wrote to *Garo* (the most important avant-garde manga journal of the 1960s) from police detention that he loved Shirato's *Ninja* and hoped the magazine could send him back issues. When it did, the student responded with a mash note. "I found it unbearable that my jailers discarded my copies of *Garo*, whose pages, one by one, I read with such care. I am tremendously glad to have those drawings so dear to me in my possession again. I was very sad to have been without them close to me."[34]

The organized Left at the time of the first *Anpo* struggle located its failure within the immaturity of its organizational theories, and was looking for new ways to effect a more powerful collusion of the intelligentsia with the masses. It is surely not coincidental that the leftist intelligentsia at this moment discovered manga and its mass appeal. If "*Ninja bugeichō* is a comic with a historical materialist point of view,"[35] then an American historian of manga may be right when he claims, "For many, *Ninja bugeichō* became a substitute for reading Marx."[36] In 1965, Takemoto Nobuhiro, at the time a Marxist student in the economics department at Kyoto University but later a leader of the Red Army Faction, wrote to *Garo* that "Shirato Sanpei's manga has made an extremely deep impression on my ideological consciousness and charged my entire being. . . . Against the desolate intellectual background of our new 'mass social theories,' Shirato's assertions are without question the most valuable initiatives we now possess."[37] One might raise the specter of life imitating art here. One ground observer of the 1968 uprising at the University of Tokyo, when students were reading Shirato's *Kamui den* (Tale of Kamui, 1964–71) for its purported *kakumei shisō* (revolutionary thought), said that campuses "were reminiscent of the days when the sword ruled Japan. . . . The Tokyo University struggle evoked strong images of Japan's violent past, and the establishment of the student struggle as a distinctive sub-culture of its own was assured."[38]

By the late 1960s, manga were firmly established as a product for and about Japanese youth subcultures, and especially that of the radical student, and soon not just at the universities. The controversial manga sensation of 1968, Nagai Gō's *Harenchi gakuen* (Saint Shameless Academy) panicked local PTAs in Japan into emergency meetings on account of its depictions of high school teachers being killed by their students and sold as meat in butcher's shops.

Despite a vocal anti–*Harenchi gakuen* movement—Mie prefecture, for instance, declared the manga officially *akusho* (bad writing)—*Harenchi*'s scenes of explicit sex made a commercial success of its sponsoring magazine *Shōnen junpu* (Boys Jump). It also spawned additional *harenchi* comics, and more. The word *harenchi* would soon show up on protest placards erected by student radicals at the gates of the University of Tokyo.[39] Noting that "television and comics were firmly intertwined in a symbiotic relationship" by the mid-sixties,[40] Minami Hiroshi wrote, "The most popular television programs among the youth are those programs characterized as *harenchi*. . . . These programs tell stories about resistance to the existing code of ethics and moral standards, and about the search for freedom."[41] Entertainment that is satirical but commercial risks the charge of complicity, and manga historians in Japan now bemoan the disappearance, come the 1970s, of the political, anti-establishment comics of the decade before. But as others point out, manga seldom address real life. It is often said, with hostility but also some truth, that American academics today are "tenured radicals." The student movement in the United States does seem to have sent an unusual number of its veterans to the same institutions it assailed. What about Japan? What happened to the majority of student radicals who did not become terrorists in the 1970s? They did not easily join the ranks of white-collar workers at Japan's more prestigious firms. Many would have refused the chance. In an essay on manga artist/writer Tsuge Yoshiharu (1937–), Yoshimoto Takaaki talks about the appeal of Tsuge's antiheroes to a generation of frustrated political youth (*seiji seinen*) for whom dealing in secondhand books or cameras appealed as professions precisely for their marginality.[42] "Contrary to popular belief," notes political scientist Ellis Krauss, "former leaders and activists in Zengakuren . . . have not flocked to Mitsui and Mitsubishi." Krauss mentions one who ended up running something called the "Let's Go Sailing Club."[43] "Beginning in 1969," writes Patricia Steinhoff, "Japanese corporate employers

Figure 8.2. Cover of volume 4 of Nagai Gō's *Harenchi gakuen* (Saint Shameless Academy; 1968)

systematically excluded ex-student radicals in their recruitment, a practice up-
held by a 1973 Supreme Court ruling." "The thousands," according to her, "who
have arrest records or have been screened out of corporate employment for
student activism have been marked by their participation and cannot extricate
themselves simply by not being students anymore. They have been declared
deviant and may have to take specific action or deliberately hide their pasts in
order to be restored to normalcy."[44]

Some did go into university careers, and some exchanged their helmets for
business suits. Oguchi Akihiko trained as a lawyer to defend unions and the
poor. A handful became novelists. Fukuda Takeshi may have become a successful businessman who leads a famously lavish lifestyle, but many veterans of the
student movement were absorbed into, as the *Asahi jānaru* put it, "the lumpen
proletariat."[45] While most student radicals simply disappeared from view, a
number went into publishing, even starting their own small companies that
produced alternative journalism and manga. One popular destination was the
Takarajima publishing company, which flourished under the leadership of Hasumi Seiichi, a veteran of the Chūkakumaruha (the Middle Core Faction of the
Japan Revolutionary Communist League). He brought comrades with him. His
alma mater, Waseda University, was not only site of some of the most vociferous
student protests starting with a strike over tuition in January 1966, but it is also
the school that has produced the most manga writers and other contributors
to the counterculture that found a home at the house magazine *Takarajima*.
It pushed the publishing industry's envelope as its founder's student politics
had once pushed the university; there was, to cite an example, a special issue
on cannabis. By 1970, the stalwart left-wing weekly *Asahi jānaru* was carrying
manga in its pages, but *Takarajima* took things further in the new decade. In the
1980s, the readership "changed one-hundred percent," says sociologist Inamatsu
Tatsuo, as the magazine moved aggressively to court a younger and more female
audience with coverage of fashion and foreign trends.[46] But Takarajima, one of
the foremost chroniclers of manga and its subcultures in the 1970s, preserved
relics of the late-sixties student movement, such as pornographic comics and
books (*erohon*). Ōtsuka Eiji recalls being impressed by how the New Left's
propaganda (*ajibira*) stylistically resembled *gekiga* comics, a keen observation
for literary history.[47] Both student activists and 1960s manga writers described
themselves as *gerira* (guerillas). Looking back on the 1960s, it was the world of
manga, not literature, that gave birth to epic works depicting class struggle.[48]

For several reasons, the workplace culture of the manga writer appealed to ex-radicals alienated from the disciplined, hierarchical structures of Japanese white-collar professions. Unlike U.S. cartoonists, most Japanese cartoonists come out of their country's elite universities. Tenured radicals in the United States may be monitored lest they propagandize students with subversive ideas harbored since the barricades. But how are Japanese ex-radicals who migrated to the manga industry recognizably "Left" in their work? When, not despite but maybe *because* of the immense commercial success of Japanese comics, political and editorial cartoons are now said to be nonexistent in Japan?[49]

In the early 1970s, some manga did describe the sort of ideological rivalries associated with the work of Shirato Sanpei and others. But if we look for evidence of an original politics at work during this period, we need to consider manga as a formal as well as thematic challenge to orthodoxy. When a PTA condemned Nagai's *Harenchi gakuen* as *akusho* in a full-throated moral panic, it invoked language with a long history in Japan. Referring to "harmful books" and meant to censor, the word *akusho* goes back to the Tokugawa period, like manga itself. "Bad writing": perhaps the distinction between high-, middle- and low-brow culture in Japan is now so minimal that it makes no sense of talk about manga as a decadent literacy. But that is a question of value, and whatever one decides about the heights or depths of the thematic content and graphic details, manga as text that is truncated, elliptical, onomatopoeic, cinematic, disposable, silly and often in the worst of taste has to be called bad insofar as it rejects conventional or standard modes of literacy by purposefully bastardizing them. Worst of all for unhappy parents, time spent reading manga was time not spent on school studies, that is, not spent on training for assimilation into the juggernaut of the high-growth Japanese economy.[50]

Is this the connection between the student Left in Japan and the growth of the manga industry in the 1970s? The *gekiga* phenomenon in postwar Japan, for which the *Anpo* struggles were a frequent theme, was not the outgrowth of modern humanism but instead, as Ishiko Junzō put it, pure *zokuakusei* (vulgarity).[51] The historical significance of postwar manga may lie less in their tales of historical revolt—nothing new there—than in their irreverent language, cheap paper, and gaudy colors, or in the claustrophobic and dank ambience of the lending libraries, cafés, and occupied classrooms where students read them. Is this why some self-styled Marxists moved from zigzagging in the streets to illustrating, with air brushes, an equally carnivalesque parade of cartoon characters? There is an articulated synchronicity to posit between the purposeful vulgarity of a bourgeois antibourgeois student movement and its verifiable links with a manga industry meaning to profit by being just as offensive.

You can visit a university campus in Japan today and see other kinds of bad writing besides manga. The worst of this *akusho* is graffiti (*rakusho* or *rakugaki* in Japanese), described by Susan Stewart as simultaneously "writing, painting, dirt, and crime," because, depending upon your perspective, it is any one of those things.[52] Another definition of graffiti starts: "pictorial or written inscriptions for which no official provision is made and which are largely unwanted"[53]— much like the anonymous, delinquent authors of same. In the 1970s, Norman Mailer made cultural heroes out of New York City adolescent vandals sporting tags such as "Taki 183" (and yes, one called "Japan") who were defacing subway cars. Mailer saw "panic in the act, a species of writing with an eye over one's shoulder for the oncoming of authority."[54] Graffiti from one point of view may be vandalism; from another they are minor terrorism, or as Dick Hebdige put it, "an expression of both impotence and a kind of power."[55] Jean Baudrillard, apropos of 1968 Paris, wrote that graffiti respond "there, on the spot, and breach the fundamental role of non-response enunciated by all the media," that they do not led themselves "to deciphering as a text rivaling commercial discourse," and that they present themselves as "a transgression."[56]

Notoriously and deliberately hard to comprehend, graffiti—"decentralized and decentered insubordination"[57]—make fascinating reading because their language is private yet on display. Like Japanese manga of the same period, graffiti fairly constituted an alternative literacy. "They draw attention to themselves," Hebdige has pointed out, with "the power to disfigure."[58] As Baudrillard suggests, graffiti's efficacy lies not in their retort but in their refusal, their rude usurpation to exist where they ought not, in their near-indecipherable and impudent dare to signify. Others have rejoined they are "clumsy, untutored, willfully destructive, and ignorant of pretense to commercial utility. Across the shiny surface of progress's *yes*, [they] scrawled a stubbornly atavistic *no*. . . . [T]his kind of scrawl has now become an inevitable, inescapable fixture of modern experience."[59]

Nowadays the impulse to deface anonymously finds its outlet on the Internet, but university walls in Japan still bear traces of the old graffiti. Much of what remains legible is dull sloganeering mixed with references to cheeky children's comics such as *Doraemon* or the lyrics of then-current pop music, in particular the *gotōchi songu* (hometown songs) that Kasagi Shizuko's "Tokyo Boogie-Woogie" pioneered decades earlier. Fuji Keiko's bluesy "Shinjuku no onna"

(Shinjuku woman, 1969) was close to an anthem for a sulky New Left with its line, "I was deceived" (*damasarechatte*).[60] But some of the graffiti are brilliantly original, untranslatable. Student radicals adorned their school walls in their struggle to destroy and create at the same time. "Poetic ironies vis-à-vis authority" were scrawled as graffiti "on walls, pillars, doors, desks, chairs and hallways, on every space in the world [*ari to arayuru kūkan*]."[61] In handwriting stylized to suggest both militancy and a generational break with history, students at Japan's best schools harnessed the worst writing to gesture a grand refusal. Art historian Matsueda Itaru, citing both *rakugaki* and manga as *itazuragaki* (mischievous writing), said graffiti

> are something written as a pleasure *for just that time and place*, as a certain kind of diversion. They are not anything we write because we are required to do so. An occasional breather, something for fun. In the margins of our notebooks, on train station walls, schoolroom desks, restrooms. A shape comes of hands in motion simply to fill up a free moment. We have no aim in mind. There is neither a beginning nor end. The end of the scribbling and the end of our looking at it are simultaneous, but there is no end where we sign our names to it. There's just a fade-out loosely linked to other things we do: a temporary end, a respite. A pleasure without completion—that is the meaning of graffiti.[62]

Tsurumi Shunsuke thought that manga preserved the tradition of graffiti and kept their essence alive. Like postwar comics (which were fond of lampooning the police), graffiti were "anonymous texts that rebuke authority."[63] Neither Tsurumi nor I claim student graffiti resemble or prefigure manga, though look hard enough and there are commonalities—lexical, graphic, and political—deriving from their totemic function. As a 1960s university student wrote in a letter, manga are "an anonymous anti-aestheticism that had their start on the walls of our university buildings during the war of the barricades. Those graffiti were the first sketches for our manga of today." Ishiko Junzō, the recipient of this letter, recalled how university walls in late-sixties Japan, as in Paris (the May Revolution) and Beijing (the Cultural Revolution), were covered with graffiti as well as with posters and flyers "from the classrooms to the toilets." He says that this student was right to refer to those scribbles as outcries (*sakebi*) rather than as writing. In such graffiti, Ishiko "wants to see the original drawings [*genga*] of manga to follow." "They share," he said, "anonymity, spontaneity, rawness, and surreptitiousness" and are capable of constituting a critique of a society otherwise governed by convention and rule.[64] Baudrillard makes a similar observation about France's graffiti in its May Revolution:

> The real revolutionary media during May were the walls and their speech, the silk-screen posters and the hand-painted notices, the street where speech began and was exchanged—everything that was an *immediate* inscription, given and returned, spoken and answered, mobile in the same space and time, reciprocal and antagonistic. The street is, in this sense, the alternative and subversive form of the mass media, since it isn't, like the latter, an objectified support for answerless messages, a transmission system at a distance. It is the frayed space of the symbolic exchange of speech—ephemeral, mortal: a speech that is not reflected on the Platonic screen of the media. Institutionalized by reproduction, reduced to a spectacle, this speech is expiring.[65]

Ishiko wrote that "the origin of manga is ancient graffiti," and "one sees the start of today's manga in the graffiti found on the campuses of universities now in the midst of struggle." He nonetheless understood that the point of radical student graffiti was never as simple as communication or propaganda. The audience for them was already other radical students who hardly needed convincing. "'Looking' at it was screaming the same scream as 'writing' it." The value of graffiti was the experience of the graffiti writer at the time of defacing property. There was never so much a message as an actualization, a demonstration of selfhood. Graffiti were written words and drawn pictures, but free from all the rules of poetry and fiction, manga and painting.[66] "*Gekiga*," Ishiko insisted, "did not derive from modern humanism, or even from the theme of the *Anpo* Treaty. They came from the very vulgarity of postwar Japanese manga."[67]

In January 1969, the University of Tokyo settled student and staff strikes on campus, but the Yasuda Amphitheater remained occupied. Renamed by students the 1968 Liberation Lecture Hall (1968 Kaihō Kōdō), it was overrun by thousands of heavily armed police (*kidōtai*) in the bloody days of 18–19 January 1969. Among the five hundred students holding out inside it were the most violent, the Trotskyist Chūkakumaruha. Its announced agenda included direct democracy, university autonomy, an end to the Security Treaty, and solidarity with liberation movements around the world. None of these goals was accomplished but the Chūkakumaruha did not meekly surrender. Under assault, the students threw furniture and Molotov cocktails against the police; the police in turn used tear gas and water hoses. Thirty-five hours later nearly four hundred students, people posing as students, and their supporters were arrested. Live television coverage of the battle earned the highest ratings in Japanese television history.[68]

The amphitheater was famously festooned with graffiti during its long student-led occupation. Many of the graffiti were sectarian and militant and required hermeneutics to decipher. There were ad hominem attacks on faculty. Some of the messages were strictly utilitarian, such as "Wash any dishes you use." Some were fatuously penned in foreign languages: a Hölderin verse scrawled on the clock tower, lines lifted from Rimbaud, Shakespeare, and Goethe. Quotations from the Chinese Four Books and Five Classics, ironic and otherwise, were not uncommon. Sōseki was parodied with the graffito "Waga-hai wa keshigoma de aru" (I am a blackboard eraser). One graffito was a flippant test: "Explain the difference between Marx and Marcuse in eight words." Some of it was sentimental; messages to girlfriends and parents were scribbled on walls. No small amount was sardonic. But references to popular culture such as club sports (rugby), the movies (cult actor Takakura Ken was a favorite), television (the students staged their own mock virtual *Kōhaku* song contest on New Year's Day)[69] and manga were rife. Twenty volumes of boys' comics (*shōnen manga*), including Shirato's *Ninja bugeichō*, were found interspersed on library bookshelves.[70]

The contemporary compendium of student graffiti, *Daigaku gerira no uta* (Songs of the University Guerillas, 1969), catalogs *rakugaki* and other jottings gathered during the University of Tokyo uprising. As my own singular rebellion, in 1974 I shoplifted it from the Kyoto Maruzen, a bookstore notorious for its usurious markups. It remains the most complete record of late-sixties student graffiti we have, and it features the most oft-quoted graffito found at the main entrance to the amphitheater: "In search of solidarity, we have no fear of isolation. We do not shrink from failure for lack of fortitude. We refuse to be daunted, our strength unspent."[71] There is nothing untutored about this graffito. Its first line was lifted from a 1958 essay by the Communist poet Tanigawa Gan (1923–95) on the problem of everyday speech and political struggle.[72] Tanigawa's early essays had a notable impact on the New Left in the 1960s, but he was hardly a household name; the allusion was likely available only to the well schooled. Ishiko saw this graffito in person and subsequently argued, in perfectly modernist terms, that it "reflected the selfhood" (*jiko hyōshutsu*) of those who wrote it. Little in the scrawls seemed directed toward motivating political

Figure 8.3. Graffiti in the Yasuda Amphitheater: "In search of solidarity, we have no fear of isolation." (Photograph: The Mainichi Newspapers/AFLO.)

action among fellow travelers.[73] Sassa Atsuyuki, entering the building after the battle, saw rooms with books scattered on the floor, shards of glass, *ajibira*, broken desks, manga, half-eaten rice balls, discarded chopsticks, and, everywhere, artlessly scrawled political graffiti.[74] The graffiti were a display of an anonymous, collective subjectivity articulated through references to the demands of the times constituting an "expression of a principle of identity [*jidōritsu*]." If graffiti, as Ishiko claimed, constitute expression formally prior to other genres ("poetry or literature, manga or paintings"), then it is a medium that is purely concrete and material, direct and unmediated and therefore wholly unlike anything such as conventional satire: it was what Ishiko "specifically sought from manga today."[75]

On the eve of the assault on the Yasuda Amphitheater, and in a review of Julien Besançon's *Les Murs ont la parole*, writer Nada Inada (a penname based on the Spanish anarchical phrase *nada y nada*) urged student radicals to deploy the irreverent humor of graffiti as a weapon. "Graffiti need the power of the imagination," he wrote in *Asahi jānaru*. "From time to time, it makes the impossible possible."[76] Nada meant that bad writing, the perennial charge against the texts of popular culture, can elevate the criminal, the transgressive, or merely the tasteless into high style while not suffering the loss of its critique. Graffiti on canvas purchased in an art gallery will still get their makers into trouble if duplicated on (someone else's) private property. A manga that details the dismemberment of a teacher by his pupils can be funny, revolutionary, or both. But it is certainly *bad*, and not in terms of salacious content but instead mischievous form. Graffiti may be called a "guerilla news channel" that "gives us raw news from society's margin,"[77] but that is not always the case. Like student radicals, cheap manga and much of popular culture itself (rock 'n' roll?), graffiti have to be rude to say what they mean. As one anonymous bathroom artist once put it, "The only difference between philosophy and graffiti is the word 'fuck.'"[78]

Right-wing writer Mishima Yukio publicly debated the students who had occupied the Yasuda Amphitheater for two and a half hours on 13 May 1969. Mishima, who by that time had already recruited his private army to seize power from the parliamentary democracy he believed had corrupted the pure direct rule of the emperor, invited his New Left audience to join him in his mission. Mishima recalls when he entered the classroom and looked about. "By the entrance there was a manga of a gorilla that was meant to be a portrait of me. I was labeled 'A Modern Gorilla.' . . . That's when I realized that this assembly was going to include laughter, whether it was derisive or sneering was fine with me." Mishima's invitation to join his revolutionary restoration, despite its failure to charm the crowd, was performed in a room whose walls were covered with graffiti drawn in this spirit of action—action that meant the long occupation of the most prestigious seat of higher learning in Japan, action that would shortly lead Mishima to commit the most literally spectacular act of terrorism in postwar Japan, and action that would in a few years' time find its way into the comic books feeding the delinquent fantasies of some Japanese young people. When he asked to be shown the restroom to wash his hands and he saw all the graffiti on its walls, he noted, "It's as if pissing and a 'liberated zone' [*kaihōku*] are one and the same."[79]

There are examples of graffiti in Japan going back to what the workers who built the seventh-century Hōryūji temple in Nara left behind. *Rakusho* is mentioned in the fourteenth-century *Taiheiki* (*A Chronicle of Medieval Japan*). It is all *itazuragaki*, that "mischievous writing" in either words or pictures found where neither belong. Scribble something nasty on the morning newspaper before it's been read? Certainly not. But the next day? By all means. Avant-garde poet and filmmaker Terayama Shūji (1935–83), in a seminal text of the Japanese 1960s tied to the political struggles of the time, heralded graffiti as aborted language, as homeless children, and as writing fated not to be read but to "disappear."

"Graffiti," he wrote, "are the law of their time" and our "new poetry." He likened serial graffiti found in restrooms with Japanese traditional linked verse, *renga*,[80] recycling an old word to name a "modern poetics . . . found where only immemorial, unregenerate vandalism seemed to lie."[81] Echoing French thinkers, Terayama said graffiti "point to the possibility of new poetry while it is also a record of social protest."[82] At the same time, Norman Mailer, impressed by the "Chinese and Arabic calligraphies" of New York graffiti artists, waxed poetic in the spirit of Terayama that "graffiti linger on our subway door as a memento of what it may well have been, our first art of karma, as if indeed all the lives ever lived are sounding now like the bugles of gathering armies across the unseen ridge."[83]

Just as the New Left in Japan failed in the late sixties to transform any part of the Japanese social order, so did manga in the 1970s fail to deliver on any of the subversive promises they had insinuated. Like graffiti, manga are meant not to last but to be discarded. Andreas Huyssen said of 1968 Paris, "The imagination did not come to power."[84] In hindsight the reason for this failure is clear enough. The year 1965 was the start of Japan's third boom in postwar manga sales, but it was different from the previous two. With increasing tie-ups between the various media, and with improved retailing, a commodified manga industry gave rise to a larger hold over Japanese commercial culture, which to an even greater extent than America's is in the hands of major corporations. "Only in the sixties," writes Guy Yasko, "did electronic media and comic books completely dislodge the itinerant story-teller."[85] People in real life began to imitate their favorite manga heroes, or listen to pop music inspired by them, or play the games those characters were notorious for. Nagai's *Harenchi gakuen*, for example, led to a nationwide rash of *sūkato-meguri*, or "skirt-raising," by naughty schoolboys.

Manga after the mid-sixties became a repository for stories and characters that were deployed widely throughout Japanese popular culture. If cultural studies had anything to teach us in its heyday, it is that the project of reconstructing historical contexts or organization of practices is *not* a search for any underlying economy of causes and effects. It is a search for a model in which myriad structures, practices, and effects circulate and come to align with each other in unpredictable ways. My model here juggles student activism, graffiti, and manga, all of which is informed by a truth not below but dispersed over surfaces. The manga of the late sixties, observed Yoshihiro Kōsuke, was akin to the graffiti in public bathrooms,[86] but the point was not to be scatological or pornographic. This rise of a manga culture—as opposed to manga themselves—fundamentally changed manga as a medium. "It is important to remember," writes Susan Stewart, "that the crime of graffiti is a crime in a mode of production. Unlike pornography, graffiti [are] not a crime of content,"[87] though graffiti can certainly be salacious. Tezuka Osamu's works stressed the spirit of graffiti in manga and insisted "graffiti are the essence of manga,"[88] but the subsequent mass commodification of comics meant their once-celebrated potential for critical transgression, like that of graffiti, was converted into benign entertainment. "Manga that are mass produced as part of a corporation's strategy," regretted Ishiko, "are, aside from attesting to the power of the mass media to create a manga boom whenever the opportunity presents itself, in fact no longer manga at all."[89]

The action (kōdō) romantically linked in the 1960s with student upheavals, graffiti, and the bold exploits of manga heroes such as Shirato's Kagemaru, was inconceivable without the possibility of alternative collectivities, such as groups of young people demonstrating or communicating to each other via slogans on walls or sharing comic books in their boarding houses. Manga in post-1970 Japan, however, is as different as the younger generations' popular politics are. Manga is something as private now as graffiti were public. Katō Makirō, a literary critic writing about 1980s manga, casts its social function (more precisely, its nonfunction) this way:

> In the case of fiction, an author can be asked to come before a group of
> students and read his or her works. In the case of film, you can manage to have
> a movie shown in a properly outfitted classroom with the curtains drawn.
> But a manga cannot be shared with even one class of young people. Manga is
> always directed toward the individual. . . . Manga is never manga except when
> you direct your gaze at someone who is no other but you. . . . While manga
> are one of consumer culture's most celebrated media, it is also one of the most
> private.[90]

Commenting on the debate between Mishima and students occupying the Yasuda Amphitheater, Guy Yasko notes that while "comics provided a seemingly 'natural' alternative to mass culture dominated by [American] film, television and radio . . . as mass culture, manga cannot be divorced from their modes of production and consumption, both of which draw from and depend on the high wages and techniques of postwar Fordism."[91] This means manga, as a medium, socializes (desocializes), as television began to do a decade earlier. Veterans of the student movement would certainly write serious fiction about it. There is

Mita Masahiro's (1948–) *Boku tte nani* (What Am I?, 1977), for example. His well-regarded if juvenile novel reduces the student movement to a sad substitute for the companionship (platonic and otherwise) students from the country-side yearned for in the cities—the narrator spends a lot of time missing his mother—but it is usefully ethnographic in how it notes radicals read nothing but their sect's "organ propaganda [*kikanshi*] and manga."[92] Kuroko Kazuo was not complimentary when he called Mita's novel *manga-chikku*, or "cartoonish."[93] Still, when the culture of that period is told in mainstream fiction, it loses some of what manga and graffiti were: "a composite phenomenon, part childish prank, part adult insult. . . . whimsical and political, amused and angry, witty and obscene, often tending toward the palimpsest, and made up of elements of imagery, writing, and simple marking."[94]

In 1970, at a time when he must have been planning the details of his own *manga-chikku* death, Mishima Yukio cleared his schedule to write about manga. Mishima's musings on manga always commenced with nostalgic regret. They were so much better in the old days, during the American Occupation, when you had to go to *kashihon'ya* in seedy alleys to get them. Now, major newspapers and magazines carry them. Back then their contents were so much more raw and violent than they are now. Today, *gekiga* are available everywhere in convenient pocket-sized editions. They are not the bad writing (*akusho*) they were once. There was a time, Mishima complained, when university students were embarrassed to be seen reading *anything* but the most serious, highbrow books—that was their vanity of the time—but today, everyone reads manga openly, not only soldiers in the Self-Defense Forces but even the young men in his own private army, the Tate no kai (Shield Society). Nowadays everyone prefers to read the facile over the difficult. Mishima recalled visiting America for the first time in 1952, and was shocked to see comics everywhere. He was even more surprised to see that adults were reading them. That, he reported, is the situation in Japan today.

Mishima blamed the student movement. People told him it was Shirato Sanpei who got to the students, but Mishima thought there must be more to it. He was not immune himself to manga's appeal, and *he* was never a left-wing student. His children brought manga home, and he admitted he had become a fan of Nyarome the Cat. Why is that? Because the *gekiga* that tell of the past share something in common with the same *hakaishūgi* that he has sought. Meaninglessly rendered "destructionism" in English, this word signifies closer to "vandalism," and vandalism is at the root of much bad writing—it is where the power of graffiti resides. Mishima, had he lived longer, would not have been happy to see graffiti vandals like Keith Haring turn into artists who exhibited in fancy galleries, just as he was not happy at the end of his life when left-wing Japanese teachers' unions were, he claimed, the master of manga's contents. That, Mishima would object, removes bad writing from the realm of action and relegates it to the realm of words. In his last essay on manga, Mishima wrote, "Action demands pattern and archetype. Action and archetype, it is abundantly clear to everyone, depend more on visual figuration [*shikakuteki keishō*] than they do on script [*moji*]."[95] Less than a year later Mishima starred in his own ultimate action before an assembled Ichigaya garrison and on television screens across the country, as he retreated indoors to disembowel himself in ways equaling the most grotesque manga. As Dennis Washburn summarized, it was a death whose staging was all "out of proportion with the finality of the event," "a forgery, a simulacrum, a work of kitsch art."[96] Manga historian Satō Tadao recalls he was writing about Shirato Sanpei when the news of Mishima's suicide suddenly broke on radio and television. Shirato's aesthetics are often discussed, Satō notes, but never Mishima's. Severed heads are judged quite differently in the two men's work. Mishima, Satō reminds us, died in a designer uniform.[97]

November 1970 was no longer the 1950s or even the 1960s. In a book devoted to the year 1972, Tsubouchi Yūzō claims it was "the end of the beginning, the beginning of the end" insofar as history would subsequently mean less and less to the younger generations.[98] No visitor to Japan fails to be struck by the numbers of people found in public who are wholly engrossed in manga, be it in traditional print format or on cell phones. The cacophony of trivial conversations heard in the public transport of other countries is eerily absent in a Japan where one's fellow passengers are half-watching the silent flow of commercials and weather reports on the flat television screens common in carriages, or wordlessly flipping real or digital pages of a comic book, or tapping away on a game inspired by the same. In a 1990s statistic that resonates with the U.S. publishing industry today, of the 130 companies that publish manga in Japan, just 5 firms control 80 percent of production. Japanese comics will never be the "reading-drug" that Félix Guattari disparagingly called them,[99] but the blame he attributed for the atomization of public life in Japan, the isolation of an earphone-wearing, manga-reading population, is an ironic sequel to the political culture of the 1960s and the manga epics that encouraged and reflected it. After the students' rout in the Yasuda Amphitheater and their loss of "most

public support for its increasingly violent tactics,"[100] they found themselves dis-
armed to be taken up in mass culture as a form of marketing. "They appeared
in advertisements, comedy shows, family serials, manga."[101] They will, in time,
surrender their place to their younger Japanese sisters; their "modernism in the
streets," as Lionel Trilling called Columbia University's student protests of the
time,[102] will capitulate to what will be called their postmodernism with no fewer
conundrums than the West's.

The Japanese state maintained a crudely disciplinary attitude toward popular culture. In early 1984, the Diet called for an inquiry into the sexual content
of girls' comics, and some publishers closed down or selectively censored their
products. There was a public movement against manga again in the early 1990s,
once more over sexual content. Violence was no longer the issue. There were
controversial, nationwide police arrests in 1991 when pedophilic manga came
under renewed scrutiny in the wake of Miyazaki Tsutomu's serial murders of
young girls. In 2004, Suwa Yūji (1968–), author of *Misshitsu* (Honey room,
2002), was convicted of obscenity, and manga in Japan would never be the
same again. But by then manga had not been revolutionary or avant-garde for
decades (though it will, predictably, be endlessly new as it recycles itself). That
ended with the sixties. Manga, writes Yomota Inuhiko, went from being countercultural to just cultural.[103] In the United States the turning point was when
underground cartoonists began to copyright their work. In Japan it was with
the heavy capitalization and consolidation of the industry.[104] After the 1960s the
combined pressure of television, anime, and the major publishing firms effectively put an end to the informal underground manga culture of the *kashihon'ya*.
Comics became available everywhere and at every hour, but something was lost
along the way. By 1991, asserts one scholar, one-third of everything published in
Japan was manga; but, he adds, manga is less satirical and more entertainment
(*asobi*).[105] Publishers such as Takarajima moved into *shōjo* manga from nearly
the start, a trend that accelerated with the cult of cute (*kawaii*) and its late-1970s
translation into the profitable business of Sanrio's "fancy goods." As I explore
in the next chapter, the young, male-centered popular culture of the 1960s
moved to a young, female-centered popular culture in the 1970s, as the history
of Takarajima discloses. Takemiya Keiko (1950–), one of the first women to
create girls' comics (she is also credited with depicting the first male-male kiss
in manga history), entered university in 1968 and participated in radical student
activities until she dropped out of school two years later. She has written about
how formative the movement was for her and others, not just fellow manga

artists but writers, composers, and those who became ordinary white-collar workers. Dissenting from the view that Japan's radical politics ended in frustration, she asserts that "everyone fought on alone, wherever they were."[106] Fighting alone, however, seldom means winning. "From the perspective of 1993," writes one critic, "the era when we all watched television together at home, sang the same pop songs, and took pleasure in the same manga is now a thing of the distant past."[107] Katō Shūichi once characterized Japan's modern culture as one in which everyone reads the same things.[108] But after the 1960s, contemporary Japanese culture, including its literature, was less "by all of us" (*warera ga*) and more "just for you" (*anata dake ni*). And with that, Japan started to edge past its short-lived, modern forms of literary colloquy and now approaches the precipice of what comes next.

Yoshimoto Banana in the Kitchen

The July 1993 summit in Tokyo of the leading industrial democracies (then the G-7) was another routine media performance by a select international cast of politicians intended for global consumption. Yet despite a full schedule of meetings, receptions, banquets, and public declarations, something seemed missing. The G-7 leaders were seven characters in search of an author. The well-made play they intended us to view via the proscenium stage that is the television set was a disappointing drama missing both antagonist and protagonist. Pre-9/11 but without a villainous Soviet empire or a rapacious Arab cartel, there could be no dramatic resolution, no tragedy or comedy. Presidents and prime ministers struck poses before high-tech footlights nonetheless, thoroughly high-bourgeois, worthy of Ibsen but without the luck of his scripts—ready for a modernist plot that, like Godot, did not come.

Directing and starring center-stage in this particular production was the host country, whose Foreign Ministry went to the usual unusual lengths to explain Japan to those in attendance and those watching around the planet. As it turned out, the ministry meant to decipher more than just Japan. Something new, we learned, was afoot worldwide. Added to each press kit for foreign journalists was a copy of the recent English translation of Yoshimoto Banana's (1964–) prizewinning novel, *Kitchin* (*Kitchen*, 1988). The slender first work slighted by many critics at home for its kinship with girls' manga, *Kitchin* would hardly seem the stuff of summit reading. But the Foreign Ministry, eager to edify as well as entertain, thought otherwise. "There should be some element in her book that can be shared, not only by the Japanese, but by the younger generation all over the world," explained a ministry spokesman. But as to what element—reporters pressed Amano on just this point—all he could respond was "I don't know."

Others shared the Foreign Ministry's sense of *Kitchin*'s importance and its confusion over just what that importance is. Tersely described by the *Wall Street Journal* as the story of "a young Japanese woman with a kitchen fetish,"[1] its original publication in Japan was a milestone event, both in its commercial success and in the dumbfounded consternation it occasioned among critics. Less than two years after it initially appeared in the highbrow literary journal *Kaien*, the novel was already in its fiftieth printing, and the combined sales of Banana's Japanese-language editions alone totaled some six million copies. But her award from *Kaien* for best new writer of the year was an exceptional event in Japanese literary history not on account of her youth—submissions to literary prizes in Japan are fairly swamped by adolescent hopefuls—but because, in the published summary of their deliberations, none of the judges praised the work. At a loss of what to say about this scant story so redolent of Japan's low-cultural female adolescent (*shōjo*) culture, the judges seemed resigned to award the prize on the basis of their nebulous impression that they were witness to something new in Japanese literature—even if they did not know exactly what, and even if they were disturbed by that failure of reading. "This is a work," wrote senior critic Nakamura Shin'ichirō, "written on a theme and with a sensibility that the older generation of which I am a part could not have imagined. . . . Its naïve rejection of the very question of whether it does or does not conform to conventional concepts is precisely what makes it strike me as a new sort of literature."[2]

Most critics in Japan ignored Banana or treated her works with scarcely concealed contempt. The reason for this may have been that they could not discern anything in Banana's works to discuss, that is, that they were functionally illiterate when it came to reading her.[3] This was an author who credited comics, especially those by Iwadate Mariko (1957–), with being her greatest literary influence.[4] "We were raised on manga and television," Banana writes. "That's why we only understand those things that go fast."[5] Other of her debts are to Stephen King, but in hindsight what helped propel *Kitchin* to the ranks of award-winning fiction was doubtless its author's bankable parentage. Banana's father, Yoshimoto Takaaki, was himself a prominent and controversial poet and critic whose ruminations on that same Japanese mass culture that his daughter epitomized were standard reading for intellectuals in the 1960s and 1970s. By 1980, Takaaki had posed as a fashion model for women's fashion magazine *An an*, but among the left-wing student radicals in the late 1960s and 1970s were plenty of "Yoshimoto-istes" (*Yoshimotoshugisha*) loyal to his antisectarian Marxism. As Ian Buruma quipped of Takaaki's daughter when he reviewed *Kitchin*, it is "as though there were a young German novelist called Banana Habermas."[6]

Both Banana and *père* Takaaki raised the ire of critics alarmed by Japan's consumer culture and worried about the prospect of ever challenging its drive to commodify and reify. Masao Miyoshi and H. D. Harootunian dismissed Takaaki's suggestion that consumption might work to undermine capitalism as an "absurdist conviction."[7] Miyoshi declared Banana's writings—which he admitted sell by the millions—"as baby talk, uninterrupted by humor, emotion, idea, not to say irony or intelligence."[8] What excites such censure is surely the nervous fear that the potential of intellectual discourse on one hand, and modernism on the other, to conceptualize and critique the ways we live is now nearly impossible under the relentless onslaught of the commodity, and under the terms of the postmodern cultural logic it has inspired. But as others have reminded us, mass cultural artifacts are contested terrain critics walk away from at their peril. As Andreas Huyssen has pointed out, "Mass culture has always been the subtext of the modernist project,"[9] and the success of *Kitchin* is yet another opportunity to consider the premises of this perennial mortal combat between the forces of popular taste and those of its intellectual conscience. We can begin with the irrefutable. *Kitchin* and its marketing do exhibit many characteristics of an expanding consumerism—and not just in Japan, though the boom that surrounds Banana's works is a perfect example of how, in the words of Mitsuhiro Yoshimoto (no relation), "the massive forces of commodification currently at work in Japan" are structured by booms in order to create (marketable) differences.[10] What is new for Japanese *literature* is the globalization of that boom. Quickly translated first into Italian and then many other languages, that Japanese novel traveled like few others—although, aside from the Chinese, the original English title *Kitchen* was retained in every version. (The German publisher, Diogenes Verlag, considered the option of entitling it *Küche* "offenbar zu banal."[11]) The publishing industry, despite the linguistic barriers posed by

Figure 9.1. Publicity material for Yoshimoto Banana's *Kitchen* (1993). Courtesy of Drew Friedman.

its products, was becoming as multinational as the oil majors. "Publishers in New York and Tokyo," wrote Herbert Mitgang in 1990 on the eve of *Kitchin*'s international debut, "are making a fresh effort to internationalize the market for Japanese fiction."[12] Grove Press marketed Banana's work in North America on an unprecedented scale, and did so without coloring it exotic. "Bananamania Arrives," trumpeted full-page ads designed by, among others, Art Spiegelman. Run in newspapers and weeklies across the United States, such copy recalls the similarly pop Beatlemania campaign a generation earlier. But such frenzy was soon and predictably tamed. *Kitchin* became a featured selection in a popular book-of-the-month club whose come-ons, in contrast to the *Wall Street Journal*'s more pathological blurb, described it blandly as "a novel of a young Japanese woman who finds comfort in the warmth of kitchens."[13]

One might marvel that any novel whose story can be reduced to an affection for a room sells at all. But sell it did. In 1989, a popular Japanese business journal asked just why sales were doing so well,[14] and as I write in 2016 the work is still being hailed in the American press as one of the five "essential Japanese novels."[15] The literary journal that launched the Banana Phenomenon (*Banana genshō*) within Japan—*Kaien*—and the scholarly journal *Kokubungaku* devoted their February 1994 issues to the spectacle of "Yoshimoto Banana in the World" and "Yoshimoto Banana Around the World," respectively. Both journals convened a panel of critics, including an unusual number of foreign ones (the usual being zero) to comment upon the event of a new Japanese writer whose works were being marketed globally with remarkable dispatch. This event was a riddle from the start. "Why, among the numerous writers in Japan today, is Yoshimoto Banana the first to go global?"[16] Global, that is, commercially, if not always critically. Speaking specifically of *Kitchin*'s success in Italy, Suga Atsuko pondered in 1994, "Why, in a country with cultural traditions, tastes, lifestyles and social customs so utterly different from Japan's has a novel such as *Kitchin* achieved in Italy unprecedented sales on the order of 90,000 copies? . . . No other book has sold so spectacularly well."[17] Part of the answer lies simply in the amount of money spent promoting *Kitchin* in the West. The attention lavished on Banana meant that the demand for *Kitchin* owed much to its global marketing and not the other way around. With no clue as to the novel's content other than that Bananamania was coming, the collaboration of the publishers with the media fostered a curiosity about a young Asian woman thought to have taken the name of a tropical fruit that only the exchange of cash for a commodity could satisfy. Critics who contributed to the special World Banana issues of Japanese highbrow journals were, however, unanimous in their view that *Kitchin* communicated something new and popular worldwide, and thus could attribute its success to something other than the sheer manipulation of the marketplace. An American, Elizabeth Floyd, called Banana's writings "something that young people around the world can enjoy." While Italian Donnatella Natili and Chinese Yin Hui'e noted that some part of *Kitchin*'s appeal in their countries was the novel's embodiment of a new, postmodern Japan with less cultural uniqueness and more economic clout ("From samurai to computers," as Natili put it), both noted that there was something distinctly non-Japanese about the book that was universal to the extent it was deracinated. "The name Banana, along with her works, are known by many people around the world regardless of national borders," claimed Yin.[18] Natili described the setting of the novel, Tokyo, as an international city without a strictly Japanese identity.[19] Most insistent on the changed character of a once provincial Japanese literature after Banana was the German scholar Hilaria Gössman. She acknowledged that *Kitchin's* "German edition marked an important shift among publishers in German-speaking countries. Rather than present the work as one with a uniquely Japanese theme, we were told that here was a novel to which young people all over the world could relate." Gössman speculated the twenty thousand copies that sold immediately were "evidence that those who read it were not only people with an interest in Japan, but indeed included those with a broad interest in the lives of young people."[20]

The Foreign Ministry spokesman's claim that *Kitchin* contained "some element . . . that can be shared . . . by the younger generation around the world," however inexplicable that element was to Amano and others, appears to be widely accepted. *Kitchin* may have been Japan's first intellectual global commodity, a status attested not by its critics' comments but by Amano's boast that his government's purchase of eight hundred copies of the English translation was proof that Japan was import-oriented. As the *Kaien* judges uneasily observed, something new is at work here, and whatever it is, literature is not exempt from its logic, a logic that is poorly understood but which surely exists, if only because nothing less basic could puzzle critics yet motivate millions to purchase. The key to what happened is found at home, the homes not only where Banana's bizarre families composed of orphans and gender changelings reside but where her older critics' own journies toward personal and intellectual adulthood unfolded according to the script of an even older, and scarcely more plausible, Greek myth.

"The people recognize themselves in their commodities," wrote Herbert Marcuse in *One-Dimensional Man*; "they find their souls in their automobiles, hi-fi sets, split-level homes, kitchen equipment."[21] Marcuse's scorn might seem justified if only in the case of *Kitchin*, where Sakura Mikage, the novel's narrator, is told by a new friend to "pick a room, then I'll know what kind of person you are"[22] and goes directly to the disdained kitchen equipment. "Lots of tea towels, dry and immaculate," a giant white American-style (but assuredly Japanese-made) refrigerator stuffed with delicacies enough "to get through a winter" (3);

the open cupboards crammed with English country crockery, Swiss cutlery, and futuristic Japanese home appliances; "a Silverstone frying pan and a delightful German-made vegetable peeler"; the dense tableau of colors and shapes is the late-twentieth-century Japanese update of a classic Dutch still life. This is the kitchen that Mikage claims she "fell in love with at first sight" (9–10).

She has competition. Shortly after Banana published *Kitchin*, her exact contemporary Bret Easton Ellis published his own highly controversial novel, *American Psycho*, which graphically depicts a sadistic serial murderer-protagonist, New York investment banker Patrick Bateman. Early in *American Psycho* Bateman surveys his luxury Manhattan kitchen:

> Next to the Panasonic bread baker and the Salton Pop-Up coffee maker is the Cremina sterling silver espresso maker (which is, oddly, still warm) that I got at Hammacher Schlemmer (the thermal insulated stainless-steel espresso cup and the saucer and spoon are sitting by the sink, stained) and the Sharp Model R-1810A Carousel II microwave oven with the revolving turntable which I use when I heat up the other half of the bran muffin. Next to the Salton Sonata toaster and the Cuisinart Little Pro food processor and the Acme Supreme Juicerator and the Cordially Yours liqueur maker stands the heavy-gauge stainless-steel two-and-one-half-quart teakettle, which whistles "Tea for Two" when the water is boiling. . . . For what seems like a long time I stare at the Black & Decker Handy Knife that lies on the counter next to the sink, plugged into the wall: it's a slicer/peeler with several attachments, a serrated blade, a scalloped blade and a rechargeable handle.[23]

As this history of modern Japanese literature becomes more focused on how Japanese fiction participates in a globalized world, it would be tempting to compare Banana and Ellis and note their common celebration of a narcissistic consumerism, but that would be misleading. Banana's Mikage is a 1980s *shōjo*, and Ellis's Bateman is a 1980s yuppie, but they are different. Bateman's kitchen is where he will arm himself to torture and murder his victims. He lives alone in his apartment, isolated and psychopathic. Banana's imaginary kitchen is the "best in the world," but not *of* the world, at least of any we are apt to inhabit. Banana will bring others into Mikage's kitchen to nurture, not kill. Her novel will be a comedy where Ellis's is a tragedy. *Kitchin* launched a literary panic, *American Psycho* a moral one. Together they share a comic-book texture. There are mutual insights into a late-model capitalism that might unite the former's

Japan and the latter's America, but those novels also prove how cultural logic works out different calculi for that capitalism.

Like Bateman's kitchen, Mikage's is a room that one might fancy, a luxurious home, but one that reeks with nostalgia for family and its old-fashioned comforts, a place where the bread rises, the cookies bake, and the *miso* soup simmers. Outside of those Nescafé and Vermont Curry commercials on Japanese television, it is a room that hardly exists, least of all in Japan, where the exigencies of modern life mean that many meals come out of the microwave, if not the corner convenience store. (Bateman, by the way, eats nearly all his meals out.) Ironically, since it is via modern media such as television (then) and the Internet (now) that the individual is socialized, such evocations of the old-fashioned hearth and the possibility of a family assembled beside it are the modern consumer's dream, and as a dream, it is unreal and powerful. "Dream kitchens," muses Mikage. "I will have countless ones, in my heart or in reality" (43). Banana's spare prose describes a place as amiably crowded with things as those California households staged by her favorite Hollywood director, Steven Spielberg. It celebrates a warehouse of culinary tools that the novel's *New Yorker* reviewer observes is "under-utilized."[24] Banana's kitchen is a place that can only be imaginary, as any desire must, yet at the same time it is the material product of a consumerism that has generated an aesthetic as well as profits.

That it is a teenage woman in *Kitchin*, and not her housewife mother, who surveys this kitchen is paradigmatic within the logic of this Japanese consumerism and something of an exception to the way in which many have theorized consumerism in the West. In the United States it has been the practice to read the relationship between women and consumption in two different and not wholly compatible contexts. First is that of a woman as the passive *object* of consumption, herself an article of (kinship, sexual, economic) exchange. The second is that of a woman as the groomed *subject* of consumption, that smart housewife in the ads who buys the newest detergent, the easiest floor wax. This double function has been dubbed a paradox, an essential tautology,[25] one where the female consumer "is the subject of a transaction in which her own commodification is ultimately the object."[26] The conflation of sexual value and material value with its converse — sexual desire and material desire — is one that is constituted in Japan with significant difference, if only because the adolescent female (*shōjo*) is not precisely a woman (*onna*). (The cult of the *shōjo* from the 1960s on existed alongside that of the highly sexualized *onna no ko* [girl], but that is never Banana's theme.) One might argue that *shōjo* constitute their own gender, neither male nor female but something importantly detached from the productive economy of heterosexual reproduction. Anthropologist Jennifer Robertson points out that "Literally speaking, shōjo means a 'not-quite-female female.' . . . Shōjo also implies heterosexual *inexperience* and homosexual *experience*,"[27] presumably homosexual because the emotional life of the *shōjo* is narcissistic in that it is self-referential, and self-referential as long as the *shōjo* is not employed productively in the sexual and capitalist economy. A distinct gender, a distinct age cohort, and a distinct status as a consumer: the Japanese *shōjo* is a sign, one uniquely positioned as a master trope for all consumption. Sociologist Merry White correctly notes, "Japanese define teenagers as a category because they are a *market*. . . . Japanese teens have appeared and been identified . . . as the economic boom of the late 1970s and 1980s targeted and reached a new 'youth market,'"[28] but Japanese social scientists have proposed something more. "The Japanese are no longer producers," writes pop anthropologist Ōtsuka Eiji, but instead are this: "Our existence consists solely of the distribution and consumption of 'things' brought us from elsewhere, 'things' with which we play. Nor are these things actually tangible, but are instead only signs without any direct utility in life. . . . What name are we to give this life of ours? The name is *shōjo*."[29]

The theory of the female consumer in the West typically declines to implicate men in its terms or distinguish adolescent women as a distinct group or subject. The situation is quite different in Japan, where the idea of the *shōjo* in some analyses has assumed the status of a hegemon, one that extends to other ages and genders. Critic Horikiri Naoto, for example, speculates, "I wonder if we men shouldn't now think of ourselves as *shōjo*, given our compulsory and excessive consumerism, a consumerism that in recent years afflicts us as if sleepwalking. We are driven night and day to be relentless consumers. . . . The *shōjo*, that new human species born of modern commodification, has today commodified everything and everyone."[30] Yoshimoto Banana and her characters are said to be archetypes of this new human species (*shinjinrui*). She was born in 1964, the year not only when Japan's Summer Olympics spectacle celebrated its rehabilitation among the more developed nations but also when Japanese consumer capitalism and the subculture of the *shōjo* were being articulated with each other and when, in a related trend, there were "major shifts . . . in the attitudes and behavior of the Japanese with respect to marriage and the family."[31] Banana has defined her generation—male, female, and *shōjo* alike—as one that "came into contact with exactly the same kinds of consumer products,"[32] including Toyota automobiles as well as Hello Kitty notebooks. Banana recognizes that her own works, hardly examples of high literature but more like "this year's model," are commodities. She has stated that she wants all of her previously published books removed from bookstore shelves whenever she comes out with something new.[33] But the contents of these books so easily consumed and discarded are filled with expressions of an intense longing for times and places that never existed. "I was seized with nostalgia," thinks Mikage with her usual fervor, "a nostalgia so sharp it was painful." And it is here that Japan, so famously distinct from other advanced nation-states, begins to look familiar. The *New York Times*, for instance, reported once on the trend among Southern Californians to seek out simpler lives in rural Montana and Idaho. As one such internal immigrant explained, "There's this desire to return to a simpler, nostalgic life, even though we don't really have any idea what that is."[34]

But they do have images of it, those pictures of the last corral projected or beamed onto screens: images as real as Mikage's, who understands that her life to date has been "total science fiction" (4) and who has to refer to an American movie (*The Miracle Worker*) in order to explain how something seemed real to her (12). Despite the intriguing ubiquity of the *shōjo* unique to contemporary Japan (though spreading throughout the world), *Kitchin* does seem to suggest the Japanese version of the late-capitalist, postmodern cultural logic sketched by Fredric Jameson. That comic books should inspire a novel which in turn goes on to win high-cultural literary awards *and* become a schlocky movie does seem to confirm the blurring of distinctions between high and mass cultures that Jameson takes as one sign of the postmodern. Mikage's inability to perceive anything without linking it to a mass-produced image (her favorite sofa "looked like something out of a commercial. An entire family could watch TV on it" [9]) certainly suggests the postmodernist blank parody that Jameson calls pastiche. Moreover, nowhere in *Kitchin* is found the sort of nuclear family that he associates with modernist ideologies of individualism. Instead, in a phrase to which I will return, both postmodernism and Banana's stories are schizophrenic in that one's sense of time, and of life, is, according to Jameson, no longer processed linearly but rather with attention to each individual signifier.

Such postmodernism is also our consumer society's logic, he argues, because its aesthetic is employed in commodification. If Mikage cannot conceptualize any part of her life as anything but the replay of a commodified image, it may be because, as Jameson says, "Cultural production . . . can no longer gaze directly on some putative real world, at some reconstruction of a past history which was once itself a present; rather, as in Plato's cave, it must trace our mental

images of that past upon its confining walls." This is because "aesthetic production today has become integrated into commodity production generally," since
aesthetic innovation is now required to move goods and services. Banana, who
wants her older books taken off shelves when new ones come out, appears to
testify to this. That she chose to be a writer as whimsically, she says, as she might
have become an airline stewardess also makes Jameson's point that late capitalism has destroyed the privileged semi-autonomy of the cultural realm, and so
too has eliminated the critical distance that once separated art from the rest of
modernity. This, states Jameson, is the predictable consequence of the "third
great original expansion of capitalism around the globe," an event that sponsors
a cultural/social system realistic and diversionary in that it mimics commodity
production even while it obscures its own status as commodity.[35]

In his 1990 essay "Disjuncture and Difference in the Global Cultural
Economy," Arjun Appadurai makes additional observations about the status
of postmodern, late-capitalist culture that may make *Kitchin*, despite its eccentricity, the perfect proof-text for such theorizing. Appadurai rethinks Jameson's
assertions to make the important point that global cultural flows are radically
context dependent (as opposed to being rigidly predetermined—think again
of how different the usages of Mikage's and Bateman's kitchens turn out to be)
in ways that could make Japan's *shōjo* culture more tractable within Jameson's
general outline. In a comment useful for how I will explain *Kitchin*'s queasy
reception, Appadurai wants us to recall how "if 'a' global system is emerging,
it is filled with ironies and resistances, sometimes camouflaged as passivity
and a bottomless appetite in the Asian world for things Western." But most
significant for *Kitchin*, Appadurai shifts his attention to what he terms a classic
human problem: the status and function of the home in this new set of global
cultural processes. "How do small groups, especially families, the classic loci
of socialization, deal with these new global realities as they seek to reproduce
themselves, and in doing so, as it were by accident, reproduce cultural forms
themselves?" Appadurai wonders how reproduction (of knowledge, of social relations, of everything) can be ensured, since nowadays "family relationships can
become volatile, as new commodity patterns are negotiated. . . . Most important,
the work of cultural reproduction in new settings is profoundly complicated by
the politics of representing a family as normal."[36] These are questions we might
expect an anthropologist to pose, but they are also questions that should occur
to any reader of Yoshimoto Banana, whose stories in general and *Kitchin* in particular raise in their own fashion the crucial query of the family, reproduction

and late capitalism—as well as those ironies and resistances that Appadurai predicts must occur even in a global system. We should look for answers where family relationships, we have been told, are always volatile—Freud called them hostile—but are uncannily calm wherever Banana's people live.

"In Yoshimoto Banana's stories, girl baby talk drones on about the cool and abundant delights of gourmet commercial life," complained the late Masao Miyoshi. "Yoshimoto's imaginary space is filled with floating zombies defined by the blurs of the brand goods they choose to buy."[37] Such a zombie is not, however, *Kitchin*'s Sakura Mikage. Mikage makes unambiguous fun of such rampant consumerism. "Truly strange" (8) is how she first describes the plethora of consumer goods in the novel's eponymous kitchen when she first visits. "I should have known these people would have a photocopier stashed away," she sardonically observes. "These people," she concludes, "had a taste for buying things that verged on the unhealthy" (26–27).

How Mikage ends up in a strange apartment with its suspicious inhabitants is the first part of *Kitchin*'s narrative. The novel opens with the news of the death of Mikage's last surviving relative, her grandmother. A young college student who must now make ends meet on her small inheritance, Mikage sinks into lonely melancholy until the day that Tanabe Yūichi, a young acquaintance of her late grandmother, invites Mikage to visit his and his mother's nearby home one evening. When she does, she is immediately charmed by the Tanabe apartment's warm coziness, especially that of the kitchen ("everything was of the finest quality," but with none of the cold stainless steel Ellis's Bateman so clearly appreciates in his). She spends the night on the Tanabe sofa ("so big, so soft, so deep") at the kind insistence of Yūichi's mother, Eriko (9).

But into this homey *Gemütlichkeit* comes the revelation that Eriko is not Yūichi's mother, but his transgender father. Yūichi explains that Eriko "had everything done, from her face to her whatever" (14). Living as a woman since the early death of his wife, Yūichi's biological mother, Eriko now runs a bar where she tends to the other transwomen working for her and the men who patronize them. None of this news bothers Mikage, though she does admit to some initial surprise. ("I've never see a woman that beautiful" [12].) She soon welcomes Eriko's affection as genuine, and their friendship (one partly sisterly, partly filial) is consecrated over a breakfast that Mikage prepares for the two of them in that kitchen she so admires. Although Mikage eventually moves into a new place of her own once she quits school and takes a job as an assistant at a cooking school, the half-year that she spends with the Tanabes is the time that, even as she is in the midst of it, she nostalgically savors as time with the sort of family she never had. "Someday, I wondered, will I be living somewhere else and look back nostalgically on my time here? Or will I return to this same kitchen one day? But right now I am here with this powerful mother, this boy with the gentle eyes. That was all that mattered" (42).

It thus shocks Mikage to learn from Yūichi, months after the actual incident, that a crazed admirer has murdered Eriko. ("He had spotted her on the street, and liked what he saw.") At first she has a hard time accepting this as true. "I pictured a scene from a war movie" (44–45). But soon commiseration brings Mikage and Yūichi together again in a "complicated, fragile relationship" that Mikage recognizes as both "brother and sister" and "man and woman in the primordial sense." Eriko's death, coming so soon after that of Mikage's grand-mother, makes the two of them orphaned sibling-lovers standing on the edge of what Mikage calls "the cauldron of hell" (66), into whose fires any family can disappear in an instant. "For some reason," Mikage remarks to Yūichi, "there's always death around us" (27). Later she describes the two of them as living at "the epicenter of death." Their mutual solitude—Mikage cries at "having been left behind in the night, paralyzed with loneliness" (67)—makes both of them miserable, disconsolate without the odd maternal love that Eriko provided.

In the last pages of *Kitchin* (for several reasons one cannot call it a climax), Mikage acts to fill this void. At the same time she is on a business trip to the resort area of the Izu peninsula with the owner of her cooking school, Yūichi is at another inn some fifty kilometers away licking his emotional wounds. Neither Mikage nor Yūichi seems to be enjoying her- or himself. A phone call between the two reveals that both inns have served them almost inedible dinners. A fam-ished Mikage is in a nearby restaurant that makes exceptionally delicious *kat-sudon* (fried pork atop rice with broth—Japanese comfort food) when she has an idea: she'll get another order of *katsudon* to go and take it by taxi, despite the extravagant cost, to Yūichi. When Mikage arrives at Yūichi's inn, she must figure out how to gain entrance to his locked room. Making her way via the garden— "The scene reminded me of the Jungle Cruise at Disneyland" (95–96)—she scales the inn's exterior wall with no little difficulty to reach Yūichi's window. An appreciative Yūichi attacks the food with gusto as Mikage, bloodied with wounds suffered on her ascent, watches with joy: "My spirits began to lift; I had done all I could" (100). Yūichi's mood, too, improves suddenly and just as mark-edly. "It must be because we are family," he theorizes, and, as Mikage observes,

"Even in the absence of Eriko," their past happiness has resumed (101). While Yūichi enjoys his simple repast, Mikage tells him that the future is theirs to enjoy together if only they want it. "Yūichi's smiling face seemed to sparkle. I knew I had touched something inside him" (102). But her waiting cab means that she has to leave before Yūichi can give her a definite yes or no. Mikage is still uncertain of Yūichi's intentions for them when the following night she gets a phone call from him in his Tokyo apartment. As soon as he says he will meet her at the station the next day, Mikage knows the answer. The last paragraph of *Kitchin* is this happy ending: "The room was warm, filling with steam from the boiling water. I launched into what time I'd be in and what platform I'd be on" (105).

The banality of this simple story, with its overwrought sentimentality and its embarrassing excess of adolescent anxieties and passions, is unquestionably hard to take seriously—despite Grove Press's attempt to convince us that *Kitchin* recalls the early Marguerite Duras, or the Italian translator's valiant comparison of its style to that of Nobel Prize winner Kawabata Yasunari. But "seriously" is exactly how a panel of distinguished arbiters of literary merit did take it, and *Kitchin* remains a work that intrigues critics in Japan and abroad. On the one hand, it represents the novelization of the *shōjo* comic book—Banana's sister is a prominent cartoonist—that has played such an important role in postwar Japanese popular culture and as such underscores how the affective tenor of the *shōjo* has come to typify some part of the experience of everyday life in Japan, and not just that of teenage girls. One of Banana's critics, male and middle-aged, has written of his and his wife's startling and exciting experience of identification with the vacuous sense of life communicated in Banana's works.[38] On the other hand *Kitchin* is also the manga-fication of mainstream fiction, a transformation that is said to degrade an accomplished art form and destroy its potential to conceptualize and critique that same everyday life. Consequently, *Kitchin* appears simultaneously as an advance for contemporary fiction and its parody.

Conspicuous to both *Kitchin*'s fans and detractors is its stubborn, thematic obsession with kitchens—a room indispensable to everyday life, whether that life is something we want nowadays to celebrate or denigrate. "The place I like best in the world," reads the novel's first line, "is the kitchen" (3)—an opening that would hardly endear it to readers who would prefer fiction aspire to grander utopias. *Any* kitchen will apparently do: clean or dirty, large or small. Mikage's penchant for kitchens is a fetish, an obsession with a part that stands for a whole. Only sleeping near the refrigerator consoles Mikage after her grandmother's death. The kitchen is where, when her own time comes, she hopes to die. Just why this should be is unclear to Mikage. "To me a kitchen represents some distant longing engraved on my soul" (56). But even the least attentive reader will conclude that the kitchen is a metonym for the family, the sign of a nostalgic desire for what the orphan Mikage has lost.

That underutilized kitchen in the Tanabe household provides Mikage with the opportunity to put its many appliances and features to their fullest use. During her stay, Mikage gives full vent to her culinary ambitions. She perfects her recipes on two happy consumers of them. "For the whole summer I went about it with a crazed enthusiasm: cooking, cooking, cooking. I poured all my earnings from my part-time job into it, and if something came out wrong I'd do it over again till I got it right. Angry, fretful, or cheery, I cooked through it all." Why? Because she has others to cook for, an audience for her performance. "I lived like a housewife," exults Mikage. "I was thrilled" (21). But like the clichés she summons to name each of her experiences, this too is merely a role she plays. Her joy seems genuine, her desire to please authentic, but these are just feelings that can be easily disassembled and reassembled, never tied to any biological family or permanent home. The referent of that joy and desire—the experience of family—might seem distinctly postmodern. In her essay "Famirii" (Family, 1989), Banana says that "usually the world is a terribly difficult place to be, and lots of times we end up living our lives apart from each other. That's why the family is a fort built for us to flee into. Inside that fort both men and women become symbols, and there protect the home."[39]

These are certainly the sentiments of Banana's Sakura Mikage, and certainly her predicament, where in the Tanabe home notions of mother and brother—not to mention the male and female genders—seem distinctly rehearsed. When the Victorians called the family "a tent pitch'd in a world not right," "the place of peace; the shelter, not only from all injury, but from all terror, doubt, and division,"[40] it was the *natural* family that compensated the individual for his labor spent in the *unnatural* arena of the factory. Yet in Banana's world, what renders "the world a terrible place to be" is not the smokestack but the precarity of the familial relations that once promised nurturing sanctuary from it. What makes her English loanword *famirii* a "fort" is its production, not any refuge it offers from the same. This is why a three-dimensional space—the kitchen—and not any biological relation defines the family. What remains constant is that space named "kitchen," or rather that such space exists. In New York City today, where Patrick Bateman is not alone in eating all his dinners out, real estate brokers' windows still feature photos of sleek, immense kitchens in their advertisements for luxury apartments.

One could argue that the final pages of *Kitchin* effectively turn the Izu peninsula into a kitchen as Mikage races across it with her hot dinner to go for lover-sibling Yūichi. Via a trip no different, other than in sheer distance traversed, from taking a casserole from the oven to the table, Mikage may have found the traditional way to her man's heart. But the upshot is a most untraditional family. Just as there is no fixed inside to Banana's families, nor is there any unnecessary outside to them either. The strict isomorphism once imposed upon the units in which we dwell has given way to something more polymorphous. This story, while fictional, does occur in a country, Japan, where ersatz family members can be rented by the hour to perform ritual obligations one is just too busy to do oneself anymore, such as visit aged parents or attend funerals; where the small place that industrial capitalism once exempted from commodification is, under it present successor, no longer excused. This is a story that seems to confirm just that sort of postmodernism in which Jameson says "the logic of the simulacrum, with its transformation of older realities into television images, does more than merely replicate the logic of late capitalism; it reinforces and intensifies it."[41] If these older realities include the family, then we have arrived at just what it is that fascinates some readers of Banana and irritates others for its diversionary tactics in masking the allegedly late-capitalist underpinnings of such vacuity. Then again, we might look further at what happens in *Kitchin*. We have to ask a little more about what occurs when Banana, or anyone else, begins to question our literal legitimacy as the sons or daughters of our families and of a progenitive modernity for which some literary critics wistfully pine.

Early in *Kitchin*, Mikage tells the reader that she "is tied by blood to no creature in this world" (10). With the death of Eriko (who, according to Mikage, "didn't look human" [11]), neither is Yūichi. Neither adolescent is the issue of any certain genealogy; neither descends from parents unproblematically fathers or mothers. The typical denouement of such situations in literature is the orphan's happy reunion with long-lost family. But in Yoshimoto Banana's novels, orphans are happy to be orphans.

This is not a new ending for Japanese literature. Critic Fujimoto Yukari has pointed out that not only did Japanese girls' comics in the early 1970s began the transgender experiment recognizable in *Kitchin*, but that these comics depict a changing family structure: no longer natural, but nonetheless happy and normal. Fujimoto notes of such families that there is "an increasing number . . . in which, unlike the traditional family, there are absolutely no blood or kinship relations."[42] The evolution of (late-)capitalism in the U.S. as well as Japan has freed us to form social units, or none, on the basis of chosen rather than assigned affiliations. Nonetheless, such carefree indifference to parentage in Banana (indifference that parallels her own to those literary traditions noted by Nakamura) has to raise psychoanalytical speculation. *Kitchin* describes a fertile ground for all manner of neuroses. Yūichi—narcissistically described as an effeminate "long-limbed young man with pretty features" who works in a flower shop—is suspected by Mikage of being her grandmother's secret lover (7–8). But this is only the first of many taboos to be transgressed. The quasi-sibling, quasi-sexual relationship between Mikage and Yūichi teeters on the incestuous. Their relationship repeats that long ago of Eriko and her deceased wife. From Yūichi we learn that Eriko, an apparent orphan him/herself, was as a child "taken in by [his future wife's] family. I don't know why. They grew up together" (14). Then, once Eriko becomes a woman, that all-important phallus—the threatened loss and promised transfer of which Freud tells us is the currency required for the successful resolution (repression) of the Oedipus complex—disappears. The only thing made in the Tanabe apartment are Mikage's meals; any other reproduction is impossible. The situation, in other words, is hardly set up for any normal, Freudian development of either Yūichi's or Mikage's adult sexuality.

Given the steady reference to kitchens, food, and eating in this novel, one might be tempted to suggest that its characters are stalled in the oral stage and are thus regressively pre-oedipal. "Why is it that everything I eat when I'm with you is so delicious?" ponders Yūichi. "Could it be," suggests Mikage, "that you're satisfying hunger and lust at the same time?" (100). The child who sucks at his mother's breast does not yet know the terror of the father and his power. No small part of *Kitchin*'s charming innocence comes from this idyllic ignorance. But what we may have in *Kitchin* is an anti-oedipal scenario, one in which the kitchen and Mikage's recipes have superseded the traumatic conflicts which Freudians predict for us; in which *Kitchin*'s warm and fuzzy feelings have replaced the struggles that the script for sexual development mandates.

Why would such an environment be appealing to Mikage, Yūichi, and Eriko? For one, it does away with the stern discipline, enforced by punishment, associated with the fear of castration by the father. Eriko willingly surrendered her own penis when she became a woman in order, she tells us, "to adopt a sort of muddled cheerfulness" (81) apparently unavailable to her as a man.

Masculinity of any sort seems in short supply in this novel, as does femininity predicated on essential difference from masculinity. Brief and thoroughly unpleasant cameo appearances by Mikage's former boyfriend and then by Yūichi's former girlfriend are the two emphatically heterosexual exceptions that prove the rule. One is struck by the absence of explicit gender contrast—like the absence of sex itself—from *Kitchin*. Mikage and Yūichi, like the so-called boy-girl pairs in other Banana stories, retain unarguable signs of maleness and femaleness only in the putative gender of their names.

But one is also struck by the narcissism rife in the Tanabe household, where every character seems to mirror every other. We can imagine another rationale for the popularity of *Kitchin* with the Japanese Foreign Ministry and public alike. Perhaps it is not coincidental that the way we consume commodities to express ourselves also resembles how we enjoy a dangerous intimacy with the images we perceive. Commodity fetishism is usually situated as a form of narcissism. Could the Tanabe household—dephallicized, yes, but very much in love with itself—represent a paradigm for how we are to submit to the allure of consumer capitalism and its demands for our psychic identification with those things we are thus convinced to buy? But such an analysis, in implying that the psychology of consumer capitalism is somehow a deformed psychology, still takes the oedipal trajectory as the norm even if it is resisted or reworked. If narcissism, which Freud ruled a stage that we ordinarily pass through on our voyage to adult heterosexuality, is now to double as the state of how we exist as consumers, then our development (or rather, our lack of it) has to be regarded suspiciously as "arrested." I would propose instead that our stubborn commitment to the Oedipus myth has much to do with the evident frustration of intellectuals over the queer story that Banana tells in *Kitchin*. Her novel's absurd situation upsets some as the unraveling of the same transfer of psychic identification that underlies not only classic psychoanalytic theory but modernity—whose master trope has been the struggle against chaos or control—and the self-sowing critique of self.

Freud calls Oedipus a revolutionary event. He means that it sets into motion the development of our civilized selves. It is no less revolutionary for modern writers and critics, whose anxiety of influence, we are told, leads to literary and intellectual innovation. No liberation, in other words, without repression. A modern novel without Oedipus is a novel without the scripted wherewithal to wrest power from that social or political authority that modernism is said to contest. But none of this can be found in *Kitchin*. It provides no model for how we are to become such fully wrought individuals, and therein lies one cause for panic. *Kitchin* would frighten any critic worried about how we are to oppose the tendency of modern consumer capitalism to reduce our ken of action to that of simply choosing the colors of our cars. But before we object to Yoshimoto Banana too strenuously, we should consider two things. One, is our own position as dissenting critics linked to the same Oedipus that engenders the commodification we would oppose? And two, does a post-oedipal cultural logic really deny us all opportunity to resist that commodification?

Gilles Deleuze and Félix Guattari long ago argued that Oedipus is our very modern story and one that indispensably seduces us to desire our own repression. *Anti-Oedipus: Capitalism and Schizophrenia* provides some clue to the real issues at stake in the dissonance not only between *Kitchin*'s global success and its critical ill-repute, but between the capitalism we inherited and the one we now see unfolding before us. Deleuze and Guattari's cynical historicization of Oedipus and their disclosure of how it duplicates the structure of our capitalist economy as well as accounts for that of our psyches, can from afar predict the moment that has produced Yoshimoto Banana and the anxiety she prompts in critics. I begin with Deleuze and Guattari's insight that political economy and the Freudian libidinal economy are not unrelated. Insofar as they similarly manage our desires, they overlap. "The flows and production of desire will simply be viewed as the unconscious of the social reductions. Behind every investment of time and interest and capital, an investment of desire, and vice versa." Hence, Deleuze and Guattari must return repeatedly to Oedipus, to what they deride as "the holy family: daddy-mommy-and-me," for it is in the oedipal code that the libido "is converted into the phallus as detached object, the latter existing only in the transcendental form of stock and lack," just as in the capitalist code and its own triangular expression, where "money as detachable chain is converted into capital as detached object."[43] The phallus works in Oedipus much as the commodity does in capitalism, another system whose tendency is to substitute for fixed and limiting relations between people and things an abstract unit of equivalence that allows for the free exchange of everything for everything. Consequently the oedipal family structure becomes the means of disciplining desire; the Oedipus complex/system guarantees that human desire will be housed within the modern nuclear family, while only a commodified desire will invest the larger social field.

In their section of *Anti-Oedipus* subtitled "Oedipus at Last," Deleuze and Guattari speculate on just how such a synchronization of codes has come to be. Once, in those systems (the primitive, the despotic) that existed before (or

now exist alongside) capitalism, "social economic production was never independent of human reproduction, of the social form of this representation." The
family is the real and not just virtual (re)production. But with capitalism comes
a real and symbolic privatization and semioticization of the family. Just as Marx
saw when he understood wealth as the representative of productive activity,
representation generally and including that of the family "no longer relates to a
distinct object, but to the productive activity itself." "The family is now simply
the form of human matter or material that finds itself subordinated to the autonomous social form of economic reproduction." Consequently it is a trope, a
figure best "suited to expressing what it no longer dominates.... Father, mother
and child thus become the simulacrum of capital ('Mister Capital, Madame
Earth,' and their child the Worker)."

Once the social field is reduced symbolically to this triangle of the family,
then and only then "Oedipus arrives: it is born in the capitalist system of the
application of first-order social images to the private familial images of the second order." When capitalism turns the family from that place where things are
made to the place where things are consumed, Oedipus is required to produce
those cannibalistic desires that would have us identify with our mothers and
fathers: it is father-mommy that we consume. Oedipus is not only linked with
capitalism, it is inconceivable *without* capitalism. "It is not via a flow of shit
or a wave of incest that Oedipus arrives, but via the decoded flows of capital-
money." Mother must become the simulacrum of our origins, and father that
of the "despotic Law"—and we, with our "slashed, split, castrated ego, are the
products of capitalism.... The family has become the locus of retention and
resonance of all the social determinations."[44] Just as, according to Marx, capital
fools us into thinking that it is responsible for production (rather than the other
way around), Oedipus tricks us into thinking that it is what makes the family
reproduce itself, when in fact it is what makes things *not* happen.

Such a grim collusion of the psychoanalytic and capitalist regimens that
make us adult and modern is not without its advantages. For Deleuze and Guattari, the oedipal code—like the capitalist code—is not primitive or despotic,
which is to say rigid and without fluidity. Rather, it is the nature of capitalism to
encourage desires even as it works to restrict them. "Capitalism therefore liber-
ates the flows of desire, but under the social conditions that define its limit and
the possibility of its own dissolution, so that it is constantly opposing with all its
exasperated strength the movement that drives it toward this limit." The same
then is also true of the oedipal code. It is a "poorly closed triangle, a porous or

seeping triangle from which the flows of desire escape in the direction of other territories."[45] The breakdown before our eyes of Oedipus is evident in Banana's *Kitchin*, where we find plenty of what had to be diagnosed with psychoanalytical theory in order to be repressed: the schizophrenic, whose schizophrenia is the extreme limit to the interior limit of capitalism-Oedipus. Schizophrenia in this usage is not a clinical diagnosis. It is the name Deleuze and Guattari give happily to the escape any of us make into what Brian Massumi termed "the unstable equilibrium of continuing self-invention."[46] It is the schizophrenic who explodes the oedipal genealogy because he or she (the "or" here assumes special significance) refuses to understand his or her desire by threatening to deprive others of what it had. The delirium of the father simply does not work here. His/her desire does not submit to such reasoning, or structure; the schizophrenic is not simply bisexual, for Freud could easily agree with that—the schizophrenic is "between the two, or intersexual. He is transsexual."[47]

And so we are back to *Kitchin*. Not just in the schizophrenic/transgender Eriko, who gladly paid to have himself castrated for the sake of a "muddled cheerfulness" and so lose the leverage of the phallus with which to organize and discipline his or her family, but also in Mikage and Yūichi, who are just as schizophrenic and just as anti-oedipal. Neither can imagine the issue of daddy-mommy-me. The lack of overt sexual difference between the two is not really a lack. They are different genders, but as Deleuze and Guattari indicate, such difference is not the basis of (different) subjectivity—"Mikage" and "Yūichi" are only oppositional terms. Is their sexuality, too, "muddled"? The products of bad object-choices, or of no object-choices at all? Wrong: they are the orphans of whom Deleuze and Guattari speak as one of the directions in which anti-oedipal schizo flows may go, and go gladly. "For what is the schizo," they say, "if not first of all the one who can no longer bear 'all that': money, the stock market, the death forces," those things that capitalism and psychoanalysis convinced us of?[48] These people, too, "can no longer bear all that." Eriko becomes a woman after the death of his wife; Mikage and Yūichi become a family after the death of Eriko. But in the end, the consequence of giving up "all that" seems to be the gain of something. What family in modern Japanese literature, after all, is as happy as Mikage, Yūichi and Eriko? None.

Still, *Kitchin* has its moments of anxiety, though that anxiety can now be thought the consequence of its anti-oedipal verve. What frightens Mikage and Yūichi after the deaths of the former's grandmother and Eriko is the immediacy of those deaths and their demonstrated potential to leave one family-less at any time. "Someday, without fail," muses Mikage, "everyone will disappear, scattered into the blackness of time" (21). What both fear is the disappearance of just that social field once ruled over by Oedipus, for even if we were orphaned, we were still someone's *daughter*, someone's *son*: titles that, even when Mikage and Yūichi assume them, are roles and not identities. Mikage's blackness is one that Deleuze and Guattari predict as precisely the consequence of being anti-oedipal. "Oedipus informs us: if you don't follow the lines of differentiation daddy-mommy-me, and the exclusive alternatives that delineate them, you will fall into the black night of the undifferentiated."[49] The deaths that surround Mikage and Yūichi—so many that the latter gloomily jokes that they should rent themselves out as "*deconstruction workers*" (50)—deterritorialize the oedipal triangle and its penchant for wrecking the assemblage of desire.

What remains is reterritorialization. The response of the characters, and that which completes the bizarre comedy that is *Kitchin*, is to refashion that field for themselves. "What a muddle, what an emulsion the family is," warn Deleuze and Guattari, "agitated by backwashes, pulled in one direction or another, in such a way that the oedipal bacillus takes or doesn't take."[50] But remember that it is for the sake of a "muddled *cheerfulness*" that Eriko undergoes the knife to make himself a woman and a mother. There is something to be gained in breaking the rules. When Mikage first hears the news of Eriko's death, she feels "powerless to stop the energy rushing out of my body; it seemed to dissipate with a hissing sound into the darkness" (48), but that energy is the flow of a liberated desire, and the darkness is the anti-oedipal void in which she will indulge it. When she orders *katsudon* to go and races to Isehara to deliver it, she binds herself and Yūichi in that fort that author Banana calls the *famirii*, a word taken from English precisely to deterritorialize it. Mikage and Yūichi's relationship is not easily schematized as boyfriend and girlfriend, or mother and son, or brother and sister. It is undifferentiated in the way that Deleuze and Guattari characterize the world of the schizophrenic; it is anti-oedipal in the way that they would schizo-analyze capitalism. One can debate whether all this is genuinely liberating or hopelessly repressive/regressive. If *Kitchin's* is a family that can be compared to any other, it is the family composed of all those images, nostalgic, cinematic, and otherwise, of the family that Mikage is heir to. One could, with Jameson, see such a production as the mark of the postmodern, namely the "transformation of the real into so many pseudo-events." (Although if the real in this instance must be the oedipal real of the family, this could still be cause for celebration.) But I do not mean to suggest that the schizo-anything of *Kitchin* is the potential for revolution that Deleuze and Guattari see in the schizo process elsewhere. *Kitchin* is rife with the diversionary intensities that Jameson warns "tend to be dominated by a peculiar kind of euphoria"[51] in the style that accommodates late capitalism. Mikage does recall, after all, "that one summer of bliss. In that kitchen" (59).

Can we say this: that the nuclear family—so carefully curated by the Japanese state with its 1959 marriage of the Crown Prince and Michiko, so flippantly ridiculed by Fukazawa Shichirō—reaches its expiration date a scant twenty years later? That the moment we now inhabit, one Appadurai aptly characterized as rhizomatic and where the ideas of consumer and producer are fetishes, is also one that can be, per Banana, ambivalently anti-oedipal? Workers in Japan and other developed nations are told today that the new global economy means that they will need several different careers over the course of their lives, that they will have to adapt constantly, abandon identities as forever *one* sort of worker or another. The polymorphous shape of our economic lives finds its equivalent in families likewise more affinitive and less filial. Just how bizarre is the Tanabe household really?

It could be that the immensely protean and adaptive nature of capital and labor is reflected in the practices of the postnuclear family, no longer spawned and contained by the father but instead infinitely pliable, in ways once unimaginable but now intuited by the Japanese Foreign Ministry when it handed out copies of *Kitchin* to the world media as a way of "understanding the younger generation all over the world." If "there is no disproportion between the life of the family and the life of the nation," according to Frantz Fanon, then there is pause here for us and not just when we read Yoshimoto Banana.[52] Her global boom will eventually pale in comparison to Murakami Haruki's, the most widely read Japanese writer in history and the subject of my next chapter, but the mystery of just what captures the tenor of the times in these writers' works, despite the revealing befuddlement of many critics, marks simultaneously the success of the last phase of modern Japanese literature and the fact that it *will* be the last phase, to be replaced with something now emerging but, just like whatever is succeeding capitalism and the families it spawns, we have not yet named.

10

Murakami Haruki and
Multiple Personality

The 1980s media blitz surrounding Yoshimoto Banana had competition. In early August 1989, just as Japan was entering its Heisei period under a new emperor, the Japanese press reported that Miyazaki Tsutomu had been arrested the previous month on suspicion of abducting, mutilating, and murdering a young girl. A twenty-six-year-old printer with a history of child molestation, Miyazaki was soon charged with the homicide of three more victims, each of them juvenile, female, and dismembered. The police discovered in Miyazaki's bedroom at his parents' home 5,793 videotapes, most of them television shows but some of his victims. The authorities confiscated his copying machines, computer, and a word processor; the room was as full of appliances as the Tanabe kitchen in Banana's debut novel. These hoarded possessions sufficed to identify Miyazaki in the popular press with the 1980s keyword of *otaku*, slang used to describe introverted young men (and some women) fond of video games, computers, and comics in lieu of normal human contact. His defense team would eventually argue his crimes were "closely related to . . . the overflow of information and goods" in Japanese society.[1] "I'm part of the manga generation,"

Miyazaki would tell a judge. "I'm not good at printed words" (*katsuji ni yowai*). The panic over Banana's *shōjo* culture for literature was met, in other words, with a complementary panic over her generation's male *otaku* withdrawal from, and renunciation of, healthy social intercourse and indeed of traditional literacy. The unspoken apprehension was that life in Japan now had a video game–like, hyperreal, and simulated quality to it; and that the distinction between the imaginary and the real was trivialized to the point of irrelevancy.

Miyazaki's trial commenced on 30 March 1990, in Tokyo district court and concluded after thirty-eight court sessions on 14 April 1997, at which time he was sentenced to death. His last words to the bench were: "I want my things back."[2] Miyazaki's guilt was never the issue. Few details of the murders were presented in evidence. In his court testimony Miyazaki was specific only about his favorite anime, brand names, and manga. The proceedings focused instead on Miyazaki's mental state. Examined over the course of four years by two teams of forensic psychiatrists from prominent universities who produced three sets of diagnoses, Miyazaki was variously declared in the 1,300 pages of psychological profiles submitted to the court as (1) normal and capable of distinguishing right from wrong, (2) afflicted with the early stages of schizophrenia and (3) in a final report written by psychiatrist Dr. Uchinuma Yukio, suffering from depersonalization syndrome (*rijinshō*) and hysterical dissociation (*hisuteriisei kairi shōjō*)—a conclusion the press instantly translated into the more colloquial and sensational "multiple personality disorder" (*tajū jinkaku*), or MPD.[3]

Uchinuma held that Miyazaki had been raised in a dissociative family (*kairisei kazoku*), a term that like *kairisei shakai* (dissociative society) Uchinuma coined especially for Miyazaki and which he implicitly blamed for his subject's emotional distress and adult criminality.[4] Miyazaki thus became the first defendant in the history of Japanese criminal justice to invoke MPD as a defense. In his testimony Uchinuma explained that Miyazaki had at least four, possibly five, distinct personalities (alters), including one group known as the Rat Men (*nezumi ningen*) whom Miyazaki said were present during the murders.[5] In a classic demonstration of dissociation, Miyazaki told his doctors that everything that happened to him seemed to happen to "another person," somewhere on "a far island" or "in a dream." As the years went by Miyazaki was popularly portrayed as less the dysfunctional *otaku* and more the newly fashionable embodiment of dissociation at its worst, the multiple. By the time of his execution, Miyazaki Tsutomu enjoyed cult status in Japan as a multiple. Celebrities and prominent intellectuals openly declared they identified with him.

The diagnosis of MPD, as old as the practice of modern psychiatry itself, has long lingered as its most controversial disorder,[6] real, if rare, in the minds of some clinicians, feigned or iatrogenic (i.e., the adverse effect of therapy) in the minds of others. Today it remains a more provocative psychiatric diagnosis than any other, and popular authority Ian Hacking wryly concedes that it may have simply "provided a new way to be an unhappy person."[7] To start, medicine's problem is that there is no definition of a multiple, only a prototype, and "personality" is a term that has always resisted scientific rigor. But thousands of cases are now treated in the United States, the center of the epidemic, and some believe that as many as 5 percent of patients admitted to psychiatric hospitals suffer from MPD and that 1 percent of the American population may suffer from it in full-blown, quasi-, or latent form.[8]

Japan has usually been cited as a counterexample to the spread of MPD, or as the *Diagnostic and Statistical Manual of Mental Disorders* has referred to it since its fourth edition (1994), dissociative identity disorder (DID). Hacking curiously rules the disorder must be a uniquely Western phenomenon since only in the West does there exist "an integrated and unique self" that can be multiplied in the first place,[9] and MPD/DID in Japan is indeed seldom diagnosed. "I recognize that it is common abroad [*mukō ni*]," conceded a Japanese expert when asked during Miyazaki's trial if MPD existed in Japan, but later he amended his testimony to say he meant America.[10] When Japanese research into multiple personality disorder began in 1919, there were only two highly dubious cases of MPD/DID in the country from which to extrapolate.[11] In 1990, one Japanese researcher wrote that the "recent consensus among psychiatrists is that MPD is a very rare disorder."[12] By October 1996, there were apparently no more than thirty documented cases of it in all of Japanese medical history, nearly all diagnosed after 1990.[13] Japanese psychiatry has boasted of this small number with hubris, claiming that the healthier Japanese family, with its lower incidence of reported child abuse than in America, means incidences of MPD/DID, too, are fewer. But by the end of the twentieth century it was on the rise. Psychiatrist Katsumasa An and his colleagues suggest that "DID and child abuse are not as rare in Japan as commonly believed," and that it may be as common in Japan as in the United States.[14] Sociologist Miyadai Shinji notes cases of MPD rose dramatically in Japan between 1995 and 2005,[15] and as recently as 2007, psychiatrists Kataoka Satomi and Tanaka Kiwamu confirmed that dissociative disorders across the board were steadily increasing in Japan.[16]

Michael Kenny claims without controversy that "multiple personality is a culturally specific metaphor, not a universally distributed mental disorder."[17] If MPD/DID and related dissociative afflictions began to attract greater notice in both 1980s Japan and America, one might ask if something besides global popular-culture flows is responsible for this roughly simultaneous surge in the world's two largest capitalist nations. Explanations of MPD/DID, which will have to be historical in addition to clinical, have already gone beyond biomedical hypotheses. When Fredric Jameson wrote about Lacan's account of schizophrenia, it was not for any clinical accuracy but because, as description rather than diagnosis, schizophrenia offered "a suggestive aesthetic model."[18]

I am not interested in the clinical accuracy of MPD/DID or its availability as an aesthetic model, but I am concerned with the present-day alienation of functional selfhood in contemporary Japan and its expression as illness. Given ongoing neurological research into MPD/DID, it is premature to discount organic factors, but our interest here must focus on, as Jeremy Hawthorn phrased it, "the importation of social contradictions into the individual as well as for their subsequent projection back into society." He argues that the childhood trauma often said to instigate MPD/DID is related to "the disintegration of the values at the heart of the family," which must involve the wider social sphere,[19] all of which suggests we should think of MPD and its virtual representations as phenomena linked to something larger in scale than the small dramas of dysfunctional households.

Multiple personalities abound in American popular culture, from novels (Chuck Palahniuk's *Fight Club*), to film (Sméagol/Gollum in *The Lord of the Rings*), to television (Showtime's *United States of Tara*) and comic books (Harvey Dent/Two-Face in *Batman*). In Japan the examples are more plentiful. As psychiatrist and critic Saitō Tamaki notes, they range from Japan's many subcultures to the realm of literature.[20] The ubiquity of the topic of MPD/DID in popular culture is seen in the immensely popular manga series *MPD-Psycho* and its spin-offs in other media. But MPD/DID is not, in Colin Ross's phrase, pleasant entertainment.[21] The Japanese press speaks openly of dissociative disorders afflicting members of the imperial family (Empress Michiko, Crown Princess Masako), even comparing them to the nation's most tabloid-worthy sumo *yokozuna*, Asashōryū, who was diagnosed with a dissociative disorder in the summer of 2007.[22]

"Second selves" have been widespread in Japanese fiction since the late 1980s. The compromised mental health of the characters who people contemporary Japanese literature runs the gamut of dissociative disorders, with MPD/DID only the most dramatic. For Saitō Tamaki, dissociation is quite broadly "the loss of temporal and spatial continuity in the human psyche."[23] Dissociation is not always pathological, dysfunctional, or maladaptive, but often a perfectly normal and even welcome way of being in the world, as we daydream, drive a car while talking to a passenger or, in Saitō's example, use our cell phones.[24] But in the clinical setting, dissociation usually refers to one or more of four roughly divisible disorders: dissociative amnesia (lapses in memory too extensive to be explained by ordinary forgetfulness), dissociative fugue (sudden and unexplained travel, accompanied by amnesia or confusion) and depersonalization disorder (persistent or recurring feeling of detachment from one's mental processes or body), and finally dissociative identity disorder. A fifth category, "dissociative disorder not otherwise specified," is simply a catchall.[25] All of these categories have colonized Japanese psychiatric discourse, and depersonalization disorder (*rijinshō*) enjoys a special prominence in discussions of contemporary Japanese fiction and culture. Saitō defines *rijinshō* as the experience of seeing oneself elsewhere—something he and other commentators on everyday life in Japan at the end of twentieth century note is rife in Uchinuma's soi-disant dissociative society. The question is, what do we then make of such a diagnosis? If, "like other psychiatric and psychological terms," one psychologist observes, "dissociation is an attempt by members of a social group to describe, explain, or otherwise account for the world they live in,"[26] how might we at large translate their language of hurt and trauma, of pathologies and pain, into our language of the historical and the material? Perhaps by lingering in their realm of feeling; I propose to make a methodological contribution to how recent Japanese fiction should be read by reviving a key tool in the cultural materialist project of the late Raymond Williams.

Williams had frequent recourse in his analysis of cultural trends in Britain to his concept of a structure of feeling, a phrase that combines the solidity of "structure" with the imprecision of "feeling." Just so: the concept from its inception was "applied by Williams specifically to problems of addressing the difficulty of articulating that which was not yet articulable." In his mature treatment of it, say, in his 1977 *Marxism and Literature*, he defined it "as a particular quality of social experience and relationship, historically distinct from particular qualities, which gives the sense of a generation or period"[27]—a quality, many have noted with frustration, that resists easy characterization. Williams, who admitted discomfort with his concept's elusiveness,[28] was quick to add that structures of feeling, "although they are emergent or pre-emergent, they do not have to await definition, classification, or rationalization before they exert palpable pressures and set effective limits on experience and on action."[29] The bold subjectivism of the concept, which led many critics to reject it, was Williams's goal.

As early as the 1954 *Preface to Film*, Williams wrote, "The structure of feeling, as I have been calling it, lies deeply embedded in our lives; it cannot be merely extracted and summarized."[30] Dismissed as a poor renomination of ideology or false consciousness, structure of feeling was an effort by Williams to bring people and their lived experience back into history, not occasionally but always. In his mid-career *The Long Revolution*, he declared that every "new generation will have its own structure of feeling, which will not appear to have come 'from' anywhere." Its advent cannot be predicted or summarized—"It is as firm and definite as 'structure' suggests, yet it operates in the most delicate and least tangible parts of our activity."[31] "The category has been stigmatized for its imprecision," Michael Moriarty concedes, "but it has this merit, that it is an attempt to affirm at once the intelligibility of history and the forces of desire and revulsion that traverse it."[32] Williams's most successful application of the term may have been in his analysis of class in 1840s British fiction, and I mean to stage something similar despite the hurdles of historicizing the present when I argue Japanese literature in the late twentieth century insinuates a structure of feeling that is, in Alan O'Connor's distillation, "something like an emergent pattern of general experience" "loosely associated with a generation of writers or artists."[33] That pattern among Japanese novelists today is dissociation, and its plainest index are tales of multiple personality.

Stuart Hall defined Williams's structure of feeling as "the way meanings and values were *lived* in real lives, in actual communities."[34] This is no utopian fantasy. Sean Matthews realizes that "the structure of feeling is commonly apparent in the experience of deadlock, obstruction and failure,"[35] precisely the predicament of the heroes of late-twentieth-century Japanese fiction caught unaware in their dissociative disorders, a crisis we readers encounter as an unironic monologue of *feeling*, a word bestowed theoretical valence by Williams when he reacted against what he saw as the basic error in Marxist literary theory, "the reduction of the social to fixed forms." Williams chose the concept of feeling to emphasize a distinction from more formal concepts of 'world-view' or 'ideology,'" but he was not in the business of psychologizing or psychoanalyzing our emotive intuitions. "The actual alternative to the received and produced fixed forms is not silence: not the absence, the unconscious, which bourgeois culture has mythicized. It is a kind of feeling and thinking which is indeed social and material, but each in an embryonic phase before it can become fully articulate and defined exchange." Part of the problem is that the specifically affective elements of consciousness and relationships are initially not recognized as social at all, "but taken to be private, idiosyncratic, and even isolating."[36] This is likely the case with the late-twentieth-century surge in the diagnoses of dissociative disorders in Japan. We can interpret them as clinical and amenable to therapy long before we understand feelings as the poorly articulated expressions of a new social order accompanying neoliberal economics circling the globe. The current structure of feeling as multiple becomes perceptible, in fiction, via the inchoate thoughts that literary characters somehow sense are not always their own—the ventriloquism of capital.

"The issue of trauma and dissociation," notes Asada Akira, "is not only a matter for psychiatry: it is a concern for society as a whole," and it has been for some time.[37] None of this is news. It is an old commonplace, even a cliché, to say in modernity the human individual is neither unitary nor internally consistent, but complex, contradictory, and divided. We could hardly expect it to be otherwise—however attractive the concept of unified consciousness may be, it "does not hold up under examination."[38] But contemporary dissociation and its epitome in MPD/DID are not quite the same as this, and certainly not an opportunity to celebrate any newfound, nuanced psychic dissonance. We are dealing with a phenomenon that, after all, either makes people ill or think themselves ill. "Every age develops its own peculiar forms of pathology," wrote Christopher Lasch in 1977 apropos of narcissism,[39] but twenty years later Anthony Cohen suggested that our pathology is now MPD, whose rise "reflects an homology between the dissociation of society and that of the individual."[40] At this point we should be substituting the word "contradiction" for "pathology" and so make it available for historical dialectics.

Saitō Tamaki moves in just that direction when he promotes dissociation as a keyword in thinking through the contemporary state of mind (gendaiteki na shinsei), which, he says, we cannot understand simply as symptoms (shōjō).[41] Taking Saitō's cue, we are talking about a structure of feeling embedded in the larger machinery of everyday life, just as Emily Martin did when writing about bipolar disorder in the United States: "Structures of feeling are actively felt sensibilities that can be vague rather than explicit, informally sensed rather than formally codified. . . . Small scale and amorphous they may be, structures of feeling can still play an important part in producing larger-scale phenomena."[42]

Martin is on to something, but she may have it backward. It could be the "larger-scale phenomena" producing the structure of feeling. To understand the articulation better, we should think about a novelist who has earned global acclaim for his best-selling stories foregrounding the dissociative tenor of daily life in Japan: Murakami Haruki.

Murakami wins international prizes as a postmodern novelist with a unique style, to quote the president of Yale, who awarded him an honorary doctorate in 2016 to the surprise of his modern Japanese literature faculty. In fact, Murakami is not thoughtful enough to be postmodern (though he would like to be) and does not have a unique style (it's familiar, recycled American literary minimalism). At home he has been described more accurately as a "smug, affected writer" (osumashi na sakka). But of interest to us here, he has been called Japan's preeminent dissociative author.[43] From the start of his career in the late 1970s his work has been characterized by bifurcated worlds, the kochiragawa (this side) and achiragawa (that side) between which his characters migrate with shifting identities and piecemeal, unreliable memories. His characters are notoriously forgetful, so much so they might be diagnosed with dissociative amnesia, and to the chagrin of his critics (though not his fans) there is the chronic social dysfunctionality of his protagonists, whom Matthew Strecher says "are so self-absorbed and socially isolated that we cannot help wondering if they exist at all." Strecher decries Murakami's people as "so lethargic at times as to be maddening"; sociologist Nakano Osamu is impatient with their "dithering attitudes toward life" (hikettei no jinsei taido) and their propensity to linger in some nondescript middle ground where they can go on living indecisively forever. These characters are only rarely capable of understanding what is happening around them. Strecher counts Murakami's most commonly recurring phrase to be Boku ni wa wakaranakatta—"None of it was clear to me."[44]

Saitō states that from the 1990s there has been no writer for whom the theme of dissociation has been more central than Murakami, setting a new high-water mark for coupling trauma with dissociation.[45] The trauma, however, is often no more evident at first to the reader than the patient's is to the therapist. In his short story "Nemuri" ("Sleep," 1989), the narrator describes a typically disembodied Murakami life. "I went through the motions—shopping, cooking, playing with my son, having sex with my husband. It was easy once I got the hang of it. All I had to do was break the connection between my mind and my body. While my body went about its business, my mind floated in its own inner space. . . . [I]t occurred to me what a simple thing reality is, how easy it is to make it work. It's just reality."[46] As Murakami's career progressed, specific dissociative disorders in his work became more frequent and distinct. Katō Norihiro sees them in Murakami's 2002 *Umibe no Kafuka* (*Kafka by the Shore*),[47] but signs are found earlier. There is dissociative fugue when Sumire disappears, for example, in his 1991 *Supūtoniku no koibito* (*Sputnik Sweetheart*) and then literally spectacular dissociative depersonalization when the heroine Miu sees her doppelgänger having sex with a man she detests. But Murakami's *Nejimaki-dori kuronikuru* (*The Wind-Up Bird Chronicle*, 1994–95) warrants special scrutiny for its reiteration of various dissociative behaviors and disorders in light of the author's prepublication declarations that this masterwork would mark a significant departure for him. The media heralded it as the author's turn to serious fiction, by which was meant a newfound attention to history, and predicted that serious critics would finally recognize Murakami's worth. Some said this would be his Nobel Prize–winning novel. What is certain about *Nejimaki* is that it was Murakami's longest novel to date (over 1,200 pages in Japanese) and the most complex in terms of story lines, which number three but are intricately intertwined.

The first is that of Okada Tōru, who has already lost his cat and is now worried he is losing his wife Kumiko, and in fact does. Reviewer Jamie James calls Okada "a lost man-boy in his early 30's who has no job, no ambition, and a failing marriage,"[48] and thus he is a familiar narrator-protagonist, a Murakami type Rebecca Suter generically defines as a male from his mid-twenties to early thirties, "working in advertising, or a writer, journalist or translator."[49] Okada was once something of a paralegal in a law office, but by the time we meet him he is unemployed—though, as Jay McInerney noted of a similar social failure in an earlier Murakami novel, he hangs on to his "run-of-the-mill house, small yard, Toyota Corolla."[50]

Okada's subsequent search for his errant wife, like Orpheus's for Eurydice, is the classic quest always found in Murakami's novels, but it is periodically interrupted by the second of *Nejimaki*'s story lines, namely, the revelations of atrocities committed just before and during the Second World War in Mongolia and Manchuria. Here is where Murakami promised to do something new— inserting real Japanese history into what had heretofore been dismissed as a corpus of light entertainment literature. While history will be important in this novel, it is the late twentieth century's, not the midcentury's. Critic after critic faulted Murakami for getting his facts wrong about the Second World War (or dispensing with them altogether—one writer called the mix a "disquieting jux-taposition of fantasy and history").[51] Hasumi Shigehiko declared that though *Nejimaki* was supposed to be about Japanese history, history is wholly absent (*issai fuzai*).[52] Murakami himself writes in *Nejimaki* that "the question of which parts of a story were factual and which parts were not was probably not a very important one."[53] The charge against Murakami is that he reduces history to a catalog of grotesquery (a man is skinned alive in the novel), leading Ōtsuka Eiji to dismiss it as a B-grade horror film.[54] What one might want to call history in *Nejimaki* is, in fact, a misnomer for the trauma that permeates the novel. It is especially evident in its third story line, that of the mother-son duo of Akasaka Nutmeg and Akasaka Cinnamon, whose family were witnesses to, and possibly participants in, atrocities during the war and after. The result is dissociation. As in most of Murakami's novels, there are distinct worlds between which char-acters, usually in alternative guises, drift. In *Nejimaki* Okada moves between the wartime 1930s and 1980s Tokyo. The *New York Times*'s Michiko Kakutani criticized *Nejimaki* as "a fragmentary and chaotic book,"[55] but that is less the result of Murakami's artistic shortcomings and more the novel's ambition to put dissociation on display. Citing Saitō Tamaki's analysis of *Nejimaki* in psychoan-alytic terms, Michael Seats concedes dissociation is "one of the most apposite tropes for our consideration of the text's significance for contemporary Japanese writing."[56] Why this is true is traceable to the traumas that fairly saturate the work.

In his study of contemporary Japanese literature focusing on Murakami, Carl Cassegård defines traumatization as "a mental state in which inner nature has ceased to stir and is felt to be dead." It is not necessary for such a state to be induced by actual trauma. The word will suffice if we understand it names the generation of an affect—a structure of feeling—among people today who are not simply alienated from life or work, as is Okada Tōru, but from a subjective comprehension of sovereign selfhood, which then can lead to the spurious gen-eration of multiple selves, as light is refracted through a prism into colors that are only spectrally real. Okada's life is functionally inanimate since, as Cassegård notes of Murakami's characters in general, "each second is as good as the next and nothing ever seems to change."[57] This is a problematic which produces the pronounced minimalism of Murakami's style. For his characters, "to communi-cate a trauma is difficult or impossible."[58] The scenes in the novel that involve him and his flashbacks to life with Kumiko (a woman described as "a piece of luggage that had been left in the wrong place" [23]) establish the trajectory of alienation to dissociation and back again in the paramount movement of the novel.

Okada suffers from amnesia that interferes with the compulsory tasks of everyday life. Other characters in the novel remark upon it—Okada is warned at one point that he "must have some kind of blind spot" in his memory (129). It is apparent to him as well. "Until the moment the telephone rang, I had been thinking of something," he tells us, "but now I couldn't remember what it was. . . . Something I had been trying unsuccessfully to recall for the longest time" (33). Kumiko, a probable survivor of trauma (her childhood is described as "warped and difficult" [72]), finds herself equally blocked at times. "What she did then was shut herself off from the outer world. She closed her eyes. She closed her ears. She shut her mind down. She put an end to any form of thinking or of hoping. The next several months were a blank" (70). Their marriage does nothing to bridge the dissociation both experience separately. The first time the two make love, it is as if neither were present: "There was something oddly lucid there, a sense of separation, of distance, though I don't know exactly what to call it. I was seized by the bizarre thought that the body I was holding in my arms was not the body of the woman I had had next to me until a few moments earlier" (230). Later Kumiko writes Okada that she never experienced sexual pleasure in his company. "All I ever felt was a vague, far-off sense that almost seemed to belong to someone else" (278). Their alienation is soon complete. Abandoned by Kumiko, Okada spends his time alone in a deep abandoned well on a nearby property, a well like one mentioned in an account of wartime atrocities told him by a veteran, Lieutenant Mamiya. While in the well, Okada's conscious mind begins to slip away from his physical body and he realizes that "this person, this self, this me, finally, was made somewhere else. Everything had come from somewhere else, and it would all go somewhere else. I was nothing but a pathway for the person known as me" (264). As "time ceased being a continuous line and became instead a kind of formless fluid" (267), Okada's psychological integration falls apart. "Then, before I knew it, I was talking to myself, mumbling fragmentary thoughts that I didn't know I was having. I couldn't stop myself. I heard my mouth forming words, but I could hardly understand a thing I was saying. My mouth was moving by itself, automatically, spinning long strings of words through the darkness, words the meaning of which I could not grasp" (267–68).

By the end of book 2, Okada's disintegration reaches the point where, in reality or a dream (from the start of *Nejimaki*, he has trouble distinguishing the two, a common cofactor in multiple personality), "he" attacks another man. "I couldn't stop. There were two of me now, I realized. I had split in two, but *this* me had lost the power to stop the other me" (338). Okada resolves, unusually for a Murakami character, that he must take action to get Kumiko back "because if I didn't, that would be the end of me. This person, this self that I thought of as 'me,' would be lost" (340). It is left to Okada in book 3 to find Kumiko, but he is obstructed by a progressive dismantling of unified consciousness and with it the agency to act. Unable to tell the difference between his waking life and his dreams, Okada recalls, "I had only the most distant sense of reality. I felt strongly detached, as if trying to leap from one moving vehicle to another that was moving at a different speed" (372). At the same time he is spatially dissociating. Isolated in the well for long stretches of time, he reflects on his inability to maintain continuity. "Part of my consciousness is still *there* as an empty house. At the same time, I am still *here*, on this sofa, as me. I think, what should I do now? I can't decide which one is reality. Little by little, the word 'here' seems to split in two inside me. I am *here*, but I am also *here*. Both seem equally real to me. Sitting on the sofa, I steep myself in this strange separation" (373). As the novel moves toward its conclusion, Okada starts to dream of, and through, the character of "boy," one of his alters. In a dream where he experiences depersonalization, Okada is aware that "someone was sleeping in his bed, under the covers, in his place. . . . [T]he one he found in the bed was himself. . . . Yet something was different. He felt as if his self had been put into a new container. He knew that he was still not fully accustomed to this new body of his. There was something about this one, he felt, that just didn't match his original self" (422–25).

Eventually Okada comes to intuit the material real of his multiplicity. In a hotel room he frequents "on the far side," he learns from the television news that his nemesis, Kumiko's brother Wataya Noboru, has been assaulted by someone with a baseball bat who looks exactly like Okada. "Could I have done such a thing without being aware of it?" he asks himself. "No, certainly not—unless there existed another me" (575). In this same hotel room Okada will finally be reunited with his wife, and she will present him with the baseball bat that his other self used to pummel her brother. That other threatens to dominate and so replace the host self. "My voice," Okada realizes, "had begun to take on a somewhat different tone in the deep darkness, as if someone lurking down there were speaking in my place" (585). He thinks, "*I am not here*, I told myself. I am not here. I am not anywhere" (587).

Kumiko, who appears to suffer from dissociation disorders akin to her husband's, admits to the trauma she experienced as a child at the hands of her brother, a trauma which Murakami remarked early in the novel "she had no memory of" (70). But now, at the end of *Nejimaki*, she finally explains in a letter to Okada:

> Inside of me, of course, there was another self that wanted to escape, but at the same time there was a cowardly, debauched self that had given up all hope of ever being able to flee from there, and the first self could never dominate the second because I had been so defiled in mind and body. . . . Do I have any sound basis for concluding that the me who is now writing this letter is the "real me"? I was never able to believe that firmly in my "self," nor am I able to do so today. (606)

Kumiko's difficulty in recovering integrated memory at the end of *Nejimaki* rehearses the classic scenario of childhood trauma–induced MPD/DID, and she is not the only character in the novel to do so. Lieutenant Mamiya, in recalling the vast expanse of the Mongolian steppes in 1938, tells Okada that "the surrounding space is so vast that it becomes increasingly difficult to keep a balanced grip on one's own being. I wonder if I am making myself clear. The mind swells out to fill the entire landscape, becoming so diffuse in the process that one loses the ability to keep it fastened to the physical self" (138–39). But no character aside from Okada and Kumiko is so plagued by multiplicity as Creta Kano, who looks to Okada disturbingly like his wife and early on confides to Okada that her body seems at moments to have a life of its own. "I felt as if my spirit had taken up residence inside a body that was not my own. I looked at it in the mirror, but between myself and the body I saw there, I felt a long, terrible distance" (99). In book 2 she shows up naked at Okada's house, unsure how she got there and displaying all the signs of dissociative fugue. "This is not the first time that something like this has happened to me, when I can't recall where I have been or what I was doing. It doesn't happen often, but it does happen to me now and then" (299).

Like Kumiko, Creta was sexually traumatized as a child. Forced into prostitution, she recalls, "No matter what anyone did to me, the sensations I felt did not belong to me. My unfeeling flesh was not my flesh" (300). One of her clients was Kumiko's brother, Noboru, whose forced insertion of a large physical object in her vagina results in response dissociation akin to clinical MPD/DID. At the time Creta felt "as if my physical self were splitting in two from the inside out. . . .

[F]rom between the two clearly split halves of my physical self came crawling a thing I had never seen or touched before" (303). Eventually Creta understands the identity of that "thing." She observes, "I could no longer connect my body's movements or sensations with my own self. They were functioning as they wished, without reference to my will without order or direction"; "I realized I had become a new person.... This was my third self. My first self had been the one that lived in the endless anguish of pain. My second self had been the one that lived in a state of pain-free numbness.... After I passed though that strange period of transition, what emerged was a brand-new me" (305–6).

When psychiatrist-critic Saitō Tamaki wants proof of his contention that MPD/DID is on the rise in Japan, he cites Murakami Haruki's fiction in general and *Nejimaki* in particular.[59] For literary history, what may make Murakami noteworthy is that his work rewrites the perennial question of modern literature's pursuit of individuated subjectivity—Who am I?—as, in Matthew Strecher's rephrase, "What happens to me when I am no longer me?"[60] Why this question should be posed now at the end of the twentieth century and into the start of the next is itself a query best addressed by thinking about what Raymond Williams might name the structure of feeling in millennial Japan.

We start with the banal observation that Okada does not actually have many feelings. He is numb, befuddled, and hapless in the face of his unemployment and abandonment. He is as superfluous a hero as there is in modern Japanese literature—and there are many. A minor character in *Nejimaki*, the thug Ushikawa, pays a threatening call on Okada and tells him, "This may sound odd, but you are basically a really ordinary guy. Or to put it more bluntly, there's absolutely nothing special about you" (457). Okada describes himself as having no defining characteristics (35), but in fact he does. Most Japanese males of working age do not stay at home, read women's magazines, and endlessly make themselves "light lunches." Okada is wholly outside the productive wage economy of his fellow Japanese. When he goes to a park and spots others in their business suits, he remarks, "I saw lots of men my age, but not one of them wore a Van Halen T-shirt [like me]" (82). What he does in lieu of work is perform mindless pseudo-chores at home:

> I vacuumed the floors and straightened the house. I tied our old newspapers in a bundle and threw them in a closet. I put scattered cassette tapes back in their cases and lined them up by the stereo. I washed the things piled in the kitchen. Then I washed myself: shower, shampoo, clean clothes. I made fresh coffee

and ate lunch: ham sandwich and hard-boiled egg. I sat on the sofa, reading
the *Home Journal* and wondering what to make for dinner. I marked the recipe
for Seaweed and Tofu Salad and wrote the ingredients on a shopping list. I
turned on the FM radio. Michael Jackson was singing "Billy Jean." (83)

Like Yoshimoto Banana's character Mikage in *Kitchin*, Okada spends a lot of
time fussing about at home. But Mikage had a paying job as well. Okada's only
income is earned when, urged by his friend and psychic Kasahara Mei 'May
Kasahara' (who will tell Okada that he is not "*totally* useless" [327]), they go to
Ginza one day to survey men's bald spots for a toupee manufacturer. He is un-
compensated for any of his household errands, which might raise the question
how he supports himself. He is an aging Peter Pan: a mid-thirties male who,
like Mary Martin flying across the stage, has no visible means of support. What
happens in the real world is of no moment to him. Watching the news on TV,
he thinks, "These were all events from some other distant world. The only thing
happening in my world was the rain falling in the yard. Soundlessly. Gently"
(292). Okada, in giving himself up "to the languid flow of time" (537), surrenders purpose in his life. There are scenes in the novel where life is productive
and fulfilling, but none involves him. May Kasahara, the bald-spot surveyor,
finds work in an industrial-capitalist wig factory, where in good Fordist fashion
she may do "the same thing over and over again, day in, day out" but doesn't
"feel the least alienated from life. . . . by not thinking about myself I can get
closer to the core of myself. . . . [A]ll I've done since I came to this factory is
work, work, work. Like an ant" (450–51). Another such scene is Mamiya's
memory of his time in a POW camp where "efficiency was everything in the
camp: it was the law of the jungle, the survival of the fittest" (564). Neither is
an attractive alternative to the life Okada chooses to lead, the one in his tidy
kitchen or the one at the bottom of a dark well. But when Murakami ends this
long novel with the sentence, "In a place far away from anyone or anywhere, I
drifted off for a moment" (611), the reader understands Okada Tōru will forever
deal with his predicament in life by dissociating from it. And then the reader
must decide whether this is a comedy or a tragedy.

Okada is as befuddled by late capitalism as is Fredric Jameson, who wrote
on the eve of the millennium in his essay "Culture and Finance" that "after
the disappearance (or brutal downsizing) of heavy industry, the only thing
that seemed to keep [the U.S. economy] going (besides the two prodigious

American industries of food and entertainment) was the stock market. How was this possible, and where did the money keep coming from?"[61] We now know for sure what Jameson suspected. This is a new age of finance capitalism, and a new period of capitalism's accelerated growth and unsustainability. While it is risky to conflate Japan's 1980s—its boom years—with the 1990s—the collapse of the bubble—in both decades it was fashionable to understand everyday life as schizophrenic on account of how people lived divided lives under late-model consumer capitalism. As a clinical term, schizophrenia can be an unwieldy convenience for a volatile range of severe mental disorders including hallucinations, delusions, blunted emotions, disordered thinking, and a withdrawal from reality. People diagnosed with it can be variously withdrawn, hebephrenic, catatonic, paranoid, or any combination thereof. But in Japan in the 1980s and 1990s, application of the term was expanded and served as a metaphor for any evidence of psychic exhaustion or stress in everyday life. As early as 1982, widely read psychiatrist Nakai Hisao noted that medicine was encountering schizophrenia in forms unknown to the nineteenth century.[62] It was left to later critics to make this a social rather than strictly medical diagnosis. By the late 1980s, just as North American observers were speaking of schizophrenia as a cultural epidemiology[63] and counting it among the principal psychopathologies of life in capitalism,[64] their Japanese counterparts were claiming "the present day is the age of schizophrenia" and that schizophrenia is our "way of life" (wei obu raifu). The rhetorical range of schizophrenia's meanings were proliferating at the same time, Karatani Kōjin averred, that it had arrived as an historical problem.[65] In a lecture delivered in retrospect, Miyadai Shinji estimated that the 1980s boom in personality disorders (jinkaku shōgai) paralleled the "evacuation of everyday life" evident in the onslaught of the "commercialization of media."[66] By the 1990s, when Japan's flaws were touted more than its merits, the impulse to describe contemporary life as schizophrenic only accelerated. Yutaka Nagahara described the decade, with its "skyrocketing information stock market and the homeless in Shinjuku station" as a schizophrenic state.[67] Certainly the popularity of the term owed something to Deleuze and Guattari's loose adaptation of it in the 1970s to nominate their absolute or exterior limit of capitalism, where schizophrenia functioned as a social institution both the product of capitalism and the possibility of its overthrow, though the Japanese never imputed any "euphoric qualities to the hallucinogenic rush of intoxicating experience behind the surface appearance of anxiety and neurosis," as David

Harvey regrets some in the West did.[68] Or as R. D. Laing put it, "No one has schizophrenia like having a cold."[69]

The epithet remained popular until the new millennium, when it gave way to multiple personality disorder as a resuscitated Zeitgeist keyword. In the clinical setting, schizophrenia and MPD/DID overlap and often are only subjectively differentiated. "The borders between schizophrenia and multiplicity," states Ian Hacking, "are contested,"[70] and medical specialists Brad Foote and Jane Park concede "the symptom overlap between MPD/DID and schizophrenia is considerable." MPD/DID's hallmark depersonalization and derealization are found in schizophrenics as well as PTSD sufferers. Both typically hear antagonistic voices, for example.[71] Nonetheless, Japanese critics such as Saitō make a clear distinction. The borderline schizophrenia that characterized earlier decades gave way to dissociation by the late 1990s as a "change in the spirit of the times" (*jidai seishin no henka*).[72] One of his examples is the contrast between Murakami Haruki's *Sekai no owari to hādo-boirudo wandārando* (*Hard-Boiled Wonderland and the End of the World*, 1985), in which schizophrenia is manifested not in a fragmented subject (*boku*) but rather the shattered world he navigates, and the dissociative impairments within *Nejimaki*'s characters themselves.

In her book *Tajūka suru riaru* (The Multiplying Real, 2002), psychiatrist Kayama Rika asks why cases of MPD/DID have increased so much since the 1990s. She does not believe, and the clinical evidence bears her out, that trauma is always a necessary instigation. Defining dissociation as a disconnect between the self in the present moment and past selves, she suggests two possible etiologies. One, common in the popular literature on the topic, is that electronic media such as television and the Internet have multiplied the real and the self, thus prompting dissociation. The other is that contemporary society has become a system (*shisutemu*) that requires us to dissociate in order to execute our social and work obligations. Kayama further speculates that MPD/DID might be the *healthiest* way for us to inhabit that society. Faced with the collapse of any singular reality, dissociation proposes itself as a survival strategy for all of us today, not just the adult survivors of childhood abuse.

Picking up from others in Japan and the West who assert things such as cell phones, text-messaging and the blogosphere encourage their users to assume different personalities at different times, Kayama concludes, "Since the advent of the modern, we have taken as a premise the existence of a 'unified self' and constructed a social system upon that premise. But were we right to have done so? 'A single psyche, a single reality' may have been nothing but an illusion of our own making; and the self and the real always something in fact many-layered and multiple."[73] Fellow psychiatrist Saitō also declares, "The present day is the age of dissociation." He believes that MPD/DID as a social phenomenon as well as a psychological one has contributed something to the terrorist Aum Shin-rikyō cult, the rise of *otaku*, cell phone culture (*keitai bunka*), and the apparently motiveless crimes of young people. Saitō proposes *otaku* like Miyazaki Tsutomu as a new breed of human being, one with altered faculties of perception much in common with fellow mutants Bill Gates and Michael Jackson, all part of the *kairikei shakai* (dissociative-type society) that the media associates with post-modernity. "Multiple personality disorder is the perfect 'illness as metaphor.' . . . The model subject for our present day is surely that of multiple personality."[74]

Fredric Jameson warned against any banal "cultural-and-personality diagnosis of our society," and it is endemic in Japan.[75] The trauma of Japanese culture or society that has allegedly resulted in dissociation and its ultimate expression in MPD/DID cannot be found in any specific historical mega-event (such as defeat in the Second World War, Aum Shinrikyō, or Fukushima), nor does multiple personality disorder seem reducible to the much-heralded fractured post-modern subject. A person with multiples has alternating but surprisingly whole subjects. Nothing is in pieces, unlike the mind of a schizophrenic. It might be more precise to argue that current talk of MPD/DID is an imaginative response that refutes *and* confirms a late-capitalist, carceral society. A redundant Okada Tōru is equally trapped in his neat home and abandoned well. Multiple personality might be construed as a culturally sanctioned form of bodily escape that is a real experience *and* an ironic expression of paradoxical social tensions at a time of increasing functional differentiation in postindustrial societies where we regularly migrate from one task or role to another in the latest configuration of a mobile, elasticized labor force. This does not go smoothly. "The 'mental health plague' in capitalist societies," writes Mark Fisher, "would suggest that, instead of being the only social system that works, capitalism is inherently dysfunctional, and that the cost of it appearing to work is very high."[76]

Our materialist accounting for MPD/DID might reach back in economic history to the shift from competitive to monopoly capitalism and its replacement of rivalry among autonomous individuals with the entropic utopia of endlessly proliferating consumer goods. "Problems such as multiple personality disorder," writes psychologist Oliver James, "are very largely caused by industrialisation and are virtually unknown in pre-industrial communities."[77] James may be mistaking clinical diagnoses for medical incidences, but in any case we need to think hard about what Williams would call the critical social facts underlying MPD/DID's extensive alienation expressed across the symptomatic horizon of, as James Glass enumerates them, "fragmentation, deadness, emptiness and numbness."[78] Such social facts have gone under a variety of names. Decades ago Robert Jay Lifton, after noting the "real possibility that the actual number of [MPD/DID] cases has radically increased," suggested "that increase could be related to the historical forces responsible for contemporary proteanism." "Multiple personality," Lifton continued, "may well be part of a pathological edge of our historical confusions."[79] At the same time, sociologist Kai Erikson was writing that "'trauma' has to be understood as resulting from a *constellation of life experiences* as well as from a discrete happening, from a *persisting condition* as well as from an acute event." "Once we realize this," he concludes, "the term 'trauma' becomes useful to social scientists as well as clinicians."[80]

When, for example, Yumiko Iida says, "contemporary Japan finds itself locked in the double bind of late modernity, torn between two contrary aesthetic solutions to its dilemma: the nihilistic and ironic positioning of simulated identities, and the attempted recovery of 'true' identity and meaning by means of an existential leap into the realm of imagination,"[81] her analysis is in no way wrong but moves us too quickly to aesthetics. The dilemma's origins and its social morphology lie in the material phenomena of multiplicity, which I provisionally call a problem of *excess*, in the sense that multiples' selves are in surplus of themselves—no more than a single alter is required at any one time, but none is required *all* the time. Note that many psychiatric illnesses, unlike neurological ones, lack biomedical explanations but are a problem of quantity; depression is too much sadness, mania is too much euphoria. Capitalism knows what to do with surpluses, namely, invest them. But MPD/DID is a surplus with nowhere to go, no place to be purposefully redeployed. Instead, it promiscuously reproduces, and so multiples today can have hundreds of alters, including cats and dogs. Murakami Haruki has found an inexhaustible career theme.

The epidemic of MPD/DID may be little more than the local eruption of a bigger history now unfolding. "The idea of the unified, bounded, internally consistent 'self,'" Paul Antze and Michael Lambek write, "is so central to our thinking that the only way to go beyond it is to have multiple persons, each a unity of the same order, rather than accept the idea of an amorphous or poorly bounded whole. . . . Multiplicity is thus over-determined or predetermined by the very idea of the unified identity it shatters."[82] That overdetermination is currently spoken of in medical terms that are ideological as well as scientific. In *Illness as Metaphor*, Susan Sontag almost inadvertently has an insight into how the notion of the pathological and our current mode of capitalism are linked in terms of malignant growth:

> Early capitalism assumes the necessity of regulated spending, saving, ac-counting, discipline—an economy that depends on the rational limitation of desire. . . . Advanced capitalism requires expansion, speculation, the creation of new needs (the problem of satisfaction and dissatisfaction); buying on credit; mobility—an economy that depends on the irrational indulgence of desire. Cancer is described in images that sum up the negative behavior of twentieth-century *homo economicus*: abnormal growth; repression of energy, that is, refusal to consume or spend.[83]

Okada Tōru does not have cancer in Murakami's novel, but he might as well. A "twentieth-century *homo economicus*," he is as listless as a patient undergoing chemotherapy, as detached from production and consumption as might be a housebound invalid. In place of a tumor's "abnormal growth," we have a pro-liferation of selves. There is no competitive workplace, no factory or office, in Okada's life. Rather, the competition is thoroughly interiorized and performed by himself (the two of them) "here" on this side, and "there" on the other. This struggle among selves suggests a "late-model" alienation, if you will. The dis-sociation we witnessed in so much of everyday life in Japan at the millennium may be the consequence of the shattering of the integral, solitary self before the onslaught of a post-postindustrial capitalism; its nature is unknown to us and thus traumatic. Then again, it may be part of the machinery of some new regime we are now registering in terms of illness because none other is yet avail-able to us. In a parallel argument, Emily Martin's work on mania and bipolar disorder makes just this pitch; her disorder's irrational heights and depths are entwined in the present-day cultural imaginary with economic success and economic failure. Martin notes it is precisely the characteristics of mania that make for success in the corporate world, if demanding palliative treatment in the proletarian one. For Martin, the irony is that real afflictions like mania have "emerge[d] onto the political economic stage as an object of desire,"[84] as possibly have multitasking, multitech, multimedia, multi-everything, including multiple personality. In Japan, Azuma Hiroki has similarly celebrated Japanese society's multiple-personality model of partial alterities (*bubunteki na tasha*) he extrapolates from such 1990s multisite computer games as *Yu-No*, *Desire*, and *Eve*.[85]

Paul Antze and Michael Lambek cleverly compared MPD/DID to "a state with several reified ethnic groups envisaged in permanent conflict with one another or with the state itself. . . . Contestations by multiples and by ethnic groups make use of the same forms."[86] The comparison is a stretch and soon falls apart, but the squaring of multiplicity (alters, ethnic groups) with the politics of *surplus* pursing *equilibrium* is instructive. That our present structure of feeling should manifest itself as multiple personality stakes out the troubled extreme of that structure; at the other end, we are told young people in Japan are happily part-time, temporary workers (*furiitā*) and that young Americans look forward to oxymoronic serial careers. "The separate functioning of alter identities can in certain circumstances," reasons Jeremy Hawthorn, "be a more effective way of surviving than the creation of a consistent and integrated personality." This is now so because "human beings collaborate in production and compete in ownership of the means of production," but this détente is precarious. There is "an increasing awareness of a tension *within* people between the cooperative and the competitive mode."[87] When, in a time such as ours, social collective and competitive elements become confused, we will be torn in different directions—one of which is often dissociation and occasionally MPD/DID, the latter a condition Colin Ross would have called "a microcosm of our culture."[88] Multiple personalities are thus "a real experience *and* an ironic *expression* of paradoxical social tensions at a time of increased 'functional differentiation' in society."[89]

In *The Long Revolution*, Raymond Williams wrote, "The experience of isolation and of self-exile is an important part of the contemporary structure of feeling, and any contemporary realist novel would have to come to real terms with it."[90] But as Williams observed, once a structure of feeling is formalized, which is to say iterable, another one is usually on its way.[91] It is coming. When the *New York Times*'s Michiko Kakutani complained that "Mr. Murakami has written a fragmentary and chaotic novel" in her review of *Nejimaki*'s translation, she explained, "Art is supposed to do something more than simply mirror the confusions of the world."[92] But why? As confusing as late capitalism is to those of us in the midst of it, that alone would be quite an achievement. As Matthew Strecher says of Murakami Haruki, and Ōtsuka Eiji of Miyazaki Tsutomu, it is difficult to find much distinction of reality from fantasy in them. Ōtsuka goes on to assert that throughout Japan, post-Aum Shinrikyō and post-MPD/DID, reality no longer sustains the real, it is fantasy that does.[93] It is little wonder that psychiatrists now moonlight as Japan's cultural and literary critics as well as provide expert testimony at the murder trial of contemporary Japan's most iconic young man. "We are all Miyazaki Tsutomu" was the rallying cry of his celebrity support group.

Psychiatrists also tell us that fewer clients come to them today with self-diagnoses of MPD/DID, though the symptoms they present may be the same as before. But it would be a mistake to conclude MPD/DID is disappearing, any more than hysteria has disappeared. As Elaine Showalter notes, "It has simply been relabeled for a new era."[94] I suggest that MPD/DID and other dissociative phenomena, whether real or fantastic, are linked to how labor and production are changing in a postindustrial Japanese economy, and it demoralizes Murakami's witless characters. At least Flaubert's Madame Bovary managed to clumsily kill herself rather than live with her nineteenth-century ennui. Our postmodern Okada Tōru, dazed to the very end, just "drifts off," neither committed to the world nor impatient with his marginal place within it. What one reviewer called Murakami's "low-maintenance, attention-deficit prose" is finally the perfect vehicle for his dysfunctional-functional themes: a slacker style for a somnolent and inconsequential surreality.[95]

Another Murakami global blockbuster, *Ichikyūhachiyon* (*1Q84*, 2009–11), exceeded *Nejimaki* in both length and sales. The *New York Times* dismissed it as a "stupefying" "1,000 uneventful pages,"[96] but fans found it familiar territory. Tengo, an underemployed twenty-something with "second-rate erections . . . *not even second-rate ones*,"[97] "lives in his own little world" having "learned early in life to make himself inconspicuous" (245, 252–53). Like Okada before him, he spends "day after day feeling uneasy and muddled" (285). "Thinking," he tells himself, "is something I can save for later" (264). Having "lost interest in anything" (399), Tengo "could no longer distinguish how much of this present world was reality and how much of it was fiction" (588). Aomame, the novel's other main character, is burdened with the typical Murakami worry that she exists in two alternate worlds (1984 versus "1Q84") she cannot easily distinguish. Like Tengo, she may watch television news and read the papers, but "not a single thing had occurred that had a direct bearing on her" (814). Like Tengo, she "was not opposed to losing her identity. If anything, she welcomed it" (373). Early in the book, both characters, each with his or her own history of childhood trauma, dissociate. Tengo's first memory is seeing himself as a third person (13), and Aomame is aware "she had become split in two. . . . *I'm here, but I'm not here.*

I'm in two places at once" (38). "Which one was the real person," a confused Tengo asks himself after sex with a teenager, "and which the alter ego?" (795).

In the more recent Murakami hit, *Shikisai o motanai Tazaki Tsukuru to, sono junrei no toshi* (*Colorless Tsukuru Tazaki and His Years of Pilgrimage*, 2013), the title character, another listless loner in life, "was himself then, but at the same time, he was not . . . [H]e distanced himself from his body and from a nearby, painless spot, observed Tsukuru Tazaki enduring the agony."[98] Dissociation, fugue, trauma: above all, multiplicity. Little in Murakami's fiction is ever singular. There are usually two or more of everything, similar but never quite identical. A young girl with an important role to play in *1Q84* will never give birth, for example—she has too many human eggs in her with "nowhere to go" (241), a condition akin to capitalism's problem with excess accumulation. But looming over all the novel's multiplicities is this astral one: two moons, one familiar but the other small and greenish. Aomame may be the one to see them first, but eventually Tengo will find himself drawn to writing a story "about a world with two moons" (196, 307). The unexplained, mismatched satellites have personalities; they look at Aomame and know what she is going to do next (345). "The moons kept a close watch over her" (608) and are "listening carefully" (882). It is hard not to conclude that these moons are alters, and that Murakami has placed them high in the sky to make the world(s) Tengo and Aomame inhabit inexplicable wherever they go. An American psychiatrist ended her effusive review of *1Q84* by asking, "Does it take 2 moons to know that things are no longer the same?"[99] The question is rhetorical and it isn't. Of course, we reply, we don't need two moons to tell us this. But Murakami's characters stare at the moons nonetheless, hoping for a surer sign of just what has changed, and why.

Conclusion
Takahashi Gen'ichirō's Disappearing Future

Murakami Haruki and Yoshimoto Banana, writes critic Tatsumi Takayuki, do not enjoy their popularity in the English-speaking world because they are "icons of 'Japan.'" In a routine reduction of "English-speaking world" to the United States, he says instead, "They write about an America that no American writer has noticed."[1] Tempting— though misleading—as it is to bundle Murakami and Banana together (Murakami has proven the better impresario), we nonetheless know what Tatsumi is getting at. "Without the Japanese names," their works could be taken "as purely American,"[2] yet somehow they are not. If the Japanese are sending us neo-American fiction these days, it is because "American" is shorthand for the stripped-down, deracinated writing recently dubbed "The Dull New Global Novel."[3]

It is a mistake for foreign readers, for whom little is translated, to conclude that Murakami and Banana represent the best of Japanese writing today, or that their global dullness marks the end of whatever was once Japanese about the modern Japanese novel. I'm talking about the older, Orientalist dull, which held nothing, such as history, ever happens in Japanese fiction. But this is not the case, despite American reviewers whose knowledge of Japanese literature ("nearly invisible abroad," says Tatsumi[4]) does not extend past a Manhattan publisher's press release. This last chapter alights on another writer, Takahashi Gen'ichirō, and on the literary turn he is pioneering. This turn is not unique to Japan—nothing is—but it is well underway there. The outside world is vaguely aware of it. The efforts of Arthur Golden's best-selling *Memoirs of a Geisha* ("A Cinderella story set in a mysterious and exotic world"[5]) notwithstanding, foreign readers are pretty much clued into the fact that amateur "compensated dating" (*enjo kōsai*) by Shibuya schoolgirls in loose socks long ago replaced kimono-clad Gion *tayū* in the Japanese literary imagination. Banana's *shōjo* are capable of burying their boyfriends alive, and Murakami's men commit war crimes.

Where is Japanese literature now? Statistics from 2015 estimate that Japan's high school girls use their cell phones an average of seven hours a day,[6] and their phones not only carry voice and text messages, selfies, Instagram images, and dating apps but also transmit original literary works (*keitai shōsetsu*, or "cell phone novel"), most of which push the limits of Banana's schoolgirl *shōjo* world with increasingly violent and sexually abusive storylines. (Here and there a male *otaku* is thrown in.) In 2008, the *New York Times* reported that Japan's "cell phone novels, republished in book form, have not only infiltrated the mainstream but have come to dominate it."[7] The point is that the cell phone may have replaced much in Japan, but not reading fiction. In any case the cell phone novel was already in commercial decline by the time foreign media, always ready to confirm their conviction Japan does all things topsy-turvy, stumbled upon it. Young people are hardly the aliterate (*katsuji-banare*) generation they are decried to be, as when a panicked Diet passed silly legislation in 2005 to promote analogue reading and designated a National Print Culture Day. In fact, more blogs are written in Japanese than any other language, including English, and it was the blogging community out of which cell phone novels arose: everyone can be a *sakka* (published writer) now, if only on a homepage.[8] The author isn't dead, she is everywhere. Nonetheless, it would be naïve to think that literature is quite the same pastime it was even in Banana's or Murakami's 1980s. In a 2001 Los Angeles lecture, cultural theorist Azuma Hiroki, who argues "game realism" (*gēmuteki riarizumu*) underlies contemporary writing,[9] told his audience about the computer-based "Novel Game" (*Noberu gēmu*) popular in Japan, the forerunner of what are referred to now as "visual novels" (*bijuaru noberu*). It "consists of a multi-ending story expressed as a textual novel. . . . The player (generally male) reads sentences on the screen, selects choices and aims to accomplish the sexual relationship with a girl he has chosen."[10]

Whether interactivity or newer innovations will be more than fads and warrant "end of literature" *cris de coeur* is the inevitable question, and a tired one. Tsubouchi Shōyō asked it in the late nineteenth century, Nagai Kafū and Natsume Sōseki asked it in the early twentieth century, and others asked it after Mishima's 1970 suicide. Karatani Kōjin asks it frequently and has a ready, discouraged answer.[11] The end of literature, unlike the end of the world, is never a prediction. It is an assertion. One literary history, which dates the demise to the mid-1970s, is entitled *Bungaku no horobikata*, or "How Literature Became Extinct." In 1999, Masao Miyoshi gave a grumpy lecture entitled "Japan Is Not Interesting" and included its recent novels. A decade later Mizumura Minae labeled the same "juvenile."[12] Talk of the end of literature in Japan typically cites one or more of the following reasons: fewer readers, fewer sales; a decline in social prestige; the loss of political engagement; the abandonment of realism; disinterest in moral or ethical questions; and the turn away from subjective interiority. Interestingly, these are all lamented *subtractions* from, rather than unwelcome *additions* to, literature. They say nothing about what remains behind or takes its place. Whatever it is, the bookstores are full of it. And in any case, some of these complaints are easily discounted with counterexamples and counterstatistics. Others can be dismantled with the demonstration that what is gone was never there in the first place.[13] Less easily dismissed perhaps is the view that little cultural production in Japan since 1945 has been free of Americanization, directly or contextually, and that Japan has independently taken the process to boorish extremes. But if true, this means your position in this "end of literature" pseudo-debate ("pseudo" because no one argues the converse) is finally a matter of taste. When Americaphile Murakami debuted with his *Kaze no uta o kike* (*Listen to the Sound of the Wind*, 1979), critics bemoaned its missing parts: lack of story, irony, psychological depth. The threat, they warned, is the degradation of high-cultural literacy. Postwar Japanese fiction, which I will abbreviate below by using "Ōe Kenzaburō" as a synecdoche, had been influenced by America, too. Fitzgerald, Carver, Pynchon, Capote, Miller, and Mailer—all their footprints are there. But by the 1980s the American presence was more low-cultural and less high-literary. The influences were no longer authors, but comics, sports journalism, television, graphic magazines, pop music, and Hollywood. This happened as America entered its own decline. By the time President

George H. W. Bush vomited on Prime Minister Miyazawa Kiichi's lap in 1992, it was hard to take the United States as seriously as Ōe's generation had. "Japanese intellectuals, including students at the major universities," Ōe laments, "no longer look to serious literary writing for new models of the future."[14] But that has little to do with Americanization because the questions Japanese literature pose would not be "Who am I?" or "How should I live my life?" anyway. Those questions ultimately hinge on the theological belief that our species worldwide has a future, another thing on which we may no longer count.

When Ōe won the 1994 Nobel Prize for literature, his petulant acceptance speech included a condemnation of Tokyo's consumer culture and the influence of the global "subcultural" that challenged "the creation of serious literature."[15] Elsewhere Ōe diagrammed modern Japanese literature into three lineages: (1) Japanese literature such as his own, apprenticed to the rest of the world; (2) that which stood independent from the West and the rest of Asia; and (3) the "Murakami Haruki–Yoshimoto Banana line." This last, Ōe says, sells two thousand times more than the first. Murakami and Banana are "truly the typical writers of an age in which all the world's subcultures have become one" with the global spread of consumer capitalism. In the *Economist* Ōe cited *Kitchin* as the perfect example of this. His protest, elitist and paranoid, encapsulates the widespread perception that Japanese literature today is not really Japanese anymore, but instead the local edition of world pop culture.[16] This is a replay of the long-standing division of literary production in Japan into the highbrow, the middlebrow, and the popular, and it is neither original nor particularly perceptive. We might as well go back to Adorno and Horkheimer. When has storytelling ever been independent of its time's hegemonic media, and when has hegemony never produced antagonists?

The late critic Etō Jun, who fairly dominated literary criticism in post-1945 Japan, wrote a book review every day from 1958 to 1978. But he stopped when, over his protests, Murakami Ryū's novel of the drug and sex subculture surrounding U.S. military bases in Japan, *Kagirinaku tōmei ni chikai burū* (*Almost Transparent Blue*), was awarded a literary prize in 1976. He complained it was the first "subcultural" novel to appear in Japan. It was not, but we might guess what he meant. Surely aware of similar complaints about American literature, Etō defined *sabukaruchā* writing as literature in which a specific social group—determined by region, age, or national origin, for example—stands in for what he called the "total culture."[17] No such thing exists, and Etō missed the point. It is meaningless to think of the Bananas and Murakami Harukis in Japan as pure literature (*junbungaku*) or fret that they are not. It is time to apply different criteria to what is at stake. Critic Katō Norihiro read Banana, Murakami, and other contemporary Japanese writers and came to this conclusion: after the collapse of radical politics in the 1970s and Communism in the 1980s, after Japan's 1995 Hanshin earthquake and the Aum Shinrikyō sarin gas attack (I would add the triple disasters of 11 March 2011), he despairs, "I wondered if something has withered in Japanese literature and Japanese society. To refute the world we have inherited; to spit contemptuously in the face of reality; to entrust ourselves to hopes for the future: these are things we now recoil from."[18] Katō is describing an end not simply literary but social. I agree but decline to echo the underlying complaint that Japanese writing now is bereft of the armory of modernist critique and has not replaced it with anything else. The political and economic realities of Japan in the new millennium are admittedly less than robust: an economy in perennial crisis, an aging population, the rise of antagonistic neighbors in Asia, a surge in jingoistic nationalism at home, a reliance on a superpower on the skids, an inability to contribute much more than the puerile to world culture: certainly, these things can be associated with an impoverished contemporary Japanese literature, film, and art. But that implies countries without such unlucky problems are doing better in the cultural sweepstakes, and that is hard to prove.

The death of the novel, notes D. A. Miller in a different context but true enough here, "has really meant the explosion everywhere of the novelistic, no longer bound in three-deckers, but freely scattered across a far greater range of cultural experience."[19] In Japan, fiction in the broadest sense and the imagination that inspires it, and its consequences, are everywhere. In fact Japan is fairly saturated with fib-telling. "All lies?" (*Minna uso?*) Takahashi asks in one of his poems. "Yeah, probably" (*Aa, tabun*).[20] From the rewriting of its wartime history as make-believe to the notion that Japanese men have sexual relationships with computer games, life-sized dolls, or even just *dakimakura* (love pillows) (the *New York Times* finds all this entirely plausible),[21] Japan is a wonderland of stories with little relationship to lived experience, where we are to believe "hypermedia have helped to blur the distinction between reality and fiction as never before."[22] Novels, as commodities sold in bookstores, have a reduced but important role to play: less pedagogic, certainly, but still a playground for new social imaginaries. We are free to call this contemporary literature (*gendai bungaku*), because the adjective now means what modern once did, that is, whatever is happening in the present moment. The modern, on the other hand, has taken on the character of a fixed historical period. Its use now refers to a sensibility and style that never obtained true coherence, while "contemporary" is simply a term of neutral reference, which does not hope for definition yet. My task is to explain how the modern in Japan's modern literature is giving way to an unnamed *something else*. That is not easy, since Japan continues to be seen as an outlier to history, a made-up place where, since Marco Polo, nothing familiar is supposed to ever happen. "What, then, is this Japan," asked Claude Lévi-Strauss, "which from our perspective short-circuits genres, telescopes periods"?[23] But to place Japan, *pace* Lévi-Strauss, in the same history as the rest of the world, I need to return to a theme running through the history of modern Japanese literature: the twin burlesques of satire and parody.

Japanese literature at the end of the millennium has been fairly accurately—if not entirely so—called a literature of parody.[24] This is coordinate with the observation that parody is ubiquitous in all twentieth-century arts as "ironic inversions."[25] Ogino Anna (1956–) and Shimada Masahiro (1961–) skewered Kawabata and Sōseki; Tsutsui Yasutaka (1934–) and Kobayashi Kyōji (1957–) took on Japan's vaunted institutions from its universities to its amusement parks. Even Murakami Haruki, for whom parody is an uphill climb, managed to mock Ōe Kenzaburō in his *1973-nen no pinbōru* (*Pinball 1973*, 1980). All this may be fun to read, but it is driven by something serious even if the effect is not. The best of Japanese writing today is not so much a literature of degraded ambitions as it is inventively parodic with a purpose.

The novelistic form was always impious. Bakhtin noted that *Don Quixote* opens with parodies of sonnets. In ironic repetitions and doubles there is an implied generic fixture, some sober original from which the laughing double is descended. Parody has to be, Bakhtin wrote, "an intentional hybrid."[26] These terms are slippery. If we start with an understanding of parody as a subset of satire because it is the imitative reference of one text to another (often with an implied critique of the first text), it is reduced not only to a parasitic practice but to one that cannot be described formally. Parody takes its formal elements from preceding texts and so cannot possess defined characteristics. Incongruity sets parody apart from simpler citation or imitation. We can describe it but not programmatically define it because the future is unknowable. It is parody, minus satire, where the proliferation of dissonant possibilities commences. A topographic description of parody at the end of modern Japanese literature and the start of something else tells us that it is accompanied by comedy. "The final phase of a world-historical form," says Marx, who learned from Hegel that we parody the past when we are ready to dissociate ourselves from it, "is its comedy. . . . Why does history proceed in this way? So that mankind will separate itself from its past."[27]

In this book I have looked at classic satire in Sōseki's *Neko* and moved on to the unstable, explosive mixture of satire and parody in Fukazawa Shichirō. I now note that contemporary Japanese literature's primary rhetorical mode has shifted wholly to parody, which in my reading of literary history marks a turning point in, not the exhaustion of, a genre, whether we know it at the time or not. Parody, writes critic Takahashi Toshio, "would seem to tell us 'everything has come to an end'; in fact it narrates the precise opposite via its 'halfway' differentiation. If this is so, then this narrative 'all is halfway, and all is over' is the story of the parody of parody itself."[28] To wit: there have been at least 150 parodies of Sōseki's signature satire since it appeared in 1906. *Neko*'s cat has been urine, a virus, a turtle, an alien from outer space, a purebred Huskie, a rotten egg, and any number of times a duck (*kamo*), Japanese slang for sucker. It has been a frock coat, a stowaway to San Francisco, a horse, a detective, a cow, a socialist, a rat, Confucius, the voyeur in a porn movie, a baseball bat, a *chef de cuisine*, and recently a serial murderer[29]—just about anything, in fact, other than the drowned cat Sōseki made of it.

If parody has been the lifeblood of modern Japanese literature, we might expect literary history to tell us why. A meta-discourse, it is supposed to be able to tell us about what *went* on in literature without falling prey to contingencies *going* on while we write it. Histories of modern Japanese literature by Nakamura Mitsuo, Usui Yoshimi, and Hirano Ken were wedded to organizing their narratives around the political division of Japanese history as a whole into imperial reign periods (Meiji, Taishō, Shōwa). Even younger historians with a more theoretical take, such as Komori Yōichi and Kōno Kensuke, never abandoned the schema.[30] The idea behind this world-unique periodization lies in a worldwide unarticulated and even absent theory of history that should frame all literary historicization. No one speaks of post-1989 Heisei period literature, though a few have tried. The 1970s were the last time Japanese literary history spoke in terms of parochial reign periods or their consequent schools of writers. Not only do most literary historians come to Japan's 1980s, with its Bananas and Murakamis, methodologically empty-handed, they are unable to reconcile the invasion of parody as well as mass culture into them. Without that reconciliation, literary history becomes passé because it seems to lack any interesting story to tell us.

"But if literary history as the history of literature has become unfashionable," anthropologist Eric Gans observes, "as the assertion of the literarity of history it is so fashionable as to have become invisible."[31] Not so invisible in Japan, however. As I write this in 2016, Fujii Sadakazu's *Nihon bungaku genryū shi* (History of the Origins of Japanese Literature) has just come out to ask, ritually, "What is literary history?" Fujii ends his history with the expected citation of global and domestic events in 1989 and shortly afterward as a closing (*shūen*)—the death of Hirohito, the collapse of Communism in Eastern Europe, the rise of apocalyptic cults in Japan, the end of the classic Cold War, crises in the Gulf.[32] But we are a quarter-century past those events, and they look less epochal than they once did. We need to look where wider speculation is permitted us. Takahashi Gen'ichirō is the Japanese novelist most interested in the supposed dead horse of literary history because, for him, it does not end with the present day. He is interested in the temporality of the past *and* the future, which is not to be confused with believing there actually is one. He has made the literariness of literary history the stuff of his fiction, and in doing so has disclosed the constellation of "modern, Japanese, literary, history" to be a teetering edifice. Like Banana and Murakami, Takahashi owes a debt to Japanese and American mass culture. He is better known in Japan for his essays on Japanese literature and for his rogue vitae than for his fiction. He has worked in the porn industry both behind and in front of the camera. When he is on television, it is usually to comment on horse racing. Born during the Occupation period, he was a young man in college at the height of the student movement in the late sixties and, like Murakami, has been described as a member of the late-sixties radical student generation. But unlike Murakami, who avoided activism, Takahashi was arrested in November 1969 for making Molotov cocktails and spent nearly ten months in jail. He says that aphasia cost him his ability to speak while incarcerated in what he dubbed *Kōchiso Kyōwakoku* (the Prison Republic),[33] and that he began to write as a form of rehabilitation, rebuilding his vocabulary in a project that took almost a decade, from 1971 to 1978, before he returned, in fragments (*danpen*), to "normal, everyday" language.[34]

Takahashi debuted as a fiction writer in the 1980s. He started with *Sayōnara, gyangu-tachi* (Goodbye Gangsters, 1981) and was praised by the high critical establishment, including Banana's father, Takaaki. Subsequent works include

Jon Renon tai Kaseijin (John Lennon versus the Martians, 1985)—his first work exploring violence and celebrating pornography, starting with a scene of Hansel of Gretel fame sodomizing his own father and moving on to special moments with Tatum O'Neal[35]—and *Gōsutobasutāzu/bōken shōsetsu* (Ghostbusters/An Adventure Story, 1997), whose main characters are poet Matsuo Bashō and bandit Butch Cassidy. All his novels attack the traditions of modern Japanese literature, not by ignoring them as do Banana/Murakami but by parodying them. The 1980s, Takahashi recalls, was a decade unlike the 1960s and 1970s. Nothing seemed clear to him: not the environment he was living in nor the literature he was reading. The 1990s proved worse. History was bracketed in quotes: "When you don't understand 'now,' writing fiction becomes difficult. . . . [H]istory and the awareness of the historical disappears."[36]

Inverted commas are a hallmark of Takahashi's writing. Without understanding their purpose, noted one Japanese critic, "you cannot read one sentence" of his work.[37] His disengagement with a bracketed "now" is why, however, Takahashi is the Japanese writer today most interested in literary history, which is not to say he is confident of it. He is fairly obsessed with it, as a critic, theorist, and practitioner.[38] His entire career, Takahashi has felt he experienced things late in life, as if everything new to him was already history for everyone else. One of his examples is the Beatles. He says he listened to their music like others listened to Hirohito's radio speech ending the war in 1945, as a present moment inscribed in the past. John Lennon and Paul McCartney's 1968 "Lady Madonna" was the instant (*shunkan*) in which he "encountered history." As a schoolboy he was taught that history was a succession of "great men, such as Napoleon and Nobunaga," but that they grow fewer in number as we approach the present day to, now, none. Anything remarkable, Takahashi concluded, "had to have happened in the past."[39] When young he thought that literature was something that didn't change much over time, and that it was odd to speak of it having a history. But in a series of novels starting with his award-winning *Nihon bungaku seisuishi* (The Rise and Fall of Japanese Literature, 1997–2000) and continuing with *Gojira* (Godzilla, 2001), *Kannō shōsetsuka* (A Voluptuous Novelist, 2002), and *Kimigayo wa chiyo ni yasodai ni* (Our Sovereign's Reign, One Thousand to Eight Thousand Generations, 2002), Takahashi has brought the past (e.g., great men) into the present and simultaneously taken things from today and let them play (*asobi*) in the past. In *Seisuishi*, Meiji writers Futabatei Shimei, Sōseki, Tōson, Ishikawa Takuboku, Kunikida Doppo, and others are made close friends and their great works fancifully entwine with each other.

Takuboku and Ōgai meet though they never did; Tayama Katai watches porn movies on technology that didn't exist. If Takahashi's ambition was to destroy an Arnoldian dichotomy between high and low culture—his high-cultural novel was inspired by low-cultural manga[40]—that had been accomplished long before. Rather, Takahashi is up to something historical though his concept of it may be unrecognizable to us. In *Seisuishi*, Takahashi shares a hospital room with Sōseki and travels on a train with his famous character Sanshirō; and in his *Gojira*, Sōseki is still alive at the end of the twentieth century. In *Seisuishi's* quasi-sequel, *Kannō shōsetsuka*, Higuchi Ichiyō, a fourteen-year-old schoolgirl, is linked in occasional pornographic detail with a forty-eight-year-old Mori Ōgai. In its chapter "Takekurabe," we learn Ichiyō's mother works as a hostess in Ginza's Copacabana nightclub alongside a young Dewi Sukarno, née Nemoto Naoko, today a daytime television B-list celebrity. In the novel's last chapter, set in the beginning of the twenty-first century, Ōgai and Sōseki gather around Ichiyō's hospital bed where she lies unconscious after overdosing on sleeping pills. Takahashi's ahistorical historical novels share a common focus on the Meiji period, not because it was the putative start to modern Japanese literature, though it was, but because from Takahashi's late-millennial perspective the Meiji period's historicity for him is plainest in the 1990s, when he was writing them. In *Kannō shōsetsuka*, Ōgai tells Takahashi things were not so different in the Meiji period, writers were already drinking in bars at their publishers' expense and badmouthing each other.[41] But the Japanese language, Takahashi insists more soberly elsewhere, was at its most alive in Meiji, and that vitality will not return. Takahashi's real protagonist might be *Nihongo* (Japanese) itself, an invention he says was required for the establishment of the *kindai kokka* (modern nation-state): Japanese words, like *kuni* (country), that he intends to rob of their prestige and authority.[42]

Takahashi serialized *Seisuishi* in forty-one installments over the course of more than three years. "It is a long, strange, uncanny work," Takahashi wrote on the occasion of its publication as a complete volume in 2001, "that is somewhat Meiji, somewhat fiction, somewhat criticism, somewhat poetry, somewhat history, somewhat manga and somewhat pornography."[43] Takahashi tried something unprecedented for literary historiography: he improvised it as a novel. With no clear perspective or theme in mind, he inserted things happening in his own life as he wrote, though he started with Itō Sei's literary history, *Nihon bundanshi* (The history of the Japanese literary establishment, 1953–78) as his outline, the same work after which Donald Keene modeled his own modern

Japanese literary history, *Dawn to the West*. Takahashi, like Itō and others, took *bundan* gossip as his archive. But unlike Itō or Keene, Takahashi jumps about the Meiji period, leaping from one decade to an earlier one and then back again. Readers will first think Takahashi has placed historical figures in the present, or that contemporary scenarios are being inserted into a Meiji setting. Both views err if they assume chronology matters. Historical writers are key to Takahashi, but he believes history should be approached as if it were a plaything (*omocha*).[44] In *Seisuishi*'s Meiji period, *tamagotchi*, handheld Japanese digital toys that sold nearly one hundred million units in the 1990s, arrive from the future. "I knew I would write about the dismemberment of the modern literary language created by Shimei and his generation, continuing through Takuboku and concluding with *tamagotchi*."[45] "No one knows," Takahashi said at the start of the new millennium, "if the modern is over or not," but he writes as if it is. When he calls the *kindai* an illusion for which he feels no sense of loss,[46] we can say in response: this is what we usually call the future.

Seisuishi lacks a single unifying theme, story, or plot, but it can be divided into three parts, all told in narratological real time. Chapters 1 through 19 are most closely based on Itō Sei's literary history. In the first chapter, "Shinda otoko" (A Dead Man), it is 1909 and Shimei is being buried. Shimei is the closest thing Takahashi has to a hero. He was remarkably contemporary (*gendaiteki*), and he understood the age in which he lived as joyless (*kairaku o kanjirarenai*)[47] and schizo (*bunretsu*).[48] But *Seisuishi* is not a biography. Ōgai, Takuboku, Sōseki, and others attend Shimei's funeral, as does practically everyone who created Japan's modern fiction as a national enterprise. Sōseki asks Ōgai if he knows where he can buy a *tamagotchi*—his daughter wants one. A bored Takuboku composes poems about Doraemon, the anachronistic cartoon figure. As the novel moves beyond the first chapter, Takuboku's depression worsens. He lives in poverty, a friend commits suicide, and when he is almost hit by a streetcar he thinks of the similar scene in a Jean-Luc Godard film sixty years in the future. The date is 8 April 1909 in the journal Takuboku keeps, but he writes about making cell phone calls, pop poet Tawara Machi (1962–), Shibuya's Tokyu Fashion Community 109, *enjo kōsai*, love hotels, and karaoke. Takuboku ekes out poems while watching porn and hiring teenage prostitutes he recruits through dating chat lines.[49]

The skewering of Meiji literati continues. Kitamura Tōkoku (1868–94) asks Tōson if he's going skinhead or punk and listens to Janis Joplin, Jimi Hendrix, and Jim Morrison on his headphones. When Tōkoku's corpse is discovered after he has hanged himself at home, he is still wearing headphones with the Doors' "Light My Fire" playing through them. With Takuboku gone, Takahashi's attention turns to poet Iroka Seihaku (1877–1946), who is also feeling despondent. He quits his job selling insurance, abandons his pregnant wife, and flees to Shimane prefecture where he listens to the news of the 1985 crash of JAL jumbo jet flight 123, the first Gulf War, and the divorce of Princess Diana from Prince Charles.

In the ninth chapter, Sōseki tells us, via Takahashi's parody of his style, that he is curious what people are reading nowadays. It turns out to be pornography and Game Boys, and so not quite reading at all. Meeting up with a resurrected Takuboku in a public bath, Sōseki discusses the 1997 hit movie *Mononoke hime* (*Princess Mononoke*), just as Doppo (who is writing a screenplay for Beat Takeshi) and Shimei will discuss wind surfing. When Doppo dies, Katai in turn enters the novel. Work starts on a porn version of his novel *Futon* (*The Quilt*, 1907) starring an actor known as Tsubouchi. No one on the set has read the book, only seen manga versions of it. Real Meiji literary events are continually referred to—canonical works are published, famous authors are buried—but they are sequestered among descriptions of, for example, Katai's wife experiencing female ejaculation as someone digitally arouses her, her moans so loud they bring a security guard to the hotel room where they are surreptitiously filming. Meanwhile there are rumors a dejected Takuboku is not dead but now running a *burusera* (used panties) fetish boutique in Shibuya.

The second section of *Seisuishi* is about illness, Sōseki's and Takahashi's own. Similarly afflicted with stomach ulcers, they share a hospital room. Author Takahashi inserts into his novel endoscopic photographs of his own stomach lining. While hospitalized, character Takahashi begins writing *Seisuishi*, and Sōseki learns a lot about the current state of Japanese literature from his roommate and his visitors, who include Tōson and Tōkoku. Tōson goes out drinking in a Shinjuku karaoke joint accompanied by Takahashi's contemporary, Mita Masahiro, who tells Tōson about J-Pop music while he sings lines from Tōson's pioneering collection of modern poetry, *Wakanashū* (Collection of Young Herbs, 1897). More absurdity follows in *Seisuishi*, much of it risqué. If Itō Sei's literary history was a serious film, says critic Katō Norihiro, then Takahashi's is a cartoon.[50] It is a simulacrum that mixes, with haphazard heteroglossia, present-day adult popular culture with the higher tradition of Meiji and Taishō literature. Itō Sei's telling of an evening Takuboku spent with Japanese bar hostesses becomes Takahashi's retelling of it with Thai sex workers; reading books is replaced by masturbating to pornographic video tapes; references to movie actresses give way to the virtual women of anime and manga. In Katō Norihiro's words, Takahashi has taken literature and "thrown it away like garbage,"[51] but interred it would be more accurate. Near the end of his literary-historical novel, Takahashi embeds obituaries for Tōkoku, Ichiyō, Kōyō, Kawakami, Doppo, Shimei, Takuboku, Sōseki, Ōgai, Katai, Tōson, and others. In other words, everyone's had his funeral.

Or is bedridden. In both *Seisuishi* and *Kannō shōsetsuka*, Meiji *bungō* (literary luminaries) spend a lot of time indisposed. At *Seisuishi's* end, the hospital bed around which they are left standing is not a comatose Ichiyō's, it is Nakagami Kenji's, a writer whose works Takahashi says elsewhere tell the entire story of a millennium of Japanese literary history, both its heights and depths (*nitsumatte iru tokoro*).[52] But the visitors arrive too late. No one comes back from the beyond, Takahashi writes. We misunderstand the dead, even as we soon enough join them. While Takahashi does not mention it, the open secret was that Nakagami, oft-cited as Japan's last serious writer, died of AIDS complications, not liver cancer—even deaths are fiction. The scene shifts and the novel ends when Takahashi goes home to look in on his newborn child. "Maybe his first memory will be, when I am dead, this visit to him," he writes. "I'll be dead when he's my age now. I hear my own voice among the cries of the future dead" (595). Takahashi, as we will see, is turning his attention to what comes after.

What is he staging? Can *Seisuishi* even be called a parody? If parody is fiction fashioned from fiction with the aim of purposeful degradation, then Takahashi's novel takes Japanese literary history as literature. If realism is really exhausted, then literature and art these days have little choice but to take their own histories, and not the world, as their subject. Parody, the rhetorical mode of late-modern Japanese fiction, has tandem gestures—that of mocking a model as a gesture of contempt, while *imitating* it to pay sympathetic homage, repudiating and animating at the same time. Parody reproduces what it parodies, and so its ideological work is subtle. But this predictable insight risks promoting parody as smug aporia, presupposing a law only to infringe upon it. *Seisuishi* looks like parody, and it is. But that is not all it is. Takahashi does not capitulate to parody. He has more to tell us. Time in prison meant it took Takahashi a decade to regain his command of "normal, ordinary" language, but in fact he never has, and that is one reason why it is incomplete to view him as a parodic writer. "What would happen if one no longer believed in the existence of normal language, of ordinary speech?" Fredric Jameson asks. He answers his own question:

That is the moment at which pastiche appears and parody has become impossible. Pastiche is, like parody, the imitation of a peculiar or unique style, the wearing of a stylistic mask, speech in a dead language: but it is a neutral practice of such mimicry, without parody's ulterior motive, without the satirical impulse, without laughter, without that still latent feeling that there exists something *normal* compared to which what is being imitated is rather comic.

Parody and pastiche mimic styles and mannerisms, but parody relies on the authenticity of an unironic original. That is no longer available to Takahashi and other contemporary Japanese writers of his ilk. "Here, once again, pastiche," says Jameson, "in a world in which stylistic innovation is no longer possible, all that is left is to imitate dead styles."[53] Takahashi says we have returned to being children nowadays. It is the Meiji period all over again. Saying "half a century after the Second World War" means nothing anymore.[54] The word Takahashi is looking for in his *shunkan* (instant) is Jameson's pastiche. The reasons have to do with the fragmentation not so much of everyday life but of the language in which we would speak of it. The transparency of the modern written vernacular (*genbun'itchi*), Takahashi's theme in *Seisuishi*, does not suffice any more. It is not Japan that bothers Takahashi so much, he says, as its *language*.[55] Our vocabulary may be polished, but it is impoverished. It is, if I may speak for Takahashi, a language of pastiche, not parody. Parody is never a constant; it appears at certain historical junctures to dismiss cynically a present overburdened by a past or to expedite the development of modern forms. Parody refers, said Wayne Booth, "at every point to historical knowledge that is in a sense 'outside itself'—that is, previous literary works—and thus to more or less probable genres."[56] Takahashi is up to something and he does so in a less probable genre. Valiant attempts have been made to distinguish between modernist parody and a postmodern one that foregrounds "ironic quotation, pastiche, appropriation or intertextuality." Postmodern parody "is a value-problematizing, denaturalizing form of acknowledging the history (and though irony, the politics) of representations," but in my view that is asking the one word "postmodern" to do too much.[57] If Takahashi means to parody literary history in *Seisuishi*, the genre must have passed its historical prime. But what has retreated into history for Takahashi is bigger than just fiction.

In the early 1990s, Takahashi wrote "I am the nation" (*Watakushi wa kokka da*),[58] an assertion that begs the question just what "nation" can mean for him. His character Takuboku in *Seisuishi* does not believe that the nation (*kokka*) is anything real you can touch (9). In a 2002 lecture Takahashi reiterated that, like Kawabata and Tanizaki, he is "a writer from the nation called Japan," but he doesn't quite know what that is,[59] which may be why he has written the words for Japan (ニホン) and country (クニ) in emptied *katakana* rather than with familiar Sino-Japanese graphs. This is quite a change for a writer in Japan where, writes John Mertz, "it is typical of much Japanese fiction starting in the 1880s for the fate of literary personae to resonate symbolically with the fate of the nation, with the consequence that such fiction could not be 'ended' without somehow closing off the full range of possibilities that lay ahead for Japan's future."[60]

Just so. The concept of a modern Japanese literature, launched with the piecemeal manufacture of a national language (*kokugo*) for a national citizenry (*kokumin*) for a modern nation-state (*kindai kokumin kokka*) for the newly minted Japanese (*Nihonjin*) after the Meiji Revolution, does not present that project today with an end, but instead the other way around. Modern Japanese literature has lost its sinecure because the nation-making project is over. The debates over *kokumin bungaku* (ethno-national literature) that commenced in the 1880s with Tsubouchi Shōyō, like the debates over the *kokumin kokka* (ethno-national state), are at an end because the *kindai* (modern) that presided over both is also at its end. On the one hand, there are now more nominal nation-states than ever. The break-up of the Soviet Union and the Balkans and the continuing reassemblage of Africa after colonialism have made it so. On the other hand, many of these are, in Masao Miyoshi's words, located in a post–Cold War "vacant space that is ideologically uncontested and militarily constabularized" as nation-states "undefined and inoperable." But a quarter-century on, Miyoshi's early prediction of a coming transnational corporate world has to be amended. When he claimed the nation-state "no longer works; it is thoroughly appropriated by transnational corporations," one of his examples of the latter was the retail group Yaohan. He could not have known it would collapse and be devoured piecemeal by some very old-fashioned national corporations.[61] "The legitimacy of the nation-state is still generally accepted, even insisted upon," wrote Benedict Anderson some years after Miyoshi. "For a fair part of the past two hundred years, narrating the nation seemed, in principle, a straightforward matter." This was predicated on the axiom that there was a necessary future for it. "The novelty of the novel as a literary form lay in its capacity to represent synchronically this bounded, intrahistorical society-with-a-future." The unstated assumption was that "the deep original affinity between nation-ness and the novel meant they would always be adequate for each other: that the nation would continue to serve as the natural if unspoken frame of the novel, and that the novel would always be capable of representing, at different levels, the reality and the truth of the nation." That is no longer true. Nowadays, said Anderson, we have ministries of culture that are responsible for representing the nation. Writing from what he called "the ruined New England town of New Haven,"[62] Anderson reworked existing translations of Walter Benjamin's "The Story-teller" to make plain his insight into the *Erzähler*, who is "by no means a contemporary presence. He has already become something remote from us and something that is getting ever more distant . . . the art of storytelling is coming to an end."[63]

But not yet. The storyteller is no more dead than the nation-state, which, despite the assault of transnational corporations on its sovereignty, continues its constitutional functions though displaced to another level.[64] Takahashi Gen'ichirō has read his Benedict Anderson. He tells us that Anderson, after reading Max Weber's 1895 lectures at Freiburg, went to New Haven's East Rock Park and saw the memorial there to the National Dead for four different American wars, with no distinction between the morality of any of them—all just for the national dead (*kuni no tame no shisha*). Takahashi embraces the same view of the national as Anderson. He reminds us that *Imagined Communities* argues the modern nation-state is inseparable from modern fiction.[65] Japanese literature has to speak for the dead, Takahashi insists, while conceding such a thing is impossible. Without the nation-state the dead are just corpses and not icons of our fraternity.

The end of the nation-state is not to be confused with the triumphant cant of globalization espoused by apologists for it, such as Takahashi's fellow countryman Kenichi Ohmae, for whom "the nation-state is increasingly a nostalgic fiction." For Ohmae, Takahashi and his work are, in what Ohmae dismisses as the "emotional nexus" of culture, obstacles in our way forward to a neoliberal future[66] where we "put global logic first"[67]—perhaps that future "united under a single logic of rule" foreseen by Michael Hardt and Antonio Negri.[68] In the meantime, Tawada Yōko (1960–) has built a literary reputation celebrating the fact she has no idea what country she belongs in. "I do not linger in any one locale, I have no place for anyone; I seek and then move on."[69] For many writers that might be a problem, but not for Tawada. She lives most of the time now in Berlin and writes in German, a German called "creolistic" by Marjorie Perloff, which means that it both is and isn't creole at all.[70] Poet and translator Suga Keijirō (1958–) bails Perloff out and defines "creolistic" as literature that "even when written in a single language" is "omniphone exilography," a phrase which

in turn demands its own rescue. Suga refers us back to Édouard Glissant's neologism *echos-monde* (world echoes), a literary poetics which is both local and
no longer so.[71] But Tawada's celebrity among her Japanese compatriots stems in
part from her successful intercontinental escape from them: still a local, if you
will, but no longer quite. And in a perfect twist for contemporary Germany, she
is as close to being a *Nationaldichter* as any writer in her new homeland.

Content to stay in Japan, "holed up in the corner of an apartment," in the
early 1990s Takahashi turned to literary history as his country's economic
bubble burst and a series of calamities man-made and natural ensued.[72] He was
pessimistic about literature in Japan, complaining that nothing was selling. The
complaint is an ancient one and not the full picture. The publishing industry
was in decline but bookstore shelves hardly bare. What Takahashi meant was
that modern Japanese literature's task was, as he put it, done (*yōzumi*).[73] In his
Nobel Prize acceptance speech, Ōe Kenzaburō had stated that his basic approach to literature deploys individuality (*kojinteki gutaisei*) to capture "society,
the nation, the world."[74] For Takahashi, that mission of modern Japanese literature is over. "The twentieth century was so traumatizing," Takahashi offers, "that
the 'nation-state,' nationalism and modern civil society are beyond repair. And
since that is so, a modern literature with deep, inseparable ties to those things is
so wounded that it cannot recover."[75]

There is a wider context here. Fredric Jameson may have meant Japan when
he exempted "the great eastern empires" from making every modern novel
an allegory of the nation, but he needn't have.[76] "The process of constructing
literary history," observes one Japanese scholar, "is a process of rethinking and
re-interpreting Japanese modernity in its relationships with the West," and it is a
process that involves forgetting as well as remembering.[77] It has been argued that
postmodernity is an experience of historical time's finality, not the appearance
of a different, or newer stage of history itself. Any attempt, we are told, to name
the precise historical moment when modernity comes to an end is therefore
destined to fail. Philosopher Gianni Vattimo said in the 1980s, "We see the postmodern not only as something new in relation to the modern, but also as a dissolution of the category of the new—in other words, as an experience of 'the end
of history'—rather than as the appearance of a different stage of history itself."[78]
Early in the new millennium, Fredric Jameson began an essay asking "After the
end of history, what?" But in the same essay, Jameson needs to remind us that
"even the possibility of stepping, for an 'instant,' outside history is a possibility
that is itself profoundly historical and has its properly historical preconditions."[79]

When Yokoyama Yūta wrote his 2014 prizewinning *Wagahai wa neko ni naru* (I Will Be a Cat), a work inspired by Sōseki's 1906 original because "everyone knows it," he used modern Chinese vocabulary in addition to Japanese.[80] The text is glossed for the benefit of the Japanese reader, but Yokoyama's point is clear. The Japanese language is hardly sufficient or even necessary for Japanese writers anymore. The dismantling of the modern Japanese novel continues apace. In *Imagined Communities*, Anderson could write with confidence that "in the modern world, everyone can, should, will 'have' a nationality, as he or she has a gender."[81] But then there is Hoshino Tomoyuki's (1965–) novel *Naburiai* (Playing Together, 1999), in which the main characters, Grande, Medio, and Puti, have no recognizable anatomical gender or sexual orientation. The only hint to their nationality is their red passports. "Our group [*kyōdōtai*]," Hoshino writes, "comes before the nation [*kuni ni yūsen*]."[82] The assault on the nation-state comes from many quarters, from the *mukokusei* (nonnationality) touted by its globally promoted popular culture to the ridicule of the state's rhetoric of masculinity with which modern Japan was fashioned.[83] At the same time, Hoshino's 1990s was the decade in which the publishing industry, stealing from phraseology such as J-Pop music and J League soccer, marketed contemporary fiction as *J-bungaku* (J-Literature) and banking on consumers agreeing there was some need to update Japanese literature. But behind that agreement must loom some additional notion of a *J-koku* (J-Nation) that redefines what was formerly a country but now a brand niche, one fatuously hailed in the pages of *Foreign Policy* as "Japan's Gross National Cool."[84]

Franco Moretti, in his own attempt at literary history (described by one reviewer as "a rather unfashionable activity"),[85] called the novel "the symbolic form of the nation-state."[86] That is not to say there is no future for it. But is there? William Gibson thought that Japan, "booted down the timeline," "is the global imagination's default setting for the future."[87] This is also the country Alexandre Kojève called posthistorical.[88] It cannot be both. This question matters in a history of modern Japanese literature. It was tautological, with nineteenth-century determinisms long in doubt, for H. D. Harootunian to announce "a conception of the future that is simply unknowable in advance." But he points us in a profitable direction when he refers to our present "removal of the conception of the future, or at least its indefinite deferral."[89] What does it mean if we *abandon* the future because it is unknowable? Still, something *will* come next, after the novel and after the nation-state, after the modern and all its post- elaborations and, yes, after the uneven leveling work of globalization.

Takahashi has given us the end of modern Japanese literature, sort of. "This country has everything," fellow novelist Murakami Ryū quotes a junior high school student. "Japan really has everything. Everything, that is, except hope."[90] Takahashi would never write such a line. Ryū still anthropomorphizes the nation as something that might possess the entirely human sentiment of hope, a theme on which he wrote a best-selling novel. In *Kibō no kuni no ekusodasu* (Exodus of the Country of Hope, 2000), a sixteen-year-old renounces his Japanese citizenship to join the Pashtuns on the Pakistan-Afghanistan border. "Japan," the teenager tells a CNN news team, "is a dead country."[91] Takahashi is beyond telling us that. His theme is not the nation, hopeless or otherwise. He does not write about a Japan that has failed. He thinks about the future and its slow cancellation in a process that began some time ago. Were he to have written a conventional history, time would have moved resolutely forward to the present and then, gingerly, into what looms ahead. He did not. Time in *Seisuishi* loops back onto itself, short-circuiting future-time. "Future" here refers not solely to the direction of time, but instead to the loss of the expectation of progress in postbubble, post-Fukushima Japan. Really new things simply do not happen anymore; "anachronism is now taken for granted."[92] We can find examples in Japanese literature today, where pastiche is what we would like to map our present with but can't. Takahashi's *Nihon bungaku seisuishi* confirms this about the time we now occupy: the montaging of earlier eras no longer occasions comment. We don't even notice it.

In a prescient work entitled *Shūen no owari* (The End of the End, 1992), novelist and onetime student radical Kasai Kiyoshi (1948–) takes up Murakami and Banana. His title may be a riff on Francis Fukuyama's popular *The End of History*, a work that Kasai summarily dismisses as vulgar Hegelianism and which, as Perry Anderson noted, has us moving nowadays "in a vast dream where events are already familiar before they happen." Kasai will have none of Fukuyama's optimistic end of history with the triumph of "the civilization of the OECD"[93] over its alternatives. But Kasai does number it among the many discussions of the end (*shūen*) sparked by Hirohito's death in 1989 and the collapse of Communism in Eastern Europe. We have arrived at *some* end, Kasai concedes, even if we are not trying very hard to comprehend it. When he tells us that Yoshimoto Takaaki tried to imagine what would happen to fiction as our polar ice caps melt and the continents are submerged by rising oceans, he was thinking in the classical terms of a writer's reality (*zengenjitsu*) inexorably overwhelming his human interiority (*naimen*). More is needed, Kasai suggests, but then fails to provide us any.[94] I don't blame him. Fredric Jameson knows "our imaginations are hostages to our mode of production (and perhaps to whatever remnants of past ones it has preserved),"[95] so even our science fictions are never really about the future.

One of the few highbrow literary journals remaining in Japan, *Gunzō*, is devoting its current issue as I write to the theme "The World Thirty Years from Now." Contributor Takahashi is not optimistic. Japan is not the planet's most rapidly aging society—that distinction belongs to economic upstart China, he says, whose "prosperity will not be long-lived"—but Japan's "future is extremely dark" nonetheless. As the apparatus of the nation-state recedes and neoliberalism advances, there are still enough countries around that in thirty years' time we may be in the midst of war (*senchū*) again and no longer postwar (*sengo*). Takahashi does not say that the nation-state may be so minimized by neoliberalism that wars will be waged by corporations, but a younger Tawada Yōko does in her post-Fukushima sci-fi story "Fushi no shima" ("The Island of Eternal Life," 2012). "In 2015 the Japanese government was privatized; an organization calling itself the Z Group became the major government shareholder and began running the thing as a corporation."[96]

Modern literature, all it does notwithstanding, no longer serves as a reliable interlocutor of modern nationhood. With historical consciousness at risk in fiction and the nation-state, Takahashi proposes that we cannot think the present *or* the future as we have in the past.[97] So what is modern Japanese literature supposed to tell us? Michael Stipe, lead singer of R.E.M., said that contemporary Japan is "the end of the world as we know it."[98] He implies another world is out there waiting for us, after Japan goes first, which is also why William Gibson told Tatsumi Takayuki that he thinks Japanese are already living in the future.[99] ("Tokyo now and forever!" Jameson notes of Gibson.[100]) Japan manages the neat trick of being both an outlier *and* a trailer of coming attractions. By placing the future's debut so far away from the West, we don't notice its "wholesale liquidation," which Jameson says is the real message behind any Hegelian end of history. "In Japan," Jameson writes and apparently believes, "the cell phone has abolished the schedule and the time of day. We don't make appointments any more, we simply call people whenever we wake up."[101] If there is an evacuation of temporality in how we live today, it has an ultimate horizon. We know something will not *always* come next, not after human consciousness ends along with the Anthropocene in the wake of climate change, or, minus human agency, after Murakami's two moons collide and lunar debris smothers us. We think about this often now. The terms of our fall are not apocalyptic because no heavenly deliverance awaits. "Do I think understanding the looming meltdowns will help avoid them?" J. Hillis Miller asked. "I doubt it . . . But at least we may have a clearer understanding as the water rises up to our chins."[102] That this strikes Miller as somehow consoling indicates just where we are today.

A recent study insists that contemporary literature is still interested "in what the future may look like in Tokyo," but then fails to mention a single Japanese work that might tell us about it.[103] Let me do so. The techno-Orientalism once entrusted to Japan has been trumped by a series of disasters, which one might think would inspire, reluctantly, new themes or new vehicles for Japanese literature. To some extent they have. In Takahashi's 2011 novel *Koi suru genpatsu* (Reactors in love), a film crew makes porn films to raise money for Fukushima survivors. Other books have been composed entirely of haiku-like post-3/11 social media tweets. The future is now *sōteigai* (unforeseeable), the alibi exploited by the state and insurance companies to evade indemnity for Japan's catastrophes. In *Uma-tachi yo, sore de mo hikari wa muku de* (*Horses, Horses, In the End the Light Remains Pure*, 2011), Fukushima native Furukawa Hideo (1966–) returns to devastated beaches to see what remains. "A typewriter. Also destroyed. No surprise in that. Someone had typed, pounded on this, but now, with this, no more typing, no more pounding, I thought." "Only that massive wave of water; after that, nothing."[104] But in Furukawa's thin novel, written too soon to grasp the full lesson, there *is* something: his everyday. After 3/11 he flies to New York, sees friends, keeps writing. Fukushima was and is terrible, but only a rehearsal for worse disasters. (In Tawada's story, Japan is finished off by a much more powerful earthquake in 2017.) For the present, "the Kafkaesque sense of the absurd that permeates much of life in Fukushima today," as historian Tessa Morris-Suzuki puts it, is no more absurd than Takahashi's modern Japan since its start.[105] "Was modernity doomed to spawn disaster?" asks Julia Thomas, another historian of Japan.[106] The answers are sundry, of course, but the two undeniably travel in tandem.

Japan's contribution to our preview of the future is not Murakami's "end of the world" (*sekai no owari*, half the title of one of his novels) because it is never really the end. "Your existence isn't over," Murakami writes encouragingly. "You'll enter another world."[107] Murakami's end of the world is a phrase lifted, somehow without irony, from a schmaltzy pop song by the 1970s duo Richard and Karen Carpenter, who go on to tell us the world may have "ended when I lost your love" but hearts "go on beating." Murakami, the upbeat storyteller, sells millions worldwide, but Takahashi is hardly known away from home, as obscure and unassimilated as future-time. No one takes Takahashi Gen'ichirō too seriously, including himself. That's part of the point. We may think we have arrived at the end of everything, including Japanese literature, because neither it nor we can see what lies around the corner, but Takahashi's reaction is less alarmed than bemused. We might dismiss talk of the "end of Japan" and its literature as just more drivel from the chattering classes, except that our finale of nations is unfolding against the backdrop of a *world* under manifold assaults. Takahashi's droll bafflement is an entirely reasonable response to an unfathomable future for which we will nonetheless be judged responsible, having willed it modernity's ambivalent gifts.

There is a novel that Takahashi says he has read several times. It is fifteen hundred pages bound in five volumes.[108] Pseudonymous Numa Shōzō's *Kachikujin Yapū* (Yapoo, the human cattle, 1956–91) was first serialized in an underground sado-masochist fetish magazine specializing in what Numa called *akusho* (bad writing),[109] akin to 1960s manga and graffiti.

But Tatsumi Takayuki hails the sci-fi *Kachikujin* as the best Japanese work of the second half of the twentieth century; a contributor to the Internet site 2channel goes further and declares it the greatest work of Japanese literature ever (*Nihon bungakushijō saikō*). Sylvain Cardonnel's French translation won the Prix Sade in 2006. Its fans over the years have grown from what a fairly scandalized Tomoko Aoyama called a "happy few" to a great many more;[110] a translation is said to have sold ten million copies in mainland China.[111] Still, few critics talk about it despite an impact one acknowledges as "profound."[112] Written in a complex layering of Japanese, English, German, and pseudo-Sinitic compounds that Numa admitted discouraged readers (5:341), it describes a creolized future where the only inviolable purity is racial. It is set thousands of years after a 1978 Third World War that lasted all of one day when America launched super-hydrogen bombs against the Communist bloc. A Soviet doomsday machine then retaliated with germ warfare around the world. The English survived by evacuating to their dominions in the southern hemisphere while Japan lost half its population and the other half was irradiated. Some Japanese fled to South America only to be enslaved. Numa describes the fate of those who remained behind in Japan:

> The core functions of the nation-state were lost. Government first stalled
> and then totally collapsed. Without police forces, crime skyrocketed; the

Figure C.1. *"Mein Hund! Komm mit*, Rin!" From the manga by Numa Shōzō et al., *Kachikujin Yapū*, vol. 4 (Yapoo, the human cattle) (Tokyo: Kadokawa Shoten, 2007), 228–29.

world became one where only the fittest survived. Material resources ran out immediately. All Japanese territory was devastated. There was no longer enough food to feed the citizenry. The weak and infirm were abandoned by their children, who in turn were abandoned by their own children. Death by starvation, murder by those hunting for food, mass suicides by those with no hope, the spread of the epidemic. Death was rampant. In the briefest of a moment, all ordinary Japanese disappeared within the nation's borders.

"Japan" ceased to exist. (2:270)

White people, their numbers decimated, assemble regardless of nationality in South Africa, where the English launch one hundred space arks to colonize a planet in the Alpha Centauri system. In time a matriarchal Aryan galactic regime called the Empire of a Hundred Suns (EHS) returns to earth to enslave the remaining blacks and bioengineer the Japanese as livestock (Yapoo) to serve as Caucasians' living commodes, sex machines, clothing, furniture, door mats and even meals (*shokuyō Yapū*). Yapoo are *kokuyū no zaisan* 'national property' (3:62). When no longer of use, they are recycled as fertilizer.

The distant future is tied to the distant past. Passages from the *Kojiki* and the *Man'yōshū* line up beside explanations of interstellar travel, and the EHS conserves other odd vestiges of Japanese culture without always knowing it. As in Takahashi's *Seisuishi*, people from different eras—such as Tang poet Li Po and Iron Lady Margaret Thatcher—live in the same era. Throughout *Kachikujin*, real and imagined history is warped, twisted, doubled back on itself. The Yapoo are impossibly ancestors and descendants of themselves in a work that is said to parody Charles Darwin[113] but does no such thing: it takes Darwinism quite seriously. "There is only one future for the Yapoo," Numa writes early in his saga, and it isn't really a future at all since evolutionary change has been ceded to another species. "The Yapoo will never be anything but the material and the tools for the maintenance and development of human (white) society" (1:84). One chapter ("No Lavatory World") is given over to explaining how bodily eliminations have been reworked into the food chain, with whites at the top, black slaves (who are allowed to dine on white people's dirty underwear) in the middle, and the formerly Japanese Yapoo at the literal bottom—solving, as has been pointed out, what French philosopher Charles Fourier, a contemporary of the Marquis de Sade, considered the biggest problem for any nation-state: managing human excrement.[114]

"Yapoo," Takahashi Gen'ichirō says in an afterword to *Kachikujin*'s latest edition, "violate so many *taboos*" that he likens Numa's novel to a star "in a black nebula accompanied only by Sade's *The 120 Days of Sodom* and Leopold von Sacher-Masoch's *Venus in Furs*."[115] Takahashi, whose own fiction has tested plenty of sexual taboos, is thinking of *Kachikujin*'s edgy eroticism, of course, as do many others; to celebrate the novel's final revisions in 1991, fans held a huge bondage-and-discipline party on the Tokyo waterfront.[116] Translator Cardonnel thinks the novel a "dystopie grandiose,"[117] but at least one critic has hailed it as Japan's first perfectly realized *utopian* fiction.[118] Numa himself called it a "utopia utterly divorced from everyday reality" (5:340). With no resistance to authority anywhere in the EHS—the more oppressive the sadistic ruling class becomes, the more the masochistic Yapoo presumably enjoy it—the social order is static. "Utopia," writes novelist Aramata Hiroshi (1947–) in an essay on

Numa, "does not require us to be superior beings. There are utopias in which we are half-human."[119] Or not human at all. In *Kachikujin* the Japanese are reified into household utensils, history has come to an end, and futurity is moot. There may be a better word for this than "utopia." After the sadistic Sade and the masochistic Masoch, Deleuze says, "the function of literature is not to describe the world, since this has already been done, but to define a counterpart of the world capable of containing its violence and excesses."[120] That counterpart may be Numa's EHS: no violence without pleasure, and no excess too much.

A generation before Donna Haraway's *Cyborg Manifesto*, which popularized the ambiguous boundary between human, animal, and machine, *Kachikujin* had already mapped such a futureless future. The white-ruled EHS supersedes the nation-state but not all its functions, above all the maintenance of hierarchal structures optimized for production. EHS preserves a nineteenth-century, pseudoscientific regime of a racial pyramid, with an Anglo-Saxon leisure class at the top with nothing but drug-fueled, Yapoo-enabled pastimes to enjoy. Class struggle in the future has been replaced by species struggle, and the Japanese have lost. At the same time, Numa's story is riddled with odd congruencies of Japan's mythical past with its abject present-into-future. Poems from the eighth century now make new, terrible sense in the fourth millennium, as everything is reimagined as fanciful elaborations of Japan's twentieth-century postwar domestication (*kachikuka*) under American hegemony Numa experienced while writing. "Our most energetic imaginative leaps into radical alternatives," writes Fredric Jameson, and are "little more than the projections of our own social moment and historical or subjective situation,"[121] which may be why, as is often noted by Jameson and others, we are better at imagining the end of the world than we are the end of capitalism.[122] There is no money or any evident political economy, in the EHS sci-fi future. We might say that literary and filmic forecasts of our imminent demise as a species or a planet are the principal melodramas of the twenty-first century in large measure because, in the absence of any signal event, we simply won't know when capitalism is done with us. Our first thought when faced with diminishing resources will always be our extermination—Numa's question is, could we be so masochistic that we might actually enjoy it?

Mishima Yukio, who initially fancied the novel so much he tore installments out of the fetish magazine to bind his own copy, urged the Chūō kōron publishing firm to issue an edition of *Kachikujin* for mainstream readers, but the scandal over Fukazawa Shichirō's "Fūryū mutan" scuttled the idea.[123] Numa's public spokesman counts the novel—along with Fukazawa's story—as one of the few anti-emperor works in Japanese literary history.[124] One of its subsequent publishers, Toshi shuppan, was the target of right-wing terrorists who accused the novel, correctly, of being a *kokujoku* (national insult) (5:375). Numa, an enthusiastic masochist himself, admitted he regretted Hirohito hadn't been humiliated by a U.S. military trial and doubted the emperor system would survive into the twenty-first century (5:335, 357). By *Kachikujin*'s fortieth century, the "chrysanthemum throne" (*kikuza*) sobriquet for the emperor is not only still slang for anus, that is *all* it means, though EHS archives suggest it was once the symbol of some Yapoo "tribal chief" (4:123–24).

Kachikujin's popularity may be due to its specialized eroticism, but that is not the entire story. Any true masochist reading this novel for erotic titillation will be frustrated by its chaste discourses on evolution, technology, and interstellar history. In fact, Mishima Yukio praised it as "the greatest novel of ideas [*kannen shōsetsu*] written by any Japanese since the war," and Mishima wrote quite a few himself.[125] But Mishima, who looked backward his whole career, may have endorsed Numa's masochistic novel of the future because it so accurately represented Mishima's anachronistic *now*. Whoever the author of *Kachikujin*— his or her steadfast refusal to come forward another sadistic pleasure?—he or she certainly read Jonathan Swift's *Gulliver's Travels*, with its humanoid Yahoos enslaved in the land of Houyhnhnms, and understood how satire of the remote depends upon a critique of the familiar. "The most characteristic SF," writes Jameson, "does not seriously attempt to imagine the 'real' future of our social system. Rather, its multiple mock-futures serve the quite different function of transforming our own present into the determinate past of something yet to come."[126] In 1970, Numa identified him- or herself to readers as a sexual fetishist first and a Japanese citizen only second, foretelling where things have been heading since.[127] Mishima's death that year was more that of a fellow masochist, after all, than of an ultranationalist. On the eve of his suicide, and in a critical assessment of modern literature around the world, Mishima concluded that Numa's scatological *Kachikujin* "touches on the essential function of literature" when it uses masochism "to terrify readers,"[128] just as Mishima's own curtailed life's denouement was choreographed to scandalize a nation.

In the future, Yapoo, reduced to being household appliances plugged into wall sockets by invisible, fourth-dimensional electric cords connected to their rectums, have no time or inclination to write, or even speak. Japanese script has fallen into disuse, and Yapoo are silenced with lip fasteners attached to their mouths. In any case, they lead no private lives (*shiseikatsu kaimu*) to talk about. On the contrary—one future human uses a whip to lash words from the dictionary into the backs of the Yapoo, not to edify them but for his own amusement. Human women still have books: scholarly tomes, textbooks, dictionaries, encyclopediae, biographies, and memoirs. Anything literary—and there isn't much—is left to an emasculated male second sex. The loss of literacy in postapocalyptic fiction is a familiar trope, but here it is *utopian*. It might as well be: Tawada Yōko once speculated with something other than regret that a thousand years from now, the writer, in her own time already disappearing along with the ephemeral electronic text, will be nonexistent.[129] "Die Zukunft ist die Zeit nach der Trennung, die Zeit nach dem Tod der Autorin,"[130] she writes in German, her chosen language, which is as rapidly dwindling in speakers as the one she was born into. In Numa's novel all languages are dying. A pill is required to understand Chinese. Wordless telepathy has replaced much oral communication, but humans and their Negroid slaves speak English, after a fashion. The Japanese language (Yapoon) survives only as crude commands used with the Yapoo. The Empire of a Hundred Suns does not govern metaphors so much as it has simply eliminated them: rhetoric banished, words mean exactly what they say, which is very little. An unnamed amanuensis in *Kachikujin*, whose real author was once imagined to be from another time or world,[131] writes to us readers (*dokusha shokun*) from the future in postapocalyptic Japanese: dry, utilitarian, free of beauty.

Tatsumi Takayuki notes that today we read *Kachikujin* less as a novel of debauchery and more as the depiction of a future society both "grotesque and appealing." "It is," he also states, "the most significant (and perhaps the only) example of a Japanese work that succeeds in questioning what the term 'Japanese' signifies."[132] Numa may have called it the tale of "the decline and fall of our ancestral homeland" (*sokoku no suitai metsubō*),[133] but it would be an error, Tatsumi wrote in 1992, to think *Kachikujin* foresaw the "end of history" debates then raging post-Francis Fukuyama.[134] Tatsumi does not want us to mistake an aporia of the past and the future for any kind of conclusion, but it seems that some sort of aporia might well be where we are stalled until things *really* end. Tawada Yōko, for one, is not afraid to write about a future bereft of a future. "Fushi no shima" posits a Japan in environmental ruins two decades after Fukushima. The narrator, who lives in European exile, still has a Japanese passport but no immigration officer will touch it, fearing nuclear contamination. Only the Japanese are affected and no one else. Her future and Numa's are not so dissimilar in their common abasement: "The Japanese homeland no longer exists in the twenty-first century" (5:304). In American sci-fi, the United States is often the only nation to survive; in Japanese, Japan is the first to go.

Numa's Yapoo have "no concept of nation" (3:277) because nations no longer exist in the future. Like Takahashi and others, Numa writes "Japan" in ironic *katakana*. The present decline of the importance of the nation-state to modern Japanese literature, its *sine qua non*, is not solely the consequence of any globalization or neoliberalism advancing in lockstep worldwide. It might be traced back to a very local failure to erect sturdy scaffolding for a modern national identity in a Western-centered world that often militated against it; to a revolution in which the Japanese *demos* played no part; to a succession of feeble emperors at the helm of a poorly crafted constitutional monarchy; to a mismanaged empire that lost a disastrous world war; to a national language with its legitimacy always in doubt; to a boom economy gone bust amid a shrinking population exacerbated by xenophobia; and now, to new natural and man-made catastrophes. Japanese writers have already told us about these troubles, and will again, when the crises are unthinkable without their imagination or maybe even with it. Millennia hence, muted and illiterate like the Yapoo, the descendants of present-day Japanese may still tell stories: with sticks scratching in dirt, drums beaten around a fire, or just fists shaking in the air. Perhaps everything will start all over again, if we are lucky; it will be a remake of Hollywood's *Planet of the Apes*, a Takahashi favorite.

Takahashi is currently undertaking a long-term project to explore a future world bereft of our words. He began with a 2015 collection of stories in which humans have surrendered their faculty of speech to animals. *Dōbutsuki* (Accounts of Animals) starts with a failed attempt by creatures of the forest to free their comrades in a zoo, a folktale but in typical Takahashi fashion irreverently peppered with references to Japanese and American pop culture. Bill Clinton and Donald Trump are mentioned along with *West Side Story*, karaoke, the Discovery Channel, Nakajima Miyuki, and Bose sound systems.[135] In the opposite of *Kachikujin Yapū*'s conclusion but akin to *Planet of the Apes*, animals now rule the world in a series of events explained in a piecemeal fashion throughout the collection. In "Uchū sensō" (War with outer space), an alien invasion of earth is underway. NHK news reports it is the end of the world (*sekai no owari*). The story's dumbfounded human narrator is not sure why the planet is being attacked, but it may be because his species is "polluting the environment, contaminating the earth, behaving immorally, eating too many sweets, undergoing cosmetic surgery, discriminating against temporary workers, has too many NEETs, and is slaughtering whales." Or, it might be because of "pornographic videos, SM, celebrity sisters Kyoko and Mika Kano, Janet Jackson's wardrobe malfunction, Britney Spears's appearance at a 'no-panties' party, or of course the very fact of Paris Hilton."[136] When NHK obtains footage of a flying saucer landing in Nevada, the aliens that emerge from the vessel are first a dog, then a monkey, and lastly a rabbit. In another of the stories, all that remains of us are giant anteaters, vicuñas, and one-hump camels that, in the reverse of Kafka's Gregor Samsa, wake up one morning to find themselves transformed into humans who talk. Takahashi's point is *not* that these animals have stopped being animals, but that now they are human-animals. As insouciant as ever, his postmodern frivolity is proof, one supposes, for that older generation of modernist critics bemoaning serious literature's downfall. I have resisted using the English phrase "postmodern novel" in this literary history because I think it is oxymoronic, but the Japanese term *posutomodan shōsetsu* is entirely agreeable to me and it describes Takahashi's work. Still, his assault on anthropocentrism in the wake of our current ecological crises—global warming comes up in *Dōbutsuki*—is earnest as well as playful. He recognizes that our fate is now conjoined with that of other entities on this planet, including the ones he makes up.

Human exceptionalism has relied on the speciesist prejudice that only humans possess language. "All the philosophers," wrote Derrida of everyone from Aristotle to Levinas, "all of them say the same thing: the animal is deprived of language."[137] The posthuman turn today pivots toward animals less because we are actually concerned with them than because animals are a way to critique this exceptionalism, which of course is a way to keep talking about humans. But Takahashi seems genuinely interested in animals, and that is why he experiments with granting them language. In one of the *Dōbutsuki* stories, for example, we are transported back to 1909 when Futabatei Shimei, literary history's putative first modern Japanese novelist, is dying aboard ship in the Bay of Bengal. Shimei, however, is recast as a canine: "Tatsunosuke the Shiba Inu Dog" recalls in his last hours the day when dogs' masters all over the world disappeared after strange events in the sky. Dogs, once kept as near-slaves, had to assume human duties—including the use of a new language, the same mission for which Takahashi's mock literary history credited the historical Futabatei Shimei (née Hasegawa Tatsunosuke) and his first-modern-Japanese-novel *Ukigumo*—the novel that, in another first, used the word *dōbutsu* (things that move) in its Western sense of all nonhuman sentient beings.[138]

In *Neko*, Sōseki personified a cat in an anthropomorphic literary tradition that goes back to the earliest Japanese literature. There's a talking hare in the *Kojiki*. At the other end of literary history, Murakami Haruki, famed felinophile, is fond of cats who talk. Furukawa has talking cats, too, but his novel *Doggumazā* (Dog Mother, 2012) stars a canine that, like Takahashi in *Seisuishi*, rearranges Meiji history (the dog, named Itō Hirobumi, is "a retriever with the face of a Shiba Inu"[139]) to arrive at the post-3/11 conclusion that an emperor-centered modern Japanese nation-state has always been unworkable. Furukawa's earlier *Beruka, hoenai no ka* (Belka, Why Don't You Bark?, 2005) tells twentieth-century history through its warring nations' military dogs, their shifting citizenships a matter of which army is their master even if they are roaming the unclaimed arctic or are in outer space aboard Sputnik. Here on earth, a spell-casting waitress in an Akihabara maid café turns the half-Chinese, half-Japanese protagonist of Yokoyama Yūta's *Wagahai wa neko ni naru* into a cat of no noted nationality. In 2013, Tawada Yōko published a play in which only animals—a cat, a dog, a fox, a bear, a rabbit, and a squirrel—survive a great flood that wipes out humanity.[140] In hindsight, Numa Shōzō's fanciful future viewed from 1956 was still anthropocentric. Numa's was a racialist universe in which Japanese are rendered the four-legged pets of a purebred Anglo-Saxon matriarchy. But writers nearer the close of modernity are up to something different. Furukawa's dogs are poised at the end of *Beruka* to declare war on the twenty-first century,[141] for example, and Takahashi Gen'ichirō is happy to reject anthropocentrism altogether to flirt with zoocentrism. When, shortly after the carnage of the Second World War, Alexandre Kojève announced our race had returned to animality, he meant barbarity. If he bizarrely exempted Japan under the shoguns because it lived for three hundred years "at the end of History,"[142] more recently Azuma Hiroki returns postmodern Japan to Kojève's "animalized" (*dōbutsuka*) fold.[143] Takahashi thinks better of animals. "Men in novels may behave as beasts, but beasts in novels may not behave like men," Mary McCarthy lectured. "That takes care of *Gulliver's Travels*, in case anyone were to mistake it for a novel."[144] Takahashi might agree but not feel badly about it, so little will McCarthy's proper novels matter in the coming posthuman world. But while we are still here, *Gulliver's Travels*, like *Planet of the Apes*, is among Takahashi's favorites.

Worldwide, dogs often survive humanity in science fiction, somehow riding out nuclear fallout, pandemics, asteroid impacts, or extinction crises. In *Dōbutsuki*, we never quite learn what happens to *Homo sapiens*. Apparently it's a rather bloodless end to our species. Tatsunosuke the Shiba Inu Dog can talk but he doesn't tell us our fate. In real life today, there is a cryptocurrency whose meme is a Shiba Inu encircled with indecipherable English. A digital image of *Canis lupis familiaris* is already replacing the nation-state's banknotes and their portraits of Ichiyō and Sōseki. The future of Japanese literature need not be its extinction but its handover to the next species in line.

In Takahashi's sci-fi, that species is not ethereal. His animals howl and growl. In *Dōbutsuki*'s last piece, an autobiographical essay rather than a fictional story, Takahashi reflects with uncharacteristic sobriety on the deaths of favorite animals, friends, and family over the course of his life. At the essay's end he pictures his own last hour. Sitting alone under the shade of a tree ("I have encountered enough human beings for a lifetime"), he watches some beast-like creature appear and stare at him with dark eyes only to turn and leave. Takahashi will have no idea what the animal is thinking or feeling, but he imagines that he will feel thankful it was there at the moment he surrenders life.

> I remember hearing that my father's older brother, whom I never met, died this way. He was a soldier in retreat when he left formation and sat under a tree, telling a friend he just couldn't go on. The friend grabbed my uncle's arm and urged him to keep going, but he said no, you go ahead. All this happened in 1945 on Luzon island in the Philippines. There is no way for me to know if, at the end of his life, my uncle came face to face with a living creature or not.[145]

Takahashi's fanciful stories of an animal future conclude with one unique reference to any real human past: the closing months of the Second World War and the slow expiry of an uncle witnessed, or not, by one of the beasts with whom we share the planet. Takahashi hopes there will be an animal present at his own death, scrutinizing him with that opaque animal gaze which has challenged thinkers throughout history. We need animals now more than ever because, as Derrida says, "the most powerful philosophical tradition in which we live has refused the 'animal' *all of that* . . . speech, reason, experience of death, mourning, culture, institutions, technics, clothing, lying, pretense of pretense, covering of tracks, gift, laughter, crying, respect, etc.," and these are the things Takahashi might want to deed our successors.[146] If wild animals were ever removed from modernity's view, they are back and they are in our future, even if humans are destined to be the animals, even if it is Numa's utopia in wait for us rather than Takahashi's. In either case it will be, in ecocritic Christine Marran's unnerving phrase, "literature without us."[147]

Takahashi makes no mention of Japan in his melancholy family anecdote from 1945, the most catastrophic year for his country's history *ima made* (so far). This is a lacuna unthinkable for Takahashi's predecessors, but the modern nation-state is not the terrain of mind he inhabits. Animals roam oblivious to man-made borders and so does he, unlike those Japanese writers who merrily wave to us when they cross them. The differences do not end there. With Takahashi, the days are over of speaking of modern Japanese literature to make just the usual troubled sense of those shibboleths. "There's no such thing as the future," an embittered Ōgai tells Takahashi while seated at a bar drinking with an equally discouraged Sōseki in *Kannō shōsetsuka*. "Get it, you idiot? History is nothing but the past and the present."[148] But new things, making the future's history for us, appear on the horizon as old ones disappear. We don't know what they will be, since many more things can happen than actually do. But here's my guess, and I'll bet Takahashi's, too: they will be things not modern anymore, probably not Japanese, possibly not human, and hardly literature; and no future perfect work of fiction today, however prescient, can foretell what guise those things will assume when they come to stalk us.

Acknowledgments

I am grateful to Alan Thomas at the University of Chicago Press, my teachers at Yonsei University's Korean Language Institute, and librarians at the University of Washington and Yale; all of you were patient. The Stanford Humanities Center, where I had the opportunity to share my early research with an extraordinary cohort of graduate students, awarded me the Mary Weeks Senior Fellowship. The Social Science Research Council subsidized my studies in Seoul, and the Japan Foundation underwrote a short-term research stay in Japan in 2003. Reiko Abe Auestad invited me to spend a month in Oslo thinking about Sōseki with her students, the upshot of which is chapter 3. Mimi Yiengpruksawan and I taught the arguments in chapter 4 together in a Yale seminar. Kuroko Kazuo encouraged me to write chapter 5, and Dr. Manō Neri kindly spoke with me about her late father, Abe Kōbō, for chapter 6. Joel Cohn, John Haley, Jeff Johnson, and Ed Kamens commented on the essay that became chapter 7. I am indebted to Kobayashi Motoo for bringing Fukazawa Shichirō to my attention, as did Kushibuchi Tadashi the work of Yoshimoto Banana. Pat Steinhoff opened her University of Hawai'i archives to me, and

Jon Holt read the resulting chapter 8. Kathy Lu and Jay Rubin reviewed an early draft of the tenth chapter; Christopher Lowy and Christine Marran commented on the conclusion. Former students Michael Chan, Ryan Cook, Nikki Floyd, Arthur Mitchell, and Matthew Strecher said things over the years that made me think harder about this book. Adam Kern reminded me what animal spoke first. Mizumura Minae confirmed a suspicion of mine. Mark McLelland helped translate a word. A brief parking lot conversation with David Wang and Carlos Rojas about Chinese literary history gave me an idea. Haruko Nakamura doggedly researched what year a neglected writer died. Seth Jacobowitz went through much of the manuscript for me at a busy time in his own work. Martha Lane Walsh and Mary Tong found errors and inconsistencies in my writing. Two anonymous readers were generous with their advice.

Fellow Asianists, thank you for your fellowship: Anne Allison, Marie Anchordoguy, Tani Barlow, Beth Berry, Davinder Bhowmik, Linda Chance, Kang-i Chang, Rachel DiNitto, Jim Dorsey, Charles Exley, Aaron Gerow, Yukiko Hanawa, Sue Hanley, Irmela Hijiya-Kirschnereit, Linda Hoaglund, Ken Ito, Mellie Ivy, Earl Jackson, Bill Kelly, David Knechtges, Kōno Kensuke, Laurie Sears, Mike Shapiro, Ann Sherif, Doug Slaymaker, Stephen Snyder, Bruce Suttmeier, Suga Keijirō, Julia Thomas, Jing Wang, Dennis Washburn, and Angela Yiu. Later in my career I learned from newer colleagues: Andrea Arai, Srinivas Aravamudan, Dani Botsman, Will Fleming, Inderpal Grewal, Todd Henry, Chris Hill, Ted Mack, Sam Malissa, Murakami Yōko, Hala Nassar, Steve Poland, Vicente Rafael, Steve Ridgely, Tsuboi Hideto, Keith Vincent, and Ran Zwigenberg. Laura Wexler, I declare you an honorary Asianist. Jill Levine, *hermana mayor*, has stood by me for years. Lastly, I dedicate this book to my husband, Doug Lind.

❆   ❆   ❆

Earlier versions of the following chapters were previously published: chapter 7 appeared as "The Beheaded Emperor and the Absent Figure in Contemporary Japanese Literature," in *PMLA* 109.1 (1994): 100–15, reprinted by permission of the Modern Language Association of America; chapter 9 appeared as "Yoshimoto Banana's *Kitchen*, or the Cultural Logic of Japanese Consumerism," in *Women, Media, and Consumption in Japan,* ed. Lise Skov and Brian Moeran (Abingdon, UK: Curzon Press, 1995), 274–98; and chapter 10 appeared as "Murakami Haruki and the Cultural Materialism of Multiple Personality Disorder," in *Japan Forum* 25.1 (2012): 87–111.

Notes

INTRODUCTION

1. Clifford Geertz, *Local Knowledge*, 161.

2. Saitō Minako, "'Bungakushi' o kettobase," 3–4, 8.

3. René Wellek, *The Attack on Literature*, 77.

4. David D. Roberts, *Nothing but History*, ix.

5. Lawrence Buell, "Literary History as a Hybrid Genre," 217, 227.

6. Michel Foucault, *The Order of Things*, 219.

7. E. B. Tylor, *Primitive Culture, vol. 1*, 1.

8. Michael McKeon, *The Origins of the English Novel*, 20.

9. Isoda Kōichi, *Rokumeikan no keifu*, 28.

10. W. G. Beasley, *The Modern History of Japan*, 154.

11. Jürgen Habermas, *The Philosophical Discourse of Modernity*, 2.

12. Miyoshi Yukio, *Nihon bungaku no kindai to hankindai*, 97.

13. Victor Koschmann, "Modernization and Democratic Values," 236.

14. Katō Shūichi, quoted in John Whitney Hall, "Changing Conceptions of the Modernization of Japan," 20.

15. Ibid., 20.

16. Michel Foucault, *The Birth of the Clinic*, 90–91.

17. Anthony Giddens, *Consequences of Modernity*, 1.

18. Hayden White, *Tropics of Discourse*, 126.

19. Timothy Brennan, "The National Longing for Form," 44.

20. Paul de Man, "Literary History and Literary Modernity," 392.

21. Lawrence Buell, "Literary History as a Hybrid Genre," 222.

22. Kamei Hideo, "Bungakushi no naka de," 66.

23. Yanagida Izumi, *Meiji bungaku kenkyū 4*, 316.

24. Taguchi Ukichi, *Nihon kaika shōshi*, 127. Unless otherwise noted, all translations are the author's own.

25. Quoted in Hiraoka Toshio, *Nihon kindai bungaku no shuppatsu*, 13.

26. Ronald P. Dore, *Education in Tokugawa Japan*, 69, 16.

27. Suzuki Sadami, *Nihon no "bungaku" o kangaeru*, 69, 61.

28. Isoda Kōichi, *Rokumeikan no keifu*, 20–22.

29. Suzuki Sadami, *Gendai Nihon bungaku no shisō*, 72.

30. Fujii Sadakazu, "Kokubungaku no tanjō," 62.

31. Isoda Kōichi, *Rokumeikan no keifu*, 30.

32. Ibid., 20–21.

33. Basil Hall Chamberlain, *Things Japanese*, 69.

34. Mary Elizabeth Berry, *Japan in Print*, 209.

35. Orikuchi Shinobu, "Kokubungaku no hassei," 10–82.

36. Ronald Griger Suny and Michael D. Kennedy, *Intellectuals and the Articulation of the Nation*, 15.

37. Mikami Sanji and Takatsu Kuwasaburō, quoted in Heekyoung Cho, *Translation's Forgotten History*, 88.

38. Mikami Sanji and Takatsu Kuwasaburō, *Nihon no bungakushi (jōkan)*, 1–2.

39. Ibid., 13.

40. Ibid., 3.

41. Ibid., 17–18.

42. Fredric Jameson, "Third-World Literature in the Era of Multinational Capitalism," 71.

43. Larzer Ziff, *Writing in the New Nation*, xi.

44. Fredric Jameson, *A Singular Modernity*, 29.

45. David Perkins, *Theoretical Issues in Literary History*, 254.

46. Roland Barthes, *S/Z*, 5.

47. Roy Andrew Miller, "The Lost Poetic Sequence of the Priest Manzei," 171.

48. David Perkins, *Theoretical Issues in Literary History*, 254.

49. Stephen Greenblatt, *Shakespearean Negotiations*, 3.

50. Michael Foucault, "Truth and Power," 55–56.

51. Hayden White, *Content of the Form*, 24.

52. Stephen Greenblatt, in Catherine Gallagher and Stephen Greenblatt, *Practicing New Historicism*, 6.

53. Nakamura Mitsuo, *Japanese Fiction in the Meiji Era*, 4.

54. Harold Bloom, quoted in Rey Chow, "Theory, Area Studies, Cultural Studies," 103.

55. Ralph Cohen, "Generating Literary Histories," 50.

56. David Perkins, *Theoretical Issues in Literary History*, 5.

57. Kamei Hideo, "Bungakushi no gijutsu," 2–3.

58. David Perkins, *Is Literary History Possible?*, 33.

59. Donald Keene, *Dawn to the West, vol. 1*, 283, 499, 527, 1183, xii.

60. Ibid., 260.

61. See Seth Jacobowitz's *Writing Technology in Meiji Japan*.

62. Fredric Jameson, *A Singular Modernity*, 57.

63. Edward Said, *Culture and Imperialism*, 73.

64. Nishi Masahiko, "Kureōru na bungaku," 228.

65. Marleigh Grayer Ryan, *The Development of Realism*, 22.

66. Kawanishi Masaaki, *Shōsetsu no shūen*, i.

67. Azuma Hiroki, *Gēmuteki riarizumu no tanjō*, 101.

68. Nakamata Akio, *Kyokusei bungakuron*; Hibi Yoshitaka, *Bungaku no rekishi*.

69. Horikoshi Hidemi, *Moeru Nihon bungaku*.

70. Henri Lefebvre, *Introduction to Modernity*, 185.

CHAPTER ONE

1. Kubota Hikosaku, *Torioi Omatsu kaijō shinwa*, 164.

2. Ibid., 167.

3. Ibid., 182.

4. Matsuyama Iwao, "Dokufu to enzetsu," 19.

5. Tamenaga Shunsui, quoted in Okitsu Kaname, "Bakumatsu kaikaki gesaku," 154.

6. Uchida Roan, quoted in Nagamine Shigetoshi, *"Dokusho kokumin" no tanjō*, v–vi.

7. Maeda Ai, *Kindai dokusha no seiritsu*, 35, 38.

8. Maeda Ai and Okitsu Kaname, eds., *Meiji kaikaki bungakushū*, 25–27.

9. Konishi Jin'ichi, *Nihon bungeishi 5*, 60.

10. Okitsu Kaname, *Meiji shinbun kotohajime*, 97.

11. Maeda Ai, *Kindai dokusha no seiritsu*, 48–49.

12. Sasaki Tōru, "*Torioi Omatsu kaijō shinwa* no seiritsu," 80.

13. Togawa Shinsuke, in Robert Campbell, Tomiyama Takao, Togawa Shinsuke, et al., "Tsuzuku . . . shinbun shōsetsu no tsūro," 19.

14. Albert Altman, "The Press," 54–55.

15. Gerald Groemer, "Singing the News," 245.

16. John Reddie Black, quoted in Yamamoto Taketoshi, *Kindai Nihon no shinbun*, 60–61.

17. Konita Seiji, "Nyūsu gengo no Edo—Meiji," 46.

18. James L. Huffman, *Creating a Public*, 47–48, 81.

19. Lennard Davis, *Factual Fictions*, 58.

20. Maeda Ai, *Kindai dokusha no seiritsu*, 119.

21. Maeda Ai, quoted in Sasaki Tōru, "Seinan sensō to kusazōshi," 52.

22. Marshall McLuhan, *Understanding Media*, 205.

23. Nakamura Mitsuo, *Japanese Fiction in the Meiji Era*, 19.

24. Michael McKeon, *The Origins of the English Novel*, 50.

25. James L. Huffman, *Creating a Public*, 63.

26. Katō Hyōko, quoted in Kamei Hideo, *Meiji bungakushi*, 33–34.

27. Nozaki Sabun, quoted in Sasaki Tōru, "*Kinnosuke no hanashi* no ninki o megutte," 107.

28. Tamai Kensuke, "Shinbun shōsetsushi," 567.

29. Edward Seidensticker, *High City, Low City*, 250.

30. Ozaki Hotsuki, *Taishū bungaku*, 112–14.

31. Rinbara Sumio, "'Koshinbun' to 'tsuzukimono,'" 14.

32. Konita Seiji, "Nyūsu gengo no Edo—Meiji," 81–82.

33. Honma Hisao, "Ese-akumashugi," 177.

34. Kamei Hideo, *Meiji bungakushi*, 31.

35. Kitagawa Tetsuo, *Buraku mondai*, 14.

36. Rinbara Sumio, "Kindai bungaku to 'tsuzukimono,'" 40.

37. Nobutaka Ike, *The Beginnings of Political Democracy in Japan*, 36.

38. Lawrence Ward Beer, *Freedom of Expression in Japan*, 47.

39. Michael McKeon, *The Origins of the English Novel*, 268, 20.

40. Marleigh Grayer Ryan, *The Development of Realism*, 36.

41. For a fuller account of poison women and female criminality in modern Japanese literature, see Christine Marran, *Poison Women*.

42. Gunji Masakatsu, "'Akuba' to 'dokufu,'" 10.

43. Matsumoto Kappei, *Watakushi no furuhon daigaku*, 280.

44. Honma Hisao, "Dokufumono," 98.

45. Jürgen Habermas, *Structural Transformation of the Public Sphere*, 181.

46. George Bailey Sansom, *The Western World and Japan*, 409.

47. Maeda Ai, *Genkei no Meiji*, 13–14.

48. Marshall Berman, *Everything That Is Solid Melts into Air*, 5.

49. Lucien Goldmann, *Towards a Sociology of the Novel*, 2.

50. D. A. Miller, *The Novel and the Police*, xii.

51. Maeda Ai, *Genkei no Meiji*, 16.

52. Hirata Yumi, "'Dokufu' no tanjō," 238.

53. Ibid.

54. Kawabe Kisaburō, *Press and Politics in Japan*, 21.

55. Yamamoto Taketoshi, *Kindai Nihon no shinbun*, 70.

56. Albert Altman, "The Press," 245–46.

57. Kanagaki Robun, quoted in Nakamura Mitsuo, *Japanese Fiction in the Meiji Era*, 12.

58. Yamada Shunji, "'Riaritii' no shūjiteki haikei," 69.

59. Nakayama Yasumasa, ed., *Shinbun shūsei Meiji hennenshi 9*, 161.

60. John Reddie Back, quoted in James L. Huffman, *Creating a Public*, 81.

61. Yanagida Izumi, *Meiji bungaku kenkyū 4*, 101.

62. Lennard J. Davis, *Factual Fictions*, 213.

63. Okitsu Kaname, *Meiji kaikaki bungaku no kenkyū*, 6–7.

64. Quoted in Okitsu Kaname, *Meiji shinbun kotohajime*, 96.

65. Sasaki Tōru, "*Torioi Omatsu kaijō shinwa* no seiritsu," 65.

66. Rinbara Sumio, "'Koshinbun' to 'tsuzukimono,'" 19.

67. Graham Law and Morita Norimasa, "Sekai no shinbun shōsetsu," 72–73.

68. P. F. Kornicki, "The Enmeiin Affair," 529, 531.

69. Okitsu Kaname, *Meiji kaikaki bungaku no kenkyū*, 31, 56.

70. Watatani Kiyoshi, *Kinsei akujo kibun*, 80–81.

71. Honda Yasuo, "Shinbun shōsetsu no hassei," 300.

72. "Hillary Clinton Adopts Alien Baby: Secret Service Building Special Nursery in the White House." *Weekly World News,* 15 June 1993.

73. James L. Huffman, *Creating a Public*, 16, 22.

74. Gerald Groemer, "Singing the News," 245.

75. James L. Huffman, *Creating a Public*, 22.

76. Gregory Kasza, *The State and Mass Media in Japan*, xii.

77. W. G. Beasley, ed., *Modern Japan*, 59.

78. Ibid., 62.

79. Paul Heng-Chao Ch'en, *The Formation of the Early Meiji Legal Code*, 18–26.

80. Yanagida Izumi, *Meiji bungaku kenkyū 4*, 92.

81. Ishii Ryosuke, ed. *Japanese Legislation*, 16.

82. Centre for East Asian Cultural Studies, *Meiji Japan 1*, 34.

83. Rinbara Sumio, "'Koshinbun' to 'tsuzukimono,'" 20.

84. Ishii Ryosuke, ed., *Japanese Legislation*, 356.

85. Kawabe Kisaburō, *Press and Politics in Japan*, 66.

86. Hirata Yumi, "'Onna no monogatari' to iu seido," 175–176.

87. Michel Foucault, *Discipline and Punish*, 112.

88. Kubota Hikosaku, *Torioi Omatsu kaijō shinwa*, 157–58; Michel Foucault, *Discipline and Punish*, 170.

89. Nagai Kafū, "Kōcha no ato," 321–22.

90. Michael McKeon, *The Origins of the English Novel*, 20.

91. Ibid., 98.

92. James A. Fujii, *Complicit Fictions*, 47.

93. Lennard Davis, "A Social History of Fact and Fiction," 143–44.

94. Kōno Kensuke, *Shomotsu no kindai*, 57.

95. James L. Huffman, *Creating a Public*, 2.

96. Nagamine Shigetoshi, *Zasshi to dokusha no kindai*, 3.

97. Yamada Shunji, "Meiji shoki shinbun zappō no buntai," 115.

98. Wolfgang Iser, *The Fictive and the Imaginary*, xiv.

99. Cathy N. Davidson, *Revolution and the Word*, 12.

100. Nicos Poulantzas, *State, Power, Socialism*, 115.

101. Rinbara Sumio, "Kindai bungaku to 'tsuzukimono,'" 43.

102. Yanagida Izumi, *Meiji bungaku kenkyū 4*, 209.

103. Fredric Jameson, *Marxism and Form*, 262.

CHAPTER TWO

1. Cecilia Segawa Seigle, *Yoshiwara*, 195.

2. Maeda Ai, *Maeda Ai chōsakushū 3*, 287.

3. Kan Satoko, *Jidai to onna to Higuchi Ichiyō*, 224.

4. Sata Ineko, quoted in Maeda Ai, *Maeda Ai chōsakushū 3*, 303.

5. Itō Sei, *Nihon bundan shi 4*, 110.

6. Robert Lyons Danly, *In the Shade of Spring Leaves*, 148.

7. Matsusaka Toshio, *Higuchi Ichiyō kenkyū*, 138.

8. Sata Ineko, "'Takekurabe' kaishaku," 163.

9. J. E. De Becker, *The Nightless City*, 245.

10. Komori Yōichi, *Buntai to shite no monogatari*, 257–58.

11. Jonathan E. Zwicker, *Practices of the Sentimental Imagination*, 122.

12. Takayama Chogyū, "Ichiyō joshi no 'Takekurabe' o yomite," 28.

13. Robert Lyons Danly, *In the Shade of Spring Leaves*, 145–46; Timothy Van Compernolle, *The Uses of Memory*, 25.

14. Gerald Graff, "Co-Optation," 176–77 (original emphasis).

15. Hugues Krafft, quoted in Christopher Reed, *Bachelor Japanists*, 23; Sir Henry Norman, quoted in Christopher Reed, *Bachelor Japanists*, 30.

16. Maeda Ai, *Maeda Ai chōsakushū 3*, 341–43.

17. J. E. De Becker, *The Nightless City*, 4.

18. Cecilia Segawa Seigle, *Yoshiwara*, 106, 70–71.

19. Leslie Pincus, *Authenticating Culture in Imperial Japan*, 16.

20. Nishio Kunio, *Nihon no bungaku to yūjo*, 215, 224.

21. Yukichi Fukuzawa, *Fukuzawa Yukichi on Japanese Women*, 140.

22. J. E. De Becker, *The Nightless City*, 165.

23. Sheldon Garon, "The World's Oldest Debate?," 713.

24. Basil Hall Chamberlain, *Things Japanese*, 156.

25. Edward Seidensticker, *High City, Low City*, 199.

26. Marshall Berman, *Everything That Is Solid Melts into Air*, 152.

27. Quoted in Edward Seidensticker, *High City, Low City*, 11.

28. Higuchi Ichiyō, "Child's Play," 270.

29. Ōkubo Hasetsu, *Hanamachi fūzokushi*, 53.

30. Yukichi Fukuzawa, *Fukuzawa Yukichi on Japanese Women*, 90, 88–89.

31. Bernard S. Silberman, "The Bureaucratic State," 226.

32. Cecilia Segawa Seigle, *Yoshiwara*, 182.

33. Sheldon Garon, "The World's Oldest Debate?," 714.

34. Maeda Ai, *Genkei no Meiji*, 95.

35. Yukichi Fukuzawa, *Fukuzawa Yukichi on Japanese Women*, 79.

36. Edward Seidensticker, *High City, Low City*, 171.

37. Kazuko Tsurumi, *Women in Japan*, 3.

38. Pierre Loti, quoted in Maeda Ai, *Genkei no Meiji*, 97.

39. Komori Yōichi, *Buntai to shite no monogatari*, 256.

40. Ronald P. Dore, *Education in Tokugawa Japan*, 313.

41. Yukichi Fukuzawa, *The Autobiography of Yukichi Fukuzawa*, 190.

42. Douglas Howland, *Translating the West*, 85, 95-96, 119.

43. Yukichi Fukuzawa, *Fukuzawa Yukichi's An Encouragement of Learning*, 16.

44. Sugiyama Chūhei, *Meiji keimō ki no keizai shisō*, 3, 19, 7.

45. Osanai Kaoru, quoted in Edward Seidensticker, *High City, Low City*, 168.

46. J. E. De Becker, *The Nightless City*, 22.

47. Henry Norman, *The Real Japan*, 285.

48. Higuchi Ichiyō, quoted in Robert Lyons Danly, *In the Shade of Spring Leaves*, 23.

49. Yasue Aoki Kidd, *Women Workers*, 1.

50. Thomas C. Smith, *Political Change and Industrial Development in Japan*, 54.

51. Louise A. Tilly and Joan W. Scott, *Women, Work and Family*, 63.

52. Koji Taira, "Economic Development," 619.

53. Jon Halliday, *A Political History of Japanese Capitalism*, 62.

54. Thomas Smith, "The Right to Benevolence" 589.

55. Patricia Tsurumi, *Factory Girls*, 47.

56. Higuchi Ichiyō, "Child's Play," 270.

57. Gilbert Rozman, "Social Change," 515.

58. Murakami Nobuhiko, *Meiji josei shi chūkan kōhen*, 137; Kazuo Okochi, *Labor in Modern Japan*, 16.

59. Hosoi Wakizō, *Jokō aishi*, 380–81.

60. Gail Lee Bernstein, "Women in the Silk-reeling Industry," 65.

61. Patricia Tsurumi, *Factory Girls*, 182.

62. Andrew Gordon, *The Evolution of Labor Relations in Japan*, 48.

63. Higuchi Ichiyō, "A Snowy Day," 177.

64. Karl Marx, "Theses on Feuerbach IX," 14–15.

65. Gilbert Rozman, "Social Change," 525.

66. Carmen Blacker, *The Japanese Enlightenment*, 36.

67. Yukichi Fukuzawa, *Fukuzawa Yukichi on Japanese Women*, 35, 52–53.

68. Ueno Chizuko, *Kindai kazoku no seiritsu to shūen*, 113.

69. Yukichi Fukuzawa, *Fukuzawa Yukichi on Japanese Women*, 82.

70. Murakami Nobuhiko, *Meiji josei shi—chūkan zenhen*, 297–98.

71. Bernard S. Silberman, "The Bureaucratic State," 249.

72. James L. Huffman, *Creating a Public*, 124.

73. Eiichi Shibusawa, *The Autobiography of Shibusawa Eiichi*, x.

74. Kōno Kensuke, *Tōki to shite no bungaku*, 154.

75. Maruyama Masao, "Patterns of Individuation," 530.

76. Theodor Adorno and Max Horkheimer, "The Culture Industry," 41.

77. Koji Taira, "Economic Development," 3.

78. Sumiya Mikio, *The Social Impact of Industrialization in Japan*, 37.

79. Bryon K. Marshall, *Capitalism and Nationalism in Prewar Japan*, 52.

80. Matsuzawa Tessei, "Street Labor Markets," 153.

81. Yukichi Fukuzawa, *Fukuzawa Yukichi on Japanese Women*, 37.

82. Andrew Gordon, *The Evolution of Labor Relations in Japan*, 36, 2 (emphasis added).

83. Ardath W. Burks, "The Politics of Japan's Modernization," 564–65.

84. Sumiya Mikio, *The Social Impact of Industrialization in Japan*, 47.

85. Andrew Gordon, *The Evolution of Labor Relations in Japan*, 33.

86. Mikio Sumiya, *The Social Impact of Industrialization in Japan*, 51.

87. Bryon K. Marshall, *Capitalism and Nationalism*, 51–76.

88. Yasue Aoki Kidd, *Women Workers*, viii–ix.

89. Sheldon Garon, "The World's Oldest Debate?," 723 (emphasis added).

90. David T. Evans, *Sexual Citizenship*, 38.

91. John Whitney Hall, "Changing Conceptions of the Modernization of Japan," 20.

92. Jürgen Habermas, *Structural Transformation of the Public Sphere*, 79.

93. Alain Touraine, *Critique of Modernity*, 119–20.

94. Jürgen Habermas, *The Philosophical Discourse of Modernity*, 39 (original emphasis).

95. Higuchi Ichiyō, "Encounters on a Dark Night," 196, 204.

96. Karl Marx, *The Communist Manifesto*, 63.

97. J. E. De Becker, *The Nightless City*, 183.

98. Patricia Tsurumi, *Factory Girls*, 188, 196.

99. Michel Foucault, *The Order of Things*, 254.

100. Henry Norman, *The Real Japan*, 285.

101. Kōra Yumiko, "Muishiki no kagaisha-tachi—'Takekurabe ron,'" 216.

102. Jürgen Habermas, *The Philosophical Discourse of Modernity*, 38.

103. Carole Pateman, *The Sexual Contract*, 3, 2, 4.

104. Ibid., 54.

CHAPTER THREE

1. Edwin McClellan, *Two Japanese Novelists: Sōseki and Tōson*, 16.

2. Itō Sei and Yamamoto Kenkichi, quoted in Asano Yō and Ōta Noboru, eds., *Sōseki sakuhinron shūsei 1*, 14, 21.

3. Natsume Kyōko, *Sōseki no omoide*, 194.

4. Umehara Takeshi, "'*Wagahai wa neko de aru*' no warai ni tsuite," 172.

5. Hibi Yoshitaka, *Bungaku no rekishi*, 105.

6. Komori Yōichi, *Sōseki o yominaosu*, 8.

7. Yoshimoto Takaaki, "Uzumakeru Sōseki (1) *Wagahai wa neko de aru*," 8.

8. Natsume Sōseki, quoted in Matsumura Tatsuo, "*Natsume Sōseki shū 1* kaisetsu," 27.

9. Kamei Hideo, "Bungakushi no naka de," 68.

10. Hasegawa Nyozekan, "Sōseki to Edokko bungaku," 367.

11. Yamamoto Yoshiaki, "Kaikaki no media to bungaku," 190–91.

12. Karatani Kōjin, *Sōseki ron shūsei*, 198, 218.

13. Karatani Kōjin, ed., *Kindai Nihon no hihyō 3*, 95.

14. Natsume Sōseki, quoted in Ishii Kazuo, "*Wagahai wa neko de aru* no 'warai' no kumitate ni tsuite," 1.

15. Takahashi Yasuo, *Wagahai wa neko de aru den*, 9.

16. Minae Mizumura, *The Fall of Language*, 138.

17. Tetsuo Najita, "Introduction," 19.

18. Jay Rubin, *Injurious to Public Morals*, 183.

19. Katō Shūichi, "Japanese Writers and Modernization," 431.

20. Karatani Kōjin, *Sōseki ron shūsei*, 245, 215.

21. Alain Touraine, *Critique of Modernity*, 177.

22. Etō Jun, *Etō Jun bungaku shūsei 1*, 213.

23. Takahama Kyoshi, quoted in Mizukawa Takao, *Sōseki to rakugo*, 84–85.

24. Takahashi Yasuo, *Wagahai wa neko de aru den*, 45.

25. Ozaki Hotsuki, *Taishū geinō no kamigami*, 8–9.

26. Edward Seidensticker, *High City, Low City*, 154.

27. Ozaki Hotsuki, *Taishū geinō no kamigami*, 43.

28. Okitsu Kaname, "Taishū bungaku zenshi," 227.

29. Heinz Morioka and Miyoko Sasaki, "The Blue-Eyed Storyteller," 133.

30. Heinz Morioka and Miyoko Sasaki, *Rakugo*, 8.

31. Andrew Lawrence Markus, "The Carnival of Edo," 501.

32. Gerald Figal, *Civilization and Monsters*, 26.

33. Teruoka Yasutaka, *Rakugo no nenrin*, 210.

34. Heinz Morioka and Miyoko Sasaki, *Rakugo*, 139–40.

35. Anonymous, quoted in Edward Fowler, *San'ya Blues*, 61.

36. Mizukawa Takao, *Sōseki to rakugo*, 84–86.

37. Ochi Haruo, "'Mizumakura' o megutte," 119.

38. Mizukawa Takao, *Sōseki to rakugo*, 83.

39. Natsume Kyōko, *Sōseki no omoide*, 102.

40. Jukichi Inouye, *Sketches of Tokyo Life*, 3–4.

41. Okitsu Kaname, *Rakugo—warai no nenrin*, 124, 123; "Sōseki to Edo bunka," 14.

42. Okitsu Kaname, *Rakugo—warai no nenrin*, 124.

43. Tsurumi Shunsuke, "Enchō ni okeru miburi to shōchō," 832.

44. Walter J. Ong, *Orality and Literacy*, 12.

45. Mizukawa Takao, *Sōseki to rakugo*, 34.

46. Okitsu Kaname, "Sōseki to Edo bunka," 14.

47. Angela Yiu, *Chaos and Order*, 100.

48. Jay Rubin, "Sōseki on Individualism," 28.

49. Okitsu Kaname, "Taishū bungaku zenshi," 232.

50. "Mister Kataoka," quoted in J. Scott Miller, "Japanese Shorthand and *Sokkibon*," 474.

51. Andrew Gordon, *Labor and Imperial Democracy*, 16.

52. Wakabayashi Kanzō, "Joshi."

53. Ochi Haruo, "Enchō tsuiseki," 23.

54. Ri Takanori, *Hyōshō kūkan no kindai*, 110–34.

55. Nanette Twine, *Language and the Modern State*, 136.

56. Teruoka Yasutaka, *Rakugo no nenrin*, 175.

57. Andrew Gordon, *Labor and Imperial Democracy*, 42.

58. Geinōshi kenkyūkai, ed., *Nihon geinōshi 7*, 39.

59. J. Scott Miller, "Japanese Shorthand and *Sokkibon*," 477.

60. See Takahashi Yasuo, *Wagahai wa neko de aru den*, 31–40; Mizukawa Takao, *Sōseki to rakugo*, 83–130.

61. Hyōdō Hiromi, *"Koe" no kokumin kokka Nihon*, 117.

62. Yamamoto Yoshiaki, "Kaikaki no media to bungaku," 195.

63. Futabatei Shimei, "Yo ga genbun'itchi no yurai," 372.

64. Ludwig Wittgenstein, quoted in Fredric Jameson, *The Political Unconscious*, 8.

65. Kindaichi Haruhiko, quoted in Roy Andrew Miller, *The Japanese Language*, 32.

66. Mikhail Bakhtin, *The Dialogic Imagination*, 381.

67. Kamei Hideo, *Meiji bungakushi*, 76.

68. Nanette Twine, *Language and the Modern State*, 87, 97.

69. James Fujii, *Complicit Fictions*, 103–25.

70. Antonio Gramsci, *Selections from Cultural Writings*, 183–84.

71. Ōtsuka Eiji, *Shōjo minzokugaku*, 65–66.

72. Emily Groszos Ooms, *Women and Millenarian Protest*, 64.

73. Makoto Ueda, *Modern Japanese Poets and the Nature of Literature*, 131–32.

74. Michel Foucault, *The Order of Things*, 300.

75. Kamei Hideo, "Enchō kōen," 30.

76. Ochi Haruo, "San'yūtei Enchō ni tsuite," 94.

77. Yamada Shunji, "Shinbun kairyō to Enchō sokki," 81–82.

78. Okitsu Kaname, "Taishū bungaku zenshi," 247–48.

79. J. Scott Miller, "Japanese Shorthand and *Sokkibon*," 486–87.

80. Nomura Masaaki, *Rakugo no gengogaku*, 128, 112.

81. Natsume Sōseki, quoted in Takahashi Yasuo, *Wagahai wa neko de aru den*, 42.

82. Ishihara Chiaki, *Sōseki no kigōron*, 31–32.

83. Walter Benjamin, quoted in Benedict Anderson, *The Spectre of Comparisons*, 351–52.

84. Maeda Ai, "Neko no kotoba, neko no rinri," 94.

85. Kojin Karatani, *The Origins of Modern Japanese Literature*, 178.

86. Marleigh Grayer Ryan, *Japan's First Modern Novel*, 88–90.

87. Senuma Shigeki, "'WAGAHAI WA NEKO DE ARU' (I Am a Cat)," 25.

88. Suzuki Sadami, *Nihon no "bungaku" o kangaeru*, 157.

89. Ozaki Hotsuki, *Taishū geinō no kamigami*, 87.

90. Ōkuma Shigenobu, quoted in Jay Rubin, *Injurious to Public Morals*, 82.

91. Jay Rubin, *Injurious to Public Morals*, 93.

92. Noma Seiji, *Watakushi no hansei*, 231.

93. Edward Seidensticker, *High City, Low City*, 157.

94. J. Scott Miller, "Japanese Shorthand and *Sokkibon*," 484.

95. Natsume Sōseki, *I Am a Cat, vol. 1*, 121–22.

96. Jürgen Habermas, *Structural Transformation of the Public Sphere*, 50.

97. Richard H. Mitchell, *Censorship in Imperial Japan*, 84–85.

98. Andrew Gordon, *Labor and Imperial Democracy*, 26, 33, 30, 41.

99. Andrew Gordon, "The Crowd and Politics in Imperial Japan," 155.

100. Yamamoto Yoshiaki, "Kaikaki no media to bungaku," 192.

101. Shumpei Okamoto, *The Japanese Oligarchy*, 206–10.

102. Heinz Morioka and Miyoko Sasaki, *Rakugo*, 248.

103. Hinotani Teruhiko, "Shiki to Enchō," 198.

104. Richard H. Mitchell, *Censorship in Imperial Japan*, 9–10.

105. Heinz Morioka and Miyoko Sasaki, *Rakugo*, 251.

106. Honoré Balzac, quoted in James Scott, *Domination and the Arts of Resistance*, 120.

107. Heinz Morioka and Miyoko Sasaki, *Rakugo*, 250.

108. Patrick Parrinder, *Nation and Novel*, 9.

109. Inoue Takuya, quoted in Jay Rubin, *Injurious to Public Morals*, 94.

110. Mizukawa Takao, *Sōseki to rakugo*, 38.

111. Natsume Sōseki, "Philosophical Foundations of the Literary Arts," 197.

112. Timothy Brennan, "The National Longing for Form," 49 (original emphasis).

113. Mikhail Bakhtin, *The Dialogic Imagination*, 7.

114. Stephen Greenblatt, *Shakespearean Negotiations*, 177.

115. Jonathan Zwicker, *Practices of the Sentimental Imagination*, 159–60.

116. Yoshimoto Takaaki, "Uzumakeru Sōseki (1) *Wagahai wa neko de aru*," 10, 17.

117. Okitsu Kaname, *Rakugo—warai no nenrin*, 154.

118. Denis Diderot, quoted in Jürgen Habermas, *Structural Transformation of the Public Sphere*, 257.

119. Johann Wolfgang von Goethe, quoted in Friedrich A. Kittler, *Gramophone, Film, Typewriter*, 8.

120. Nanette Twine, *Language and the Modern State*, 256.

121. Seth Jacobowitz, *Writing Technology in Meiji Japan*, 254.

122. Kōno Kensuke, *Shomotsu no kindai*, 90.

123. Nagamine Shigetoshi, *Zasshi to dokusha no kindai*, 35–76.

124. Octave Uzanne, "The End of Books."

125. Imanishi Junkichi, *Sōseki bungaku*, 128.

126. Walter J. Ong, *Orality and Literacy*, 136.

127. Marshall McLuhan, *The Gutenberg Galaxy*, 32.

128. Hyōdō Hiromi, *"Koe" no kokumin kokka Nihon*, 8.

129. Takeyama Akiko, *Rajio no jidai*, 44.

130. Michel Foucault, "What Is an Author?," 118.

131. Nagamine Shigetoshi, *Zasshi to dokusha no kindai*, 69, 4.

132. Ayako Kano, *Acting Like a Woman*, 56.

133. Natsume Kyōko, *Sōseki no omoide*, 349.

134. Hibi Yoshitaka, *Bungaku no rekishi*, 91–94.

CHAPTER FOUR

1. Azuma Tamaki, *Kishida Ryūsei to sono shūhen*, 11.

2. Furui Yoshikichi, quoted in Edward Fowler, *The Rhetoric of Confession*, 273.

3. Howard Hibbett, "The Portrait of the Artist in Japanese Fiction," 347.

4. Edward Fowler, *The Rhetoric of Confession*, 128.

5. Miyoshi Yukio, *Nihon bungaku no kindai to hankindai*, 227.

6. Edward Fowler, *The Rhetoric of Confession*, 238.

7. William James, quoted in Reuben Fine, *Narcissism, the Self and Society*, x.

8. Usui Yoshimi, *Taishō bungakushi*, 5.

9. Edward Fowler, *The Rhetoric of Confession*, xix.

10. Paul de Man, "Autobiography as De-Facement," 121.

11. Natsume Sōseki, *I Am a Cat*, vol. 1, 31, 48

12. Xavier F. Salomon, "Portraits," 40–42.

13. Natsume Sōseki, *I Am a Cat*, vol. 1, 61–62.

14. Kōjin Karatani, *The Origins of Modern Japanese Literature*, 26.

15. Jürgen Habermas, "Modernity—An Incomplete Project," 8.

16. J. Thomas Rimer, *Pilgrimages*, 25.

17. H. D. Harootunian, "Late Tokugawa Culture and Thought," 179.

18. Minoru Harada, *Meiji Western Painting*, 29.

19. Hibi Yoshitaka, *"Jiko hyōshō" no bungakushi*, 177.

20. Arthur Waley, quoted in Ivan Morris, ed., *Madly Singing in the Mountains*, 242.

21. Norbert Schneider, *The Art of the Portrait*, 6.

22. Shunsuke Tsurumi, *A Cultural History of Postwar Japan*, 30.

23. Ludwig Goldscheider, ed., *Five Hundred Self-Portraits*, 20–21.

24. Kuroi Senji, *Jigazō to no taiwa*, 4.

25. Haga Tōru, *Kaiga no ryōbun*, 10, 13, 12.

26. Takahashi Yuichi, quoted in Tōru Haga, "The Formation of Realism in Meiji Painting," 238.

27. Kuwabara Sumio, *Nihon no jigazō*, 17.

28. Ishiko Junzō, *Kitchu ron*, 287.

29. Yamada Akio, "'Kaiga no yakusoku' ronsō sobyō," 15.

30. Sadoya Shigenobu, *Sōseki to seikimatsu geijutsu*, 67–68.

31. Motoo Kobayashi, "Merging of Voices," 11.

32. Nanette Twine, *Language and the Modern State*, 155.

33. Richard Torrance, *The Fiction of Tokuda Shusei*, 47.

34. Haga Tōru, *Kaiga no ryōbun*, 374.

35. Mary Layoun, *Travels of a Genre*, 121.

36. Kuwabara Sumio, *Nihon no jigazō*, 22.

37. Kobayashi Hideo, *Kindai kaiga*, 102–3.

38. Aeba Takao, *Nihon kindai no seikimatsu*, 13.

39. Norbert Schneider, *The Art of the Portrait*, 113.

40. Gustave Courbet, quoted in Robert Folkenflik, *The Culture of Autobiography*, 12.

41. Takumi Hideo, *Kindai Nihon no bijutsu to bungaku*, 117.

42. Donald McCallum, "Three Taishō Artists," 90.

43. Kitazawa Norio, *Kishida Ryūsei*, 17.

44. Azuma Tamaki, *Taishō-ki no seishun gunzō*, 95.

45. Atsushi Tanaka, "Kishida Ryūsei," 152.

46. Haga Tōru, *Kaiga no ryōbun*, 548, 541.

47. Kishida Ryūsei, "Uchi naru bi," 29–30.

48. Lionel Trilling, *The Liberal Imagination*, 179.

49. Kuroi Senji, *Jigazō to no taiwa*, 2.

50. Awazu Norio, *Jigazō wa kataru*, 110.

51. Kishida Ryūsei, "Uchi naru bi," 28–29.

52. Kishida Ryūsei, "Jiko no geijutsu," 39.

53. Kishida Ryūsei, "Jiko no sekai," 287–92.

54. Mushanokoji Saneatsu, "Jiko no tame no geijutsu," 228.

55. Mushanokoji Saneatsu, quoted in Tomi Suzuki, *Narrating the Self*, 52–53.

56. Yanagi Sōetsu, "Kakumei no gaka," 4.

57. H. W. Janson and Anthony F. Janson, *History of Art*, 535.

58. Theodor Adorno and Sigmund Freud, quoted in C. Fred Alford, *Narcissism*, 26.

59. Sigmund Freud, "On Narcissism," 94.

60. Mushanokoji Saneatsu, quoted in Shūji Takashina, "Natsume Sōseki," 277.

61. Sigmund Freud, *Leonardo da Vinci*, 75.

62. Irmela Hijiya-Kirschnereit, *Rituals of Self-Revelation*, 141, 273.

63. Shiga Naoya, quoted in William Sibley, *The Shiga Hero*, 31.

64. William Sibley, *The Shiga Hero*, 81.

65. Sigmund Freud, *Leonardo da Vinci*, 74.

66. Sigmund Freud, quoted in William Sibley, *The Shiga Hero*, 63.

67. Sigmund Freud, "On Narcissism," 87.

68. William Sibley, *The Shiga Hero*, 121.

69. Heinz Kohut, *The Analysis of the Self*, 25 (original emphasis).

70. J. Thomas Rimer, "Introduction: Satō Haruo," 1.

71. Satō Haruo, *The Sick Rose*, 95.

72. Sigmund Freud, "Mourning and Melancholia," 132.

73. Satō Haruo, "Enkō," 22.

74. Ibid., 26.

75. Christopher Lasch, *The Culture of Narcissism*, 50.

76. Kuroi Senji, *Jigazō to no taiwa*, 44.

77. Ken K. Ito, *Visions of Desire*, 95.

78. Donald F. McCallum, "Three Taishō Artists," 94; Kitazawa Norio, *Kishida Ryūsei*, 17.

79. Yokota Yōichi, "Shirakaba-kai," 94.

80. Kishida Ryūsei, *Bi no hontai*, 185.

81. Jacques Derrida, *Memoirs of the Blind*, 65 (original emphasis).

82. Murakami Kumi, quoted in Michael Lucken, *Imitation and Creativity*, 76.

83. Bernard Denvir, *Vincent, A Complete Portrait*, 7.

84. Sigmund Freud, "On Narcissism," 91.

85. Stephen Z. Levine, *Monet, Narcissus, and Self-Reflection*, 143.

86. Manuel Gasser, *Self-Portraits*, 11, 16.

87. Edward Fowler, "Shishosetsu in Modern Japanese Literature," 16.

88. Anthony J. Cascardi, *The Subject of Modernity*, 90.

89. André Gide, quoted in Steve Z. Levine, *Monet, Narcissus, and Self-Reflection*, 143.

90. Naoya Shiga, *A Dark Night's Passing*, 400–1.

91. Ovid, *Metamorphoses*, 63.

92. Julia Kristeva, *Tales of Love*, 121.

93. Marshall W. Alcorn, Jr., *Narcissism and the Literary Libido*, 164.

94. Hans-Georg Gadamer, *Truth and Method*, 127–29.

95. Reuben Fine, *Narcissism, the Self and Society*, 3.

96. Aeba Takao, *Nihon kindai no seikimatsu*, 14.

CHAPTER FIVE

1. Arishima Takeo, quoted in Kim Hŭi-jŏng, "Arishima Takeo to Kankoku bungaku (1)," 47.

2. Karatani Kōjin, ed., *Kindai Nihon no hihyō 3*, 155–56.

3. George Akita, *Foundations of Constitutional Government*, 16.

4. Samuel Smiles, *Self-Help*, 234.

5. Nakarai Tōsui, *Kosa fuku kaze* (The Wind Blows Yellow Sand, 1891).

6. Haga Tōru, "Senzen Shōwa no Nihon bunjin to Kankoku," 158.

7. Kawamura Minato, *Ajia to iu kagami*, 160.

8. Tsurumi Shunsuke, "Chōsenjin no tōjō suru shōsetsu," 189.

9. Kawamura Minato, *Ikyō no Shōwa bungaku*, 18–19.

10. Kawamura Minato, *"Yoidorebune" no seishun*, 143.

11. Kawamura Minato, *Ikyō no Shōwa bungaku*, 19.

12. Edward Said, *Culture and Imperialism*, 188, 70.

13. Wanyao Zhou, "The Kōminka Movement in Taiwan and Korea," 53.

14. Minami Jirō, quoted in Miyata Setsuko, *Chōsen minshū to "kōminka" seisaku*, 148.

15. Carter J. Eckert, *Offspring of Empire*, 240.

16. Michael Robinson, *Cultural Nationalism*, 31.

17. Ibid., 109.

18. Ibid., 21.

19. Miyata Setsuko, *Chōsen minshū to "kōminka" seisaku*, 158–59.

20. *Kaizō* editorial board, quoted in Im Chŏn-hye, *Nihon ni okeru Chōsenjin*, 202.

21. Hayashi Fusao et al., "Chōsen bunka no shōrai," 273.

22. Tanaka Hidemitsu, "Chōsen no sakka," 389.

23. Tanaka Hidemitsu, "Hantō bundan," 384.

24. Tsurumi Shunsuke, "Chōsenjin no tōjō suru shōsetsu," 198.

25. Im Chŏn-hye, *Nihon ni okeru Chōsenjin*, 13.

26. Kim Tal-su, quoted in Sofue Shōji, *Kindai Nihon bungaku*, 28–29.

27. Nayoung Aimee Kwon, *Intimate Empire*, 33.

28. Paek Ch'ŏl, quoted in Kim Yun-sik, *Shōkon to kokufuku*, 168.

29. Hayashi Fusao et al., "Chōsen bunka no shōrai," 279.

30. Ueda Kazutoshi, quoted in Yasuda Toshiaki, *Teikoku Nihon*, 6.

31. Ueda Kazutoshi, quoted in S. Robert Ramsey, "The Polysemy of the Term *Kokugo*," 41.

32. An Ushiku, "'Teikō no sakka' no shōgai," 210.

33. Ronald Paulson, "Non-European Foundations of European Imperialism," 120–21.

34. Kim Sŏk-pŏm, *Tenkō to shinnichiha*, 92–93.

35. Bruce Cumings, "The Legacy of Japanese Colonialism," 494–95.

36. Kim Ku, quoted in Mark Gayn, *Japan Diary*, 433.

37. Miyata Setsuko, *Chōsen minshū to "kōminka" seisaku*, 161–62.

38. Kim Sŏk-pŏm, *Tenkō to shinnichiha*, 49.

39. Kim Mun-jip, quoted in Kwak Hyoungduck, "Kin Shiryō *Tenma*," 127.

40. Kim Yŏng-dal, "Kimu Munjipu to 'Inukuso,'" 70.

41. Changsoo Lee and George De Vos, *Koreans in Japan*, 42.

42. Kawamura Minato, *Manshū hōkai*, 133–36.

43. Kim Chong-guk, *Chin'il munhangnon*, 199.

44. Kawamura Minato, *Manshū hōkai*, 142.

45. Kim Mun-jip, "Chōsen bundan no tokushūsei," 156, 152, 160.

46. Kim Mun-jip, quoted in Kawamura Minato, *Manshū hōkai*, 133.

47. Kim Chong-guk, *Chin'il munhangnon*, 199.

48. Kobayashi Hideo, quoted in Kawamura Minato, *Manshū hōkai*, 132.

49. Kim Mun-jip, *Arirantōge*, 27. Further page references to this source are made parenthetically in the paragraph.

50. Kim U-chang, "The Situation of the Writers," 8.

51. Kim Yun-sik, quoted in Kawamura Minato, *Manshū hōkai*, 148.

52. Shū Shakubin, *Kin Shiryō bungaku no kenkyū*, 41–43, 73.

53. Kwak Hyoungduck, "Kin Shiryō *Tenma*," 120.

54. Kim Sa-ryang, *Tenma*, 139.

55. Kim Sa-ryang, quoted in Kim Sŏk-pŏm, *"Zainichi" no shisō*, 127.

56. Kim Sa-ryang, *Tenma*, 156. Further references to this source are made parenthetically in the following two paragraphs.

57. Kim Sa-ryang, "Chōsen bunka tsūshin," 22.

58. Kim Sa-ryang, quoted in Kawamura Minato, "Kin Shiryo to Chō Kakuchū," 216–17.

59. Neil Larsen, *Modernism and Hegemony*, 79.

60. Im Chŏn-hye, *Nihon ni okeru Chōsenjin*, 235.

61. Hayashi Fusao, quoted in Shū Shakubin, *Kin Shiryō bungaku no kenkyū*, 29.

62. Ishikawa Takuboku, quoted in Ozaki Hotsuki, *Kyū-shokuminchi bungaku*, 13.

63. Lee Yeon-suk, *"Kokugo" to iu shisō*, 13.

64. Hayashi Fusao, "Chōsen no seishin," 196.

CHAPTER SIX

1. John Dower, *Embracing Defeat*, 527.

2. Katō Shūichi, "Zasshūteki Nihon," 50.

3. Franco Minganti, "Jukebox Boys," 149.

4. Derek Bickerton, *Dynamics of a Creole System*, 175.

5. Yokota Kōichi, *Kenpō to tennōsei*, 48.

6. Kim Sa-ryang, "Kōmei," 39.

7. Nanette Gottlieb, "Language and Politics," 1178.

8. Yokote Kazuhiko, *Hisenryōka no bungaku*, 149.

9. Robert Ward, "Reflections on the Allied Occupation," 483.

10. Mark Gayn, *Japan Diary*, 493–94.

11. Kata Kōji, *Uta no Shōwa shi*, 166.

12. Minami Hiroshi, ed., *Zoku Shōwa bunka*, 183.

13. Yamamoto Akira, *Sengo fūzoku shi*, 112–13.

14. Haruhiko Fukui, "Postwar Politics," 168.

15. John Dower, *Embracing Defeat*, 377.

16. Yokote Kazuhiko, *Hisenryōka no bungaku*, 106.

17. Tsurumi Shunsuke, *Sengo Nihon no taishū bunka shi*, 13.

18. Shishi Bunroku, *Jiyū gakkō*, 438.

19. Komata Yūsuke, "Manshū, Chōsen, Taiwan."

20. Shishi Bunroku, *Jiyū gakkō*, 407–8.

21. Tanaka Katsuhiko, *Kureōrugo to Nihongo*, 19.

22. Yoshimi Shun'ya, "Nihon no naka no 'Amerika,'" 139, 141–42.

23. Carol Gluck, "The 'End' of the Postwar," 12.

24. Nanette Twine, "Language and the Constitution," 125.

25. Koseki Shōichi, *The Birth of Japan's Postwar Constitution*, 133.

26. Gayatri Spivak, "Constitutions and Culture Studies," 141.

27. Nanette Twine, "Language and the Constitution," 125.

28. Rudyard Kipling, *Sea to Sea*, 292–93.

29. Dick Hebdige, *Cut 'n' Mix*, 14.

30. John Dower, *Embracing Defeat*, 311–12.

31. Fredric Jameson, *Archaeologies of the Future*, 16.

32. John Maki, "Japanese Constitutional Style," 12.

33. Edward Seidensticker, "Japan after Vietnam," 56.

34. Dan Fenno Henderson, "Introduction," xi.

35. Mark Gayn, *Japan Diary*, 130.

36. John Dower, *Embracing Defeat*, 386.

37. Kyoko Inoue, *MacArthur's Japanese Constitution*, 37.

38. Larzer Ziff, *Writing in the New Nation*, 105, 114.

39. George Akita, *Foundations of Constitutional Government*, 61.

40. Katō Norihiro, *Kanōsei*, 235.

41. Hayashi Shirō, "Nihonkoku kenpō," 46–49.

42. Kyoko Inoue, *MacArthur's Japanese Constitution*, 81, 95.

43. Robert Ward, "The Commission on the Constitution," 401.

44. John Maki, "Japanese Constitutional Style," 12.

45. Kyoko Inoue, *MacArthur's Japanese Constitution*, 85–86.

46. Mori Arinori, quoted in Roy Andrew Miller, *The Japanese Language*, 42.

47. Isoda Kōichi, *Rokumeikan no keifu*, 45–69.

48. Ralph Willett, *The Americanization of Germany*, 90.

49. Derek Bickerton, *The Roots of Language*, 73.

50. Kata Kōji, *Uta no Shōwa shi*, 201.

51. Edward Seidensticker, *High City, Low City*, 274.

52. Suzumura Ichirō, "Jiipu wa hashiru," written by Yoshikawa Shizuo and Uehara Gento, *Jiipu wa hashiru* (King Records, March 1946, 45rpm).

53. Kurata Yoshihiro, *"Hayariuta" no kōkogaku*, 241–42.

54. Hosokawa Shūhei, "The Swinging Voice of Kasagi Shizuko," 163.

55. Futaba Jūzaburō, quoted in ibid., 159.

56. Ibid., 170.

57. Hattori Ryōichi, *Boku no ongaku jinsei*, 238.

58. Kurata Yoshihiro, *"Hayariuta" no kōkogaku*, 239.

59. Hattori Ryōichi, *Boku no ongaku jinsei*, 226.

60. Michael Bourdaghs, *Sayonara Amerika*, 31.

61. Shishi Bunroku, *Jiyū gakkō*, 514.

62. Hiraoka Masaaki, *Dai kayōron*, 648.

63. Shiozawa Minobu, "Kasagi Shizuko to Misora Hibari," 229–30.

64. Hattori Ryōichi, "Kaisō no Kasagi Shizuko," 290.

65. Komota Nobuo et al., *Shinpan Nihon ryūkōka*, 72–74.

66. Michael Bourdaghs, *Sayonara Amerika*, 113.

67. Isoda Kōichi, *Shisō to shite no Tōkyō*, 111, 112–13.

68. Shindō Ken, *"Shisetsu" sengo kayōkyoku*, 34; Uta Poiger, "American Music," 129.

69. Shindō Ken, *"Shisetsu" sengo kayōkyoku*, 35.

70. Antonio Gramsci, "Language, Linguistics and Folklore," 195.

71. Heide Fehrenbach and Uta Poiger, "Introduction," xxiii.

72. Kata Kōji, *Uta no Shōwa shi*, 185.

73. Sonobe Saburō, *Enka kara*, 146.

74. Hiraoka Masaaki, *Dai kayōron*, 643.

75. Hiraoka Masaaki, *Utairi suikoden*, 28.

76. Yamaori Tetsuo, *Enka to Nihonjin*, 77.

77. Ibid., 34, 140–56.

78. Shindō Ken, *"Shisetsu" sengo kayōkyoku*, 66.

79. Andrew Barshay, "Postwar Social and Political Thought," 289.

80. Michel Foucault, "What Is an Author?," 119.

81. Nishi Masahiko, "Kureōru na bungaku."

82. Yi Chŏng-hŭi, "Henbō suru tekisuto *Tobu otoko* kō," 86.

83. Nishi Masahiko, *Mori no gerira Miyazawa Kenji*, 16–17.

84. Mano Neri, "Sora tobu kureōru," 107.

85. Abe Kōbō, "Kureōru no tama," 296, 295–96.

86. Manō Neri, "Sora tobu kureōru," 109.

87. Odagiri Takashi, "Konseiteki Nihongo no imi," 95.

88. Prince Mikasa-no-miya, quoted in Roy Andrew Miller, *The Japanese Language*, 267.

89. Ulf Hannerz, "Scenarios for Peripheral Cultures," 127.

90. Isoda Kōichi, *Shisō to shite no Tōkyō*, 118–19.

91. Miura Nobutaka, "Kureōru to zasshū bunka ron," 45.

92. Hosomi Kazuyuki, "'Nihonjin' to kureōru no saiken," 300.

93. Slavoj Žižek, "Multiculturalism," 40.

94. Ulf Hannerz, "Scenarios for Peripheral Cultures," 128.

CHAPTER SEVEN

1. "Fanatical Rightist Youth Confesses Brutal Stabbings," *Japan Times,* 3 February 1961.

2. Fukazawa Shichirō, *Rurō no shuki*, 221.

3. Marius B. Jansen, "Changing Japanese Attitudes toward Modernization," 71.

4. Ibid., 121–22.

5. Edward Seidensticker, quoted in "Fukazawa Shichirō no mita yume," 59.

6. Satō Shizuo, *Tennōsei to gendai Nihon bungaku*, 30.

7. Nakamura Michiko, *"Fūryū mutan" jiken igo*, 10.

8. Ide Magoroku, "Shōgeki no burakku yūmoa," 186–87.

9. Kōsaka Masaaki, quoted in Andrew Barshay, "Postwar Social and Political Thought," 336.

10. John Dower, "Introduction," xxii.

11. "Rightist Terrorism," *Japan Times,* 3 February 1961.

12. David Sanger, "Mute Michiko, Sad Land (And a Contrite Press)," *New York Times,* 24 December 1993.

13. Jin'ichi Konishi, *A History of Japanese Literature 2*, 324.

14. Donald Shively, "Tokugawa Plays," 26.

15. George M. Beckmann, *The Making of the Meiji Constitution*, 151.

16. Marius B. Jansen, "Monarchy and Modernization in Japan," 617.

17. Richard H. Mitchell, *Censorship in Imperial Japan*, 91–92, 130.

18. Jay Rubin, *Injurious to Public Morals*, 58.

19. Richard H. Mitchell, *Censorship in Imperial Japan*, 223.

20. Karatani Kōjin, "History and Repetition in Japan," 34.

21. Kuroko Kazuo, "Han-tennō seido shōsetsu," 47.

22. Fukazawa Shichirō, "Fūryū mutan," 330. Further page references to this source are made parenthetically in the following paragraphs.

23. Kyōya Hideo, *Senkyūhaku rokujūichi-nen*, 141.

24. Yoshimoto Takaaki, "Fukazawa o koritsu sasete oite nan no 'genron no jiyū' zo ya," 238.

25. Sotooka Hidetoshi, "Mishima vs. Fukazawa," 19.

26. Kyōya Hideo, *Senkyūhaku rokujūichi-nen*, 165.

27. Ishihara Shintarō, quoted in Matsuura Sōzō, *Masukomi no naka no tennō*, 145.

28. Nakano Shigeharu, "Teroru wa sayoku ni taishite wa yurusareru ka," 215.

29. Suga Hidemi, Asada Akira, and Watanabe Naoki et al., "Tennō to bungaku," 24; Kawamura Minato, *Sengo bungaku*, 63.

30. Ōoka Shōhei, "Yande iru no wa dare ka," 203.

31. Kyōya Hideo, *Senkyūhaku rokujūichi-nen*, 154–55.

32. Hasegawa Izumi, "'Fūryū mutan,'" 102.

33. Takeuchi Yoshimi, "Kenryoku to geijutsu," 337.

34. Hinuma Rintarō, "Sonzai tōshiryoku," 231, 236.

35. Mikhail Bakhtin, *Rabelais and His World*, 20.

36. "Fukazawa Shichirō no mita yume," 58.

37. Nakamura Mitsuo, quoted in Karatani Kōjin, ed., *Kindai Nihon no hihyō 1*, 178.

38. Yoel Hoffmann, *Japanese Death Poems*, 43.

39. Kenneth Rexroth, "Introduction," xiv.

40. Ikari Hiroshi, "'Fūryū mutan' ron," 47.

41. Irokawa Daikichi, "The Subject Mentality," 29.

42. Hirakawa Sukehiro, "Japan's Turn to the West," 484.

43. David Titus, "The Making of the 'Symbol Emperor System,'" 567.

44. Basil Hall Chamberlain, *Things Japanese*, 377.

45. Murakami Shigeyoshi, *Kōshitsu jiten*, 19–20.

46. Kishida Hideo, "*Utakai-hajime*," 47–48.

47. Yaku Masao, "*Shikishima no michi*" *kenkyū*, 2.

48. James Scott, *Domination and the Arts of Resistance*, 58.

49. Katayama Sadami, "Futari no senchūha," 56.

50. Matsumoto Jōji, quoted in Masanori Nakamura, *The Japanese Monarchy, 1931–91*, 103.

51. Sasaki Sōichi, "Tennō no kokka-tei shōchō sei," 408.

52. Ako Nakano, "Death and History," 40.

53. Roland Barthes, *The Empire of Signs*, 32.

54. Karatani Kōjin, Kasai Shigeru, and Matsumoto Ken'ichi et al., "Tennōsei— yokuatsuteki yūwa no benshōhō," 264.

55. Kyōya Hideo, *Senkyūhaku rokujūichi-nen*, 141.

56. Kyōko Hirano, *Mr. Smith*, 16–17.

57. Takashi Fujitani, *Splendid Monarchy*, 26.

58. Masanori Nakamura, *The Japanese Monarchy, 1931–91*, 124.

59. Itō Mamoru, "Kōsō suru ōdiensu," 174–75.

60. Kizugawa Kei, "Sengo no henbō," 282.

61. Yamaori Tetsuo, *Enka to Nihonjin*, 96.

62. Takahashi Gen'ichirō, "Terebi yori ai o komete," 201–2.

63. Kiyomizu Ikutarō, "Terebishon jidai," 18–19.

64. Yun Kwon-ja, "'Zainichi' bunka to nashonarizimu," 262.

65. Yoshimi Shun'ya, "Terebi ga kazoku ni yatte kita," 27–28.

66. Andrew A. Painter, "On the Anthropology of Television," 81.

67. Kainō Michitaka, "Genron to terebishon."

68. Sasaki Kiichi, "Terebi geijutsu."

69. Jean Baudrillard, *For a Critique of the Political Economy of the Sign*, 172 (original emphasis).

70. Tsurumi Shunsuke, *A Cultural History of Postwar Japan*, 62; *Sengo Nihon no taishū bunka shi*, 135–36.

71. Fujitake Akira. *Terebi to no taiwa*, 34–35.

72. Haruhiko Fukui, "Postwar Politics," 209.

73. Marshall McLuhan, *Understanding Media*, 335.

74. Okada Susumu, "Terebi-teki ishiki," 23.

75. Carol Gluck, *Japan's Modern Myths*, 94.

76. John Fiske, *Television Culture*, 22.

77. Marshall McLuhan and Quentin Fiore, *The Medium is the Massage*, 125.

78. Nakai Hideo, "Kōtaishi," 188.

79. Yoshimi Shun'ya, "Terebi ga kazoku ni yatte kita," 35–36.

80. Shiga Nobuo, *Shōwa terebi hōsōshi (jō)*, 214.

81. Kawamura Minato, *Sengo bungaku*, 56–57.

82. Yomiuri shinbunsha geinōbu, *Terebi bangumi no yonjū-nen*, 563–64.

83. Yoshimi Shun'ya, "Terebi ga kazoku ni yatte kita," 37, 43.

84. Kiyomizu Ikutarō, "Terebishon jidai," 16.

85. Yokota Kōichi, *Kenpō to tennōsei*, 66.

86. Ibid., 128.

87. Takabatake Michitoshi, "'Rokujū Anpo,'" 71.

88. Yoshimi Shun'ya, "Terebi ga kazoku ni yatte kita," 26.

89. Fukazawa Shichirō, quoted in Katō Norihiro, "Senkyūhyakuku-nen no kekkon," 310.

90. Fukazawa Shichirō, "Kore ga oira no sōkoku da na nikki."

91. Minami Hiroshi, "Terebishon to ukete no seikatsu," 105, 107.

92. Thomas Crump, *The Death of an Emperor*, 189.

93. David Titus, "The Making of the 'Symbol Emperor System,'" 564.

94. Yokota Kōichi, *Kenpō to tennōsei*, 52.

95. Terry Eagleton, *Walter Benjamin*, 151.

96. M. M. Bakhtin, *The Dialogic Imagination*, 236.

97. Watsuji Tetsurō, *Kokumin tōgō no shōchō*, 112.

98. Inoue Kiyoshi, *Tennō*, 119.

99. Nagai Kafū, quoted in Edward Seidensticker, *Tokyo Rising*, 18.

100. John Whitney Hall, "A Monarch for Modern Japan," 64.

101. Julia Kristeva, *Desire in Language*, 31.

102. Fukazawa Shichirō, *Rurō no shuki*, 220.

103. Sōma Tsuneo, *Fukazawa Shichirō*, 181.

104. Ōe Kenzaburō, quoted in Fukazawa Shichirō, *Fukazawa Shichirō no metsubō taidan*, 85.

105. Matsuura Sōzō, "*Tensei jingo*," 175.

106. Kawamura Minato, *Sengo bungaku*, 60.

107. Helen Hardacre, *Shintō and the State*, 41.

108. Shinkai Hitoshi, *Fukazawa Shichirō gaiden*, 52.

109. Tsurumi Shunsuke, *Sengo Nihon no taishū bunka shi*, 139.

110. Fukazawa Shichirō, *Fukazawa Shichirō no metsubō taidan*, 383.

111. Takashi Fujitani, "Electronic Pageantry," 828.

112. "NHK Sees Ratings for 'Kohaku' Music Show Sink to Lowest Level Ever." *Japan Times*, 2 January 2016.

CHAPTER EIGHT

1. *Asahi jānaru* henshūbu, "Marukusu to manga (sono ichi)," 31.

2. Peter Duus, "Liberal Intellectuals," 413.

3. Patricia Steinhoff, "Hijackers, Bombers, and Bank Robbers," 733.

4. Kazuko Tsurumi, *Social Change and the Individual*, 307–9.

5. Roger Sabin, *Adult Comics*, 5.

6. Shimizu Isao, *Manga no rekishi*, ii–iii.

7. Guy Yasko, "Mishima Yukio vs. Todai Zenkyoto," 21.

8. *Asahi jānaru* henshūbu, "Marukusu to manga (sono ichi)," 31.

9. Skip Williamson, quoted in Mark Estren, *A History of Underground Comics*, 179.

10. Andreas Huyssen, *After the Great Divide*, 141.

11. Stuart Dowsey, *Zengakuren*, 7.

12. Yomota Inuhiko, *Manga genron*, 142.

13. Kure Tomofusa, *Gendai manga*, 48, 153.

14. Ishiko Junzō, *Sengo mangashi nōto*, 129.

15. Roger Sabin, *Adult Comics*, 165.

16. Okonogi Keigo, "Gendai manga," 8–9.

17. Ozaki Hotsuki et al., "Manga bunka no jidai," 461.

18. Takeuchi Osamu, *Sengo manga*, 3–4.

19. Shiomi Takaya, *Sekigunha shimatsuki*, 20–22, 42, 57, 175, 191, 225.

20. Yamaguchi Masao, "Kodomo no tame no manga," 437.

21. Tsurumi Shunsuke, *Sengo Nihon no taishū bunka shi*, 79–80.

22. Satō Tadao, *Nihon no manga*, 190.

23. Takahashi Shintarō, "*Utage no ato no isō*," 115.

24. Yamaguchi Masao, "Kodomo no tame no manga," 439.

25. Satō Tadao, *Nihon no manga*, 235.

26. Fujikawa Jisui, "Ninja zankoku monogatari," 58, 62.

27. Shimizu Isao, *Manga no rekishi*, 189.

28. Roger Sabin, *Adult Comics*, 165.

29. George Orwell, "Boys' Weeklies," 483.

30. Marilyn Ivy, "Formations of Mass Culture," 246.

31. Tanihata Ryōzō, *Anpo gekidō*, 32.

32. Satō Tadao, *Nihon no manga*, 195, 198.

33. Sakurai Tetsuo, *Shisō to shite no rokujū nendai*, 229.

34. Imai Kiyoshi, quoted in Tanihata Ryōzō, *Anpo gekidō*, 28.

35. Takeuchi Osamu, *Sengo manga*, 71.

36. Frederik Schodt, *Manga! Manga!*, 70–71.

37. Takemoto Nobuhiro, quoted in Nagai Katsuichi, *"Garo" henshūchō*, 26.

38. Sawada Yukiko, quoted in Stuart Dowsey, *Zengakuren*, 150.

39. Okamoto Masami and Murao Kōichi, eds., *Daigaku gerira*, 43.

40. Frederik Schodt, *Manga! Manga!*, 67.

41. Hiroshi Minami, *Psychology of the Japanese People*, vii–viii.

42. Yoshimoto Takaaki, "Kaisetsu—Tsuge Yoshiharu *Munō no hito* sono ta," 391–92.

43. Ellis Krauss, *Japanese Radicals Revisited*, 94, 6.

44. Patricia Steinhoff, "Student Conflict," 176, 204.

45. *Asahi jānaru* henshūbu, "Garatto shita hōrōsha," 31.

46. Maeda Tomomi, "Zasshi *Takarajima*."

47. Ōtsuka Eiji, *"Otaku" no seishinshi*, 25, 24.

48. Satō Tadao, *Nihon no manga*, 67.

49. Frederik Schodt, *Manga! Manga!*, 67.

50. Yoshihiro Kōsuke, *Manga no gendaishi*, 20.

51. Ishiko Junzō, *Sengo manga shi nōto*, 93.

52. Susan Stewart, "Ceci Tuera Cela," 162.

53. Regina Blume, "Graffiti," 137.

54. Norman Mailer, "The Faith of Graffiti," 79.

55. Dick Hebdige, *Subculture*, 3.

56. Jean Baudrillard, *For a Critique of the Political Economy of the Sign*, 183–84.

57. Jeff Ferrell, *Crimes of Style*, 197.

58. Dick Hebdige, *Subculture*, 3.

59. Kirk Varnedoe and Adam Gopnik, *High and Low*, 64.

60. Hiraoka Masaaki and Sakuma Shun, "Jakkunaifu no yō ni," 189.

61. Hirasawa Gō, "Rokujū-nendai rakugaki kō," 156.

62. Matsueda Itaru, "Shōka no supiido," 8–9 (original emphasis).

63. Tsurumi Shunsuke, *Manga no dokusha to shite*, 89.

64. Anonymous, quoted in Ishiko Junzō, *Komikku ron*, 209, 334, 214.

65. Jean Baudrillard, *For a Critique of the Political Economy of the Sign*, 176 (original emphasis).

66. Ishiko Junzō, *Komikku ron*, 241, 212.

67. Ishiko Junzō, *Sengo manga shi nōto*, 93.

68. Yomota Inuhiko, *Haisukūru 1968*, 71.

69. Okamoto Masami and Murao Kōichi, *Daigaku gerira*, 109–33, 145–60.

70. Tanihata Ryōzō, *Anpo gekidō*, 29.

71. Shima Taizō, *Yasuda kōdō*, 242. I thank an anonymous reader for help with this translation.

72. Tanigawa Gan, "Kōsakusha," 114.

73. Ishiko Junzō, *Komikku ron*, 211.

74. Sassa Atsuyuki, *Tōdai rakujō*, 185–86.

75. Ishiko Junzō, *Komikku ron*, 335.

76. Nada Inada, "Pari no heki wa kataru," 25.

77. Kirk Varnedoe and Adam Gopnik, *High and Low*, 69.

78. Ernest Abel, *The Handwriting on the Wall*, 20.

79. Mishima Yukio, *Mishima Yukio vs. Tōdai zenkyōtō*, 127, 14–15, 127.

80. Terayama Shūji, *Bōryoku to shite no gengo*, 154–55, 160.

81. Kirk Varnedoe and Adam Gopnik, *High and Low*, 69.

82. Terayama Shūji, *Bōryoku to shite no gengo*, 162–63.

83. Norman Mailer and Jon Naar, *The Faith of Graffiti*, 31.

84. Andreas Huyssen, *After the Great Divide*, 166.

85. Guy Yasko, "Mishima Yukio vs. Todai Zenkyoto," 12.

86. Yoshihiro Kōsuke, *Manga no gendaishi*, 22.

87. Susan Stewart, "Ceci Tuera Cela," 174.

88. Tezuka Osamu, *Manga no kakikata*, 14.

89. Ishiko Junzō, *Sengo manga shi nōto*, 133.

90. Katō Makirō, "Ai no jikan," 25.

91. Guy Yasko, "Mishima Yukio vs. Todai Zenkyoto," 8.

92. Mita Masahiro, *Boku tte nani*, 67–68.

93. Kuroko Kazuo, *Shukusai*, 36–37.

94. Kirk Varnedoe and Adam Gopnik, *High and Low*, 77.

95. Mishima Yukio, "Gekiga ni okeru wakamono ron," 55.

96. Dennis Washburn, *Translating Mount Fuji*, 239.

97. Satō Tadao, *Nihon no manga*, 192, 198.

98. Tsubouchi Yūzō, *Ichikyūnanani*, 13.

99. Félix Guattari, *Machinic Eros*, 14.

100. Patricia Steinhoff, "Student Conflict," 174.

101. Stuart Dowsey, *Zengakuren*, 215.

102. Lionel Trilling, quoted in Marshall Berman, "Why Modernism Still Matters," 33.

103. Yomota Inuhiko, *Manga genron*, 8.

104. Mark Estren, *A History of Underground Comics*, 287.

105. Shimizu Isao, *Manga no rekishi*, iii.

106. Takemiya Keiko, "'Ōizumi saron.'"

107. Miyadai Shinji, Ishihara Hideki, and Ōtsuka Meiko, *Sabukaruchā shinwa kaitai*, 4.

108. Tsurumi Shunsuke, *Sengo Nihon no taishū bunka shi*, 109–10.

CHAPTER NINE

1. John Bussey and Michael Williams, "'Reporters' Notebook: Sumo Champion Makes Pitch for His Adoptive Japan." *Wall Street Journal,* 7 July 1993.

2. Nakamura Shin'ichirō, quoted in Mitsui Takayuki and Washida Koyata, *Yoshimoto Banana shinwa*, 143.

3. Tsuge Teruhiko, "Yoshimoto Banana no sekaiteki na imi," 82–83.

4. Takahashi Gen'ichirō and Yoshimoto Banana, "'Sakka' no kaku," 194, 197–98.

5. Yoshimoto Banana, "Watakushi-tachi 'Chibimaruko-chan' sedai," 269.

6. Ian Buruma, "Weeping Tears of Nostalgia," 29.

7. Masao Miyoshi and H. D. Harootunian, "Introduction," xvi.

8. Masao Miyoshi, *Off-Center*, 236; "Women's Short Stories in Japan," 38.

9. Andreas Huyssen, "Mass Culture as Woman," 191.

10. Mitsuhiro Yoshimoto, "The Postmodern," 9.

11. "Verwirrte Motten," 270.

12. Herbert Mitgang, "Letter from Tokyo."

13. John Bussey and Michael Williams, "'Reporters' Notebook."

14. Yamamoto Yōrō, "'Yoshimoto Banana' wa naze ureru."

15. Jackie Copleton, "5 Essential Japanese Writers."

16. Tsuge Teruhiko, "Yoshimoto Banana no sekaiteki na imi," 78.

17. Suga Atsuko, "Bashō wa banana no ki?," 29.

18. Tsuge Teruhiko et al., "Sekai no naka no Yoshimoto Banana," 91, 92–93.

19. Donnatella Natili, "Itaria de no Yoshimoto Banana," 109.

20. Hilaria Gössman, in Tsuge Teruhiko et al., "Sekai no naka no Yoshimoto Banana," 90.

21. Herbert Marcuse, *One-Dimensional Man*, 9.

22. Banana Yoshimoto, *Kitchen*, 9. Further page references to this source are made parenthetically throughout the chapter.

23. Bret Easton Ellis, *American Psycho*, 28–29.

24. Deborah Garrison, "Day-O," 110.

25. Jane Gaines and Michael Renov, "Preface," vii.

26. Mary Ann Doane, "The Economy of Desire," 30.

27. Jennifer Robertson, "Gender-Bending in Paradise," 56 (original emphasis).

28. Merry White, *The Material Child*, 48, 7.

29. Ōtsuka Eiji, *Shōjo minzokugaku*, 18.

30. Horikiri Naoto, "Onna wa dokyō, shōjo wa aikyō," 114–15.

31. Sodei Takako, "The Fatherless Family," 81.

32. Yoshimoto Banana, "Watakushi-tachi 'Chibimaruko-chan' sedai," 239, 279.

33. Yoshimoto Banana, "Chōnōryoku tte," 279.

34. "Eastward, Ho! Disenchanted, Californians Turn to the Interior West." *New York Times*, 30 May 1993.

35. Fredric Jameson, "Postmodernism," 71, 88.

36. Arjun Appadurai, "Disjuncture and Difference," 17–18.

37. Masao Miyoshi, "Women's Short Stories in Japan," 38.

38. Matsumoto Takayuki, *Yoshimoto Banana ron*, 16.

39. Yoshimoto Banana, "Famirii," 39–40.

40. Eli Zaretsky, *Capitalism, the Family, and Personal Life*, 51.

41. Fredric Jameson, "Postmodernism," 84.

42. Yukari Fujimoto, "A Life-Size Mirror," 54–55.

43. Gilles Deleuze and Félix Guattari, *Anti-Oedipus*, xv, 73.

44. Ibid., 262–67.

45. Ibid., 139–40, 96.

46. Brian Massumi, *A User's Guide*, 92.

47. Gilles Deleuze and Félix Guattari, *Anti-Oedipus*, 77.

48. Ibid., 341.

49. Ibid., 78.

50. Ibid., 278.

51. Fredric Jameson, *Postmodernism, or the Cultural Logic of Late Capitalism*, 16.

52. Frantz Fanon, *Black Skin, White Masks*, 142.

CHAPTER TEN

1. "Child Killer's Mental State to Be Examined," *Japan Times*, 11 November 1990.

2. Miyazaki Tsutomu, quoted in Sasaki Ryūzō, *Miyazaki Tsutomu saiban (ge)*, 218, 260.

3. Yoshioka Shinobu, *M no sekai*, 58; Uchinuma Yukio, "Hitori-aruki suru 'tajū jinkaku,'" 33.

4. Uchinuma Yukio, "Hitori-aruki suru 'tajū jinkaku,'" 18.

5. Yukio Uchinuma and Yoshio Sekine, "Dissociative Identity Disorder (DID) in Japan," 155–60.

6. Colin A. Ross, *Dissociative Identity Disorder*, 226.

7. Ian Hacking, *Rewriting the Soul*, 236.

8. Ichimaru Tōtarō, "'Watakushi,'" 43; Kayama Rika, *Tajūka suru riaru*, 101.

9. Ian Hacking, "Two Souls in One Body," 843.

10. Hozaki Nobuo, quoted in Sasaki Ryūzō, *Miyazaki Tsutomu saiban (ge)*, 163, 166.

11. Nakamura Kokyō, *Hentai shinri no kenkyū*.

12. Yoshitomo Takahashi, "Is Multiple Personality Disorder Really Rare in Japan?," 57.

13. Yoichiro Fujii et al., "Multiple Personality Disorder in Japan," 299–302.

14. Katsumasa An et al., "Dissociative Identity Disorder," S113, S111.

15. Miyadai Shinji, "Kodomo o torimaku ima to mirai," 39.

16. Nakai Hisao, Iida Yoshihiko, and Fujikawa Yōko, "Kairi genshō o megutte," 14.

17. Michael Kenny, *The Passion of Ansel Bourne*, 3.

18. Fredric Jameson, *Postmodernism, or the Cultural Logic of Late Capitalism*, 26; "Postmodernism and Consumer Society," 118.

19. Jeremy Hawthorn, *Multiple Personality*, 33.

20. Saitō Tamaki, *Bungaku no chōkō*, 112.

21. Colin A. Ross, *Dissociative Identity Disorder*, 144.

22. Segawa Hiroko, "Asashōryū no 'kairisei shōgai' to Masako-sama no 'tekiō shōgai' wa nani ga chigau no?," *Nikkei shinbun*, 25 January 2008; Tanaka Kiwamu, "Kairi o megutte," 102.

23. Saitō Tamaki, "Kairi no gihō," 63.

24. Saitō Tamaki, "Kairi to posutomodan," 95.

25. American Psychiatric Association, *Diagnostic and Statistical Manual*, 477.

26. Stanley Kippner, "Cross-cultural Treatment Perspectives," 338.

27. Raymond Williams, *Marxism and Literature*, 131.

28. Paul Filmer, "Structures of Feeling and Social-cultural Formations," 211, 200.

29. Raymond Williams, *Marxism and Literature*, 132.

30. Raymond Williams and Michael Orrom, *Preface to Film*, 54.

31. Raymond Williams, *The Long Revolution*, 49, 48.

32. Michael Moriarty, "The Longest Journey," 92.

33. Alan O'Connor, *Raymond Williams*, 83–84.

34. Stuart Hall, "Culture, Community, Nation," 351.

35. Sean Matthews, "Change and Theory," 189.

36. Raymond Williams, *Marxism and Literature*, 129–32.

37. Saitō Tamaki, Nakai Hisao, and Asada Akira, "Torauma to kairi," 59.

38. Ernest R. Hilgard, "Neodissociation Theory," 38.

39. Christopher Lasch, *The Culture of Narcissism*, 41.

40. Anthony P. Cohen and Nigel Rapport, eds. *Questions of Consciousness*, 16.

41. Saitō Tamaki, "Kairi no jidai," 137–38.

42. Emily Martin, *Bipolar Expeditions*, 177.

43. Watanabe Naoki, quoted in Koyano Atsushi, "Tayama Katai," 186; Saitō Tamaki, *Bungaku no chōkō*, 48.

44. Matthew Strecher, *Dances with Sheep*, 116, 28, 12, 31.

45. Saitō Tamaki, "Kairi no gihō," 63.

46. Murakami Haruki, quoted in Rebecca Suter, *The Japanization of Modernity*, 160.

47. Katō Norihiro, *Shōsetsu no mirai*, 347.

48. Jamie James, "East Meets West," *New York Times*, 2 November 1997.

49. Rebecca Suter, *The Japanization of Modernity*, 166.

50. Jay McInerney, quoted in ibid., 42.

51. Susan Fisher, "An Allegory of Return," 165.

52. Hasumi Shigehiko, quoted in Ōtsuka Eiji, "'Boku' to kokka," 214.

53. Haruki Murakami, *The Wind-Up Bird Chronicle*, 529. Further page references to this source are made parenthetically throughout the chapter.

54. Ōtsuka Eiji, "'Boku' to kokka," 219.

55. Michiko Kakutani, "On A Nightmarish Trek through History's Web," *New York Times*, 31 October 1997.

56. Michael Seats, *Murakami Haruki*, 303–4.

57. Carl Cassegård, *Shock and Naturalization*, 164, 162.

58. Carl Cassegård, "Murakami Haruki and the Naturalization of Modernity," 90.

59. Saitō Tamaki, "Kairi no gihō," 64–65.

60. Matthew Strecher, *Dancing with Sheep*, 127.

61. Fredric Jameson, "Culture and Finance Capital," 247.

62. Nakai Hisao, Iida Yoshihiko, and Fujikawa Yōko, "Kairi genshō o megutte," 13.

63. David Michael Levin, "Introduction," 1.

64. David Michael Levin, "Psychopathology in the Epoch of Nihilism," 36.

65. Kimura Bin et al., "'Bunretsubyō' o megutte," 7, 10, 47, 12.

66. Miyadai Shinji, "Kodomo o torimaku ima to mirai," 39.

67. Yutaka Nagahara, *"Monsieur le Capital,"* 300.

68. David Harvey, *The Condition of Postmodernity*, 351.

69. R. D. Laing, *The Divided Self*, 34.

70. Ian Hacking, *Rewriting the Soul*, 103.

71. Brad Foote and Jane Park, "Dissociative Identity Disorder and Schizophrenia," 217.

72. Saitō Tamaki, *Kairi no poppu sukiru*, 115.

73. Kayama Rika, *Tajūka suru riaru*, 181.

74. Saitō Tamaki, *Kairi no poppu sukiru*, 300.

75. Fredric Jameson, *Postmodernism, or the Cultural Logic of Late Capitalism*, 26.

76. Mark Fisher, *Capitalist Realism*, 19.

77. Oliver James, *The Selfish Capitalist*, 39.

78. James Glass, "Schizophrenia and Rationality," 433–34.

79. Robert Jay Lifton, *The Protean Self*, 210.

80. Kai Erikson, "Notes on Trauma and Community," 185 (original emphasis).

81. Yumiko Iida, "Between the Technique," 458.

82. Paul Antze and Michael Lambek, "Introduction," xxiii.

83. Susan Sontag, *Illness as Metaphor*, 63.

84. Emily Martin, *Bipolar Expeditions*, 29, 9.

85. Azuma Hiroki, *Dōbutsuka suru posutomodan*, 161–69.

86. Paul Antze and Michael Lambek, "Introduction," xxiii.

87. Jeremy Hawthorn, *Multiple Personality*, 44, 116 (original emphasis).

88. Colin Ross, *Dissociative Identity Disorder*, 216.

89. Joseph Gemin, "Insiders in the Body," 265 (original emphasis).

90. Raymond Williams, *The Long Revolution*, 63.

91. Raymond Williams, *Marxism and Literature*, 132.

92. Michiko Kakutani, "On a Nightmarish Trek."

93. Matthew Strecher, *Dances with Sheep*, 61; Ōtsuka Eiji, *"Otaku" no seishinshi*, 364.

94. Elaine Showalter, *Hystories*, 4.

95. Geoff Dyer, "Marathon Man."

96. Janet Maslin, "A Tokyo with Two Moons and Many More Puzzles," *New York Times*, 9 November 2011.

97. Haruki Murakami, *1Q84*, 727 (original emphasis). Further page references to this source are made parenthetically in the following paragraphs.

98. Haruki Murakami, *Colorless Tsukuru Tazaki*, 46.

99. Judith Eve Lipton, "*1Q84*."

CONCLUSION

1. Tatsumi Takayuki, *Nihon henryū bungaku*, 251.

2. "'Kitchen' a U.S. Best Seller: Yoshimoto's Novel Becomes an American Success," *Japan Times*, 30 January 1993.

3. Tim Parks, "The Dull New Global Novel," 26.

4. Takayuki Tatsumi, *Full Metal Apache*, 171.

5. "Memoirs of a Geisha—Official Site," *Sony Pictures*. http://www.sonypictures.com/movies/memoirsofageisha.

6. Kana Yamada, "Survey: High School Girls Use Mobile Phones 7 Hours Daily," *Asahi shinbun*, 10 February 2015.

7. Norimitsu Onishi, "Thumbs Race as Japan's Best Sellers Go Cellular," *New York Times*, 20 January 2008.

8. Sugiura Yumiko, *Keitai shōsetsu no riaru*, 6, 142–43, 178.

9. Azuma Hiroki, *Gēmuteki riarizumu no tanjō*, 140–42.

10. Azuma Hiroki, "Superflat Japanese Postmodernity."

11. Karatani Kōjin, "Kindai bungaku no owari," 6.

12. Minae Mizumura, *The Fall of Language*, x, 46.

13. Itō Ujitaka, "'Bungaku no shūen' no shūen," 234, 240–54.

14. Ōe Kenzaburō, "A Novelist's Lament," *Japan Times*, 23 November 1986.

15. Ōe Kenzaburō, *Aimai na Nihon no watakushi*, 11.

16. Kimata Satoshi, "Media kankyō to bungaku," 107–8.

17. Etō Jun, quoted in Ōtsuka Eiji, *Etō Jun*, 60–61.

18. Katō Norihiro, *Shōsetsu no mirai*, 347.

19. D. A. Miller, *The Novel and the Police*, x.

20. Takahashi Gen'ichirō, "Meikinguobu," 216.

21. Andrew Pollack, "Japan's Newest Young Heartthrobs Are Sexy, Talented and Virtual," *New York Times*, 25 November 1996.

22. Takayuki Tatsumi, *Full Metal Apache*, 9.

23. Claude Lévi-Strauss, *The Other Side of the Moon*, 51.

24. Kawamura Minato, *Sengo bungaku*, 195.

25. Linda Hutcheon, *A Theory of Parody*, 1, 5.

26. M. M. Bakhtin, "From the Prehistory of Novelistic Discourse," 51, 76.

27. Karl Marx, quoted in Pavek Petr, "Marxist Theories of the Comic," 57.

28. Takahashi Toshio, "Kassō suru parodi," 73.

29. Takemoto Kenji, *Uroborosu no gisho*, 9.

30. Suga Hidemi, "Posuto 'kindai bungakushi,'" 30.

31. Eric Gans, "The End of Literature."

32. Fujii Sadakazu, *Nihon bungaku genryū shi*, 26, 435–37.

33. Takahashi Gen'ichirō, *Boku ga shimaumago o shabetta koro*, 52–54.

34. Larry McCaffery, Sinda Gregory, and Yoshiaki Koshikawa, "Why Not Have Fun?," 198; Takahashi Gen'ichirō, *Boku ga shimaumago o shabetta koro*, 44–46.

35. Takahashi Gen'ichirō, *Jon Renon tai Kaseijin*, 16–17.

36. Takahashi Gen'ichirō and Homura Hiroshi, "Meiji kara tōku hanarete," 135.

37. Aoyama Minami, "Takahashi Gen'ichirō ron," 354.

38. Takahashi Gen'ichirō, Katō Norihiro, and Nagae Akira, "Kotoba—kakumei—sekkusu," 19.

39. Takahashi Gen'ichirō, *Otona*, 1–2, 3–4.

40. Takahashi Gen'ichirō and Komori Yōichi, "Ikita bungakushi," 10.

41. Takahashi Gen'ichirō, *Kannō shōsetsuka*, 58, 418–30, 106.

42. Takahashi Gen'ichirō et al, "Zadankai Shōwa bungakushi," 204–5.

43. Takahashi Gen'ichirō, "*Nihon bungaku seisuishi* tsui ni kankō."

44. Takahashi Gen'ichirō, *Otona*, 7.

45. Takahashi Gen'ichirō and Homura Hiroshi, "Meiji kara tōku hanarete," 136.

46. Takahashi Gen'ichirō and Okuizumi Hikaru, "Kokyō e no sesshon," 190, 193.

47. Takahashi Gen'ichirō and Komori Yōichi, "Ikita bungakushi," 12.

48. Takahashi Gen'ichirō and Homura Hiroshi, "Meiji kara tōku hanarete," 150.

49. Takahashi Gen'ichirō, *Nihon bungaku seisuishi*, 32–48. Further page references to this source are made parenthetically throughout the chapter.

50. Katō Norihiro, *Shōsetsu no mirai*, 188.

51. Katō Norihiro, "Gendai shōsetsuron kōgi (15)," 61.

52. Takahashi Gen'ichirō et al, "Zadankai Shōwa bungakushi," 176.

53. Fredric Jameson, "Postmodernism and Consumer Society," 114, 115 (original emphasis).

54. Takahashi Gen'ichirō and Homura Hiroshi, "Meiji kara tōku hanarete," 140.

55. Takahashi Gen'ichirō, *Nippon no shōsetsu*, 135.

56. Wayne Booth, *A Rhetoric of Irony*, 123.

57. Linda Hutcheon, *The Politics of Postmodernism*, 89–90.

58. Takahashi Gen'ichirō, *Bungaku ja nai ka mo shirenai*, 184.

59. Takahashi Gen'ichirō, *Nippon no shōsetsu*, 135.

60. John Mertz, *Novel Japan*, 117–18.

61. Masao Miyoshi, "A Borderless World?," 743–44.

62. Benedict Anderson, *The Spectre of Comparisons*, 333–35, 363.

63. Walter Benjamin, quoted in Benedict Anderson, *The Spectre of Comparisons*, 351.

64. Michael Hardt and Antonio Negri, *Empire*, 309.

65. Takahashi Gen'ichirō, *Nippon no shōsetsu*, 367–68, 365.

66. Kenichi Ohmae, *The End of the Nation-State*, 12, 16.

67. Kenichi Ohmae, "Putting Global Logic First," 125.

68. Michael Hardt and Antonio Negri, *Empire*, xii.

69. Yoko Tawada, "Eine Heidin," 249.

70. Marjorie Perloff, "Foreword," viii.

71. Keijirō Suga, "Translation, Exophony, Omniphony," 28–29.

72. Takahashi Gen'ichirō, *Boku ga shimaumago o shabetta koro*, 236.

73. Takahashi Gen'ichirō and Okuizumi Hikaru, "Kokyō e no sesshon," 181, 189.

74. Ōe Kenzaburō, *Aimai na Nihon no watakushi*, 3.

75. Takahashi Gen'ichirō, *Nippon no shōsetsu*, 365.

76. Fredric Jameson, "Third-World Literature in the Era of Multinational Capitalism," 67.

77. Satō Izumi, "Kindai bungakushi," 182.

78. Gianni Vattimo, *The End of Modernity*, 4.

79. Fredric Jameson, "The End of Temporality," 695, 712.

80. Yokoyama Yūta, *Wagahai wa neko ni naru*, 8.

81. Benedict Anderson, *Imagined Communities*, 14.

82. Hoshino Tomoyuki, *Naburiai*, 30–31, 58, 29, 30.

83. See, for example, Christopher Hill, *National History*, 77–81.

84. Douglas McGray, "Japan's Gross National Cool."

85. Andreas Gailus, "Modern Epic," 175.

86. Franco Moretti, *Atlas of the European Novel*, 17.

87. William Gibson, "My Own Private Tokyo."

88. William Gibson and Alexandre Kojève, quoted in Eric Hayot, "Through the Mirror."

89. H. D. Harootunian, "Remembering the Historical Present," 485, 472.

90. Murakami Ryū, "'Basho : jibun' atogaki," 185.

91. Murakami Ryū, *Kibō no kuni no ekusodasu*, 8–21.

92. Mark Fisher, *Ghosts of My Life*, 7–8, 14.

93. Perry Anderson, *A Zone of Engagement*, 352, 282.

94. Kasai Kiyoshi, *Shūen no owari*, 7, 11–14.

95. Fredric Jameson, *Archaeologies of the Future*, xiii.

96. Yoko Tawada, "The Island," 7.

97. Takahashi Gen'ichirō, Okuizumi Hikaru, and Shimada Masahiko, "Teidan Okuizumi Hikaru x Takahashi Gen'ichirō, and Shimada Masahiko," 154, 156–57, 160–61, 164.

98. Michael Stipe, quoted in Larry McCaffery and Sinda Gregory, "Introduction," 20.

99. William Gibson, quoted in Takayuki Tatsumi, *Full Metal Apache*, 180.

100. Fredric Jameson, *Archaeologies of the Future*, 384.

101. Fredric Jameson, "The End of Temporality," 704, 706–7.

102. J. Hillis Miller, "Paul de Man at Work," 88.

103. Amir Eshel, *Futurity*, 16.

104. Hideo Furukawa, *Horses*, 61, 127.

105. Tessa Morris-Suzuki, "Touching the Grass," 357.

106. Julia Adeney Thomas, "The Cage of Nature," 34.

107. Haruki Murakami, *Hard-Boiled Wonderland and the End of the World*, 271.

108. Takahashi Gen'ichirō, "Kaisetsu," 378.

109. Numa Shōzō, *Kachikujin Yapū*, 5:336. Further page references to this source are made parenthetically throughout the chapter.

110. Tomoko Aoyama, *Reading Food*, 129.

111. Kō Yoshio, "*Kachikujin Yapū* hiwa," 257.

112. Thomas LaMarre, "Speciesism, Part II," 69.

113. Jason Herlands, "Rewriting History," 51.

114. Aramata Hiroshi, "Kaisetsu," 353.

115. Takahashi Gen'ichirō, "Kaisetsu," 383 (original emphasis).

116. Aramata Hiroshi, "Kaisetsu," 334–35.

117. Sylvain Cardonnel, "Nishida avec Numa," 17.

118. Maeda Muneo, "Kaisetsu," 318.

119. Aramata Hiroshi, "Kaisetsu," 338.

120. Gilles Deleuze, *Masochism*, 33.

121. Fredric Jameson, *Archaeologies of the Future*, 211.

122. Mark Fisher, *Capitalist Realism*, 2.

123. Koyama Tetsurō, "'Numa Shōzō' kaikenki," 256–57; Okuno Takeo, "Kaisetsu," 353.

124. Kō Yoshio, "*Kachikujin Yapū* hiwa," 256–57.

125. Mishima Yukio and Terayama Shūji, "Erosu," 154.

126. Fredric Jameson, *Archaeologies of the Future*, 288.

127. Numa Shōzō, quoted in Jason Herlands, "Rewriting History," 67.

128. Mishima Yukio, *Shōsetsu to wa nani ka*, 118.

129. Yoko Tawada, "Tawada Yōko Does Not Exist," 17.

130. Yoko Tawada, "Zukunft ohne Herkunft," 61.

131. Okuno Takeo, "Kaisetsu," 354.

132. Takayuki Tatsumi, "Comparative Metafiction," 14.

133. Numa Shōzō, quoted in Koyama Tetsurō, "'Numa Shōzō' kaikenki," 257.

134. Tatsumi Takayuki, "Kaisetsu," 372–73, 395.

135. Takahashi Gen'ichirō, "Dōbutsu no shanikusai," 19–21.

136. Takahashi Gen'ichirō, "Uchū sensō," 126, 128.

137. Jacques Derrida, *The Animal That Therefore I Am*, 32.

138. Takahashi Gen'ichirō, "Soshite, itsu no hi ni ka," 86–92.

139. Furukawa Hideo, *Doggumazā*, 9.

140. Tawada Yōko, *Dōbutsu-tachi no Baberu*.

141. Hideo Furukawa, *Belka*, 307.

142. Alexandre Kojève, *Introduction to the Reading of Hegel*, 161.

143. Azuma Hiroki, *Dōbutsuka suru posutomodan*, 125–28.

144. Mary McCarthy, "The Fact in Fiction," 440.

145. Takahashi Gen'ichirō, "Dōbutsuki," 271, 272.

146. Jacques Derrida, *The Animal That Therefore I Am*, 135 (original emphasis).

147. Christine Marran, "Literature Without Us."

148. Takahashi Gen'ichirō, *Kannō shōsetsuka*, 287.

Bibliography

Abe Kōbō. "Kureōru no tama." *Sekai* 500 (April 1987): 295–305.

Abel, Ernest. *The Handwriting on the Wall: Toward a Sociology and Psychology of Graffiti.* Westport, CT: Greenwood Press, 1977.

Adorno, Theodor, and Max Horkheimer. "The Culture Industry: Enlightenment as Mass Deception." In *The Cultural Studies Reader,* edited by Simon During, 314–41. London: Routledge, 1993.

Aeba Takao. *Nihon kindai no seikimatsu.* Tokyo: Bungei shunjū, 1990.

Akita, George. *Foundations of Constitutional Government in Modern Japan, 1868–1900.* Cambridge, MA: Harvard University Press, 1967.

Alcorn, Marshall W., Jr. *Narcissism and the Literary Libido: Rhetoric, Text, and Subjectivity.* New York: New York University Press, 1994.

Alford, C. Fred. *Narcissism: Socrates, the Frankfurt School, and Psychoanalytic Theory.* New Haven, CT: Yale University Press, 1988.

Altman, Albert A. "The Press." In *Japan in Transition, from Tokugawa to Meiji,* edited by Marius B. Jansen and Gilbert Rozman, 231–47. Princeton, NJ: Princeton University Press, 1986.

American Psychiatric Association. *Diagnostic and Statistical Manual of Mental Disorders: DSM-IV.* Washington, DC: American Psychiatric Association, 1994.

An, Katsumasa, Shunzo Kobayashi, Kiwamu Tanaka, Hiroyuki Kaneda, Minoru

Sugibayashi, and Junko Okazaki. "Dissociative Identity Disorder and Childhood Trauma in Japan." *Psychiatry and Clinical Neurosciences*, 52 suppl. (1998): S111–14.

An Ushiku. "'Teikō no sakka' no shōgai—Kin Shiryō no jidai." In *Nihon to Chōsen no aida*, edited by Kim Sam-kyu, 194–222. Tokyo: Asahi shinbunsha, 1980.

Anderson, Benedict. *Imagined Communities: Reflections on the Origin and Spread of Nationalism*. London: Verso, 1983.

———. *The Spectre of Comparisons: Nationalism, Southeast Asia, and the World*. London: Verso, 1998.

Anderson, Perry. *A Zone of Engagement*. London: Verso, 1992.

Antze, Paul, and Michael Lambek. "Introduction: Forecasting Memory." In *Tense Past: Cultural Essays in Trauma and Memory*, edited by Paul Antze and Michael Lambek, xi–xxxviii. London: Routledge, 1996.

Aoyama Minami. "Takahashi Gen'ichirō ron—'kakkō' bakari no sekai." *Bungei* 25, no. 5 (December 1986): 354–57.

Aoyama, Tomoko. *Reading Food in Modern Japanese Literature*. Honolulu: University of Hawai'i Press, 2008.

Aramata Hiroshi. "Kaisetsu." In Numa, *Kachikujin Yapū 4*, 334–54.

Asahi jānaru henshūbu. "Garatto shita hōrōsha." *Asahi jānaru* 13, no. 16 (30 April 1971): 31–36.

———. "Marukusu to manga (sono ichi)." *Asahi jānaru* 13, no. 13 (4 April 1971): 31–35.

Asano Yō, and Ōta Noboru, eds. *Sōseki sakuhinron shūsei*. Vol. 1, *Wagahai wa neko de aru*. Tokyo: Ōfūsha, 1990.

Awazu Norio. *Jigazō wa kataru*. Tokyo: Shinchōsha, 1993.

Azuma Hiroki. *Dōbutsuka suru posutomodan*. Tokyo: Kōdansha, 2001.

———. *Gēmuteki riarizumu no tanjō—dōbutsuka suru posutomodan 2*. Tokyo: Kōdansha, 2007.

———. "Superflat Japanese Postmodernity." Lecture given at the MOCA Gallery, Pacific Design Center, 5 April 2001. Accessed 12 November 2016. https://web.archive.org/web/20040223082912/http://www.hirokiazuma.com/en/texts/superflat_en1.html.

Azuma Tamaki. *Kishida Ryūsei to sono shūhen*. Tokyo: Higashi shuppan, 1974.

———. *Taishō-ki no seishun gunzō—hyūmanizumu no taido*. Tokyo: Bijutsu kōronsha, 1984.

Bakhtin, M. M. *The Dialogic Imagination: Four Essays*. Edited by Michael Holquist. Translated by Caryl Emerson and Michael Holquist. Austin: University of Texas Press, 1990.

———. "From the Prehistory of Novelistic Discourse." In *The Dialogic Imagination: Four Essays*, 41–83.

———. *Rabelais and His World*. Translated by Helene Iswolsky. Bloomington: Indiana University Press, 1984.

Barshay, Andrew. "Postwar Social and Political Thought, 1945–90." In *Modern Japanese*

Thought, edited by Bob Tadashi Wakabayashi, 273–355. Cambridge: Cambridge University Press, 1997.

Barthes, Roland. *The Empire of Signs*. Translated by Richard Howard. New York: Hill and Wang, 1982.

———. *S/Z*. Translated by Richard Miller. Oxford: Blackwell, 1992.

Baudrillard, Jean. *For a Critique of the Political Economy of the Sign*. Translated by Charles Levin. Saint Louis, MO: Telos Press, 1981.

Beasley, W. G. *The Modern History of Japan*. New York: Praeger, 1967.

———, ed. *Modern Japan: Aspects of History, Literature, and Society*. Berkeley: University of California Press, 1977.

Beckmann, George M. *The Making of the Meiji Constitution: The Oligarchs and the Constitutional Development of Japan, 1868–1891*. Westport, CT: Greenwood, 1975.

Beer, Lawrence Ward. *Freedom of Expression in Japan: A Study in Comparative Law, Politics, and Society*. Tokyo: Kodansha International, 1984.

Berman, Marshall. *Everything That Is Solid Melts into Air: The Experience of Modernity*. New York: Simon and Schuster, 1982.

———. "Why Modernism Still Matters." In *Modernity and Identity*, edited by Scott Lash and Jonathan Friedman, 33–58. Oxford: Blackwell, 1992.

Bernstein, Gail Lee. "Women in the Silk-Reeling Industry in Nineteenth-Century Japan." In *Japan and the World: Essays on Japanese History and Politics in Honour of Ishida Takeshi*, edited by Gail Lee Bernstein, Haruhiro Fukui, and Ishida Takeshi, 54–77. Basingstoke, UK: Macmillan, 1988.

Berry, Mary Elizabeth. *Japan in Print: Information and Nation in the Early Modern Period*. Berkeley: University of California Press, 2006.

Bhaba, Homi, ed. *Nation and Narration*. London: Routledge, 1990.

Bickerton, Derek. *Dynamics of a Creole System*. Cambridge: Cambridge University Press, 1975.

———. *The Roots of Language*. Ann Arbor, MI: Karoma Publishers, 1981.

Blacker, Carmen. *The Japanese Enlightenment: A Study of the Writings of Fukuzawa Yukichi*. Cambridge: Cambridge University Press, 1964.

Blume, Regina. "Graffiti." In *Discourse and Literature*, edited by Teun A. Van Dijk, 137–48. Amsterdam: J. Benjamins Publishing Company, 1985.

Booth, Wayne C. *A Rhetoric of Irony*. Chicago: University of Chicago Press, 1974.

Bourdaghs, Michael. *Sayonara Amerika, Sayonara Nippon: A Geopolitical Prehistory of J-Pop*. New York: Columbia University Press, 2012.

Brennan, Timothy. "The National Longing for Form." In *Nation and Narration*, edited by Homi Bhaba, 44–70. London: Routledge, 1990.

Buell, Lawrence. "Literary History as a Hybrid Genre." In Cox and Reynolds, *New Historical Literary Study*, 216–29.

Burks, Ardath W. "The Politics of Modernization: The Autonomy of Choice." In Ward, *Political Development in Modern Japan*, 537–75.

Buruma, Ian. "Weeping Tears of Nostalgia." *New York Review of Books* XL, no. 14 (12 August 1993): 29–30.

Campbell, Robert, Tomiyama Takao, Togawa Shinsuke, and Yamada Shunji. "Tsuzuku . . . shinbun shōsetsu no tsūro." *Bungaku* 4, no. 1 (January–February 2003): 2–33.

Cardonnel, Sylvain. "Nishida avec Numa: le Japon et les démons de la modernité (1/4)." *Kokusai bunka kenkyū* 13 (2009): 15–39.

Cascardi, Anthony J. *The Subject of Modernity*. Cambridge: Cambridge University Press, 1992.

Cassegård, Carl. "Murakami Haruki and the Naturalization of Modernity." *International Journal of Japanese Sociology* 10 (2001): 80–92.

———. *Shock and Naturalization in Contemporary Japanese Literature*. Folkestone, UK: Global Oriental, 2007.

Centre for East Asian Cultural Studies. *Meiji Japan through Contemporary Sources 1*. Tokyo: Yunesuko Higashi Ajia bunka kenkyū sentā, 1972.

Chamberlain, Basil Hall. *Things Japanese: Being Notes on Various Subjects Connected with Japan, for the Use of Travelers and Others*. Rutland, VT: Tuttle, 1971.

Ch'en, Paul Heng-Chao. *The Formation of the Early Meiji Legal Code: The Japanese Code of 1871 and its Chinese Foundation*. Oxford: Oxford University Press, 1981.

Cho, Heekyoung. *Translation's Forgotten History: Russian Literature, Japanese Mediation, and the Formation of Modern Korean Literature*. Cambridge, MA: Harvard University Asia Center, 2016.

Chow, Rey. "Theory, Area Studies, Cultural Studies: Issues of Pedagogy in Multicultural-ism." In *Learning Places: The Afterlives of Area Studies*, edited by Masao Miyoshi and H. D. Harootunian, 10–18. Durham, NC: Duke University Press, 2002.

Cohen, Anthony P., and Nigel Rapport, eds. *Questions of Consciousness*. London: Routledge, 1995.

Cohen, Ralph. "Generating Literary Histories." In Cox and Reynolds, *New Historical Literary Study*, 39–53.

Copleton, Jackie. "5 Essential Japanese Writers." Bookriot.com. Accessed 12 November 2016. http://bookriot.com/2015/12/11/5-essential-japanesewriters/?utm_campaign =SocialFlow&utm_source=twitter.com&utm_medium=referral.

Cox, Jeffrey N., and Larry J. Reynolds. *New Historical Literary Study: Essays on Reproducing Texts, Representing History*. Princeton, NJ: Princeton University Press, 1993.

Crump, Thomas. *The Death of an Emperor: Japan at the Crossroads*. London: Constable, 1989.

Cumings, Bruce. "The Legacy of Japanese Colonialism in Korea." In *The Japanese Colonial Empire, 1895–1945*, edited by Ramon Myers and Mark R. Peattie, 478–96. Princeton, NJ: Princeton University Press, 1984.

Danly, Robert Lyons. *In the Shade of Spring Leaves: The Life and Writings of Higuchi Ichiyō, a Woman of Letters in Meiji Japan.* New York: W. W. Norton and Company, 1981.

Davidson, Cathy N. *Revolution and the Word: The Rise of the Novel in America.* Oxford: Oxford University Press, 1986.

Davis, Lennard J. *Factual Fictions: The Origins of the English Novel.* New York: Columbia University Press, 1983.

———. "A Social History of Fact and Fiction: Authorial Disavowal in the Early English Novel." In *Literature and Society,* edited by Edward Said, 120–48. Baltimore, MD: Johns Hopkins University Press, 1980.

De Becker, J. E. *The Nightless City: Or the "History of the Yoshiwara Yūkwaku."* London: Max Nössler & Co., 1906.

Deleuze, Gilles. *Masochism: An Interpretation of Coldness and Cruelty.* Translated by Jean McNeil and Aude Willm. New York: George Braziller, 1971.

Deleuze, Gilles, and Félix Guattari. *Anti-Oedipus: Capitalism and Schizophrenia.* Translated by Robert Hurley, Mark Seem, and Helen R. Lane. Minneapolis: University of Minnesota Press, 1983.

De Man, Paul. "Autobiography as De-Facement." *MLN* 94, no. 5 (December 1979): 919–30.

———. "Literary History and Literary Modernity." *Daedalus* 99, no. 2 (Spring 1970): 384–404.

Denvir, Bernard. *Vincent, A Complete Portrait: All of Vincent Van Gogh's Self-Portraits, With Excerpts from his Writings.* Philadelphia, PA: Running Press, 1994.

Derrida, Jacques. *The Animal That Therefore I Am.* Edited by Mare-Louise Mallet. Translated by David Wills. New York: Fordham University Press, 2008.

———. *Memoirs of the Blind: The Self-Portrait and Other Ruins.* Chicago: University of Chicago Press, 1993.

Doane, Mary Ann. "The Economy of Desire: The Commodity Form in/of the Cinema." *Quarterly Review of Film and Video* 11, no. 1 (1989): 23–35.

Dore, Ronald P. *Education in Tokugawa Japan.* Berkeley: University of California Press, 1965.

Dower, John W. *Embracing Defeat: Japan in the Wake of World War II.* New York: W. W. Norton, 1999.

———. Introduction to *A Political History of Japanese Capitalism,* by John Halliday, xvii–xxxiii. New York: Pantheon Books, 1975.

Dowsey, Stuart. *Zengakuren: Japan's Revolutionary Students.* Berkeley: Ishi Press, 1970.

Duus, Peter. "Liberal Intellectuals and Social Conflict in Taishō Japan." In Najita and Koschmann, *Conflict in Modern Japanese History,* 412–40.

———, ed. *The Cambridge History of Japan.* Vol. 6, *The Twentieth Century.* Cambridge: Cambridge University Press, 2008.

Dyer, Geoff. "Marathon Man." *New York Times Sunday Book Review,* 10 August 2008, 16.

Eagleton, Terry. *Walter Benjamin; or, Towards a Revolutionary Criticism*. London: Verso, 1981.

Eckert, Carter J. *Offspring of Empire: The Koch'ang Kims and the Colonial Origins of Korean Capitalism, 1876–1945*. Seattle: University of Washington Press, 1996.

Ellis, Bret Easton. *American Psycho*. New York: Vintage Books, 1991.

Erikson, Kai. "Notes on Trauma and Community." In *Trauma: Explorations in Memory*, edited by Cathy Caruth, 183–99. Baltimore, MD: Johns Hopkins University Press, 1995.

Eshel, Amir. *Futurity: Contemporary Literature and the Quest for the Past*. Chicago: University of Chicago Press, 2013.

Estren, Mark James. *A History of Underground Comics*. San Francisco: Straight Arrow Books, 1974.

Etō Jun. *Etō Jun bungaku shūsei 1*. Tokyo: Kawade shobō shinsha, 1984.

Evans, David T. *Sexual Citizenship: The Material Construction of Sexualities*. London: Routledge, 1993.

Fanon, Frantz. *Black Skin, White Masks*. Translated by Charles Lam Markmann. New York: Grove Press, 1967.

Fehrenbach, Heide, and Uta G. Poiger. "Introduction: Americanization Reconsidered." In Fehrenbach and Poiger, *Transactions, Transgressions, Transformation*, xiii–xl.

Fehrenbach, Heide, and Uta G. Poiger, eds. *Transactions, Transgressions, Transformation: American Culture in Western Europe and Japan*. New York: Bergahn Books, 1999.

Ferrell, Jeff. *Crimes of Style: Urban Graffiti and the Politics of Criminality*. Boston: Northeastern University Press, 1996.

Figal, Gerald. *Civilization and Monsters: Spirits of Modernity in Meiji Japan*. Durham, NC: Duke University Press, 1999.

Filmer, Paul. "Structures of Feeling and Socio-Cultural Formations: The Significance of Literature and Experience to Raymond Williams's Sociology of Culture." *British Journal of Sociology* 54, no. 2 (2003): 199–219.

Fine, Reuben. *Narcissism, the Self and Society*. New York: Columbia University Press, 1986.

Fisher, Mark. *Capitalist Realism: Is There No Alternative?* Winchester, UK: Zero Books, 2009.

———. *Ghosts of My Life: Writings on Depression, Hauntology and Lost Futures*. Winchester, UK: Zero Books, 2014.

Fisher, Susan. "An Allegory of Return: Murakami Haruki's *The Wind-up Bird Chronicle*." *Comparative Literature Studies* 27, no. 2 (2000): 155–70.

Fiske, John. *Television Culture*. New York: Methuen, 1987.

Folkenflik, Robert. *The Culture of Autobiography: Constructions of Self-Expression*. Stanford, CA: Stanford University Press, 1993.

Foote, Brad, and Jane Park. "Dissociative Identity Disorder and Schizophrenia." *Current Psychiatry Reports* 10 (2008): 217–22.

Foucault, Michel. *The Birth of the Clinic: An Archaeology of Medical Perception.* Translated by A. M. Sheridan Smith. New York: Pantheon Books, 1973.

———. *Discipline and Punish: The Birth of the Prison.* Translated by Alan Sheridan. New York: Pantheon Books, 1977.

———. *The Foucault Reader.* Edited by Paul Rabinow. New York: Pantheon Books, 1984.

———. *The Order of Things: An Archaeology of the Human Sciences.* New York: Pantheon Books, 1973.

———. "Truth and Power." In *The Foucault Reader,* 51–75.

———. "What Is an Author?" In *The Foucault Reader,* 101–20.

Fowler, Edward. *The Rhetoric of Confession: Shishōsetsu in Early Twentieth Century Japanese Fiction.* Berkeley: University of California Press, 1988.

———. *San'ya Blues: Laboring Life in Contemporary Tokyo.* Ithaca, NY: Cornell University Press, 1996.

———. "Shishosetsu in Modern Japanese Literature." Working Papers in Asian/Pacific Studies, Asian/Pacific Institute, Duke University, 1986.

Freud, Sigmund. *Leonardo da Vinci: A Study in Psychosexuality.* Translated by A. A. Brill. Vintage Books, 1947.

———. "Mourning and Melancholia." In *A General Selection from the Works of Sigmund Freud,* 125–40. Edited by John Rickman, MD. Translated by Joan Riviere. Garden City, NJ: Doubleday & Company, 1957.

———. "On Narcissism: An Introduction." In *Narcissism: An Introduction,* edited by Joseph Sandler, 3–32. London: Karnac Books, 2012.

Fujii, James A. *Complicit Fictions: The Subject in the Modern Japanese Prose Narrative.* Berkeley: University of California Press, 1993.

Fujii Sadakazu. "Kokubungaku no tanjō." *Shisō* 845 (November 1994): 57–74.

———. *Nihon bungaku genryū shi.* Tokyo: Seidosha, 2016.

Fujii, Yoichiro, Kunifumi Suzuki, Tetsuya Sato, Yasuhiko Murakami, and Toshihiko Takahashi. "Multiple Personality Disorder in Japan." *Psychiatry and Clinical Neurosciences,* 52 (1998): 299–302.

Fujikawa Jisui. "Ninja zankoku monogatari—*Ninja bugeichō* ron." *Shisō no kagaku* 10 (July 1963): 58–63.

Fujimoto, Yukari. "A Life-Size Mirror: Women's Self-Representation in Girls' Comics." *Review of Japanese Culture and Society* 4 (December 1991): 53–57.

Fujitake Akira. *Terebi to no taiwa.* Tokyo: Nihon hōsō shuppan kyōkai, 1974.

Fujitani, Takashi. "Electronic Pageantry and Japan's 'Symbolic Emperor.'" *Journal of Asian Studies* 51, no. 4 (November 1992): 824–50.

———. *Splendid Monarchy: Power and Pageantry in Modern Japan.* Berkeley: University of California Press, 1996.

Fukazawa Shichirō. *Fukazawa Shichirō no metsubō taidan.* Tokyo: Chikuma shobō, 1993.

———. "Fūryū mutan." *Chūō kōron* 75, no. 13 (1960): 328–40.

————. "Kore ga oira no sōkoku da na nikki." *Gunzō* 14, no. 10 (1959): 223.

————. *Rurō no shuki*. Tokyo: Heiwa shinsho, 1963.

"Fukazawa Shichirō no mita yume." *Shūkan bunshin*, 12 December 1960, 56–59.

Fukui, Haruhiko. "Postwar Politics, 1945–1973." In Duus, *The Cambridge History of Japan*, vol. 6, *The Twentieth Century*, 154–214.

Fukuzawa, Yukichi. *The Autobiography of Yukichi Fukuzawa*. Translated by Eiichi Kiyooka. New York: Columbia University Press, 2007.

————. *Fukuzawa Yukichi's An Encouragement of Learning*. New York: Sophia University Press, 1969.

————. *Fukuzawa Yukichi on Japanese Women*. Tokyo: University of Tokyo Press, 1988.

Furukawa, Hideo. *Belka, Why Don't You Bark?* Translated by Michael Emmerich. San Francisco: Haikasoru, 2012.

————. *Doggumazā*. Tokyo: Shinchōsha, 2012.

————. *Horses, Horses, In the End the Light Remains Pure: A Tale That Begins with Fukushima*. Translated by Doug Slaymaker with Akiko Takenaka. New York: Columbia University Press, 2016.

Futabatei Shimei. "Yo ga genbun'itchi no yurai." *Gendai Nihon bungaku taikei I*, 372–73. Tokyo: Chikuma shobō, 1971.

Gadamer, Hans-Georg. *Truth and Method*. Translated by Joel Weinsheimer and Donald G. Marshall. New York: Crossroad, 1989.

Gailus, Andreas. "*Modern Epic: The World System from Goethe to García Marquez* (review)." *Modernism/Modernity* 4, no. 3 (September 1997): 175–77.

Gaines, Jane, and Michael Renov. "Preface: Female Representation and Consumer Culture." *Quarterly Review of Film and Video* 11, no. 1 (1989): vii–viii.

Gallagher, Catherine, and Stephen Greenblatt. *Practicing New Historicism*. Chicago: University of Chicago Press, 2000.

Gans, Eric. "The End of Literature and the Beginning of Literary History." *Chronicles of Love and Resentment* 135 (2 May 1998). http://www.anthropoetics.ucla.edu/views/vw135/.

Garon, Sheldon. "The World's Oldest Debate? Prostitution and the State in Imperial Japan, 1900–1945." *American Historical Review* 98, no. 3 (June 1993): 710–32.

Garrison, Deborah. "Day-O." *New Yorker*, 25 January 1993, 109–10.

Gasser, Manuel. *Self-Portraits from the Fifteenth Century to the Present Day*. Translated by Angus Malcolm. New York: Appleton-Century, 1963.

Gayn, Mark. *Japan Diary*. Rutland, VT: Tuttle, 1984.

Geertz, Clifford. *Local Knowledge: Further Essays in Interpretive Anthropology*. New York: Basic Books, 1983.

Geinōshi kenkyūkai, ed. *Nihon geinōkai 7*. Tokyo: Hōsei daigaku shuppankyoku, 1990.

Gemin, Joseph. "Insiders in the Body: Communication, Multiple Personalities, and the Body Politic." In *Transgressing Discourses: Communication and the Voice of the Other*, edited by Michael Huspek and Gary P. Radford, 251–68. Albany, NY: SUNY Press, 1977.

Gendaishi techō tokushūban Takahashi Gen'ichirō. Tokyo: Shinchōsha, 2008.

Gibson, William. "My Own Private Tokyo." *Wired* 9, no. 9 (September 2001). Accessed 12 November 2016. http://www.wired.com/2001/09/gibson/.

Giddens, Anthony. *The Consequences of Modernity.* Stanford, CA: Stanford University Press, 1990.

Glass, James M. "Schizophrenia and Rationality: On the Function of the Unconscious Fantasy." In Levin, *Pathologies of the Modern Self,* 405–38.

Gluck, Carol. "The 'End' of the Postwar: Japan at the Turn of the Millennium." *Public Culture* 10, no. 1 (1997): 1–23.

———. *Japan's Modern Myths: Ideology in the Late Meiji Period.* Princeton, NJ: Princeton University Press, 1985.

Goldmann, Lucien. *Towards a Sociology of the Novel.* Translated by Alan Sheridan. London: Tavistock Publications, 1975.

Goldscheider, Ludwig, ed. *Five Hundred Self-Portraits from Antique Times to the Present Day, in Sculpture, Painting, Drawing and Engraving.* Translated by J. Byam Shaw. Vienna: Phaidon Press, 1937.

Gordon, Andrew. "The Crowd and Politics in Imperial Japan: Tokyo 1905–1918." *Past & Present* 121 (November 1988): 141–70.

———. *The Evolution of Labor Relations in Japan: Heavy Industry, 1853–1955.* Cambridge, MA: Harvard University Press, 1988.

———. *Labor and Imperial Democracy in Prewar Japan.* Berkeley: University of California Press, 1992.

Gottlieb, Nanette. "Language and Politics." *Journal of Asian Studies* 53, no. 4 (November 1994): 1175–98.

Graff, Gerald. "Co-Optation." In *The New Historicism,* edited by Harold Aram Veeser, 168–81. New York: Taylor and Francis, 1989.

Gramsci, Antonio. "Language, Linguistics, and Folklore." In *Selections from Cultural Writings,* edited by David Forgacs and Geoffrey Nowell-Smith, 164–95. Translated by William Boelhower. Cambridge, MA: Harvard University Press, 1985.

Greenblatt, Stephen. *Shakespearean Negotiations: The Circulation of Social Energy in Renaissance England.* Berkeley: University of California Press, 1988.

Groemer, Gerald. "Singing the News: *Yomiuri* in Japan during the Edo and Meiji Periods." *Harvard Journal of Asiatic Studies* 54, no. 1 (June 1994): 233–61.

Guattari, Félix. *Machinic Eros: Writings on Japan.* Edited by Gary Genosko and Jay Hetrick. Minneapolis, MN: Univocal, 2015.

Gunji Masakatsu. "'Akuba' to 'dokufu.'" *Edo bungaku* 12 (December 1994): 4–11.

Habermas, Jürgen. "Modernity—An Incomplete Project." Translated by Seyla Benhabib.

In *The Anti-Aesthetic: Essays on Postmodern Culture*, edited by Hal Foster, 3–15. Port Townsend, WA: Bay Press, 1983.

———. *The Philosophical Discourse of Modernity: Twelve Lectures*. Translated by Frederick Lawrence. Cambridge, MA: MIT Press, 1987.

———. *Structural Transformation of the Public Sphere: An Inquiry into a Category of Bourgeois Society*. Translated by Thomas Berger with the assistance of Frederick Lawrence. Cambridge, MA: MIT Press, 1989.

Hacking, Ian. *Rewriting the Soul: Multiple Personality and the Sciences of Memory*. Princeton, NJ: Princeton University Press, 1995.

———. "Two Souls in One Body." *Critical Inquiry* 17 (Summer 1991): 838–67.

Haga Tōru. "The Formation of Realism in Meiji Painting: The Artistic Career of Takahashi Yūichi." In *Tradition and Modernization in Japanese Culture*, edited by Donald H. Shively, 221–56. Princeton, NJ: Princeton University Press, 1971.

———. *Kaiga no ryōbun: kindai Nihon no hikaku bunkashi no kenkyū*. Tokyo: Asahi shinbunsha, 1990.

———. "Senzen Shōwa no Nihon bunjin to Kankoku." In *Nikkan bunka ron*, edited by Zai-Nihon Kankoku bunkain, 157–73. Tokyo: Gakuseisha, 1994.

Hall, John Whitney. "Changing Conceptions of the Modernization of Japan." In Jansen, *Changing Japanese Attitudes toward Modernization*, 7–41.

———. "A Monarch for Modern Japan." In Ward, *Political Development in Modern Japan*, 11–64.

Hall, Stuart. "Culture, Community, Nation." *Cultural Studies* 7, no. 3 (1993): 349–63.

Halliday, Jon. *A Political History of Japanese Capitalism*. New York: Random House, 1975.

Hannerz, Ulf. "Scenarios for Peripheral Cultures." In *Culture, Globalization and the World-System: Contemporary Conditions for the Representation of Identity*, edited by Anthony D. King, 107–28. Binghamton, NY: Department of Art and Art History, SUNY at Binghamton, 1991.

Harada, Minoru. *Meiji Western Painting*. Translated by Akiko Murakata. New York: Weatherhill and Shinbundō, 1974.

Hardacre, Helen. *Shintō and the State*. Princeton, NJ: Princeton University Press, 1989.

Hardt, Michael, and Antonio Negri. *Empire*. Cambridge, MA: Harvard University Press, 2000.

Harootunian, H. D. "Late Tokugawa Culture and Thought." In Jansen, *The Cambridge History of Japan*, vol. 5, *The Nineteenth Century*, 168–258.

———. "Remembering the Historical Present." *Critical Inquiry* 33 (Spring 2007): 471–94.

———. "Visible Discourses/Invisible Ideologies." In Miyoshi and Harootunian, *Postmodernism and Japan*, 63–92.

Harvey, David. *The Condition of Postmodernity: An Enquiry into the Origins of Cultural Change*. Oxford: Blackwell, 1989.

Hasegawa Izumi. "'Fūryū mutan.'" *Kokubungaku* 21, no. 8 (June 1972): 100–2.

Hasegawa Nyozekan. "Sōseki to Edokko bungaku." *Hasegawa Nyozekan shū* 6, 360–70. Tokyo: Iwanami shoten, 1990.

Hattori Ryōichi. *Boku no ongaku jinsei—episōdo de tsuzuru wasei jazu songu shi.* Tokyo: Chūō bungeisha, 1982.

———. "Kaisō no Kasagi Shizuko." *Bungei shunjū* 63, no. 6 (June 1985): 286–90.

Hawthorn, Jeremy. *Multiple Personality and Disintegration of Literary Character: From Oliver Goldsmith to Sylvia Plath.* New York: Palgrave Macmillan, 1983.

Hayashi Fusao. "Chōsen no seishin." *Bungei* 8, no. 7 (July 1940): 194–97.

Hayashi Fusao, Akita Ujaku, Murayama Tomoyoshi, Karajima Takeshi, Furukawa Kenshū, Chŏng Ji-yong, Im Hwa, Yu Chin-o, Kim Mun-jip, Yi Tae-jun, and Yu Ch'i-jin. "Chōsen bunka no shōrai." *Bungakukai* 6, no. 1 (January 1936): 271–79.

Hayashi Shirō. "Nihonkoku kenpō no bunsho." *Gengo seikatsu* 402 (May 1985): 46–51.

Hayot, Eric. "Through the Mirror: Claude Lévi-Strauss in Japan." *Los Angeles Review of Books*, 14 April 2013. Accessed 12 November 2016. https://lareviewofbooks.org /review/through-the-mirror-claude-levi-strauss-in-japan.

Hebdige, Dick. *Cut 'n' Mix: Culture, Identity, and Caribbean Music.* New York: Methuen, 1987.

———. *Subculture: The Meaning of Style.* New York: Routledge, 2002.

Henderson, Dan Fenno. Introduction to Henderson, *The Constitution of Japan*, xi–xv.

Henderson, Dan Fenno, ed. *The Constitution of Japan: Its First Twenty Years, 1947–67.* Seattle: University of Washington Press, 1968.

Herlands, Jason. "Rewriting History: The Intoxicating Hierarchies of *Kachikujin Yapū*." In *PostGender: Gender, Sexuality and Performativity in Japanese Culture*, edited by Ayelet Zohar, 50–69. Newcastle upon Tyne, UK: Cambridge Scholars Publishing, 2009.

Hibbett, Howard. "The Portrait of the Artist in Japanese Fiction." *Far Eastern Quarterly* 14, no. 3 (May 1955): 347–54.

Hibi Yoshitaka. *Bungaku no rekishi o dō kakinaosu no ka—nijū seiki Nihon no shōsetsu kūkan media.* Tokyo: Kasama shoin, 2016.

———. *"Jiko hyōshō" bungakushi—jiko o kaku shōsetsu no tōjō.* Tokyo: Kanrin shobō, 2008.

Higuchi Ichiyō. "Child's Play." In Danly, *In the Shade of Spring Leaves*, 254–87.

———. "Encounters on a Dark Night." In Danly, *In the Shade of Spring Leaves*, 182–204.

———. "A Snowy Day." In Danly, *In the Shade of Spring Leaves*, 174–77.

Hijiya-Kirschnereit, Irmela. *Rituals of Self-Revelation: Shishōsetsu as Literary Genre and Socio-Cultural Phenomenon.* Cambridge, MA: Council on East Asian Studies, Harvard University, 1996.

Hilgard, Ernest R. "Neodissociation Theory." In *Dissociation: Clinical and Theoretical Perspectives*, edited by Stephen Jay Lynn and Judith W. Rhue, 32–51. New York: Guilford Press, 1994.

Hill, Christopher L. *National History and the World of Nations: Capital, State, and the*

Rhetoric of History in Japan, France, and the United States. Durham, NC: Duke University Press, 2008.

Hinotani Teruhiko. "Shiki to Enchō." *Bungaku* 11, no. 53 (November 1985): 190–201.

Hinuma Rintarō. "Sonzai tōshiryoku." In *Ibuse Masuji Fukazawa Shichirō*, edited by Nihon bungaku kenkyū shiryō kankōkai, 229–39. Tokyo: Yūseidō, 1977.

Hirakawa Sukehiro. "Japan's Turn to the West." Translated by Bob Tadashi Wakabayashi. In Jansen, *The Cambridge History of Japan*, vol. 5, *The Nineteenth Century*, 432–98.

Hirano, Kyōko. *Mr. Smith Goes to Tokyo: The Japanese Cinema under the American Occupation, 1945–52.* Washington DC: Smithsonian Institute, 1992.

Hiraoka Masaaki. *Dai kayōron.* Tokyo: Chikuma shobō, 1989.

———. *Utairi suikoden.* Tokyo: Ongaku no tomonosha, 1974.

Hiraoka Masaaki, and Sakuma Shun. "Jakkunaifu no yō ni." In *Bungei bessatsu Fuji Keiko*, edited by Abe Harumasa, 184–91. Tokyo: Kawade shobō, 2013.

Hiraoka Toshio. *Nihon kindai bungaku no shuppatsu.* Tokyo: Kinokuniya shoten, 1973.

Hirasawa Gō. "Rokujū-nendai rakugaki kō." *Gendai shisō* 31, no. 12 (October 2003): 156–60.

Hirata Yumi. "'Dokufu' no tanjō." In *Nyūsu no tanjō—kawaraban to shinbun nishikie no jōhō sekai*, edited by Kinoshita Naoyuki and Yoshimi Shun'ya, 238–55. Tokyo: Tōkyō daigaku sōgō kenkyū hakubutsukan, 1999.

———. "'Onna no monogatari' to iu seido." In *Nashonariti no datsukōchiku*, edited by Sakai Naoki, Brett de Bary, and Iyotani Toshio, 161–82. Tokyo: Kashiwa shobō, 1996.

Hoffmann, Yoel. *Japanese Death Poems.* Rutland, VT: Tuttle, 1986.

Honda Yasuo. "Shinbun shōsetsu no hassei—*Tōkyō e'iri shinbun* o yonde." *Kokubungaku kenkyū shirōkan kiyō* 17 (March 1991): 281–302.

Honma Hisao. "Dokufumono." In *Nihon bungakushi 10 Meiji bungakushi (jōkan)*, 83–105. Tokyo: Tōkyōdō, 1933.

———. "Ese-akumashugi—iwayuru dokufumono no kōsatsu." *Waseda bungaku* 229 (1925): 164–77.

Horikiri Naoto. "Onna wa dokyō, shōjo wa aikyō." In *Shōjoron*, edited by Honda Masuko, 108–28. Tokyo: Aoyumisha, 1991.

Horikoshi Hidemi. *Moeru Nihon bungaku.* Tokyo: Gentōsha, 2008.

Hoshino Tomoyuki. *Naburiai.* Tokyo: Kawabe shobō shinsha, 1999.

Hosoi Wakizō. *Jokō aishi.* Tokyo: Iwanami shoten, 1954.

Hosokawa, Shūhei. "The Swinging Voice of Kasagi Shizuko: Japanese Jazz Culture in the 1930s." In *Japanese Studies Around the World 2006: Research on Art and Music in Japan—A Colloquy with Foreign Scholars Resident in Japan*, edited by Patricia Fister and Hosokawa Shūhei, 159–85. Kyoto: International Research Center for Japanese Studies, 2007.

Hosomi Kazuyuki. "'Nihonjin' to kureōru no saiken." In *"Fukusū bunka" no tame ni—posutokoroniarizumu to kureōrusei no genzai*, edited by Fukusū bunka kenkyūkai, 299–320. Tokyo: Jinbun shoin, 1998.

Howland, Douglas. *Translating the West: Language and Political Reason in Nineteenth-Century Japan*. Honolulu: University of Hawai'i Press, 2002.

Huffman, James L. *Creating a Public: People and Press in Meiji Japan*. Honolulu: University of Hawai'i Press, 1997.

Hutcheon, Linda. *The Politics of Postmodernism*. New York: Routledge, 1989.

———. *A Theory of Parody: The Teachings of Twentieth-Century Art Forms*. New York: Methuen, 1985.

Huyssen, Andreas. *After the Great Divide: Modernism, Mass Culture, Postmodernism*. Bloomington: Indiana University Press, 1986.

———. "Mass Culture as Woman: Modernism's Other." In *Studies in Entertainment: Critical Approaches to Mass Culture*, edited by Tania Modleski, 188–207. Bloomington: Indiana University Press, 1986.

Hyōdō Hiromi. *"Koe" no kokumin kokka Nihon—naniwabushi ga tsukuru Nihon kindai*. Tokyo: Kōdansha, 2009.

Ichimaru Tōtarō. "'Watakushi' no naka no yotsu no 'watashi.'" In *Tajū jinkaku to wa nani ka*, edited by Asahi shinbunsha, 41–60. Tokyo: Asahi shinbunsha, 1997.

Ide Magoroku. "Shōgeki no burakku yūmoa—Fukazawa Shichirō 'Fūryū mutan.'" *Shinchō* 85, no. 12 (December 1988): 185–87.

Iida, Yumiko. "Between the Technique of Living an Endless Routine and the Madness of Absolute Degree Zero: Japanese Identity and the Crisis of Modernity in the 1990s." *positions: east asia cultures critique* 8, no. 2 (2000): 423–64.

Ikari Hiroshi. "'Fūryū mutan' ron." *Nihon bungaku* 40, no. 4 (1991): 42–50.

Ike, Nobutaka. *The Beginnings of Political Democracy in Japan*. Baltimore, MD: Johns Hopkins Press, 1950.

Im Chŏn-hye. *Nihon ni okeru Chōsenjin no bungaku no rekishi—1945-nen made*. Tokyo: Hōsei daigaku shuppankyoku, 1994.

Imanishi Junkichi. *Sōseki bungaku no shisō dainibu*. Tokyo: Chikuma shobō, 1992.

Inoue Kiyoshi. *Tennō—tennōsei no rekishi*. Tokyo: Meiseki, 1986.

Inoue, Kyoko. *MacArthur's Japanese Constitution: A Linguistic and Cultural Study of Its Making*. Chicago: University of Chicago Press, 1991.

Inouye, Jukichi. *Sketches of Tokyo Life*. Yokohama: Torando, 1892.

Irokawa Daikichi. "The Subject Mentality." *Japan Quarterly* 30 (1983): 28–38.

Iser, Wolfgang. *The Fictive and the Imaginary: Charting Literary Anthropology*. Baltimore, MD: Johns Hopkins University Press, 1993.

Ishihara Chiaki. *Sōseki no kigōron*. Tokyo: Kōdansha, 1999.

Ishii Kazuo. "*Wagahai wa neko de aru* no 'warai' no kumitate ni tsuite." *Bungei to shisō* 52 (February 1988): 1–15.

Ishii, Ryosuke, ed. *Japanese Legislation in the Meiji Period 1*. Translated and adapted by William J. Chambliss. Tokyo: Kasai Publishing & Printing Co., 1958.

Ishiko Junzō. *Kitchu ron*. Tokyo: Ramasha, 1986.

———. *Komikku ron*. Tokyo: Hokutō shobō, 1988.

———. *Sengo mangashi nōto*. Tokyo: Kinokuniya shoten, 1994.

Isoda Kōichi. *Rokumeikan no keifu*. Tokyo: Bungei shunjū, 1984.

———. *Shisō to shite no Tōkyō—kindai bungakushi ron nōto*. Tokyo: Kokubunsha, 1978.

Ito, Ken K. *Visions of Desire: Tanizaki's Fictional Worlds*. Stanford, CA: Stanford University Press, 1991.

Itō Mamoru. "Kōsō suru ōdiensu—kōyō no kioku o meguru teikō to terebishon." *Shisō* 956 (December 2003): 174–90.

Itō Sei. *Nihon bundanshi 4*. Tokyo: Kōdansha, 1953.

Itō Ujitaka. "'Bungaku no shūen' no shūen." *Gunzō* 63, no. 1 (January 2008): 230–60.

Ivy, Marilyn. "Formations of Mass Culture." In *Postwar Japan as History*, edited by Andrew Gordon, 239–58. Berkeley: University of California Press, 1993.

Jacobowitz, Seth. *Writing Technology in Meiji Japan: A Media History of Modern Japanese Literature and Visual Culture*. Cambridge, MA: Harvard University Asia Center, 2015.

James, Oliver. *The Selfish Capitalist: Origins of Affluenza*. London: Vermillion, 2008.

Jameson, Fredric. *Archaeologies of the Future: The Desire Called Utopia and Other Science Fictions*. London: Verso, 2005.

———. "Culture and Finance Capital." *Critical Inquiry* 24, no. 1 (Autumn 1997): 246–65.

———. "The End of Temporality." *Critical Inquiry* 29, no. 4 (Summer 2003): 695–718.

———. *Marxism and Form: Twentieth-Century Dialectics of Literature*. Princeton, NJ: Princeton University Press, 1974.

———. *The Political Unconscious: Narrative as a Socially Symbolic Act*. London: Routledge, 2002.

———. "Postmodernism and Consumer Society." In *Postmodern Culture*, edited by Hal Foster, 111–25. London: Pluto Press, 1985.

———. "Postmodernism, or the Cultural Logic of Late Capitalism." *New Left Review* 146 (July–August 1984): 53–92.

———. *Postmodernism, or the Cultural Logic of Late Capitalism*. Durham, NC: Duke University Press, 1991.

———. *A Singular Modernity: Essays on the Ontology of the Present*. New York: Verso Books, 2002.

———. "Third-World Literature in the Era of Multinational Capitalism." *Social Text* 15 (Fall 1986): 65–88.

Jansen, Marius B., ed. *Cambridge History of Japan*. Vol 5. *The Nineteenth Century*. Cambridge: Cambridge University Press, 2008.

———, ed. *Changing Japanese Attitudes toward Modernization*. Princeton, NJ: Princeton University Press, 1972.

———. "Changing Japanese Attitudes toward Modernization." In Jansen, *Changing Japanese Attitudes toward Modernization*, 43–97.

———. "Monarchy and Modernization in Japan." *Journal of Asian Studies* 36 (1977): 611–22.

Jansen, Marius B., and Gilbert Rozman, eds. *Japan in Transition, from Tokugawa to Meiji*. Princeton, NJ: Princeton University Press, 1986.

Janson, H. W., and Anthony F. Janson. *History of Art*. New York: Abrams, 1991.

Kainō Michitaka. "Genron to terebishon." *Shisō* 413 (November 1958): 207–15.

Kamei Hideo. "Bungakushi no gijutsu." *Bungaku* 9, no. 4 (October 1998): 2–12.

———. "Bungakushi no naka de." *Kokubungaku* 34, no. 8 (September 1982): 66–72.

———. "Enchō kōen ni okeru hyōgen to wa nani ka." *Nihon bungaku* 23, no. 6 (June 1974): 21–31.

———. *Meiji bungakushi*. Tokyo: Iwanami shoten, 2000.

Kan Satoko. *Jidai to onna to Higuchi Ichiyō*. Tokyo: Nihon hōsō shuppan kyōkai, 1999.

Kano Ayako. *Acting Like a Woman in Modern Japan: Theater, Gender, and Nationalism*. New York: Palgrave, 2001.

Karatani Kōjin. "History and Repetition in Japan." In *History and Repetition*, edited by Seiji M. Lippit, 29–46. New York: Columbia University Press, 2012.

———. "Kindai bungaku no owari." *Waseda bungaku* 29, no. 3 (May 2004): 4–29.

———. *The Origins of Modern Japanese Literature*. Edited by Brett de Bary. Translated with Yukari Kawahara, Robert Steen, Ayako Kano, Eiko Elliot, and Joseph Murphy. Durham, NC: Duke University Press, 1993.

———. *Sōseki ron shūsei*. Tokyo: Daisan bunmeisha. 1992.

Karatani Kōjin, ed. *Kindai Nihon no hihyō*. 3 vols. Tokyo: Fukutake shoten, 1992.

Karatani Kōjin, Kasai Shigeru, and Matsumoto Ken'ichi. "Tennōsei—yokuatsuteki yūwa no benshōhō." *Bungei* 25, no. 2 (1986): 250–78.

Kasai Kiyoshi. *Shūen no owari—1991 bungakuteki kōsatsu*. Tokyo: Fukutake shoten, 1992.

Kasza, Gregory J. *The State and Mass Media in Japan, 1918–1945*. Berkeley: University of California Press, 1988.

Kata Kōji. *Uta no Shōwa shi*. Tokyo: Jiji tsūshinsha, 1975.

Katayama Sadami. "Futari no senchūha." *Tanka* 25, no. 14 (December 1978): 56–59.

Katō Makirō. "Ai no jikan: ika ni shite manga wa ippanteki tōgi o kyozetsu suru ka." In Yonezawa, *Manga hihyō sengen*, 23–37.

Katō Norihiro. "Gendai shōsetsu ron kōgi (15)—Takahashi Gen'ichirō *Nihon bungaku seisuishi* (chūhen)." *Issatsu no hon* 7, no. 9 (September 2002): 57–62.

———. *Kanōsei to shite no sengo igo*. Tokyo: Iwanami shoten, 1999.

———. "Senkyūhyakuku-nen no kekkon." *Gunzō* 43, no. 9 (September 1988): 296–318.

———. *Shōsetsu no mirai*. Tokyo: Asahi shinbunsha, 2004.

Katō, Shūichi. "Japanese Writers and Modernization." In Jansen, *Changing Japanese Attitudes toward Modernization*, 425–45.

———. "Zasshūteki Nihon bunka no kibō." In *Zasshū bunka*, 49–64. Tokyo: Kōdansha, 1974.

Kawabe Kisaburō. *Press and Politics in Japan: A Study of the Relation between the Newspaper and the Political Development of Modern Japan*. Chicago: University of Chicago Press, 1921.

Kawamura Minato. *Ajia to iu kagami—Kyokutō no kindai*. Tokyo: Shichōsha, 1989.

———. *Ikyō no Shōwa bungaku—"Manshū" to kindai Nihon*. Tokyo: Iwanami shoten, 1990.

———. "Kin Shiryō to Chō Kakuchū." In *Kindai Nihon to shokuminchi 6: teikō to kutsujū*, edited by Ōe Shinobu, Asada Kyōji, Mitani Taichirō, Gotō Ken'ichi, Kobayashi Hideo, Takasaki Sōji, Wakabayashi Masahiro, and Kawamura Minato, 205–34. Tokyo: Iwanami shoten, 1993.

———. *Manshū hōkai—"Dai Tōa bungaku" to sakka-tachi*. Tokyo: Bungei shunjū, 1997.

———. *Sengo bungaku o tou—sono taiken to rinen*. Tokyo: Iwanami shoten, 1995.

———. *"Yoidorebune" no seishun—mō hitotsu no senchū—sengo*. Tokyo: Kōdansha, 1986.

Kawanishi Masaaki. *Shōsetsu no shūen*. Tokyo: Iwanami shoten, 2004.

Kayama Rika. *Tajūka suru riaru—kokoro to shakai no kairi ron*. Tokyo: Kosaidō shuppan, 2002.

Keene, Donald. *Dawn to the West: Japanese Literature in the Modern Era*. Vol. 1. New York: Holt, Rinehart and Winston, 1984.

Kenny, Michael G. *The Passion of Ansel Bourne: Multiple Personality in American Culture*. Washington, DC: Smithsonian Institution Press, 1986.

Kidd, Yasue Aoki. *Women Workers in the Japanese Cotton Mills, 1880–1920*. Ithaca, NY: Cornell University East Asian Papers No. 20, 1978.

Kim Chong-guk. *Chin'il munhangnon*. Seoul: Minjok munje yŏnguso, 2002.

Kim Hŭi-jŏng. "Arishima Takeo to Kankoku bungaku (1)." *Kanazawa daigaku kokugo kokubun* 25 (February 2000): 45–56.

Kim Mun-jip. *Arirantōge*. Tokyo: Daini shobō, 1958.

———. "Chōsen bundan no tokushūsei." *Shinchō* 3, no. 2 (February 1936): 152–60.

Kim Sa-ryang. "Chōsen bunka tsūshin." *Kin Shiryō zenshū 4*, 21–30.

———. *Kin Shiryō zenshū*. 4 vols. Edited by Kin Shiryō zenshū henshū iinkai. Kawade shobō shinsha, 1973–74.

———. "Kōmei." *Kin Shiryō zenshū 2*, 25–52.

———. *Tenma*. In *"Gaichi" no Nihongo bungakusen 3*, edited by Kurokawa Sō, 129–67. Tokyo: Shinjuku shobō, 1996.

Kim Sŏk-pŏm. *Tenkō to shinnichiha*. Tokyo: Iwanami shoten, 1993.

———. *"Zainichi" no shisō*. Tokyo: Chikuma shobō, 1981.

Kim, U-chang. "The Situation of the Writers under Japanese Colonialism." *Korea Journal* 16, no. 5 (May 1976): 4–15.

Kim Yŏng-dal, "Kimu Munjipu to 'Inukuso'—hitori-aruki suru sōshi kaimei no kidan." *Shohyō* 109 (October 1996): 70–77.

Kim Yun-sik. *Shōkon to kokufuku—Kankoku no bungakusha to Nihon*. Translated by Ōmura Masuo. Tokyo: Asahi shinbunsha, 1975.

Kimata Satoshi. "Media kankyō to bungaku." In *Iwanami kōza Nihon bungakushi* 14, edited by Kubota Jun, 87–112. Tokyo: Iwanami shoten, 1997.

Kimura Bin, Nakai Hisao, Ichikawa Hiroshi, and Karatani Kōjin. "'Bunretsubyō' o megutte—koyūmei no ketsujo—fuseiritsu." *Kikan shichō* 2 (1988): 6–47.

Kipling, Rudyard. *From Sea to Sea: Letters of Travel*. New York: Doubleday, Page and Company, 1924.

Kippner, Stanley. "Cross-Cultural Treatment Perspectives on Dissociative Disorders." In *Dissociation: Clinical and Theoretical Perspectives*, edited by Stephen Jay Lynn and Judith W. Rhue, 338–61. New York: Guilford Press, 1994.

Kishida Hideo. "*Utakai-hajime*: The New Year's Poetry Party." *Japan Quarterly* 30, no. 1 (1983): 44–49.

Kishida Ryūsei. *Bi no hontai*. Tokyo: Shinchōsha, 1961.

———. "Jiko no sekai." *Kishida Ryūsei zenshū* 1, 286–98.

———. "Jiko no geijutsu." *Kishida Ryūsei zenshū* 1, 29–43.

———. *Kishida Ryūsei zenshū*. 10 vols. Tokyo: Iwanami shoten, 1979–80.

———. "Uchi naru bi." *Bi no hontai*, 28–39.

Kitagawa Tetsuo. *Buraku mondai o toriageta hyaku no shōsetsu*. Kyoto: Buraku mondai kenkyūjō shuppanbu, 1985.

Kitazawa Norio. *Kishida Ryūsei to Taishō avangyarudo*. Tokyo: Iwanami shoten, 1993.

Kittler, Friedrich A. *Gramophone, Film, Typewriter*. Translated by Geoffrey Winthrop-Young and Michael Wutz. Stanford, CA: Stanford University Press, 1999.

Kiyomizu Ikutarō. "Terebishon jidai." *Shisō* 413 (November 1958): 2–22.

Kizugawa Kei. "Sengo no henbō." In *Nihon geinō shi* 7, edited by Geinōshi kenkyūkai, 259–99. Tokyo: Hōsei daigaku shuppankyoku, 1990.

Kō Yoshio. "*Kachikujin Yapū* hiwa—Numa Shōzō no shi ni sai shi." *Shinchō* 106, no. 2 (February 2009): 254–57.

Kobayashi Hideo. *Kindai kaiga*. Shinchōsha, 1984.

Kobayashi, Motoo. "Merging of Voices: Vernacularization of Narrative and the Invention of the Subject in the Making of the Modern Japanese Novel." PhD diss., University of Washington, 1994.

Kohut, Heinz. *The Analysis of the Self: A Systematic Approach to the Psychoanalytic Treatment of Narcissistic Personality Disorders*. New York: International Universities Press, 1971.

Kojève, Alexandre. *Introduction to the Reading of Hegel: Lectures on the "Phenomenology of Spirit."* Edited by Allan Bloom. Translated by James H. Nichols, Jr. Ithaca, NY: Cornell University Press, 1969.

Komata Yūsuke. "Manshū, Chōsen, Taiwan—shokuminchi to kureōru." *Kokubungaku kaishaku to kyōzai no kenkyū* 41, no. 13 (November 1996): 84–90.

Komori Yōichi. *Buntai to shite no monogatari*. Tokyo: Chikuma shobō, 1988.

———. *Sōseki o yominaosu*. Tokyo: Chikuma shobō, 1995.

Komota Nobuo, Yazawa Tamotsu, Shimada Yoshinobu, and Yokozawa Chiaki. *Shinpan Nihon ryūkōka shi chū*. Tokyo: Shakai shisōsha, 1970.

Konishi, Jin'ichi. *A History of Japanese Literature*. Vol. 2. *The Early Middle Ages*. Edited by Earl Miner. Translated by Aileen Gatten and Nicholas Teele. Princeton, NJ: Princeton University Press, 1986.

———. *Nihon bungeishi 5*. Tokyo: Kōdansha, 1992.

Konita Seiji. "Nyūsu gengo no Edo—Meiji." *Bungaku* 4, no. 1 (January–February 2003): 70–83.

Kōno Kensuke. *Shomotsu no kindai—media no bungakushi*. Tokyo: Chikuma shobō, 1992.

———. *Tōki to shite no bungaku—katsuji, kenshō, media*. Tokyo: Shin'yōsha, 2003.

Kōra Yumiko. "Muishiki no kagaisha-tachi—'Takekurabe' ron." In *Higuchi Ichiyō o yominaosu*, edited by Shin feminisuto hihyō no kai, 195–218. Tokyo: Gakugei shorin, 1994.

Kornicki, P. F. "The Enmeiin Affair of 1803: The Spread of Information in the Tokugawa Period." *Harvard Journal of Asiatic Studies* 42, no. 2 (December 1982): 503–33.

Koschmann, Victor. "Modernization and Democratic Values: The 'Japanese Model' in the 1960s." In *Staging Growth: Modernization, Development, and the Global Cold War*, edited by David C. Engerman, Nils Gilman, Mark Haefele, and Michael E. Lathan, 225–49. Amherst: University of Massachusetts Press, 2003.

Koseki Shōichi. *The Birth of Japan's Postwar Constitution*. Translated by Ray A. Moore. Boulder, CO: Westview Press, 1998.

Koyama Tetsurō. "'Numa Shōzō' kaikenki." *Bungakukai* 45, no. 13 (December 1991): 256–59.

Koyano Atsushi. "Tayama Katai, AV, tennōsei." In *Gendaishi techō tokushūban Takahashi Gen'ichirō*, 184–89.

Krauss, Ellis S. *Japanese Radicals Revisited: Student Protest in Postwar Japan*. Berkeley: University of California Press, 1974.

Kristeva, Julia. *Desire in Language: A Semiotic Approach to Literature and Art*. Translated by Thomas Gora, Alice Jardine, and Leon Samuel Roudiez. New York: Columbia University Press, 1980.

———. *Tales of Love*. New York: Columbia University Press, 1987.

Kubota Hikosaku. *Torioi Omatsu kaijō shinwa*. In *Meiji kaikaki bungakushū*, edited by Maeda Ai and Okitsu Kaname, 125–82. Tokyo: Kadokawa, 1970.

Kurata Yoshihiro. *"Hayariuta" no kōkogaku—kaikoku kara sengo fukkō made*. Tokyo: Bungei shunjū, 2001.

Kure Tomofusa. *Gendai manga no zentaizō*. Tokyo: Futabasha, 1997.

Kuroi Senji. *Jigazō to no taiwa*. Tokyo: Bungei shunjū, 1992.

Kuroko Kazuo. "Han-tennō seido shōsetsu no unmei." *Nihon bungaku* 34, no. 1 (1985): 41–50.

———. *Shukusai to shura*. Tokyo: Sairyūsha, 1985.

Kuwabara Sumio. *Nihon no jigazō*. Tokyo: Nanbokusha, 1966.

Kwak Hyoungduck. "Kin Shiryō *Tenma* ni okeru 'moderu mondai' saikō." *Chōsen gakuhō* 218 (January 2011): 115–43.

Kwon, Nayoung Aimee. *Intimate Empire: Collaboration and Colonial Modernity in Korea and Japan*. Durham, NC: Duke University Press, 2015.

Kyōya Hideo. *Senkyūhaku rokujūichi-nen fuyu "Fūryū mutan jiken."* Tokyo: Heibonsha, 1996.

Laing, R. D. *The Divided Self*. Harmondsworth, UK: Penguin, 1965.

LaMarre, Thomas. "Speciesism, Part II: Tezuka Osamu and the Multispecies Ideal." *Mechademia* 5 (2010): 51–85.

Larsen, Neil. *Modernism and Hegemony: A Materialist Critique of Aesthetic Agencies*. Minneapolis: University of Minnesota Press, 1990.

Lasch, Christopher. *The Culture of Narcissism: American Life in the Age of Diminishing Expectations*. New York: Norton, 1978.

Law, Graham, and Morita Norimasa. "Sekai no shinbun shōsetsu no rekishi o megutte." *Bungaku* 4, no. 1 (January–February 2003): 34–55.

Layoun, Mary. *Travels of a Genre: The Modern Novel and Ideology*. Princeton, NJ: Princeton University Press, 1990.

Lee, Changsoo, and George A. De Vos. *Koreans in Japan: Ethnic Conflict and Accommodation*. Berkeley: University of California Press, 1981.

Lee Yeon-suk. *"Kokugo" to iu shisō*. Tokyo: Iwanami shoten, 1996.

Lefebvre, Henri. *Introduction to Modernity: Twelve Preludes, September 1959–1961*. Translated by John Moore. London: Verso, 1995.

Lévi-Strauss, Claude. *The Other Side of the Moon*. Translated by Jane Marie Todd. Cambridge, MA: Belknap Press, 2013.

Levin, David Michael. Introduction to *Pathologies of the Modern Self*, 1–17.

———. "Psychopathology in the Epoch of Nihilism." In Levin, *Pathologies of the Modern Self*, 21–83.

———, ed. *Pathologies of the Modern Self: Postmodern Studies on Narcissism, Schizophrenia, and Depression*. New York: New York University Press, 1987.

Levine, Steve Z. *Monet, Narcissus, and Self-Reflection: The Modernist Myth of the Self*. Chicago: University of Chicago Press, 1994.

Lifton, Robert Jay. *The Protean Self*. New York: Basic Books, 1993.

Lipton, Judith Eve. "*1Q84*: Living in a World with Two Moons." *Psychology Today*, 2011. Accessed 12 November 2016. https://www.psychologytoday.com/blog/pura-vida /201111/1q84-living-in-world-two-moons.

Lucken, Michael. *Imitation and Creativity in Japanese Arts: From Kishida Ryūsei to Miyazaki Hayao*. Translated by Francesca Simkin. New York: Columbia University Press, 2016.

Maeda Ai. *Genkei no Meiji*. Tokyo: Chikuma shobō, 1989.

———. *Kindai dokusha no seiritsu*. Tokyo: Chikuma shobō, 1989.

————. *Maeda Ai chōsakushū 3 Higuchi Ichiyō no sekai*. Tokyo: Chikuma shobō, 1989.

————. "Neko no kotoba, neko no rinri." In *Sōseki sakuhinron shūsei I Wagahai wa neko de aru*, edited by Asano Yō and Ōta Noboru, 94–105. Tokyo: Ōfūsha, 1990.

Maeda Ai, and Okitsu Kaname, eds. *Meiji kaikaki bungakushū*. Tokyo: Kadokawa, 1970.

Maeda Muneo. "Kaisetsu—gyaku-yūtopia no eikō to hisan." In Numa, *Kachikujin Yapū 2*, 313–42.

Maeda Tomomi. "Zasshi *Takarajima*—shūkanshi e no gekidō kōkai ki." Accessed 12 November 2016. http://tkj.jp/takarajima_x/ichibachi/01.html.

Mailer, Norman. "The Faith of Graffiti." *Esquire*, May 1974, 77–58.

Mailer, Norman, and Jon Naar. *The Faith of Graffiti*. New York: HarperCollins, 2009.

Maki, John. "Japanese Constitutional Style." In Henderson, *The Constitution of Japan*, 3–39.

Manō Neri. "Sora tobu kureōru." *Kokubungaku kaishaku to kyōzai no kenkyū* 41, no. 13 (January 1996): 106–11.

Marcuse, Herbert. *One-Dimensional Man: Studies in the Ideology of Advanced Industrial Society*. Boston: Beacon Press, 1964.

Markus, Andrew Lawrence. "The Carnival of Edo: Misemono Spectacles from Contemporary Accounts." *Harvard Journal of Asiatic Studies* 45, no. 2 (December 1985): 499–541.

Marran, Christine L. "Literature Without Us." In *Ishimure Michiko's Writing in Ecocritical Perspective: Between Sea and Sky*, edited by Bruce Allen and Yuki Masami, 75–87. Lanham, MD: Lexington Books, 2016.

————. *Poison Women: Figuring Female Transgression in Modern Japanese Culture*. Minneapolis: University of Minnesota Press, 2007.

Marshall, Byron K. *Capitalism and Nationalism in Prewar Japan: The Ideology of the Business Elite, 1868–1941*. Stanford, CA: Stanford University Press, 1967.

Martin, Emily. *Bipolar Expeditions: Mania and Depression in American Culture*. Princeton, NJ: Princeton University Press, 2007.

Maruyama, Masao. "Patterns of Individuation and the Case of Japan: A Conceptual Scheme." In Jansen, *Changing Japanese Attitudes toward Modernization*, 489–531.

Marx, Karl. *The Communist Manifesto*. Edited by Frederic L. Bender. New York: W. W. Norton, 2013.

————. "Theses on Feuerbach IX." In *Marx/Engels Selected Works*, vol. 1, 13–15. Moscow: Progress Publishers, 1969.

Massumi, Brian. *A User's Guide to Capitalism and Schizophrenia*. Cambridge, MA: MIT Press, 1992.

Matsueda Itaru. "Shōka no supiido, kanki no chikara." In Yonezawa, *Manga hihyō sengen*, 3–22.

Matsumoto Kappei. *Watakushi no furuhon daigaku—shingekijin no dokusho hōkō*. Tokyo: Seieisha, 1981.

Matsumoto Takayuki. *Yoshimoto Banana ron—"futsū" to iu muishiki*. Tokyo: JICC shuppankyoku, 1991.

Matsumura Tatsuo. "*Natsume Sōseki shū I* kaisetsu." In Natsume Sōseki, *Nihon kindai bungaku taikei Natsume Sōseki shū 1*, 8–42. Tokyo: Kadokawa shoten, 1971.

Matsusaka Toshio. *Higuchi Ichiyō kenkyū*. Tokyo: Kyōiku shuppan sentā, 1970.

Matsuura Sōzō. *Masukomi no naka no tennō*. Tokyo: Ōtsuki shoten, 1984.

———. *"Tensei jingo" no tennō to sensō—"kami no kuni" hōdō kenkyū*. Tokyo: Kagyū shinsha, 2000.

Matsuyama Iwao. "Dokufu to enzetsu." *Yuriika* 21, no. 6 (May 1989): 18–27.

Matsuzawa Tessei. "Street Labor Markets, Day Laborers and the Structure of Oppression." In *The Japanese Trajectory: Modernization and Beyond*, edited by Gavan McCormack et al., 147–64. Cambridge: Cambridge University Press, 2009.

Matthews, Sean. "Change and Theory in Raymond Williams's Structure of Feeling." *Pretexts: Literary and Cultural Studies* 10, no. 2 (2001): 179–94.

McCaffery, Larry, and Sinda Gregory. Introduction to *Review of Contemporary Fiction* XXII, no. 2 (Summer 2002): 19–28.

McCaffery, Larry, Sinda Gregory, and Yoshiaki Koshikawa. "Why Not Have Fun? An Interview with Gen'ichiro Takahashi." *Review of Contemporary Fiction* XXII, no. 2 (Summer 2002): 192–99.

McCallum, Donald F. "Three Taishō Artists: Yorozu Tetsugorō, Koide Narashige, and Kishida Ryūsei." In Takashina, Rimer, and Bolas, *Paris in Japan*, 81–95.

McCarthy, Mary. "The Fact in Fiction." *Partisan Review* 27, no. 3 (Summer 1960): 438–58.

McClellan, Edwin. *Two Japanese Novelists: Sōseki and Tōson*. Chicago: University of Chicago Press, 1969.

McGray, Douglas. "Japan's Gross National Cool." *Foreign Policy* 130 (May–June 2002): 44–54.

McKeon, Michael. *Origins of the English Novel, 1600–1740*. Baltimore, MD: Johns Hopkins University Press, 1987.

McLuhan, Marshall. *The Gutenberg Galaxy: The Making of Typographic Man*. New York: New American Library, 1969.

———. *Understanding Media: The Extensions of Man*. Cambridge, MA: MIT Press, 1994.

McLuhan, Marshall, and Quentin Fiore. *The Medium is the Massage*. San Francisco: Hardwired, 1967.

"Memoirs of a Geisha—Official Site." Sony Pictures. Accessed 12 November 2016. www .sonypictures.com/movies/memoirsofageisha.

Mertz, John Pierre. *Novel Japan: Spaces of Nationhood in Early Meiji Narrative, 1870–88*. Ann Arbor: Center for Japanese Studies, University of Michigan, 2003.

Mikami Sanji, and Takatsu Kuwasaburō. *Nihon bungakushi (jōkan)*. Tokyo: Nihon tosho sentā, 1982.

Miller, D. A. *The Novel and the Police*. Berkeley: University of California Press, 1988.

Miller, J. Hillis. "Paul de Man at Work: In These Bad Days, What Good is the Archive?" In

Tom Cohen, Claire Colebrook, and J. Hillis Miller, *Theory and the Disappearing Future: On de Man, on Benjamin*, 55–88. London: Routledge, 2012.

Miller, J. Scott. "Japanese Shorthand and *Sokkibon*." *Monumenta Nipponica* 49, no. 4 (Winter 1994): 471–87.

Miller, Roy Andrew. *The Japanese Language in Contemporary Japan: Some Sociological Observations*. Washington, DC: American Enterprise Institute for Public Policy Research, 1977.

———. "The Lost Poetic Sequence of the Priest Manzei." *Monumenta Nipponica* 36, no. 2 (1981): 133–72.

Minami Hiroshi. *Psychology of the Japanese People*. Translated by Albert R. Ikoma. Honolulu: East-West Center, 1970.

———. "Terebishon to ukete no seikatsu—uketori hannō to shakai kōka no mondaiten." *Shisō* 413 (November 1958): 103–15.

Minami Hiroshi, ed. *Zoku Shōwa bunka 1945–1989*. Tokyo: Keisō shobō, 1990.

Minganti, Franco. "Jukebox Boys: Postwar Italian Music and the Culture of Covering." In Fehrenbach and Poiger, *Transactions, Transgressions, Transformation*, 148–65.

Mishima Yukio. "Gekiga ni okeru wakamono ron." In *Mishima Yukio zenshū 36*, 53–56. Tokyo: Shinchōsha, 2003.

———. *Mishima Yukio vs. Tōdai zenkyōtō, 1969–2000*. Tokyo: Fujiwara shoten, 2000.

———. *Shōsetsu to wa nani ka*. Tokyo: Shinchōsha, 1972.

Mishima Yukio, and Terayama Shūji. "Erosu wa teikō no kyoten ni nariuru ka." *Ushio* 127 (July 1970): 141–55.

Mita Masahiro. *Boku tte nani*. Tokyo: Kawade shobō shinsha, 2008.

Mitchell, Richard H. *Censorship in Imperial Japan*. Princeton, NJ: Princeton University Press, 1983.

Mitgang, Herbert. "Letter from Tokyo: Brando, the Stones and Banana Yoshimoto." *New York Times Book Review*, 8 July 1990, 13–14.

Mitsui Takayuki, and Washida Koyata. *Yoshimoto Banana shinwa*. Tokyo: JICC shuppankyoku, 1989.

Miura Nobutaka. "Kureōru to zasshū bunka ron—Katō Shūichi Gurissan taidan ni yosete." *Nichi-Futsu bunka* 69, no. 11 (2003): 32–49.

Miyadai Shinji. "Kodomo o torimaku ima to mirai." *Seishin iryō daiyonji* 44 (2006): 38–81.

Miyadai Shinji, Ishihara Hideki, and Ōtsuka Meiko. *Sabukaruchā shinwa kaitai: shōjo, ongaku, manga, sei no hen'yō to genzai*. Tokyo: Paruko shuppan, 1993.

Miyata Setsuko. *Chōsen minshū to "kōminka" seisaku*. Tokyo: Miraisha, 1985.

Miyoshi, Masao. "A Borderless World? From Colonialism to Transnationalism and the Decline of the Nation-State." *Critical Inquiry* 19 (Summer 1993): 726–51.

———. *Off-Center: Power and Culture Relations between Japan and the United States*. Cambridge, MA: Harvard University Press, 1991.

———. "Women's Short Stories in Japan." *Mānoa* 3, no. 2 (Fall 1991): 33–39.

Miyoshi, Masao, and H. D. Harootunian. Introduction to Miyoshi and Harootunian, *Postmodernism and Japan*, vii–xx.

———, eds. *Postmodernism and Japan*. Durham, NC: Duke University Press, 1989.

Miyoshi Yukio. *Nihon bungaku no kindai to hankindai*. Tokyo: Tōkyō daigaku shuppankai, 1972.

Mizukawa Takao. *Sōseki to rakugo—Edo shomin geinō no eikyō*. Tokyo: Sairyūsha, 1989.

Mizumura, Minae. *The Fall of Language in the Age of English*. Translated by Mari Yoshihara and Juliet Winters Carpenter. New York: Columbia University Press, 2015.

Moretti, Franco. *Atlas of the European Novel, 1800–1900*. London: Verso, 1998.

Moriarty, Michael. "The Longest Journey: Raymond Williams and French Theory." In *Cultural Materialism: On Raymond Williams*, edited by Christopher Prendergast, 91–116. Minneapolis: University of Minnesota Press, 1995.

Morioka, Heinz, and Miyoko Sasaki. "The Blue-Eyed Storyteller: Henry Black and His *Rakugo* Career." *Monumenta Nipponica* 38, no. 2 (Summer 1983): 133–62.

———. *Rakugo, the Popular Narrative Art of Japan*. Cambridge, MA: Council on East Asian Studies, Harvard University, 1990.

Morris, Ivan, ed. *Madly Singing in the Mountains: An Appreciation and Anthology of Arthur Waley*. London: Allen & Unwin, 1970.

Morris-Suzuki, Tessa. "Touching the Grass: Science, Uncertainty and Everyday Life from Chernobyl to Fukushima." *Science, Technology and Society* 19, no. 3 (2014): 331–62.

Murakami, Haruki. *1Q84*. Translated by Jay Rubin and Philip Gabriel. New York: Alfred A. Knopf, 2011.

———. *Colorless Tsukuru Tazaki and His Years of Pilgrimage*. Translated by Philip Gabriel. New York: Alfred A. Knopf, 2014.

———. *Hard-Boiled Wonderland and the End of the World*. Translated by Alfred Birnbaum. New York: Kodansha International, 1991.

———. *The Wind-Up Bird Chronicle*. Translated by Jay Rubin. New York: Alfred A. Knopf, 1997.

Murakami Nobuhiko. *Meiji josei shi chūkan kōhen*. Tokyo: Rironsha, 1971.

Murakami Ryū. "'Basho: jibun' atogaki." *Doko ni mo aru basho to doko ni mo inai watashi*, 184–86. Tokyo: Bungei shunjū, 2003.

———. *Kibō no kuni no ekusodasu*. Tokyo: Bungei shunjū, 2002.

Murakami Shigeyoshi. *Kōshitsu jiten*. Tokyo: Tōkyōdō, 1980.

Mushanokoji Saneatsu. "Jiko no tame no geijutsu." In *Gendai Nihon shisō taikei 13 Bungaku no shisō*, edited by Nakamura Mitsuo, 223–32. Tokyo: Chikuma shobō, 1965.

Myers, Ramon H., and Mark R. Peattie, eds. *The Japanese Colonial Empire, 1895–1945*. Princeton, NJ: Princeton University Press, 1984.

Nada Inada. "Pari no heki wa kataru—'gogatsu kakumei' no hyōgen." *Asahi jānaru* 10, no. 52 (22 December 1968): 20–25.

Nagahara, Yutaka. "*Monsieur le Capital* and *Madame la Terre* Do Their Ghost-Dance:

Globalization and the Nation-State." In *Japan After Japan: Social and Cultural Life from the Recessionary 1990s to the Present*, edited by Tomiko Yoda and Harry Harootunian, 299–330. Durham, NC: Duke University Press, 2006.

Nagai Kafū. "Kōcha no ato (shō)." In *Nagai Kafū shū Meiji bungaku zenshū* 73, 313–23. Tokyo: Chikuma shobō, 1969.

Nagai Katsuichi. *"Garo" henshūchō—watakushi no sengo manga shuppan shi*. Tokyo: Chikuma shobō, 1987.

Nagamine Shigetoshi. *"Dokusho kokumin" no tanjō—Meiji 30-nendai no katsuji media to dokusho bunka*. Tokyo: Nihon editā sukūru shuppanbu, 2004.

———. *Zasshi to dokusha no kindai*. Tokyo: Nihon editā sukūru shuppanbu, 1997.

Najita, Tetsuo. "Introduction: A Synchronous Approach to the Study of Conflict in Modern Japanese History." In Najita and Koschmann, *Conflict in Modern Japanese History*, 3–21.

Najita, Tetsuo, and J. Victor Koschmann, eds. *Conflict in Modern Japanese History: The Neglected Tradition*. Princeton, NJ: Princeton University Press, 1982.

Nakai Hideo. "Kōtaishi denka Michiko hidenka no outa." *Asahi gurafu*, 20 December 1968, 188–99.

Nakai Hisao, Iida Yoshihiko, and Fujikawa Yōko. "Kairi genshō o megutte." *Kokoro no kagaku* 136 (November 2007): 12–28.

Nakamata Akio. *Kyokusei bungakuron = Westway to the World*. Tokyo: Shōbunsha, 2004.

Nakamura Kokyō. *Hentai shinri no kenkyū*. Tokyo: Daidōkan, 1919.

Nakamura, Masanori. *The Japanese Monarchy, 1981–91: Ambassador Grew and the Making of the "Symbol Emperor System."* London: Routledge, 1992.

Nakamura Michiko. *"Fūryū mutan" jiken igo*. Tokyo: Tabata shoten, 1976.

Nakamura, Mitsuo. *Japanese Fiction in the Meiji Era*. Tokyo: Kokusai bunka shinkōkai, 1966.

Nakano, Ako. "Death and History: An Emperor's Funeral." *Public Culture* 2, no. 2 (1990): 33–40.

Nakano Shigeharu. "Teroru wa sayoku ni taishite wa yurusareru ka." *Bessatsu shinhyō* 7, no. 2 (1974): 210–15.

Nakayama Yasumasa, ed. *Shinbun shūsei Meiji hennenshi 9*. Tokyo: Zaisei keizai gakkai, 1934–36.

Natili, Donnatella. "Itaria de no Yoshimoto Banana." *Kokubungaku kaishaku to kyōzai* 39, no. 3 (February 1994): 108–12.

Natsume Kyōko. *Sōseki no omoide*. Tokyo: Kaizōsha, 1928.

Natsume Sōseki. *I Am a Cat*. 3 vols. Translated by Aiko Itō and Graeme Wilson. Rutland, VT: Tuttle, 1972.

———. "Philosophical Foundations of the Literary Arts." In *Theory of Literature and Other Critical Writings*, edited and translated by Michael Bourdaghs, Atsuko Ueda, and Joseph A. Murphy, 159–213. New York: Columbia University Press, 2009.

Nishi Masahiko. "Kureōru na bungaku—Miyazawa Kenji ron." *Gendai shisō* 25, no. 1 (January 1997): 219–29.

———. *Mori no gerira Miyazawa Kenji*. Tokyo: Iwanami shoten, 1997.

Nishio Kunio. *Nihon no bungaku to yūjo*. Tokyo: Aiiku shuppan, 1972.

Noma Seiji. *Watakushi no hansei*. Tokyo: Kōdansha, 1959.

Nomura Masaaki. *Rakugo no gengogaku*. Tokyo: Heibonsha, 1994.

Norman, Henry. *The Real Japan: Studies of Contemporary Japanese Manners, Morals, Administration, and Politics*. London: T. F. Unwin, 1892.

Numa Shōzō. *Kachikujin Yapū*. 5 vols. Tokyo: Gentōsha, 2014.

Ochi Haruo. "Enchō tsuiseki." In *Kindai bungaku seiritsuki no kenkyū*, 22–44. Tokyo: Iwanami shoten, 1984.

———. "'Mizumakura' o megutte." *Yuriika* 9, no. 12 (November 1978): 118–21.

———. "San'yūtei Enchō ni tsuite." In *Bungaku no kindai—bungaku ronshū 1*, 48–58. Tokyo: Sunagoya shobō, 1986.

O'Connor, Alan. *Raymond Williams: Writing, Culture, Politics*. Oxford: Basil Blackwell Ltd., 1989.

Odagiri Takashi. "Konseiteki Nihongo no imi." *Kōza Nihongo kyōiku* 37 (November 2001): 88–110.

Ōe Kenzaburō. *Aimai na Nihon no watakushi*. Tokyo: Iwanami shoten, 1995.

Ohmae, Kenichi. *The End of the Nation-State: The Rise of Regional Economies*. New York: Free Press, 1995.

———. "Putting Global Logic First." *Harvard Business Review* 73, no. 1 (January–February 1995): 119–25.

Okada Susumu. "Terebi-teki ishiki—futatabi dōjisei no tsuite." *Bungaku* 30, no. 1 (January 1962): 23–32.

Okamoto Masami, and Murao Kōichi, eds. *Daigaku gerira no uta—rakugaki Tōdai tōsō*. Tokyo: Sanseidō: 1969.

Okamoto, Shumpei. *The Japanese Oligarchy and the Russo-Japanese War*. New York: Columbia University Press, 1970.

Okitsu Kaname. "Bakumatsu kaikaki gesaku no dokusha sō." *Bungaku* 26, no. 5 (May 1958): 655–65.

———. *Meiji kaikaki bungaku no kenkyū*. Tokyo: Ōfūsha, 1968.

———. "Meiji kaikaki bungakushū kaisetsu." In *Nihon kindai bungaku taikei 1*, edited by Okitsu Kaname and Maeda Ai, 8–30. Tokyo: Kadokawa shoten, 1970.

———. *Meiji shinbun kotohajime—"bunmei kaika" no janarizumu*. Tokyo: Taishūkan shoten, 1997.

———. *Rakugo—warai no nenrin*. Tokyo: Kadokawa shoten, 1968.

———. "Sōseki to Edo bunka—miotosarete ita sakka no sokumen." *Asahi jānaru* 8, no. 23 (July 1966): 20–24.

———. "Taishū bungaku zenshi—kōdan rakugo sokkibon no igi." In *Meiji no bungaku*, edited by Nihon bungaku kenkyū shiryō sōsho, 227-51. Tokyo: Yūseidō, 1981.

Okochi, Kazuo. *Labor in Modern Japan*. Tokyo: Science Council of Japan, 1958.

Okonogi Keigo. "Gendai manga to moratoriamu ningen." *Kokubungaku kaishaku to kyōzai no kenkyū* 26, no. 6 (April 1981): 8–13.

Ōkubo Hasetsu. *Hanamachi fūzokushi.* Tokyo: Nihon tosho sentā, 1983.

Okuno Takeo. "Kaisetsu—*Kachikujin Yapū* densetsu." In Numa, *Kachikujin Yapū 1,* 350–58.

Ōoka Shōhei. "Yande iru no wa dare ka—jōshikiteki bungakuron (2)." *Gunzō* 16, no. 2 (February 1961): 196–203.

Ong, Walter J. *Orality and Literacy: The Technologizing of the Word.* New York: Methuen, 1982.

Ooms, Emily Groszos. *Women and Millenarian Protest in Meiji Japan: Deguchi Nao and Ōmotokyō.* Ithaca, NY: Cornell East Asia Series, 1993.

Orikuchi Shinobu. "Kokubungaku no hassei." *Kodai kenkyū 2,* 10–286. Tokyo: Ōokayama shoten, 1929.

Orwell, George. "Boys' Weeklies." In *The Collected Essays, Journalism, and Letters of George Orwell,* vol. 1, *An Age Like This 1920–1940,* edited by Sonia Orwell and Ian Angus, 460–85. New York: Harcourt, Brace & World, 1968.

Ōtsuka Eiji. "'Boku' to kokka to nejimaki-dori no noroi." In *Murakami Haruki Nihon bungaku kenkyū ronbun shūsei 46,* edited by Kimata Satoshi, 212–24. Tokyo: Wakakusa shobō, 1998.

———. *Etō Jun to shōjo feminizumu-teki sengo.* Tokyo: Chikuma shobō, 2001.

———. *"Otaku" no seishinshi—senkyūhyakuhachijū nendai ron.* Tokyo: Kōdansha, 2004.

———. *Shōjo minzokugaku—seikimatsu no shinwa o tsumugu "miko no matsuei."* Tokyo: Kōbunsha, 1989.

Ovid. *Metamorphoses.* Translated by A. D. Melville. Oxford: Oxford University Press, 1986.

Ozaki Hotsuki. *Kyū-shokuminchi bungaku no kenkyū.* Tokyo: Keisō shobō, 1971.

———. *Taishū bungaku.* Tokyo: Kinokuniya shoten, 1994.

———. *Taishū geinō no kamigami—Ikari to naki to warai to.* Tokyo: Marugei shuppan, 1978.

Ozaki Hotsuki, Satō Tadao, Nagai Katsuichi, and Nagajima Shin'ichi. "Manga bunka no jidai." In *Shōwa hihyō taikei 5,* edited by Muramatsu Takeshi, Saeki Shōichi, and Ōkubo Tsuneo, 457–66. Tokyo: Banchō shobō, 1978.

Painter, Andrew A. "On the Anthropology of Television: A Perspective from Japan." *Visual Anthropology Review* 10, no. 1 (Spring 1994): 70–85.

Parks, Tim. "The Dull New Global Novel." In *Where I'm Reading From: The Changing World of Books,* 25–28. New York: New York Review Books, 2015.

Parrinder, Patrick. *Nation and Novel: The English Novel from its Origins to the Present Day.* Oxford: Oxford University Press, 2006.

Pateman, Carole. *The Sexual Contract.* Stanford, CA: Stanford University Press, 1988.

Paulson, Ronald. "Non-European Foundations of European Imperialism: Sketch for a Theory of Collaboration." In *Studies in the Theory of Imperialism,* edited by Roger Owen and Bob Sutcliffe, 117–42. London: Longman, 1972.

Perkins, David. *Is Literary History Possible?* Baltimore, MD: Johns Hopkins University Press, 1992.

———. *Theoretical Issues in Literary History.* Cambridge, MA: Harvard University Press, 1991.

Perloff, Marjorie. Foreword to Slaymaker, *Yōko Tawada,* vii–ix.

Petr, Pavel. "Marxist Theories of the Comic." In *Comic Relations: Studies in the Comic, Satire and Parody,* edited by Pavel Petr, David Roberts, and Philip Thomson, 57–66. Frankfurt: Peter Lang, 1985.

Pincus, Leslie. *Authenticating Culture in Imperial Japan: Kuki Shūzō and the Rise of National Aesthetics.* Berkeley: University of California Press, 1996.

Poiger, Uta G. "American Music, Cold War Liberalism, and German Identities." In Fehrenbach and Poiger, *Transactions, Transgressions, Transformations,* 127–47.

Poulantzas, Nicos. *State, Power, Socialism.* London, Verso, 1990.

Ramsey, S. Robert. "The Polysemy of the Term *Kokugo.*" In *Schriftfestschrift: Essays on Writing and Language in Honor of John DeFrancis on His Eightieth Birthday,* edited by Victor H. Mair. Special issue, *Sino-Platonic Papers* 27 (31 August 1991): 37–47.

Reed, Christopher. *Bachelor Japanists: Japanese Aesthetics and Western Masculinities.* New York: Columbia University Press, 2016.

Rexroth, Kenneth. Introduction to In *One Hundred Poems from the Japanese,* ix–xx. New York: New Directions, 1964.

Ri Takanori. *Hyōshō kūkan no kindai—Meiji "Nihon" no media hensei.* Tokyo: Shin'yōsha, 1996.

Rimer, J. Thomas. "Introduction: Satō Haruo." In *The Sick Rose: A Pastoral Elegy,* by Satō Haruo, 1–14. Translated by Francis B. Tenny. Honolulu: University of Hawai'i Press, 1993.

———. *Pilgrimages: Aspects of Japanese Literature and Culture.* Honolulu: University of Hawai'i Press, 1988.

Rinbara Sumio. "Enchō bungei kō." In *Nihon bungaku kenkyū shiryō shinshū 11 Kindai bungaku no seiritsu—shisō to buntai no mosaku,* edited by Komori Yōichi, 15–23. Tokyo: Yūseidō, 1986.

———. "Kindai bungaku to 'tsuzukimono.'" *Nihon bungaku* 42, no. 4 (April 1993): 40–53.

———. "'Koshinbun' to 'tsuzukimono.'" *Nihon bungaku* 48, no. 2 (February 1999): 12–23.

Roberts, David D. *Nothing but History: Reconstruction and Extremity after Metaphysics.* Berkeley: University of California Press, 1995.

Robertson, Jennifer. "Gender-Bending in Paradise: Doing 'Female' and 'Male' in Japan." *Genders* 5 (1989): 50–69.

Robinson, Michael Edson. *Cultural Nationalism in Colonial Korea, 1920–1925.* Seattle: University of Washington Press, 1988.

Ross, Colin A., MD. *Dissociative Identity Disorder: Diagnosis, Clinical Features, and Treatment of Multiple Personality.* New York: John Wiley & Sons, 1997.

Rozman, Gilbert. "Social Change." In Jansen, *The Cambridge History of Japan*, vol. 5, *The Nineteenth Century*, 499–568.

Rubin, Jay. *Injurious to Public Morals: Writers and the Meiji State*. Seattle: University of Washington Press, 1984.

———. "Sōseki on Individualism: 'Watakushi no Kojinshugi.'" *Monumenta Nipponica* 34, no. 1 (Spring 1979): 21–48.

Ryan, Marleigh Grayer. *The Development of Realism in the Fiction of Tsubouchi Shōyō*. Seattle: University of Washington Press, 1975.

———. *Japan's First Modern Novel*: Ukigumo *of Futabatei Shimei*. New York: Columbia University Press, 1967.

Sabin, Roger. *Adult Comics: An Introduction*. New York: Routledge, 1993.

Sadoya Shigenobu. *Sōseki to seikimatsu geijutsu*. Tokyo: Bijutsu kōronsha, 1982.

Said, Edward. *Culture and Imperialism*. New York: Knopf, 1993.

Saitō Minako. "'Bungakushi' o kettobase." In *Datsu-bungaku to chō-bungaku*, edited by Saitō Minako, 1–22. Tokyo: Iwanami shoten, 2002.

Saitō Tamaki. *Bungaku no chōkō*. Tokyo: Bungei shunjū. 2004.

———. "Kairi no gihō to rekishiteki gaishō." *Yuriika* 32, no. 4 (2000): 62–71.

———. "Kairi no jidai ni aidentiti o yōgo suru tame ni." In *Datsu-aidentiti*, edited by Ueno Chizuko, 137–66. Tokyo: Keisō shobō, 2005.

———. *Kairi no poppu sukiru*. Tokyo: Keisei shobō. 2004.

———. "Kairi to posutomodan, aruiwa seishin bunseki kara no teikō." *Hihyō kūkan* 3, no. 1 (2001): 84–99.

Saitō Tamaki, Nakai Hisao, and Asada Akira. "Torauma to kairi." *Hihyō kūkan* 3, no. 1 (2001): 53–83.

Sakurai Tetsuo. *Shisō to shite no rokujū nendai*. Tokyo: Kōdansha, 1988.

Salomon, Xavier F. "Portraits." In Julian Brooks, with Denise Allen and Xavier F. Salomon, *Andrea del Sarto: The Renaissance Workshop in Action*, 36–53. Los Angeles: J. Paul Getty Museum, 2015.

Sansom, George Bailey. *The Western World and Japan: A Study in the Interaction of European and Asiatic Cultures*. New York: Knopf, 1949.

Sasaki Kiichi. "Terebi geijutsu no kyō no mondai—rakkanteki hikan to hikanteki rakkan." *Bungaku* 28, no. 2 (February 1960) 113–17.

Sasaki Ryūzō. *Miyazaki Tsutomu saiban (ge)*. Tokyo: Asahi shinbunsha, 1997.

Sasaki Sōichi. "Tennō no kokka-tei shōchō sei." In *"Tennōsei" ronshū 2*, edited by San'ichi shobō henshūbu, 407–12. Tokyo: San'ichi shobō, 1978.

Sasaki Tōru. "*Kinnosuke no hanashi* no ninki o megutte—Ōsaka to iu shiten mo fukumete." *Bungaku* 4, no. 1 (January–February 2003): 99–113.

———. "Seinan sensō to kusazōshi." *Kinsei bungei* 69 (January 1999): 52–65.

———. "*Torioi Omatsu kaijō shinwa* no seiritsu—rensai to kusazōshi no hazama de." *Edo bungaku* 21 (December 1999): 63–81.

Sassa Atsuyuki. *Tōdai rakujō—Yasuda kōdō kōbō nanajūni jikan.* Tokyo: Bungei shunjū, 1993.

Sata Ineko. "'Takekurabe' kaishaku e no hitotsu no gimon." In *Gunzō Nihon no sakka 3 Higuchi Ichiyō,* edited by Ōoka Makoto, Takahashi Hideo, and Miyoshi Yukio, 158–64. Tokyo: Shōgakukan, 1992.

Satō Haruo. "Enkō." In *Teihon Satō Haruo zenshū 3,* 21–16. Kyoto: Rinsen shoten, 1998.

———. *The Sick Rose: A Pastoral Elegy.* Translated by Francis B. Tenny. Honolulu: University of Hawaiʻi Press, 1993.

Satō Izumi. "Kindai bungakushi no kioku/bōkyaku." *Gendai shisō* 27, no. 1 (January 1991): 170–82.

Satō Shizuo. *Tennōsei to gendai Nihon bungaku.* Tokyo: Seijisha, 1988.

Satō Tadao. *Nihon no manga.* Tokyo: Hyōronsha, 1973.

Schodt, Frederik L. *Manga! Manga! The World of Japanese Comics.* Tokyo: Kodansha International, 1983.

Schneider, Norbert. *The Art of the Portrait: Masterpieces of European Portrait-painting, 1420–1670.* Translated by Iain Galbraith. Cologne: B. Taschen, 1994.

Scott, James. *Domination and the Arts of Resistance: Hidden Transcripts.* New Haven, CT: Yale University Press, 1990.

Seats, Michael. *Murakami Haruki: The Simulacrum in Contemporary Japanese Culture.* Lanham, MD: Rowman and Littlefield, 2006.

Seidensticker, Edward. *High City, Low City: Tokyo from Edo to the Earthquake.* New York: Knopf, 1983.

———. "Japan after Vietnam." *Commentary* 60, no. 3 (September 1975): 55–60.

———. *Tokyo Rising: The City since the Great Earthquake.* New York: Knopf, 1990.

Senuma Shigeki. "WAGAHAI WA NEKO DE ARU (I Am a Cat)." In *Essays on Natsume Sōseki's Works,* edited by the Japan National Commission for UNESCO, 19–31. Tokyo: Japan Society for the Promotion of Science, 1972.

Seigle, Cecilia Segawa. *Yoshiwara.* Honolulu: University of Hawaiʻi Press, 1993.

Shibusawa, Eiichi. *The Autobiography of Shibusawa Eiichi: From Peasant to Entrepreneur.* Translated by Teruko Craig. Tokyo: University of Tokyo Press, 1994.

Shiga, Naoya. *A Dark Night's Passing.* Translated by Edwin McClellan. Tokyo: Kodansha International, 1976.

Shiga Nobuo. *Shōwa terebi hōsōshi (jō).* Tokyo: Hayakawa shobō, 1990.

Shima Taizō. *Yasuda kōdō.* Tokyo: Chūō kōron shinsha, 2005.

Shimizu Isao. *Manga no rekishi.* Tokyo: Iwanami shoten, 1991.

Shindō Ken. *"Shisetsu" sengo kayōkyoku.* Tokyo: San'ichi shobō, 1977.

Shinkai Hitoshi. *Fukazawa Shichirō gaiden.* Tokyo: Shio shuppansha, 2012.

Shiomi Takaya. *Sekigunha shimatsuki.* Tokyo: Sairyūsha, 2003.

Shiozawa Minobu. "Kasagi Shizuko to Misora Hibari—kakushite hangurii seishin wa uta to natta." *Purejidento* 39, no. 9 (October 1999): 228–33.

Shishi Bunroku. *Jiyū gakkō*. Tokyo: Shinchōsha, 1953.

Shively, Donald. "Tokugawa Plays on Forbidden Topics." In *Studies in Kabuki and the Puppet Theater*, edited by James R. Brandon, 23–57. Honolulu: University of Hawaiʻi Press, 1982.

Showalter, Elaine. *Hystories: Hysterical Epidemics and Modern Culture*. New York: Columbia University Press, 1997.

Shū Shakubin. *Kin Shiryō bungaku no kenkyū—sono bungakuteki shōgai to sakuhin sekai o megutte*. Seoul: JNC, 2001.

Silberman, Bernard S. "The Bureaucratic State: The Problem of Authority and Legitimacy." In Najita and Koschmann, *Conflict in Modern Japanese History*, 226–57.

Sibley, William. *The Shiga Hero*. Chicago: University of Chicago Press, 1979.

Slaymaker, Doug, ed. *Yōko Tawada: Voices from Everywhere*. Lanham, MD: Lexington Books, 2007.

Smiles, Samuel. *Self-Help: With Illustrations of Conduct and Perseverance*. London: J. Murray, 1958.

Smith, Thomas C. *Political Change and Industrial Development in Japan: Government Enterprise, 1868–1880*. Stanford, CA: Stanford University Press, 1955.

———. "The Right to Benevolence: Dignity and Japanese Workers, 1890–1920." *Society for Comparative Studies in Society and History* 26, no. 4 (October 1984): 587–613.

Sodei, Takako. "The Fatherless Family." *Japan Quarterly* 32, no. 1 (January–March 1985): 77–82.

Sofue Shōji. *Kindai Nihon bungaku e no shatei—sono shikaku to kiban to*. Tokyo: Miraisha, 1998.

Sōma Tsuneo. *Fukuzawa Shichirō kono men'yō naru miryoku*. Tokyo: Bensei shuppan, 2001.

Sonobe Saburō. *Enka kara jazu e no Nihon shi*. Tokyo: Wakōsha, 1954.

Sontag, Susan. *Illness as Metaphor; and, AIDS and its Metaphors*. New York: Anchor Books, 1990.

Sotooka Hidetoshi. "Mishima vs. Fukazawa—Jiketsu no bigaku to notarejini no shisō." *AERA* 6, no. 19 (18 May 1993): 18–20.

Spivak, Gayatri Chakravorty. "Constitutions and Culture Studies." *Yale Journal of Law and the Humanities* 2, no. 1 (Winter 1990): 133–47.

Steinhoff, Patricia G. "Hijackers, Bombers, and Bank Robbers: Managerial Style in the Japanese Red Army." *Journal of Asian Studies* 48, no. 4 (November 1989): 724–40.

———. "Student Conflict." In *Conflict in Japan*, edited by Ellis S. Krauss, Thomas P. Rohlen, and Patricia G. Steinhoff, 174–213. Honolulu: University of Hawaiʻi Press, 1984.

Stewart, Susan. "Ceci Tuera Cela: Graffiti as Crime and Art." In *Life after Postmodernism: Essays on Value and Culture*, edited by John Fekete, 161–80. Basingstoke, UK: MacMillan Education Ltd., 1988.

Strecher, Matthew. *Dances with Sheep: The Quest for Identity in the Fiction of Murakami Haruki*. Ann Arbor: Center for Japanese Studies, University of Michigan, 2002.

Suga Atsuko. "Bashō wa banana no ki?" *Kaien* 13, no. 2 (February 1994): 28–31.

Suga Hidemi. "Posuto 'kindai bungakushi' o dō kaku ka." *Shōsetsu torippā* (Autumn 2001): 30–39.

Suga Hidemi, Karatani Kōjin, Asada Akira, and Watanabe Naoki. "Tennō to bungaku." *Hihyō kūkan* 24 (February 2000): 6–26.

Suga, Keijirō. "Translation, Exophony, Omniphony." In Slaymaker, *Yōko Tawada*, 21–33.

Sugiura Yumiko. *Keitai shōsetsu no riaru.* Tokyo: Chūō kōron shinsha, 2008.

Sugiyama Chūhei. *Meiji keimō ki no keizai shisō.* Tokyo: Hōsei daigaku shuppankyoku, 1986.

Sumiya Mikio. *The Social Impact of Industrialization in Japan.* Tokyo: Japanese National Commission for UNESCO, 1963.

Suny, Ronald Griger, and Michael D. Kennedy, eds. *Intellectuals and the Articulation of the Nation.* Ann Arbor: University of Michigan Press, 1999.

Suter, Rebecca. *The Japanization of Modernity: Murakami Haruki between Japan and the United States.* Cambridge, MA: Harvard University Asia Center, 2008.

Suzuki Sadami. *Gendai Nihon bungaku no shisō.* Tokyo: Gogatsu shobō, 1992.

———. *Nihon no "bungaku" o kangaeru.* Tokyo: Kadokawa shoten, 1994.

Suzuki, Tomi. *Narrating the Self: Fictions of Japanese Modernity.* Stanford, CA: Stanford University Press, 1996.

Taguchi Ukichi. *Nihon kaika shōshi.* Tokyo: Iwanami shoten, 1934.

Taira, Koji. "Economic Development, Labor Markets, and Industrial Relations in Japan, 1905–1955." In Duus, *The Cambridge History of Japan*, vol. 6, *The Twentieth Century*, 606–53.

Takabatake Michitoshi. "'Rokujū Anpo' no seishinshi." In *Sengo Nihon no seishinshi*, edited by Tetsuo Najita, Maeda Ai, and Kamishima Jirō, 70–91. Tokyo: Iwanami shoten, 1988.

Takahashi Gen'ichirō. *Boku ga shimaumago o shabetta koro.* Tokyo: Shinchōsha, 1989.

———. *Bungaku ja nai ka mo shirenai shōkōgun.* Tokyo: Asahi shinbunsha, 1992.

———. "Dōbutsu no shanikusai." In Takahashi, *Dōbutsuki*, 7–39.

———. "Dōbutsuki." In Takahashi, *Dōbutsuki*, 245–72.

———. *Dōbutsuki.* Tokyo: Kawade shobō, 2015.

———. *Jon Renon tai Kaseijin.* Tokyo: Kōdansha, 2011.

———. "Kaisetsu—ankoku seiun no kanata ni." In Numa, *Kachikujin Yapū* 5, 378–87.

———. *Kannō shōsetsuka.* Tokyo: Asahi shinbunsha, 2002.

———. "Meikinguobu." In *Gendaishi techō tokushūban Takahashi Gen'ichirō*, 199–217.

———. *Nihon bungaku seisuishi.* Tokyo: Kōdansha, 2001.

———. "*Nihon bungaku seisuishi* tsui ni kankō." *Shūkan asahi* (1 June 2001): 116.

———. *Nippon no shōsetsu—hyakunen no kodoku.* Tokyo: Bungei shunjū, 2007.

———. *Otona ni wa wakaranai Nihon bungakushi.* Tokyo: Iwanami shoten, 2013.

———. "Soshite, itsu no hi ni ka." In Takahashi, *Dōbutsuki*, 75–101.

———. "Terebi yori ai o komete." *Kaien* 7, no. 10 (October 1988): 200–10.

———. "Uchū sensō." In Takahashi, *Dōbutsuki*, 105–31.

Takahashi Gen'ichirō, and Homura Hiroshi. "Meiji kara tōku hanarete." *Gunzō* 56, no. 8 (August 2001): 134–52.

Takahashi Gen'ichirō, Katō Norihiro, and Nagae Akira. "Kotoba—kakumei—sekkusu—Takahashi Gen'ichirō to 80 nendai irai no gendai Nihon bungaku." In *Gendaishi techō tokushūban Takahashi Gen'ichirō*, 15–37.

Takahashi Gen'ichirō, and Komori Yōichi. "Ikita bungakushi to Sōseki." *Shōsetsu torippā* (Spring 1999): 9–17.

Takahashi Gen'ichirō, and Okuizumi Hikaru. "Kokyō e no sesshon." *Gunzō* 56, no. 2 (February 2001): 170–94.

Takahashi Gen'ichirō, Okuizumi Hikaru, and Shimada Masahiko. "Teidan Okuizumi Hikaru x Takahashi Gen'ichirō x Shimada Masahiko." *Gunzō* 71, no. 3 (March 2016): 154–66.

Takahashi Gen'ichirō, Shimada Masahiko, Inoue Hisashi, and Komori Yōichi. "Zadankai Shōwa bungakushi." *Subaru* 25, no. 7 (July 2003): 166–210.

Takahashi Shintarō. "*Utage no ato* no isō." *Kokubungaku kaishaku to kanshō* 65, no. 11 (November 2000): 112–16.

Takahashi Toshio. "Kassō suru parodi—parodi no owari." *Waseda bungaku* 195 (August 1992): 72–76.

Takahashi Yasuo. *Wagahai wa neko de aru den*. Tokyo: Hokusōsha, 1998.

Takahashi, Yoshitomo, MD. "Is Multiple Personality Disorder Really Rare in Japan?" *Dissociation* III, no. 2 (June 1990): 57–59.

Takashina, Shūji. "Natsume Sōseki and the Development of Modern Japanese Art." In *Culture and Identity: Japanese Intellectuals during the Interwar Years*, edited by J. Thomas Rimer, 273–81. Princeton, NJ: Princeton University Press, 1990.

Takashina Shūji, J. Thomas Rimer, and Gerald D. Bolas, eds. *Paris in Japan: The Japanese Encounter with European Painting*. Saint Louis: Washington University Press, 1987.

Takayama Chogyū. "Ichiyō joshi no 'Takekurabe' o yomite." In *Gendai bungakuron taikei 6*, edited by Aono Suekichi, 27–28. Tokyo: Kawade shobō, 1956.

Takemiya Keiko. "'Ōizumi saron' shōjo manga kōjō tōsō no koro." In *Rengō Sekigun "ōkami"-tachi no jidai 1969–1975*, 372. Edited by Nishii Kazuo. Tokyo: Asahi shinbunsha, 1999.

Takemoto Kenji. *Uroborosu no gisho*. Tokyo: Kodansha Novels, 1997.

Takeuchi Osamu. *Sengo manga gojūnen shi*. Tokyo: Chikuma shobō, 1995.

Takeuchi Yoshimi. "Kenryoku to geijutsu." In Nakamura Mitsuo, Karaki Junzō, Usui Yoshimi, and Takeuchi Yoshimi, *Gendai Nihon bungaku taikei 78*, 331–43. Tokyo: Chikuma shobō, 1974.

Takeyama Akiko. *Rajio no jidai—rajio wa chanoma no shuyaku datta*. Kyoto: Sekai shisōsha, 2002.

Takumi Hideo. *Kindai Nihon no bijutsu to bungaku—Meiji Taishō Shōwa no sashie*. Tokyo: Mokujisha, 1979.

Tamai Kensuke. "Shinbun shōsetsushi." *Bungaku* 6, no. 22 (June 1954): 567–87.

Tanaka, Atsushi. "Kishida Ryūsei." In Takashina, Rimer, and Bolas, *Paris in Japan*, 152–53.

Tanaka Hidemitsu. "Chōsen no sakka." In Tanaka, *Tanaka Hidemitsu zenshū 2*, 389–93.

———. "Hantō bundan no shin hassoku ni tsuite." In Tanaka, *Tanaka Hidemitsu zenshū 2*, 383–87.

———. *Tanaka Hidemitsu zenshū*. 11 vols. Tokyo: Haga shoten, 1964–65.

Tanaka Katsuhiko. *Kureōrugo to Nihongo*. Tokyo: Iwanami shoten, 1999.

Tanaka Kiwamu. "Kairi o megutte kangaete iru koto." *Kokoro no kagaku*, 136 (2007): 102–8.

Tanigawa Gan. "Kōsakusha no shitai ni moeru mono." In *Tanigawa Gan no shigoto 1*, 112–14. Tokyo: Kawade shobō shinsha, 1996.

Tanihata Ryōzō. *Anpo gekidō no kono jūnen*. Tokyo: Bungei shunjū, 1969.

Tatsumi, Takayuki. "Comparative Metafiction: Somewhere between Ideology and Rhetoric." *Critique: Studies in Contemporary Fiction* 39, no. 1 (Fall 1997): 2–17.

———. *Full Metal Apache: Transactions between Cyberpunk Japan and Avant-Pop America*. Durham, NC: Duke University Press, 2006.

———. "Kaisetsu—Numa Shōzō *Kachikujin Yapū* to Nihon shinwa no datsukōchiku." In Numa, *Kachikujin Yapū 3*, 370–402.

———. *Nihon henryū bungaku*. Tokyo: Shinchōsha, 1998.

Tawada Yōko. *Dōbutsu-tachi no Baberu*. Subaru 35, no. 8 (August 2013): 112–31.

———. "Eine Heidin einem Heidekloster." In *Poesie und Stille: Schriftstellerinnen schreiben in Klöstern*, edited by Klosterkammer Hannover, 235–50. Göttingen: Wallstein, 2009.

———. "The Island of Eternal Life." Translated by Margaret Mitsutani. In *March Was Made of Yarn: Reflections on the Japanese Earthquake, Tsunami, and Nuclear Meltdown*, edited by Elmer Luke and David Karashima, 3–11. New York: Vintage Books, 2012.

———. "Tawada Yōko Does Not Exist." Translated by Doug Slaymaker. In Slaymaker, *Yōko Tawada*, 13–19.

———. "Zukunft ohne Herkunft." In *Zukunft! Zukunft? literarische Essays*, edited by Anna Maria Carpi, 55–72. Tübingen: Konkursbuchverlag, 2000.

Terayama Shūji. *Bōryoku to shite no gengo—shiron made jisoku hyaku kiro*. Tokyo: Shichōsha, 1983.

Terdiman, Richard. *Discourse/Counter-Discourse: The Theory and Practice of Symbolic Resistance in Nineteenth-Century France*. Ithaca, NY: Cornell University Press, 1985.

Teruoka Yoshitaka. *Rakugo no nenrin*. Tokyo: Kōdansha, 1978.

Tezuka Osamu. *Manga no kakikata*. Tokyo: Kōbunsha, 1996.

Thomas, Julia Adeney. "The Cage of Nature: Modernity's History in Japan." *History and Theory* 40 (February 2001): 16–36.

Tilly, Louise A., and Joan W. Scott. *Women, Work and Family*. New York: Holt, Rinehart and Winston, 1978.

Titus, David A. "The Making of the 'Symbol Emperor System' in Postwar Japan." *Modern Asian Studies* 14, no. 4 (1980): 529–78.

Torrance, Richard. *The Fiction of Tokuda Shusei and the Emergence of Japan's New Middle Class.* Seattle: University of Washington Press, 1994.

Touraine, Alain. *Critique of Modernity.* Translated by David Macey. Cambridge: Blackwell, 1995.

Tsubouchi Yūzō. *Ichikyūnanani— "hajimari no owari" to "owari no hajimari."* New York: Bungei shunjū, 2003.

Tsuge Teruhiko. "Yoshimoto Banana no sekaiteki na imi." *Kaien* 13, no. 2 (February 1994): 78–83.

Tsuge Teruhiko, Hilaria Gössman, Elizabeth Floyd, and Yin Hui'e. "Sekai no naka no Yoshimoto Banana." *Kokubungaku kaishaku to kyōzai no kenkyū* 39, no. 3 (February 1994): 88–106.

Tsurumi, Kazuko. *Social Change and the Individual: Japan Before and After Defeat in World War II.* Princeton, NJ: Princeton University Press, 1970.

———. *Women in Japan: A Paradox of Modernization.* Tokyo: Sophia University Press, 1977.

Tsurumi, Patricia. *Factory Girls: Women in the Thread Mills of Meiji Japan.* Princeton, NJ: Princeton University Press, 1992.

Tsurumi Shunsuke. "Chōsenjin no tōjō suru shōsetsu." In *Bungaku riron no kenkyū,* edited by Kuwabara Takeo, 184–200. Tokyo: Iwanami shoten, 1974.

———. *A Cultural History of Postwar Japan, 1945–1980.* London: KPI, 1987.

———. "Enchō ni okeru miburi to shōchō." *Bungaku* 26, no. 7 (July 1958): 831–42.

———. *Manga no dokusha to shite.* Tokyo: Chikuma shobō, 1991.

———. *Sengo Nihon no taishū bunka shi.* Tokyo: Iwanami shoten, 1990.

Twine, Nanette. "Language and the Constitution." *Japan Forum* 3, no. 1 (April 1991): 125–37.

———. *Language and the Modern State: The Reform of Written Japanese.* London: Routledge, 1991.

Tylor, E. B. *Primitive Culture.* Vol. 1. New York: J. P. Putnam's Sons, 1920.

Uchinuma Yukio. "Hitori-aruki suru 'tajū jinkaku.'" In *Tajū jinkaku to wa nani ka,* edited by Asahi shinbunsha, 17–40. Tokyo: Asahi shinbunsha, 1997.

Uchinuma, Yukio, and Yoshio Sekine. "Dissociative Identity Disorder (DID) in Japan: A Forensic Case Report and the Recent Increase in Reports of DID." *International Journal of Psychiatry in Clinical Practice* 4 (2000): 155–60.

Ueda, Makoto. *Modern Japanese Poets and the Nature of Literature.* Stanford, CA: Stanford University Press, 1983.

Ueno Chizuko. *Kindai kazoku no seiritsu to shūen.* Tokyo: Iwanami shoten, 1994.

Umehara Takeshi. "*Wagahai wa neko de aru* no warai ni tsuite." In *Nihon bungaku kenkyū shiryō sōsho Natsume Sōseki 1,* edited by Nihon bungaku kenkyū shiryō kankōkai, 126–41. Tokyo: Yūseidō, 1973.

Usui Yoshimi. *Taishō bungakushi.* Tokyo: Chikuma shobō, 1963.

Uzanne, Octave. "The End of Books." *Scribner's Magazine*, August 1894, 221–31.

Van Compernolle, Timothy J. *The Uses of Memory: The Critique of Modernity in the Fiction of Higuchi Ichiyō*. Cambridge, MA: Harvard University Asia Center, 2006.

Varnedoe, Kirk, and Adam Gopnik. *High and Low: Modern Art, Popular Culture*. New York: Museum of Modern Art, 1990.

"Verwirrte Motten." *Der Spiegel* 46 (9 November 1992): 270–73.

Vattimo, Gianni. *The End of Modernity: Nihilism and Hermeneutics in Postmodern Culture*. Translated by Jon R. Snyder. Baltimore, MD: Johns Hopkins University Press, 1988.

Wakabayashi Kanzō. "Joshi." In San'yūtei Enchō, *Kaidan botandōrō*, 8–9. Tokyo: Iwanami shoten, 2002.

Ward, Robert E. "The Commission on the Constitution and Prospects for Constitutional Change in Japan." *Journal of Asian Studies* 24, no. 3 (May 1965): 401–29.

———, ed. *Political Development in Modern Japan*. Princeton, NJ: Princeton University Press, 1968.

———. "Reflections on the Allied Occupation and Planned Political Change in Japan." In Ward, *Political Development in Modern Japan*, 477–535.

Washburn, Dennis. *Translating Mount Fuji: Modern Japanese Fiction and the Ethics of Identity*. New York: Columbia University Press, 2007.

Watatani Kiyoshi. *Kinsei akujo kibun*. Tokyo: Seiabō, 1979.

Watsuji Tetsurō. *Kokumin tōgō no shōchō*. Tokyo: Keisō shobō, 1948.

Wellek, René. *The Attack on Literature and Other Essays*. Chapel Hill: University of North Carolina Press, 1982.

White, Hayden. *Content of the Form: Narrative Discourse and Historical Representation*. Baltimore, MD: Johns Hopkins University Press, 1987.

———. *Tropics of Discourse: Essays in Cultural Criticism*. Baltimore, MD: Johns Hopkins University Press, 1987.

White, Merry. *The Material Child: Coming of Age in Japan and America*. New York: Maxwell Macmillan International, 1993.

Willett, Ralph. *The Americanization of Germany, 1945–1949*. London: Routledge, 1989.

Williams, Raymond. *The Long Revolution*. New York: Columbia University Press, 1961.

———. *Marxism and Literature*. Oxford: Oxford University Press, 1977.

Williams, Raymond, and Michael Orrom. *Preface to Film*. London: Film Drama Limited, 1954.

Yaku Masao. *"Shikishima no michi" kenkyū*. Tokyo: Kokumin bunka kenkyūjo, 1985.

Yamada Akio. "'Kaiga no yakusoku' ronsō sobyō." *Nihon kindai bungaku* 14 (1971): 14–27.

Yamada Shunji. "Meiji shoki shinbun zappō no buntai—genjitsu to iu 'seido' o megutte." *Kokubungaku kenkyū* 100 (March 1990): 111–21.

———. "'Riaritii' no shūjiteki haikei." In *Kindai no retorikku*, edited by Nakamura Miharu, 69–88. Tokyo: Yūseidō, 1995

———. "Shinbun kairyō to Enchō sokki." *Bungaku* 14, no. 2 (March–April 2013): 71–85.

Yamaguchi Masao. "Kodomo no tame no manga kara—dokudanteki zokuaku-manga ron." *Bungaku* 9, no. 9 (June 1990): 436–39.

Yamamoto Akira. *Sengo fūzoku shi*. Osaka: Ōsaka shoseki, 1986.

Yamamoto Taketoshi. *Kindai Nihon no shinbun dokusha sō*. Tokyo: Hōsei daigaku shuppan-kyoku, 1981.

Yamamoto Yōrō. "'Yoshimoto Banana' wa naze ureru." *Purejidento* 27, no. 10 (October 1989): 298–305.

Yamamoto Yoshiaki. "Kaikaki no media to bungaku." In *Iwanami kōza Nihon bungakushi 11 Henkakuki no bungaku 3*, edited by Kubota Jun, 177–98. Tokyo: Iwanami shoten, 1996.

Yamaori Tetsuo. *Enka to Nihonjin*. Kyoto: PHP kenkyūjō, 1984.

Yanagida Izumi. *Meiji bungaku kenkyū 4 Meiji shoki no bungaku shisō*. Tokyo: Shunjūsha, 1965.

Yanagi Sōetsu. "Kakumei no gaka." *Shirakaba* 1, no. 3 (January 1912): 1–31.

Yasko, Guy. "Mishima Yukio vs. Todai Zenkyoto: The Cultural Displacement of Politics." Durham, NC: Asia/Pacific Studies Institute, Duke University, 1995.

Yasuda Toshiaki. *Teikoku Nihon no gengo hensei*. Tokyo: Seori shobō, 1997.

Yi Chŏng-hǔi. "Henbō suru tekisuto *Tobu otoko* kō—kankōbon *Tobu otoko* ni itaru made." *Kokubungaku* 42, no. 9 (August 1997): 86–92.

Yiu, Angela. *Chaos and Order in the Works of Natsume Sōseki*. Honolulu: University of Hawai'i Press, 1998.

Yokota Kōichi. *Kenpō to tennōsei*. Tokyo: Iwanami shoten, 1990.

Yokota Yōichi. "Shirakaba-kai no sono ato to Kishida Ryūsei." *Kindai gasetsu* 5 (March 1997): 73–97.

Yokote Kazuhiko. *Hisenryōka no bungaku ni kan suru kisōteki kenkyū shiryō hen*. Tokyo: Musashino shobō, 1995.

Yokoyama Yūta. *Wagahai wa neko ni naru*. Tokyo: Kōdansha, 2014.

Yomiuri shinbunsha geinōbu. *Terebi bangumi no yonjū-nen*. Tokyo: Nihon hōsō shuppan kyōkai, 1994.

Yomota Inuhiko. *Haisukūru 1968*. Tokyo: Shinchōsha, 2004.

———. *Manga genron*. Tokyo: Chikuma shobō, 1994.

Yonezawa Yoshihiro, ed. *Manga hihyō sengen*. Tokyo: Aki shobō, 1987.

Yoshihiro Kōsuke. *Manga no gendaishi*. Tokyo: Maruzen, 1993.

Yoshimi Shun'ya. "Nihon no naka no 'Amerika' ni tsuite kangaeru." *Kan* 8 (Winter 2002): 131–43.

———. "Terebi ga kazoku ni yatte kita—terebi no kūkan, terebi no jikan." *Shisō* 956 (December 2003): 26–48.

Yoshimoto Banana. "Chōnōryoku tte, zettai ni sonzai suru to omou. . . . ." In Yoshimoto, *Fruits Basket taidanshū*, 271–83.

———. "Famirii." In *Painatsupurin*, 39–41. Tokyo: Kadokawa shoten, 1989.

———. *Fruits Basket taidanshū*. Tokyo: Fukutake shoten, 1990.

———. *Kitchen*. Translated by Megan Backus. New York: Grove Press, 1993.

———. "Watakushi-tachi 'Chibimaruko-chan' sedai." In Yoshimoto, *Fruits Basket taidanshū*, 237–69.

Yoshimoto, Mitsuhiro. "The Postmodern and Mass Images in Japan." *Public Culture* 1, no. 2 (Spring 1989): 8–25.

Yoshimoto Takaaki. "Fukazawa o koritsu sasete oite nan no 'genron no jiyū' zo ya." *Bessatsu shinhyō* 7, no. 2 (July 1974): 238–41.

———. "Kaisetsu—Tsuge Yoshiharu *Munō no hito* sono ta." In *Munō no hito Hi no tawamure by* Tsuge Yoshiharu, 391–97. Tokyo: Shinchōsha, 1988.

———. "Uzumakeru Sōseki (1) *Wagahai wa neko de aru*." *Chikuma* 236 (November 1990): 8–20.

Yoshioka Shinobu. *M no sekai, yūutsu na sentan*. Tokyo: Bungei shunjū, 2000.

Yun Kwon-ja. "'Zainichi' bunka to nashonarizumu." In *Taishū bunka to nashonarizumu*, edited by Pak Soon-ae, Tanikawa Takeshi, and Yamada Shōji, 237–62. Tokyo: Shinwasha, 2016.

Zaretsky, Eli. *Capitalism, the Family, and Personal Life*. New York: Harper & Row, 1976.

Zhou, Wanyao. "The Kōminka Movement in Taiwan and Korea: Comparisons and Interpretations." In *The Japanese Wartime Empire, 1931–1945*, edited by Peter Duus, Ramon Hawley Myers, Mark R. Peattie, and Wanyao Zhou, 40–68. Princeton, NJ: Princeton University Press, 1996.

Ziff, Larzer. *Writing in the New Nation: Prose, Print, and Politics in the Early United States*. New Haven, CT: Yale University Press, 1991.

Žižek, Slavoj. "Multiculturalism, Or, the Cultural Logic of Multinational Capitalism." *New Left Review* 1/225 (September–October 1997): 28–51.

Zwicker, Jonathan E. *Practices of the Sentimental Imagination: Melodrama, the Novel, and the Social Imaginary in Nineteenth-Century Japan*. Cambridge, MA: Harvard University Asia Center, 2000.

Index